Integrated Science

Volume 37

The **Integrated Science** Series aims to publish the most relevant and novel research in all areas of Formal Sciences, Physical and Chemical Sciences, Biological Sciences, Medical Sciences, and Social Sciences. We are especially focused on the research involving the integration of two of more academic fields offering an innovative view, which is one of the main focuses of Universal Scientific Education and Research Network (USERN), science without borders.

Integrated Science is committed to upholding the integrity of the scientific record and will follow the Committee on Publication Ethics (COPE) guidelines on how to deal with potential acts of misconduct and correcting the literature.

Beatriz Casais
Editor

Integrated Science to Achieve Sustainable Development Goals

Springer

Editor
Beatriz Casais
School of Economics, Management and Political Science; iBMS – Centre for Research in Business, Markets & Society
University of Minho
BRAGA, Portugal

ISSN 2662-9461 ISSN 2662-947X (electronic)
Integrated Science
ISBN 978-3-031-88776-5 ISBN 978-3-031-88777-2 (eBook)
https://doi.org/10.1007/978-3-031-88777-2

This Springer imprint is published by the registered company Springer Nature Switzerland AG
The registered company address is: Gewerbestrasse 11, 6330 Cham, Switzerland

Preface

Multidisciplinary Challenges for UN Sustainable Development Goals

> As we embark on this great collective journey, we pledge that no one will be left behind. Recognizing that the dignity of the human person is fundamental, we wish to see the Goals and targets met for all nations and peoples and for all segments of society. And we will endeavour to reach the furthest behind first. (UN Declaration: Transforming our world: the 2030 Agenda for Sustainable Development, 2015)

The Sustainable Development Goals (SDGs) are a collection of 17 global goals adopted by all United Nations Member States in 2015. The declaration signed with the SDGs is a universal call to action to end poverty, protect the planet, and ensure peace and prosperity for all as an agenda of 15 years, to be achieved by 2030. SDGs represent an ambitious vision for a better future, encompassing the three dimensions of sustainability—environmental protection, social equity, and economic growth. The 17 SDGs are interconnected and complex global challenges that require a multifaceted approach that transcends traditional disciplinary boundaries and calls for the involvement of experts from various fields, such as environmental scientists, urban planning, economists, managers, marketing specialists, supply chain experts, psychologists and sociologists, and experts on political science and international relations, among others. The multidisciplinary intervention is conducted both at an upstream level of public policies and at a downstream level, where individual and community responses have an important role. This means that everyone is committed to achieving SDGs for a more sustainable future, requiring the collaboration of governments, businesses, civil society, and individuals worldwide.

The book *Integrated Science to Achieve Sustainable Development Goals* delves into the complexities of navigating global challenges. It explores multidisciplinary challenges and proposes innovative solutions necessary to achieve a sustainable and equitable future for all. The book shows a diverse range of perspectives from leading scholars or practitioners across various disciplines, who reflect on the current knowledge of their field and propose, based on such knowledge, recommendable actions to address Agenda 2030. The chapters of the book discuss innovative approaches to poverty alleviation and access to clean water, sanitation, health and education, equality, and inclusion of vulnerable populations. The book offers insights into obtaining a society with the conditions for quality of life and well-being for all, regardless of age, race, or gender. The experts also reflect on human capital and access to decent jobs as drivers for economic growth, as well as the role of technology in achieving efficient cities and how to create sustainable cities to prevent climate change. Sustainable consumption and production are also discussed to ensure sustainable markets, which are crucial to the economy. This perspective requires the management of sustainable supply chains that can, at the same time, prevent environmental degradation and assure the multidimensions of human rights. Finally, considering that peace and justice are fundamental values of sustainable development, the vision of political science and international relations regarding the current geopolitical tensions are also included in the book. Overall, the book provides a wide reflection on how the world must converge to achieve sustainable development for all. And that multidisciplinary approach is the last SDG, indeed, with establishing partnerships to achieve a sustainable world.

This book delves into diverse aspects of global development, offering valuable insights and actionable solutions into challenges and opportunities to achieve SDGs, examining the interconnectedness of social, economic, and environmental issues and highlighting the urgent need for interdisciplinary collaboration and innovative approaches to address these global challenges. Furthermore, the book also examines the importance of ethical considerations, social justice, and community engagement in achieving the SDGs. I invite readers to join us on this journey of exploration of the complexities of the SDGs and work on the actionable recommendations suggested in the book. We aim to inspire and empower readers to engage in the critical conversations and actions needed to build a more sustainable and just world by bringing together diverse perspectives and fostering interdisciplinary dialogue.

Chapter 1 emphasizes the role of social enterprises and nonprofit organizations in creating opportunities for marginalized communities. It highlights the importance of social entrepreneurship and social innovation in tackling poverty. The chapter explores how the Quadruple Helix model (government, academia, industry, and civil society) can be leveraged to maximize the impact of social projects. Chapter 2 discusses how social marketing can be used to promote, modify, or discourage behaviors that affect people's well-being, particularly in areas like health and environmental sustainability. Chapter 3 explores how choice architecture, a policy design strategy derived from behavioral economics, can be used to nudge citizens toward healthier choices, particularly to overcome challenges such as low health literacy and limited access to healthcare, especially in developing countries. Chapter 4 delves into education as a fundamental human right and a key driver of sustainable development. It examines the challenges to achieving education for all, such as inequality, social divisions, and gender disparities. The chapter explores the efforts made in Algeria to address these challenges of inclusive education. Chapter 5 discusses the issue of under/misrepresentation of women in marketing approaches, raising awareness about the importance of gender equality in marketing and encouraging the adoption of more inclusive and equitable practices. Chapter 6 focuses on the critical issue of water conservation in households. Reducing household water consumption is crucial due to the increasing water scarcity and climate change. The chapter explores how behavioral economics can be a powerful tool in promoting water-saving practices. By understanding human behavior and applying nudges or incentives, it is possible to encourage households to adopt circular economy principles. Chapter 7 examines 10 major research trends in human resources management, including remote work, diversity and inclusion, mental health, and digital transformation, advocating for a strategic alignment between these trends and the SDGs. Chapter 8 refers to the idea that economic growth is driven by decent work policies, and Chap. 9 shows that sustainable business models for the fashion industry may also contribute to economic growth and contribute to a better environment. Chapter 10 examines the demographic shift, the challenges to ensuring the quality of life and inclusion for the older population, and the implications for social and economic systems of extended life hope. Chapter 11 delves into the critical issue of social inclusion, focusing on ensuring that individuals with disabilities and women are fully integrated into society and have equal opportunities. The concept of smart and sustainable cities is highlighted in Chap. 12, where 10 key gaps are addressed to create truly sustainable urban environments. Building on this, Chap. 13 explores the importance of responsible consumption in a world of finite resources. Chapter 14 addresses the topic of climate change and the need to protect the environment as a crucial resource for economic growth and ensure access to human rights. Chapter 15 provides a framework for evaluating the environmental performance of cities and guiding their path toward sustainability. The book then shifts its focus to broader societal issues, exploring them in Chaps. 16 and 17. These chapters highlight the importance of cooperation, diplomacy, and inclusive networks in addressing global challenges and fostering peaceful and equitable societies.

This book offers a valuable resource for academics, policymakers, and anyone interested in understanding and addressing our planet's complex challenges. Exploring these diverse themes provides a roadmap for navigating the path toward a more sustainable future.

BRAGA, Portugal Beatriz Casais

Contents

About the Author

Beatriz Casais has a Ph.D. in Business and Management Studies from the University of Porto and an MSc in Marketing, with a bachelor's degree in Communication Sciences and a Post-Graduation in Health Communication. She is Currently an Associate Professor at the University of Minho in the fields of Marketing and Strategy, a senior researcher at iBMS—Centre for Research in Business, Markets, and Society, and a board member of the European Social Marketing Association (ESMA). Her research focuses on social marketing and public health advertisement, digital marketing, and tourism marketing. She was social marketing manager at the Portuguese Ministry of Health, HIV/AIDS National Prevention Program. Beatriz Casais was Vice-Dean of the School of Economics and Management of the University of Minho between 2020 and 2023, and head of the executive education unit—UMinhoExec.

Disclosure

The authors of this book retain full responsibility for the content and ideas presented. Some authors used AI-powered tools to assist with the technical aspects of writing, such as grammar and style checks, to enhance the overall readability of their chapters. While these tools can be helpful, they do not replace the human element of critical thinking and creative writing.

1 Harnessing the Social Economy for Poverty Reduction: A Quadruple Helix Perspective

Beatriz Casais and Camila Barroso dos Santos

Well-adjusted and well-implemented policies can facilitate cross-sector collaboration, resolve conflicts, and align stakeholders' interests, thereby enhancing joint initiatives' overall efficacy and sustainability.

Islam et al. [24], pp. 9–10.

Abstract

The social economy encompasses social enterprises and non-profit organizations that prioritize social impact alongside financial sustainability. Social economy organizations play a crucial role in empowering individuals, promoting social inclusion, providing essential services that may be under-served by traditional markets, and creating opportunities for marginalized communities. Social entrepreneurship and social innovation stand out as essential transformative forces for implementing a social economy and addressing poverty reduction with innovative solutions. The quadruple helix model integrates government, the private sector, academia, and civil society to provide valuable insights into developing and evaluating social projects and maximizing their impact on society.

B. Casais (✉)
iBMS – Centre for Research in Business, Markets & Society, University of Minho;
School of Economics, Management and Political Science, University of Minho,
Braga, Portugal
e-mail: bcasais@eeg.uminho.pt

C. B. Santos
School of Economics, Management and Political Science, University of Minho,
Braga, Portugal

B. Casais (ed.), *Integrated Science to Achieve Sustainable Development Goals*,
Integrated Science 37, https://doi.org/10.1007/978-3-031-88777-2_1

Graphical Abstract

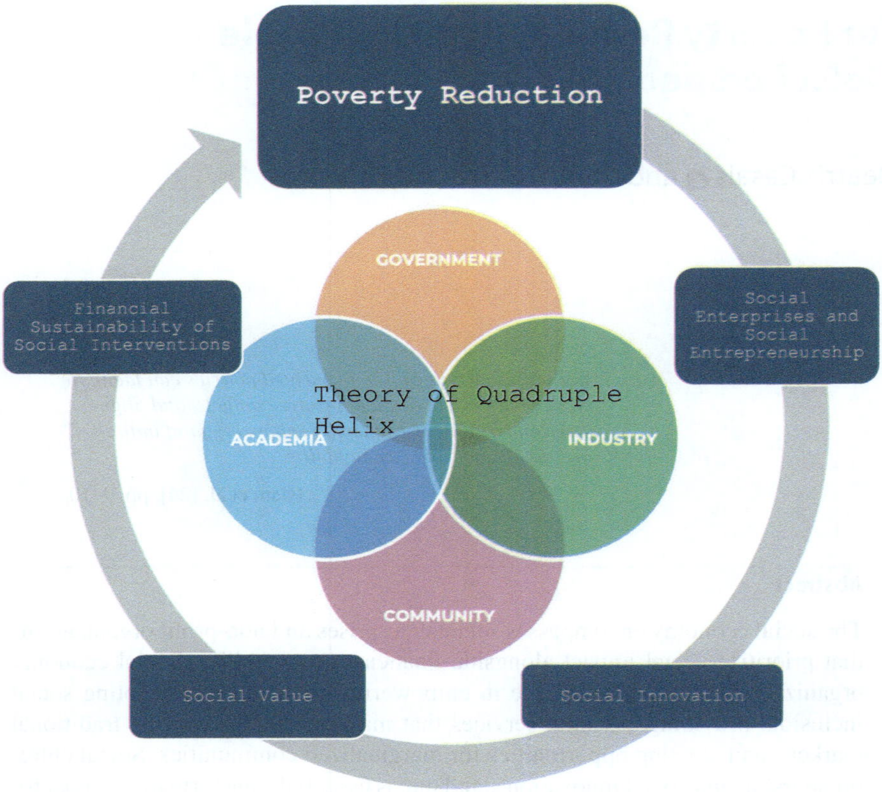

Source: Authors

Keywords

Social entrepreneurship · Social innovation · Social enterprises · Quadruple helix model · Social ecosystem · Social economy · Social development · Reduce poverty

1 Introduction

Fighting poverty and hunger correspond to the Sustainable Development Goals (SDGs) 1 and 2 and are assumed to be priorities to overcome the world cleavage between developed and developing countries, contribute to better health, and achieve minimum well-being and quality of life. There are several international poverty alleviation programs [20], policy interventions [7], and a focus on human resource development to support sustainable employment [31]. In rural areas, the development of agriculture is important in reducing poverty [2], and investment in education is a cost-effective response to poverty [4]. However, despite these efforts, poverty remains a persistent challenge. Organisations can alleviate poverty by providing resources, opportunities, and capabilities to marginalised communities [55].

Social entrepreneurship initiatives and social innovation have emerged as promising strategies to combat poverty and promote social inclusion, contributing to sustainable development [8, 27]. These approaches emphasize community-centered and knowledge-based development that engages local actors and resources [49]. This ecosystem compounds the social economy, which includes a diverse range of organizations, such as cooperatives, non-profits, social enterprises, and governmental institutions, with the purpose of developing joint interventions to engage such communities to participate in an economy that can reduce disparities [53]. The social economy considers that inclusion, social justice, and community empowerment can be more than a simple purpose but also a form to obtain business development with financial sustainability and social welfare at the same time [33].

Collaborations between different sectors are essential to fostering an ecosystem conducive to developing innovation and social entrepreneurship initiatives. The Triple Helix Model, later expanded to the Quadruple Helix Model, highlights the importance of this collaboration, stating that collaboration between government, industry, academia, and civil society generates possibilities for innovation that would not be viable if each acted in isolation [59]. Each sector promotes innovative and sustainable solutions to social problems, but only a joint response can effectively respond to local needs [10].

This chapter explores the concepts of social economy fostered by social entrepreneurship and social innovation approaches. It reflects on how the collaboration of the four sectors conceptualised in the quadruple helix model may contribute to poverty reduction and sustainable development goals in general.

2 Social Economy and Poverty Reduction

Although foreign aid has shown positive impacts on addressing poverty in developing countries [34], such response has not had long-term effects on sustainable poverty reduction without investments in human capital and occupational policies [41, 54]. Small and medium enterprises have a significant impact on this topic [44] because many corporate social entrepreneurship approaches focus on developing local social innovation initiatives that create market-based solutions [22, 57] and open social opportunities for civic participation [25, 58] with effects on poverty alleviation.

Social entrepreneurship is a promising approach to contribute to poverty reduction and sustainable development, for example, among women, through implementing microloan systems [18]. A community-focused and knowledge-based development model could effectively address poverty [49] with elements of social innovation and value creation since it is focused on social impact [3]. This means that the community's particular needs may be addressed, potentializing the specificities of human resources and upskilling human capital by investing in education [32], giving them the resources to generate value in terms of profit and social good for the community [19].

The mentioned context frames what is known as the fourth sector [17]. The joint response to social problems by government, companies, and civil society generates a fourth typology of institutions, called social enterprises, that also involve non-profit organizations and public institutions to address social development and promote profit to generate economic welfare in vulnerable populations. Soares and Casais [53] attributed this fourth sector a characteristic of uniting efforts for the common good. The fourth sector creates the environment for a social economy where only cross-sector collaboration can achieve social responses effectively [10].

3 Social Entrepreneurship

Social entrepreneurship is an important dimension of the social economy, centered on creating social value and promoting positive impacts on communities. This occurs by solving complex and persistent social issues that are often not efficiently addressed by traditional market mechanisms [40]. This concept of social entrepreneurship has gained greater visibility and recognition in recent decades, characterized by a combination of social objectives and business practices [29]. Social entrepreneurship establishes a new paradigm for addressing social issues by integrating business practices focused on generating profit with a strong social mission, aiming to increase social value by creating ventures with innovative approaches, identifying gaps in the social system, and developing effective solutions to serve marginalized groups [14]. The hybrid nature of social entrepreneurship considers the establishment of social objectives with sustainable profitable business practices. According to Doherty, Haugh, and Lyon [13], the dual mission of creating social value and financial sustainability is essential, ensuring that social projects respond to immediate needs and sustain themselves in the long term, promoting lasting solutions. Thus, profit, although not the primary objective, is seen as a means of enabling and expanding social initiatives [6]. This conscious and proactive approach reflects the pursuit of social value creation, which is considered a key indicator of success in this area, in contrast to the traditional focus on solely profit-making [36].

The assessment of social impact is essential for developing specific methods that can measure and understand the results achieved by social entrepreneurship projects [1, 30]. The impact of social entrepreneurship goes beyond meeting immediate needs, acting as a driver for systemic change [16]. Methodologies such as Social Return on Investment (SROI) have been gaining prominence to measure the social value generated [42]. SROI attempts to identify the key changes obtained due to a certain activity and attribute a monetary value to social outcomes by comparing the total monetized value of benefits with the cost of the intervention (for example, for each monetary unit invested, x monetary units of social value are created).

Social entrepreneurship is recognized for promoting innovative solutions to social problems, prioritizing collective well-being, and using creativity to drive initiatives that provide lasting benefits [40]. This perspective contrasts with charity and philanthropic initiatives by emphasizing creating market-based solutions that aim to meet social needs and generate autonomy and sustainability for the communities served [28]. In fact, social entrepreneurship should not be seen only as a solution to social issues but rather as a strategy to create new opportunities for sustainable development [27]. This implies that social innovations promoted in the context of social economy are designed to be scalable and replicable, reaching more beneficiaries and expanding their impact [47]. In this sense, identifying best practices and challenges in collaborations between different sectors is essential to build a model that promotes cooperation between the parties involved [46]. Social entrepreneurs can mobilize more resources and implement policies that favour social justice through collaborations between different public and private sectors. The collaboration between sectors favours combining complementary resources and knowledge, leading to more efficient and sustainable social innovations [10]. This approach aims to improve communities' quality of life and contributes to developing a social innovation ecosystem that can drive significant and sustainable changes in society. Thus, social entrepreneurs stand out as key agents in social transformation, creating a future where market solutions and social responsibility coexist and reinforce each other [36].

4 Social Innovation

Social innovation consists of new ideas addressing social needs that can change the way how society operates, promoting fairer and more inclusive solutions [21]. This view emphasizes innovation as an end and a means to encourage society in the search for improvements in economic sustainability and social equity, allowing different groups access to opportunities and resources [38]. Social innovation goes far beyond developing new products or services, requiring shifts in established practices and power structures [46]. This shift to a more collaborative and inclusive approach is essential to meet current social demands and create a solid foundation for the future [15].

Promoting social innovation should be a priority on the political, economic, and social agendas, ensuring that communities are equipped and empowered to face the challenges [21]. Social innovation may alter existing relationships and social dynamics by establishing collaborative networks to generate social value and promote community development [46]. Involving different agents is essential. Social entrepreneurs need to solve community problems without waiting for government or market interventions. In this sense, social entrepreneurship is a social movement that generates pressure and support for social innovation by articulating voices and demands around human rights and social justice, bringing together different organizations ranging from NGOs to social enterprises and public institutions to implement projects with a social purpose jointly. In fact, a significant aspect of social innovation is its role in fostering collaboration [56]. This interaction is facilitated by social innovation hubs, which act as catalysts for exchanging ideas and creating collaborative networks, creating an ecosystem that fosters collective innovation [10]. The most effective solutions often emerge from combining diverse knowledge and joining forces around a common problem.

Social innovation is a promising approach to combat poverty by improving access to education and finance and fostering entrepreneurship [22, 35] to create jobs, provide essential services, and drive economic growth [3]. Digital social innovations, such as prosocial P2P lending platforms, have shown success in connecting low-income individuals with lenders [48]. Women's entrepreneurship and social capital are crucial in rural poverty alleviation [45]. However, challenges remain, including weak institutional environments and the need for supportive policies [22, 38]. To maximize impact, social innovation should empower beneficiaries, transform social relationships, and develop collaborative processes [38]. This calls for policymakers to support social innovation through funding, training, and creating favourable conditions for its growth [3].

Social innovation and social entrepreneurship are strongly connected [15]. Social entrepreneurship is often seen as putting social innovation into practice, focusing on creating businesses that are not solely focused on profit but that seek to solve complex social problems [26]. Social innovation initiatives face the challenge of demonstrating their impact in a tangible way. Difficulties in measuring social outcomes and uncertainty regarding financial sustainability often hinder access to funding. Social entrepreneurs often encounter obstacles in securing investment, as traditional business success metrics do not always apply to social innovation projects [15, 46]. The ability to communicate initiatives' social and economic impact is essential to attract support from investors and grants [37].

In short, social innovation represents a path to a future where solutions are shaped and driven by the real needs of communities. By engaging multiple stakeholders and fostering creativity and collaboration, social innovation addresses pressing social problems and promotes a cultural shift in which social responsibility is seen as a priority. This collective and integrated approach is essential to addressing contemporary challenges and building a more resilient, equitable, and sustainable society [14].

5 Quadruple Helix Model

The Quadruple Helix (QH) Model emerged as a significant evolution of the Triple Helix (TH) Model, which focused on the interactions between academia, industry, and government to promote regional innovation and rural development [51]. However, this approach has faced criticism in rural contexts, where the emphasis on science may not meet local needs. The Quadruple Helix Model responds to these limitations by adding civil society and incorporating NGOs and associations that occupy strategic positions and are connected to local needs. This combination of four sectors can be effectively leveraged to promote social entrepreneurship [10].

The Quadruple Helix Model offers an innovative and inclusive framework to foster social innovation and sustainable development [12], fostering communities' economic empowerment and an inclusive future. This interdependence between four sectors creates opportunities for innovation that cannot be achieved in isolation, highlighting the importance of cooperation. In the context of the social economy, this model has effectively promoted growth and addressed social challenges [52].

The relevance of this model is evident in contexts of complex economic and social challenges. This collaboration requires the alignment of contributions from the sectors, facilitated by shared strategies [5]. However, implementing the model faces challenges, such as the need for effective coordination between sectors with different objectives. Building a common language and defining shared goals are essential to overcome these challenges, as is investing in training to understand each actor's responsibilities and contributions [5]. While the government traditionally addresses social issues, its effectiveness is enhanced with the involvement of NGOs, which can implement effective interventions, especially in the intermediate stages of projects [39]. Including society in the innovation process allows solutions shaped by local realities, promoting community empowerment. Social enterprises based on social entrepreneurship emerge as essential partners, capable of acting in collaborative networks aimed at community empowerment. Academia plays a crucial role in the model, transferring knowledge that fosters innovation and social development. The active involvement of universities, in partnership with companies, governments, and civil society, strengthens the innovation ecosystem and enables greater dissemination of sustainable practices. Chesbrough [11] argues that the interaction between academia and the private sector is crucial to creating innovative solutions that help solve social issues. The research and development stimulated by this collaboration provides new products and services and fosters an environment conducive to social innovation. By working with companies, universities can transfer relevant knowledge and technologies that address social problems such as health, education, and sustainability.

Building effective partnerships and implementing business models prioritizing social impact can pave the way for more agile and lasting solutions [9]. Human capital, social capital, and motivation obtained with the coordination of the quadruple helix benefit social entrepreneurship initiatives [23]. The model supports community-driven social innovations in rural development, emphasizing the importance of local knowledge and informal communities [43]. Engaging civil society in regional innovation strategies remains challenging, but the quadruple helix approach is promising to address rural development challenges and reduce poverty [5, 50] by leveraging the collective strengths and resources of government, academia, industry, and civil society. This model can contribute to a more equitable society by fostering collaboration, innovation, and community empowerment. Collaboration between small and medium enterprises, NGOs, and governments can promote the sustainable growth of small and medium enterprises by providing financial support, capacity building, and policy guidance [24].

6 Conclusions and Recommendations for Social Entrepreneurs

The social economy emphasizes social impact and financial sustainability. It is a crucial form of addressing contemporary challenges, particularly in empowering individuals and communities to overcome poverty. By creating opportunities, providing essential services, and fostering social inclusion, social economy organizations contribute significantly to a more equitable and sustainable society.

The quadruple helix model integrates government, the private sector, academia, and civil society, offering a valuable framework for understanding and enhancing the impact of the social economy. This collaborative approach facilitates innovation, resource sharing, and knowledge exchange, enabling stakeholders to work together towards common goals and address complex social and environmental issues more effectively. Government funding and policy support can be leveraged with private sector investment and technological expertise, while academia can provide knowledge, research methodologies, and human resources. Civil society organizations can contribute their expertise and networks to reach vulnerable communities and ensure that interventions are relevant and impactful. The involvement of local communities in the decision-making process is crucial because interventions can be more responsive to the needs and priorities of those affected by poverty. This collaborative approach can lead to more effective and sustainable poverty reduction strategies. This can empower communities to take ownership of their development and build resilience.

To implement this approach to reduce poverty effectively, we recommend creating spaces where representatives from all four helixes can come together to discuss poverty-related issues, share knowledge, and co-create solutions. This could involve regular meetings, workshops, conferences, or online forums. Also, it is important to encourage open communication and transparency among stakeholders to build trust and foster a collaborative environment. Another recommendation is to create incubators and accelerators to support the development of social enterprises that address poverty-related challenges and facilitate sharing best practices and lessons learned among different stakeholders. It is also important to involve communities in decision-making, ensuring that the voices of those affected by poverty are heard and that their needs and priorities are considered in designing and implementing interventions. Finally, it is important to establish common objectives and measurable indicators to track progress and ensure that all actors work towards the same goals.

References

1. Alomoto W, Niñerola A, Pié L (2022) Social impact assessment: a systematic review of literature. Soc Indic Res 161(1):225–250. https://doi.org/10.1007/s11205-021-02809-1
2. Angélique NC, Stany V, Lebailly P, Azadi H (2022) Agricultural development in the fight against poverty: the case of south Kivu, DR Congo. Land 11(4):472. https://doi.org/10.3390/land11040472

3. Arejiogbe OE, Moses CL, Salau OP, Onayemi OO, Agada SA, Dada AE, Obisesan OT (2023) Bolstering the impact of social entrepreneurship and poverty alleviation for sustainable development in Nigeria. Sustain For 15(8):6673. https://doi.org/10.3390/su15086673
4. Banerjee A, Duflo E, Goldberg N, Karlan D, Osei R, Parienté W et al (2015) A multifaceted program causes lasting progress for the very poor: evidence from six countries. Science 348(6236):1260799. https://doi.org/10.1126/science.1260799
5. Bellandi M, Donati L, Cataneo A (2021) Social innovation governance and the role of universities: cases of quadruple helix partnerships in Italy. Technol Forecast Soc Chang 164:120518. https://doi.org/10.1016/j.techfore.2020.120518
6. Besley T, Ghatak M (2017) Profit with purpose? A theory of social enterprise. Am Econ J Econ Pol 9(3):19–58. https://doi.org/10.1257/pol.20150495
7. Besser R, Morita J, Schwarz D (2021) We know how to fight poverty. So let's fight. Academic Pediatrics 21(8):S86–S87. https://doi.org/10.1016/j.acap.2021.07.024
8. Bornstein D (2007) How to change the world: social entrepreneurs and the power of new ideas, 2nd edn. Oxford University Press
9. Carayannis EG, Grigoroudis E, Stamati D, Valvi T (2019) Social business model innovation: a quadruple/quintuple helix-based social innovation ecosystem. IEEE Trans Eng Manag 68(1):235–248. https://doi.org/10.1109/TEM.2019.2914408
10. Casais B, Soares AM (2024) Implementing the quadruple helix towards social innovation: the case of the human power hub, Braga, Portugal. In: Thrassou A, Vrontis D, Efthymiou L, Weber Y, Shams SMR, Tsoukatos E (eds) Non-profit organisations, volume II: economy, industries and context. Springer, pp 123–145. https://doi.org/10.1007/978-3-031-62530-5_12
11. Chesbrough H (2010) Business model innovation: opportunities and barriers. Long Range Plan 43(2–3):354–363. https://doi.org/10.1016/j.lrp.2009.07.010
12. Dinata C (2023) Quadruple helix model in building communalism and social resilience in handling poverty in rural communities. J Transfor Governance Soc Justice (J-TRAG) 1(1):11–22
13. Doherty B, Haugh H, Lyon F (2014) Social enterprises as hybrid organizations: a review and research agenda. Int J Manag Rev 16(4):417–436. https://doi.org/10.1111/ijmr.12028
14. El Ebrashi R (2013) Social entrepreneurship theory and sustainable social impact. Soc Respons 9(2):188–209. https://doi.org/10.1108/SRJ-07-2011-0013
15. Farinha L, Sebastião JR, Sampaio C, Lopes J (2020) Social innovation and social entrepreneurship: discovering origins, exploring current and future trends. Int Rev Public Nonprofit Mark 17(1):77–96. https://doi.org/10.1007/s12208-020-00243-6
16. Fernández-Guadaño J, Diez RM (2024) Social entrepreneurship impact in ten EU countries with supportive regulations. J Knowl Econ 15(3):10781–10798. https://doi.org/10.1007/s13132-023-01513-4
17. Ferreira MR, Braga V, Sánchez-Hernández MI, Gomes J (2024) Framing the fourth sector–dystopia or future contours?. Int Rev Public Nonprofit Mark 1-28. https://doi.org/10.1007/s12208-024-00406-9
18. Fotheringham S, Saunders C (2014) Social enterprise as poverty reducing strategy for women. Soc Enterp J 10(3):176–199. https://doi.org/10.1108/SEJ-06-2013-0028
19. Hamby A, Pierce M, Brinberg D (2017) Solving complex problems: enduring solutions through social entrepreneurship, community action, and social marketing. J Macromark 37(4):369–380. https://doi.org/10.1177/0276146716663797
20. Hirschl TA, Mohammed A, Fagan A, Houssock C, Bergh L (2023) International comparisons in fighting poverty: the poverty stoplight program in South Africa, the UK, and the US. J Poverty 27(1):82–97. https://doi.org/10.1080/10875549.2021.2010868
21. Howaldt J, Schwarz M (2021) Social innovation and social change. In *a research agenda for social innovation*. Edward Elgar Publishing, pp 39–57. https://doi.org/10.4337/9781789909357.00010
22. Ipinnaiye O, Olaniyan F (2023) An exploratory study of local social innovation initiatives for sustainable poverty reduction in Nigeria. Sustain Dev 31(4):2222–2239. https://doi.org/10.1002/sd.2502

23. Iqbal J, Kousar S, Ul Hameed W (2018) Antecedents of sustainable social entrepreneurship initiatives in Pakistan and outcomes: collaboration between quadruple helix sectors. Sustain For 10(12):4539. https://doi.org/10.3390/SU10124539
24. Islam A, Islam MA, Hossain MI, Nimfa DT, Tehseen S (2025) Paradox of sustainable growth: the interplay between small and medium enterprises and non-governmental organizations and government helix. Business Strategy Develop 8(1):e70054. https://doi.org/10.1002/bsd2.70054
25. Islam MS, Alam K (2018) Does social capital reduce poverty? A cross-sectional study of rural household in Bangladesh. Int J Soc Econ 45(11):1515–1532. https://doi.org/10.1108/IJSE-07-2017-0295
26. João-Roland IDS, Granados ML (2020) Social innovation drivers in social enterprises: systematic review. J Small Bus Enterp Dev 27(5):775–795. https://doi.org/10.1108/JSBED-12-2019-0396
27. Kamaludin MF, Xavier JA, Amin M (2024) Social entrepreneurship and sustainability: a conceptual framework. J Soc Entrep 15(1):26–49. https://doi.org/10.1080/19420676.2021.1900339
28. Khieng S, Dahles H (2015) Commercialization in the non-profit sector: the emergence of social enterprise in Cambodia. J Soc Entrep 6(2):218–243. https://doi.org/10.1080/19420676.2014.954261
29. Klarin A, Suseno Y (2023) An integrative literature review of social entrepreneurship research: mapping the literature and future research directions. Bus Soc 62(3):565–611. https://doi.org/10.1177/00076503221101611
30. Lee EKM, Lee H, Kee CH, Kwan CH, Ng CH (2021) Social impact measurement in incremental social innovation. J Soc Entrep 12(1):69–86
31. Li J (2020) Join the fight against poverty: utilizing HRD practices to support pathways to sustainable employment and decent work. Hum Resour Dev Int 23(1):1–4. https://doi.org/10.1080/13678868.2020.1701222
32. Liu F, Li L, Zhang Y, Ngo QT, Iqbal W (2021) Role of education in poverty reduction: macroeconomic and social determinants form developing economies. Environ Sci Pollut Res 28:63163–63177. https://doi.org/10.1007/s11356-021-15252-z
33. Macías Ruano AJ, Milán-García J, Marruecos Rumi ME, De Pablo Valenciano J (2021) Scientific production on the social economy: a review of worldwide research. Volunt Int J Volunt Nonprofit Org 32(5):925–943. https://doi.org/10.1007/s11266-021-00361-7
34. Mahembe E, Odhiambo NM (2019) Foreign aid and poverty reduction: a review of international literature. Cogent Soc Sci 5(1):1625741. https://doi.org/10.1080/23311886.2019.1625741
35. Mahmuda I, Baskaran A, Pancholi J (2014) Financing social innovation for poverty reduction: a case study of microfinancing and microenterprise development in Bangladesh. Sci Technol Soc 19(2):249–273. https://doi.org/10.1177/0971721814529879
36. Mair J, Martí I (2006) Social entrepreneurship research: a source of explanation, prediction, and delight. J World Bus 41(1):36–44. https://doi.org/10.1016/j.jwb.2005.09.002
37. Martins T, Braga A, Braga V, Ferreira MR (2020) The social innovation momentum: a qualitative analysis of governance and funding processes. Int Rev Public Nonprofit Mark 17(1):97–120. https://doi.org/10.1007/s12208-019-00238-y
38. Millard J, Fucci V (2023) The role of social innovation in tackling global poverty and vulnerability. Front Sociol 8:966918. https://doi.org/10.3389/fsoc.2023.966918
39. Mulyaningsih HD (2021) Social entrepreneurship model based on quadruple helix collaboration: economic empowerment in disabilities community. J Soc Entrepreneur Theory Practice (JSETP) 1(1):1–11. https://doi.org/10.31098/jsetp.v1i1.647
40. Muñoz P, Kimmitt J (2019) Social mission as competitive advantage: a configurational analysis of the strategic conditions of social entrepreneurship. J Bus Res 101:854–861. https://doi.org/10.1016/j.jbusres.2018.11.044
41. Mwabu G (2023) Poverty reduction through growth, redistribution and social inclusion in times of COVID-19: Kenyan evidence on the underlying mechanisms. J Afr Econ 32(Supplement_2):ii69-ii80. https://doi.org/10.1093/jae/ejac042

42. Nicholls J (2017) Social return on investment—development and convergence. Eval Program Plann 64:127–135. https://doi.org/10.1016/j.evalprogplan.2016.11.011
43. Nordberg K, Mariussen Å, Virkkala S (2020) Community-driven social innovation and quadruple helix coordination in rural development. Case study on LEADER group Aktion Österbotten. J Rural Stud 79:157–168. https://doi.org/10.1016/j.jrurstud.2020.08.001
44. Nursini N (2020) Micro, small, and medium enterprises (MSMEs) and poverty reduction: empirical evidence from Indonesia. Develop Stud Res 7(1):153–166. https://doi.org/10.1080/21665095.2020.1823238
45. Osei CD, Zhuang J (2020) Rural poverty alleviation strategies and social capital link: the mediation role of women entrepreneurship and social innovation. SAGE Open 10(2):2158244020925504. https://doi.org/10.1177/2158244020925504
46. Phillips A, Luo R, Wendland-Liu J (2024) Shifting the paradigm: a critical review of social innovation literature. Int J Innov Stud 8(1):45–58. https://doi.org/10.1016/j.ijis.2023.08.003
47. Rado I, Nuchpiam P (2024) Scaling for social impact: understanding social innovation through local empowerment strategies. Soc Enterp J 20(1):54–75. https://doi.org/10.1108/SEJ-04-2023-0045
48. Ravishankar MN (2021) Social innovations and the fight against poverty: an analysis of India's first prosocial P2P lending platform. Inf Syst J 31(5):745–766. https://doi.org/10.1111/isj.12340
49. Raza A, Murad HS, Zakar MZ (2016) Contextualizing poverty and culture; towards a social economy of community centered knowledge based development. Int J Soc Econ 43(5):486–501. https://doi.org/10.1108/IJSE-04-2014-0072
50. Roman M, Varga H, Cvijanovic V, Reid A (2020) Quadruple helix models for sustainable regional innovation: engaging and facilitating civil society participation. Economies 8(2):48. https://doi.org/10.3390/economies8020048
51. Sá E, Casais B, Silva J (2019) Local development through rural entrepreneurship, from the triple helix perspective: the case of a peripheral region in northern Portugal. Int J Entrepreneurial Behaviour Res 25(4):698–716. https://doi.org/10.1108/IJEBR-03-2018-0172
52. Saiz-Álvarez JM, Palma-Ruiz JM (2019) Entrepreneurship in the solidarity economy: a valuation of models based on the quadruple helix and civil society. In: Ratten V, Jones P, Braga V, Marques CS (eds) Subsistence entrepreneurship: the interplay of collaborative innovation, sustainability and social goals, contributions to management science. Springer, Cham, pp 33–50. https://doi.org/10.1007/978-3-030-11542-5_4
53. Soares AM, Casais B (2023) Uniting marketing efforts for the common good—a challenge for the fourth sector. Springer. https://doi.org/10.1007/978-3-031-29020-6
54. Sofo F, Wicks A (2017) An occupational perspective of poverty and poverty reduction. J Occup Sci 24(2):244–249. https://doi.org/10.1080/14427591.2017.1314223
55. Soundararajan V, Sahasranamam S, Rogerson M, Bapuji H, Spence LJ, Shaw JD (2025) Organizational engagement with poverty: a review and reorientation. J Manag 51(1):62–102. https://doi.org/10.1177/01492063241234663
56. Starkbaum J, Braun R, Blok V, Schroth F, Häußermann JJ, Colonnello C et al (2024) Responsible innovation across societal sectors: a practice perspective on quadruple helix collaboration. J Resp Innov 11(1):2414531. https://doi.org/10.1080/23299460.2024.2414531
57. Zaefarian R, Tasavori M, Ghauri PN (2015) A corporate social entrepreneurship approach to market-based poverty reduction. Emerg Mark Financ Trade 51(2):320–334. https://doi.org/10.1080/1540496X.2015.1021606
58. Zhang X, Sun Y, Gao Y, Dong Y (2022) Paths out of poverty: social entrepreneurship and sustainable development. Front Psychol 13:1062669. https://doi.org/10.3389/fpsyg.2022.1062669
59. Carayannis EG, Campbell DF (2009) 'Mode 3'and'Quadruple Helix': toward a 21st century fractal innovation ecosystem. Int J Tech Manag 46(3-4):201–234. https://doi.org/10.1504/IJTM.2009.023374

Beatriz Casais has a Ph.D. in Business and Management Studies from the University of Porto and a MSc in Marketing, with a bachelor's degree in Communication Sciences and a Post-Graduation in Health Communication. She is currently an Associate Professor at the University of Minho in the fields of Marketing and Strategy, a senior researcher at iBMS—Centre for Research in Business, Markets, and Society -. and a board member of the European Social Marketing Association (ESMA). Her research focuses on social marketing and public health advertisement, digital marketing, and tourism marketing. She was social marketing manager at the Portuguese Ministry of Health, HIV/AIDS National Prevention Program. Beatriz Casais was vice-Dean of the School of Economics and Management of the University of Minho between 2020 and 2023, and head of the executive education unit—UMinhoExec.

Camila Barroso dos Santos holds a degree in Education from the University of Minho and is pursuing a Master of Science in Social Economy with a focus on social entrepreneurship and social innovation.

Social Marketing for Well-Being and Quality of Life

2

M. Mercedes Galan-Ladero

Improving the lives of all, leaving no one behind.

– United Nations [1]

Abstract

Social Marketing focuses on seeking the common good and creating social value. For this purpose, social marketing tries to promote, modify, discourage, or even reject ideas, values, attitudes, and, especially, behaviors that affect people's well-being and quality of life. Consequently, as a behavior change is needed to fulfill the Sustainable Development Goals (SDGs), social marketing can be a key tool to achieve them.

Graphical Abstract

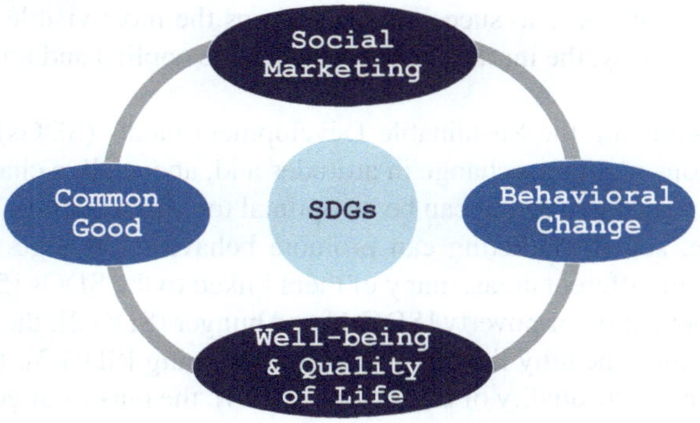

Source: Author

M. M. Galan-Ladero (✉)
University of Extremadura, Badajoz, Spain
e-mail: mgalan@unex.es

B. Casais (ed.), *Integrated Science to Achieve Sustainable Development Goals*, Integrated Science 37, https://doi.org/10.1007/978-3-031-88777-2_2

Keywords

Marketing of ideas and social issues · Attitudes · Behaviors · Behavioral change · Social change · Common good · Social good · Creation of social value · Sustainable Development Goals (SDGs) · Welfare · Social interventions

1 Introduction

With the purpose of improving the lives of all people, including everyone, the United Nations General Assembly adopted on September 25, 2015, the 2030 Agenda for Sustainable Development [2]. This Agenda, in which the 17 Sustainable Development Goals (SDGs) stand out, was intended to be a reference framework for global development programs aimed at improving the quality of life of people around the world [3, 4] and obtaining greater socially inclusive well-being for all [5].

On the other hand, social marketing, also called *marketing of ideas and social issues* [6], focuses on seeking the common good [7]. And, for this purpose, it seeks to promote, modify, discourage, or even reject ideas, values, attitudes and, especially, behaviors that affect people's well-being and quality of life [5].

In this way, social marketing, like marketing in general, is based on exchange (this is its essence). The product, in this case, is a behavior (either a behavior that, socially, is desirable and, therefore, is promoted; or a behavior that is intended to be changed, discouraged, or even eliminated because it is socially undesirable). In return, the price paid for this product can be monetary (the amount of money it costs to carry it out or not to carry it out) and non-monetary (time, effort, or inconvenience to achieve it). Achieving this behavior may or may not require the intervention of intermediaries, and omnichannel strategy could be considered [8]. And communication is also key to success (it is perhaps the most visible part of social marketing). In this way, the marketing mix can also be applied and underpins social marketing.

Moreover, achieving the Sustainable Development Goals (SDGs) proposed by the United Nations requires a change in attitudes and, above all, a change in behaviors. Therefore, social marketing can be an optimal tool for achieving the 17 SDGs.

In this sense, social marketing can promote behavioral change to respond to social problems in different areas, many of them linked to the SDGs [5], such as, for example, the eradication of poverty [SDG 1] and hunger [SDG 2], the improvement of health, to ensure a healthy life and promote well-being [SDG 3], the promotion and improvement of the quality of education [SDG 4], the pursuit of gender equality [SDG 5], the availability of water and sanitation, as well as the sustainability of their management [SDG 6], the use of clean energy and energy efficiency [SDG 7], inclusive and sustainable economic growth, as well as the promotion of decent work and the fulfillment of human and labor rights [SDG 8], building resilient infrastructure and promoting sustainable and innovation-promoting industrialization [SDG 9], reducing inequality within and between countries [SDG 10], making cities more inclusive, safe, resilient and sustainable [SDG 11], promoting sustainable consumption and production [SDG 12], combating climate change and its impacts [SDG 13], conserving the oceans [SDG 14], protecting ecosystems, sustainably managing forests, combating desertification and halting biodiversity loss [SDG 15], promoting peaceful and inclusive societies [SDG 16] and revitalizing the global partnership for sustainable development [SDG 17].

This chapter will analyze the role of social marketing and its relationship with the SDGs, as well as its influence on people's well-being and quality of life. First of all, the terms "social marketing", "well-being", "welfare", and "quality of life" will be defined, analyzing their characteristics and the relationships between them. Finally, conclusions and some final reflections will be drawn, as well as the main implications for managers of organizations and public policies.

2 Social Marketing

Although in 1951 Wiebe already raised the possibility of applying marketing tools and techniques to social issues [9], and family planning interventions to change lifestyles and behaviors were developed in India in the 1960s [10], the origin of social marketing theory dates back to 1971 [9], when Kotler and Zaltman, in an article published in the Journal of Marketing, proposed to extend the marketing concept to the field of social ideas or causes, defining *social marketing* as "*the design, implementation and control of programs calculated to influence the acceptance of social ideas and involves considerations of product planning, pricing, communication, distribution and marketing research*" [11]: 5. In this way, they also transferred the marketing mix scheme (the 4 Ps) to social marketing [12].

In its more than half a century of existence, social marketing has evolved to adopt a more holistic, strategic, and interdisciplinary approach [7], focused on creating social value [13] and targeting different stakeholders (not only citizens, but also social service providers, policy makers and others [13].

Influencing ideas, values, attitudes and, above all, behaviors [14], it aims to benefit individuals and their communities [15], as well as society as a whole [16], creating social value [13] to achieve greater social good, and even seeking social change [17] and improving individual and social well-being [18]. The main milestones in social marketing are summarized in Fig. 2.1.

In short, social marketing seeks to "*encourage a certain social behavior, fostering certain values, promoting specific attitudes, or achieving the acceptance of ideas that facilitate the desired behavior, considered beneficial for society, or for a part of it; or, on the contrary, it can also try to discourage or curb a specific behavior, as well as the attitudes or ideas that may lead to it, because it is considered harmful and, consequently, not socially desirable*" [19]: 265.

Social marketing, initially developed by public and non-profit organizations, is currently carried out by all types of organizations, including companies [3]. In the latter case, it is called *corporate social marketing* and considered as one of the main CSR initiatives [16].

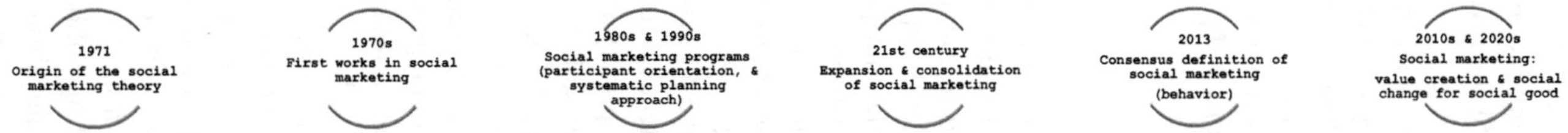

Fig. 2.1 Main milestones in social marketing. (Source: Adapted from Galan-Ladero and Alves [3])

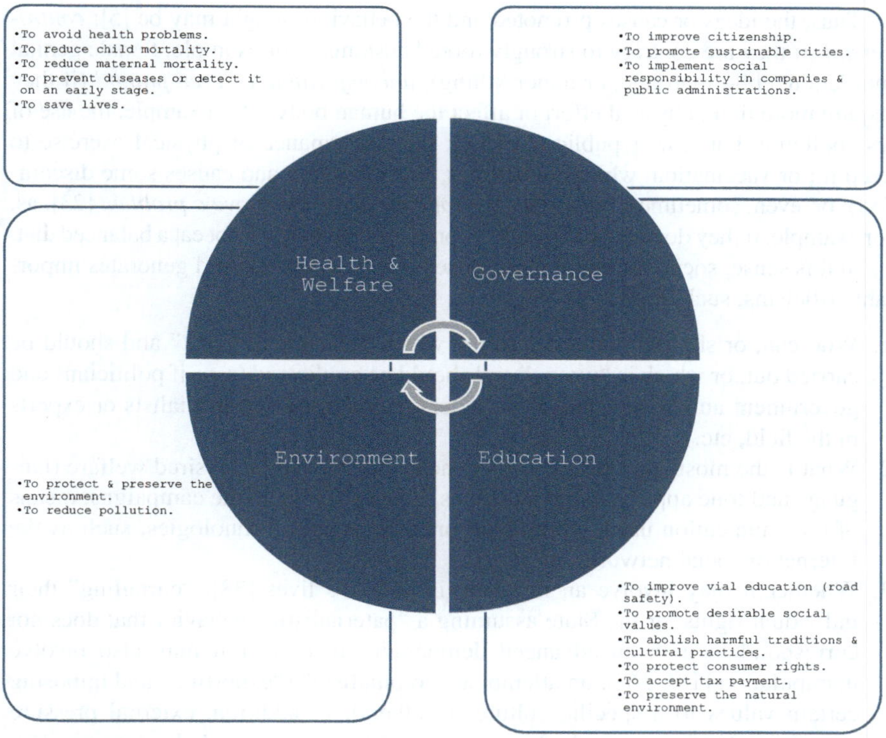

Fig. 2.2 Some areas of application of social marketing. (Source: Adapted from Galan-Ladero and Alves [3])

Throughout all this time, social marketing has been applied in numerous areas (Fig. 2.2), also incorporating in recent years the focus on the SDGs.

For behavioral change, social marketing can use different forms and strategies of intervention.

Among the different forms [20], the following classifications can be highlighted: the behavior of individuals can be influenced directly or indirectly; the focus can be on identifying causes or facilitating solutions; laws and regulations can be enacted, new technologies can be designed, information can be provided, sanctions can be imposed or, on the contrary, tax breaks and subsidies can be encouraged, and/or interpersonal interactions can be established.

As for the different intervention strategies, it is possible to reinforce the desired behavior, induce it, rationalize, and explain the reason for the desired behavior, and even confront in order to achieve the intended behavior [21].

On the other hand, and unlike other marketing modalities, a characteristic of social marketing is that it is not driven by market demand or economic value [22], nor does it seek short-term satisfaction of the target audience, but rather to improve their quality of life and well-being in the long term [3].

Thus, the ideas or causes promoted and the behaviors sought may be [5]: *controversial* (if they are contrary to strongly rooted customs—for example, female genital mutilation, child marriage, or honor killing); *uncomfortable or even painful* (if they require more time, physical effort or affect the human body—for example, the use of less polluting but slower public transport; the performance of physical exercise to keep fit; or vaccination, which, sometimes, gives reaction and causes some discomfort); or, even, sometimes *individuals do not even know they have a problem* [23], as, for example, if they do not use antibiotics correctly, or if they do not eat a balanced diet.

In this sense, social marketing also raises ethical questions and generates important criticisms, such as [5]:

1. Who can, or should, really determine which behavior is "right" and should be carried out, or which is "wrong" and should be eradicated (e.g., if politicians and government authorities, religious leaders, a committee of specialists or experts in the field, etc.).
2. What is the most appropriate way or means to achieve the desired welfare (language and tone applied in the messages, images shown in the campaigns, means of communication used—traditional or through new technologies, such as the Internet or social networks, etc.).
3. Whether it may involve an intrusion in people's lives [38], "curtailing" their individual rights, or the State assuming a "paternalistic" behavior that does not correspond to it in an advanced democratic society; or it may also involve manipulation [18]: 36 or an attempt at "colonialism" ("exporting" and imposing certain values to a specific culture on others). In addition, external pressure groups (such as corporate lobbies or political interests), could also interfere [5].

In short, and to avoid these criticisms and ethical issues, social marketing should seek a clear common good, which, ultimately, is reflected in the people's well-being and improvement of their quality of life.

3 Well-Being and Quality of Life

Based on the above, it can be stated that social marketing is linked to the concepts of well-being and quality of life. These two concepts, although closely connected, are not exactly synonymous.

3.1 Well-Being

The term "well-being" is frequently considered synonymous with "welfare" [24], and both terms are often used interchangeably. However, strictly speaking, some differences can be appreciated.

Well-being: Well-being can be considered as "*a positive state experienced by individuals and societies*" [25]; or more specifically, "*the state of the person in which the good functioning of his somatic and psychic activity is made sensible*" [26].

This is usually due to the fact that he/she has all the necessary things to live well, with peace of mind [26]. Well-being can be considered as an index of societal progress [27].

There are different theories of well-being, most of them come from psychology. They try to discover what factors contribute to people's well-being, and to identify the different forms of well-being [27]. Thus, subjective, and objective approaches can be observed in people's well-being [27]:

- Subjective approach: subjective aspects of well-being that depend on the mental state and attitudes of the person. It is related to people's evaluations of their own lives. Subjective well-being is also called *happiness*, which is defined as "*satisfaction with life in general*" [27]: 294. This subjective approach has the following main dimensions: the role of human genes, universal needs, social environment, economic environment, and political environment.
- Objective approach: objective aspects are related to observable dimensions for its measurement. They are measured through indexes and indicators (e.g., Gross Domestic Product—GDP; inflation or national income). There are also different dimensions: related to health, job opportunities, socioeconomic development, environment, safety, and politics.

Welfare: In the broadest sense, "welfare" refers to the well-being of individuals, families, and the community [25]. But it can also have an economic and institutional connotation, referring to government programs that offer protection, financial and/or social, to the most vulnerable individuals or groups, in areas related to health care, housing or unemployment benefits [24].

This concept is directly related to the "Welfare State", which designates "*a form of governance characterized by a set of institutions and policies in which the national government or State assumes a fundamental role in seeking a better redistribution of income and greater social benefits for the most disadvantaged*" [26], thus safeguarding and promoting the well-being of its citizens.

3.2 Quality of Life

Quality of Life (QoL) is a complex and interdisciplinary concept (it is used in psychology, sociology, marketing, economics, politics, healthcare, etc.). Thus, QoL is defined as the set of conditions (economic, natural, socio-cultural, political-legal, etc.) "*that contribute to making life pleasant, dignified and valuable*" [26]. QoL refers, therefore, to the notion of living a good life, a life of high quality [28].

QoL can also be defined as "*the individual's subjective perception of objective conditions related to well-being and standard of living*" [29]. But QoL goes beyond economic well-being: it is "*each individual's perception of his or her position in life, within the cultural context and value system in which he or she lives, in relation to his or her expectations, interests and achievements*" [30]: 2. In other words, QoL is often perceived differently by individuals depending on their cultural and socioeconomic environment [31], and also on the moment of time in which they live.

Consequently, the definition of QoL combines and integrates two dimensions [39]:

- Objective dimension: QoL is usually measured using indicators that represent observable and measurable conditions (e.g., durable housing, adequate water supply, availability of green areas and accessibility to schools).
- Subjective dimension: QoL sometimes requires some subjective judgment (e.g., there may be different standards for considering a dwelling inadequate).

Thus, QoL incorporates two main approaches [30]:

- Quantitative—objective approach: what people have and can be directly observed.
- Qualitative—subjective approach: what people feel and can be observed indirectly.

QoL is assessed by analyzing different areas, such as [32]: physical well-being (health, fitness, mobility, personal safety), material well-being (income, possessions, housing, transport, etc.), social well-being (interpersonal relationships—family, relatives, friends—and community involvement), development (job, leisure, education, etc.) or emotional well-being (self-esteem, fulfillment, status/respect, faith/belief, etc.).

There are numerous indicators to measure quality of life, such as the United Nations Human Development Index, the OECD's Human Development Index, or Eurostat's population and social conditions/ Quality of life indicators [33].

4 Relationship Between the Concepts of Social Marketing, Well-Being, and Quality of Life

The impact of social marketing on people's quality of life is significant [34]. But the dimensions of quality of life have also influenced the development of social marketing [29].

With social marketing, marketing techniques have been put at the service of society. They have enabled a better understanding of the different target audiences and the identification of their needs, for better planning and design of programs and strategies, thus improving the effectiveness of social interventions and the results obtained (financial as well as social and environmental [34]).

For all these reasons, authors such as Sirgy et al. [22] consider that social marketing is marketing for quality of life. An effective social marketing strategy to improve the quality of life must also increase the well-being of specific target groups and create social value for all potential stakeholders. Thus, quality-of-life oriented social marketing "*represents a powerful tool for human development and the flourishing of societies*" [34]: 13.

5 Social Marketing Approaches and Strategies, Related to the SDGs, to Achieve Well-Being and Improve People's Quality of Life

5.1 Approaches

Social marketing, to achieve well-being and improve people's quality of life, can be addressed from different approaches, with different classifications.

1. A first classification refers to the people on whom social marketing efforts are focused. This classification points to 3 approaches (see Fig. 2.3), which can also be combined and complementary [3, 18, 36]:

   – **Downstream approach**. It involves addressing the problem by facilitating access to solutions, directly influencing people's behavior.
   Efforts are focused on individuals whose behavior is to be directly influenced. For example, to combat financial exclusion, information and educational programs on digitization can be offered to vulnerable people. This would be the case for elderly people who are not familiar with new technologies: they need to learn how to make their financial transactions safely through the internet, mobile apps, or ATMs, so as not to depend on relatives or other people who have to make them, or who have to accompany them to ATMs to help them.

   – **Midstream approach**. It involves addressing the problem by acting on those who can help change behavior (e.g., family members, friends, teachers, co-workers, among others).
   Efforts are focused on people close to the individuals who have the problem. For example, to prevent cell phone addiction in children and adolescents, it can be tried to raise awareness among parents and teachers so that, together, they can help to reduce the time they spend in front of screens (control the use of cell phones at home, do not let them be used in class, etc.).

   – **Upstream approach**. It involves addressing the problem by identifying the main causes and influencing the policies, structures and decision-makers that can help prevent and mitigate the problem.
   Efforts are focused on those who can influence the system in which the behavior occurs (e.g., policy makers, authorities, experts and others whose decisions could influence the social environment of the individuals affected by the problem), in order to encourage or discourage that behavior.

Fig. 2.3 Social marketing streams. (Source: Adapted from Alves et al. [34])

For example, to encourage a healthy diet, taxes on natural or organic products could be lowered to make their final price more affordable for the general population; or in public tenders and bids, better scoring could be given to caterers in school and university canteens, or in workplaces, who offer more natural and sustainable products, or even require them not to include industrial pastries or junk food in their menus; or include in educational programs cross-cutting courses on healthy eating habits; or, from the Ministry of Health itself, prohibit, or at least recommend not to buy, certain products or large-sized packaging of certain products whose excessive consumption may cause certain diseases (for example, "supersize" fast food, since it has been shown that their continued consumption can cause problems of obesity, hypertension, diabetes, etc.).

2. A second classification would be according to the way of addressing or achieving the desired behavior (these approaches are also often combined and complementary [3, 21]):

   – **Legal approach**: based on laws, norms, regulations, etc.
   For example: creation of public aid for people with scarce resources [SDG 1 and SDG 2]; ban on smoking in public places, ban on selling tobacco or alcohol to children under 18, ban on advertising—directly or indirectly—tobacco, ban on the installation of vending machines for sugary soft drinks in educational centers, creation of a universal healthcare system [SDG 3]; obligation to put all children in school, so that they receive a basic education (free of charge) [SDG 4]; adoption of laws to enforce equal rights between men and women, reforming the penal code to condemn gender-based violence [SDG 5]; forcing public establishments to have their doors closed, and heating and air conditioning at certain temperatures to improve energy efficiency [SDG 7]; occupational health and safety standards, labor standards and worker protection, obligation to pay a minimum wage to workers [SDG 8]; creation of development cooperation agencies [SDG 10]; laws for accessibility in public buildings and places [SDG 11]; obligation to charge for single-use plastic bags requested in commercial establishments—or, directly, banning plastic bags [SDG 12 and SDG 14]; laws for the protection of natural sites and preservation of biodiversity [SDG 15]; allowing the sale of weapons only in authorized establishments and to persons who, beforehand, have obtained a weapons permit [SDG 16].
   – **Technological approach**: based on the use of technological innovations or digital technologies to alleviate the problem.
   For example, technological innovations to improve production processes (less water consumption and in a smaller area, regenerating soil and reducing the carbon footprint in the value chain) and food, ensuring food safety and increased production (fortified and functional products, probiotics, transgenics, etc.) [SDGs 1 and 2]; medicines to reduce tobacco consumption (nicotine

pills, patches, or gum), electronic devices and mobile applications to report the distance traveled when exercising, steps taken when walking, etc. [SDG 3]; new technologies (e.g., social networks, apps, etc.) applied to education [SDG 4]; innovations to improve the quality of water and sanitation systems [SDG 6 and SDG 11]; innovations and improvements in equipment installations that use clean energy and pollute less [SDG 7, SDG 9 and SDG 11]; innovations in workers' protective equipment to prevent work accidents [SDG 8]; cameras and drones to prevent fires [SDG 15].

– **Informative approach**: based on persuasive information to carry out the desired behavior (or stop doing the undesired one).
  For example: Information campaigns in the media and in supermarkets for the collection of products for Food Banks [SDG 1 and SDG 2]; information campaigns for the prevention of certain diseases, informative messages on recommended doses (labels on bottles of alcoholic beverages), unpleasant images on tobacco packs [SDG 3]; posters and videos on means of transport to identify behaviors that constitute gender-based violence [SDG 5], encourage recycling and reuse of products [SDG 12], raise awareness of climate change [SDG 13] or fight against stereotypes [SDG 16].
– **Economic approach**: reducing the cost of performing the desired behavior or, conversely, increasing the price of performing the undesired behavior.
  For example, income tax deductions for donations to nonprofit organizations [SDGs 1 and 2]; free vaccinations / fines for parents who do not vaccinate their children (mandatory vaccination schedules), taxes on sugary drinks [SDG 3]; provision of study grants [SDG 4]; penalties for companies that do not have an equality plan [SDG 5], irregular hiring [SDG 8]; aid and/or tax breaks for companies that employ people with disabilities or those belonging to the most vulnerable groups [SDG 16]; aid to companies for digitalization and/or adaptation of facilities to use clean energy and reduce the carbon footprint [SDG 7, SDG 9 and SDG 13]; tax discounts for recycling correctly/fines for not recycling correctly [SDG 12]; subsidies and vouchers for travel on public transport [SDG 12].
– **Relational approach**: based on interpersonal interactions (between family members, friends, classmates, co-workers, etc.).
  For example, to fight bullying, involve family members, teachers, influencers, and even the school's own students [SDG 4 and SDG 16]; to fight gender-based violence, involve family members, friends, co-workers and society in general, so that they report any situation of gender-based violence they witness or are aware of [SDG 5]; to raise awareness of the need to be active, do sports and lead a healthy lifestyle, involve families, health personnel, teachers [SDG 3].

5.2 Strategies

Regarding strategies to address social problems, they can be [3, 21, 37]:

Reinforcement: when attitudes are positive, and the desired behaviors are carried out.

Objective: that the desired behavior continues to be performed (e.g., with prizes, rewards, social recognition, economic incentives, legal regulations, educational activities, etc.).

For example: financial incentives to people over 18 years of age for passing school graduation or compulsory secondary education [SDG 4]; public recognition and awards for people who have donated blood the most times [SDG 3];

Induction: when the attitude is positive, but the desired behavior is not carried out.

Objective: the aim is to "induce" the desired behavior, to encourage it to take place (by providing human and material means, economic incentives, legal regulations, etc.).

For example: using mobile units to travel to university centers and workplaces, to crowded places or rural areas, and thus facilitate blood donations [SDG 3]; setting up stands on beaches to raise awareness about skin cancer [SDG 3]; installing containers and clean points near homes, to facilitate recycling [SDG 12]; creating infrastructure and public transport networks (improving the service and frequency of urban buses, and covering more points of the city; offering new rail connections, or improving existing ones) [SDG 13].

Rationalization: when the attitude is negative, but the behavior is carried out.

Objective: to "rationalize", to make the individual understand why he/she should perform the behavior and to change his/her negative attitude (not to perform only the desired behavior to avoid sanctions).

For example: with advertising and educational programs, to avoid speeding or double parking, to explain why one should wear a seat belt or not use a cell phone while driving [SDG 4 and SDG 11]; or to make people aware of the need to pay taxes.

Confrontation: when the attitude is negative and, in addition, the desired behavior is not carried out.

Objective: to change the attitude and achieve the desired behavior (this is the most difficult strategy to carry out).

For example: applying economic sanctions, or preventing access to public aid, to parents who do not vaccinate their children (SDG 3); imposing prison sentences on parents who do not send their children to school (SDG 4), who perform genital mutilation on their daughters (SDG 3 and SDG 5), who give their underage children in marriage (SDG 3 and SDG 5, if they are girls), or whoever orders and/or executes an honor killing (SDG 5); fining those companies that hire their workers irregularly, that do not pay the established minimum wage, and/or do not respect the maximum working hours or mandatory breaks (SDG 8).

6 Conclusions and Final Reflections

This chapter has attempted to highlight the importance of social marketing for improving people's well-being and quality of life, and in particular for achieving the 17 SDGs of the 2030 Agenda proposed by the United Nations.

Social marketing is not only a means to promote, modify or eliminate ideas, beliefs, values, attitudes and, above all, behaviors in search of the common good, but it also serves to promote social change, create social value and, ultimately, improve people's well-being and quality of life. Social marketing often focuses on complex problems that, in practice, can only be solved in the long or very long term (sometimes it may even take several generations to achieve the desired social change). In any case, it is important to carry out social marketing campaigns and interventions now, to at least start this transformation process as soon as possible (raising awareness, changing attitudes and, ultimately, achieving socially desirable behavior).

6.1 Implications for Managers

As noted above, social marketing can be carried out by both for-profit organizations (companies) and non-profit organizations (public administrations, NGOs, etc.), and both public and private, to respond to social problems in different areas (such as health, the environment, education, consumption and production, human and labor rights, etc.)—[5].

- **Managers of public and non-profit organizations**: social marketing can be a very useful tool to raise awareness about a particular social cause and get people to carry out the desired behavior (for example, the public health service, if it seeks to prevent cancer or detect it in its early stages, can launch a social marketing campaign to raise awareness among people of the need to have regular check-ups and provide the means to do so; or an NGO seeking to protect the environment, with social marketing campaigns, can raise awareness among people of the need to recycle and get them to carry out this behavior).
- **Company managers**: they can use social marketing within their sustainability or social responsibility policy (in this case, it is called *Corporate Social Marketing*). Especially if a company manages to link the product it sells with the social cause, it can, in addition to encouraging socially desirable behavior, improve its corporate image and even increase its sales (for example, a toothpaste company, which promotes oral hygiene; or a food company, which promotes healthy eating).

6.2 Implications for Public Policies

Social marketing can also be a key instrument for the success of public policies of all kinds (economic, social, health, environmental) and at any level (local, regional, national, or even international).

The quality of life in a region or country "*is largely determined by the political decisions taken by its leaders*" [29]. Therefore, public policies should be designed to guarantee the quality of life of the people to whom they are directed [35]. Getting citizens to behave in a socially desirable way, seeking the common good, requires that, first, people are aware of the social cause, become aware of it, adopt a favorable attitude towards it and, finally, carry out the desired behavior. Thus, social marketing works with that purpose.

References

1. The United Nations (2022) World Moving Backwards on Sustainable Development Goals, Secretary-General Tells Economic and Social Council, Deploring 'Fundamental Lack of Solidarity'. Retrieved from https://www.un.org/press/en/2022/sgsm21196.doc.htm
2. The United Nations (2015) La Asamblea General adopta la Agenda 2030 para el Desarrollo Sostenible [In Spanish]. Retrieved from https://www.un.org/sustainabledevelopment/es/2015/09/la-asamblea-general-adopta-la-agenda-2030-para-el-desarrollo-sostenible/
3. Galan-Ladero MM, Alves H (2023) Theoretical Background: Social Marketing & Sustainable Development Goals (SDGs). In: Galan-Ladero MM, Alves H (eds) Social Marketing and Sustainable Development Goals (SDGs). Case Studies for a Global Perspective. Springer, Cham. https://doi.org/10.1007/978-3-031-27377-3
4. Galan-Ladero MM, Sarmento M, Marques S (2023) Social Marketing to achieve the Sustainable Development Goals (SDGs) in 2030 Agenda by the United Nations. Int Rev Public Nonprofit Mark 20:521–527. https://doi.org/10.1007/s12208-023-00381-7
5. Galan-Ladero MM (2025) El papel de los líderes religiosos en el marketing social y su importancia para alcanzar los ODS. Revista Austral Comunicación, 14 (2): 01413. https:// doi.org/10.26422/aucom.2025.140 2 . gal .
6. Fine SH (1981) The marketing of ideas and social issues. Praeger Publishers Inc
7. French J, Gordon R (2020) Strategic social marketing for behaviour and social change, 2nd ed. SAGE Publications Ltd
8. Casais B (2023) Conceptualizing an omnichannel approach for social marketing under the assumptions of the transtheoretical model of change. Soc Mark Q 29(3):208–224. https://doi.org/10.1177/15245004231186903
9. Stewart DW (ed) (2015) The handbook of persuasion and social marketing. Volume 1: historical and social foundations. Praeger
10. Casais B, Proença JF (2023) Social marketing contributions to mitigate global epidemics. In: Rezaei N (ed) Integrated science of global epidemics, vol 14. Springer, Cham, pp 347–360. https://doi.org/10.1007/978-3-031-17778-1_15
11. Kotler P, Zaltman G (1971) Social marketing: an approach to planned social change. J Mark 35(July):3–12
12. Alves HM, Galan-Ladero MM (2019) Theoretical background: introduction to social marketing. In: Galan-Ladero MM, Alves HM (eds) Case studies on social marketing. Management for professionals. Springer, Cham. https://doi.org/10.1007/978-3-030-04843-3_1
13. French J, Russell-Bennett R (2015) A hierarchical model of social marketing. J Soc Mark 5(2):139–159. https://doi.org/10.1108/JSOCM-06-2014-0042
14. Andreasen AR (1994) Social marketing: its definition and domain. J Public Policy Mark 13(1):108–114. https://doi.org/10.1177/074391569401300109

15. Boards of the International Social Marketing Association, European Social Marketing Association, and Australian Association of Social Marketing. (2013). Social marketing definition. In ESMA (2024). Social Marketing. https://europeansocialmarketing.org/social-marketing/
16. Kotler P, Lee N (2005) Corporate social responsibility: doing the most good for company and your cause. Wiley
17. Hastings G, Domegan C (2018) Social marketing: rebels with a cause, 3rd ed. Routledge
18. Basil DZ (2019) The big picture in social marketing. In: Basil D, Diaz-Meneses G, Basil M (eds) Social marketing in action. Springer Texts in Business and Economics. Springer, Cham. https://doi.org/10.1007/978-3-030-13020-6_1
19. Galan-Ladero MM, Galera-Casquet C (2019) Capítulo XI: Marketing para el cambio social. In: Cerdá LM, Ramírez M (eds) Fundamentos para un nuevo marketing. Sindéresis, Madrid, pp 251–284
20. French J (2011) Why nudging is not enough. J Soc Mark 1(2):154–162. https://doi.org/10.1108/20426761111141896
21. Santesmases M (1999) Marketing. Conceptos y Estrategias [In Spanish]. 4th Edition. Pirámide
22. Sirgy MJ, Morris M, Samli C (1985) The question of value in social marketing. use of a quality of life theory to achieve long-term life satisfaction. Am J Econ Sociol 44(2):215–228. https://doi.org/10.1111/j.1536-7150.1985.tb02336.x
23. Rundle-Thiele S (2015) Looking back and moving forwards: an agenda for social marketing research. Recherche et Applications en Marketing (English Edition) 30(3):128–133. https://doi.org/10.1177/2051570715599338
24. Barberà-Mas E, Mañé F (2024) Defining well-being: towards common language. Working Paper No. 6. International society for quality-of-life studies. Retrieved from: https://www.isqols.org/Workingpaperseries
25. AIHW – Australian Institute of Health and Welfare (2023) Understanding welfare and wellbeing. Retrieved from https://www.aihw.gov.au/reports/australias-welfare/understanding-welfare-and-wellbeing
26. Real Academia Española (2024) Diccionario de la Lengua Española. Retrieved from: https://dle.rae.es/diccionario
27. Voukelatou V, Gabrielli L et al (2021) Measuring objective and subjective well-being: dimensions and data sources. Int J Data Sci Anal 11:279–309. https://doi.org/10.1007/s41060-020-00224-2
28. Ventegodt S, Merrick J, Andersen NJ (2003) Quality of life theory I. The IQOL theory: an integrative theory of the global quality of life concept. Sci World J 3:1030–1040. https://doi.org/10.1100/tsw.2003.82
29. Constantinescu M (2012) The relationship between the quality of life concept and social marketing development. Int J Econ Pract Theor 2(2):75–80
30. Tonon G (2020) Calidad de vida y psicología positiva. Cuadernos de pedagogía 507:6–7
31. Christie L, Venter De Villiers M (2023) The role of social marketing in promoting quality of life through the lens of sustainable consumption. J Soc Mark 13(3):419–433
32. Felce D, Perry J (1995) Quality of life: its definition and measurement. Res Dev Disabil 16(1):51–74. https://doi.org/10.1016/0891-4222(94)00028-8
33. INE – Instituto Nacional de Estadística (2024) Indicadores de Calidad de Vida. Introducción [In Spanish]. Retrieved from: https://www.ine.es/ss/Satellite?c=Page&cid=1259936854013&pagename=ProductosYServicios%2FPYSLayout&L=0
34. Alves H, Galan-Ladero MM, Rivera RG (2021) Theoretical background: social marketing and quality of life. In: Galan-Ladero MM, Rivera RG (eds) Applied social marketing and quality of life. case studies from an international perspective. Springer, Cham. DOI. https://doi.org/10.1007/978-3-030-83286-5
35. Tonon G (2010a) La utilización de indicadores de calidad de vida para la decisión de políticas públicas. Polis Revista Latinoamericana 26
36. Donovan R, Henley N (2010) Principles and practice of social marketing: An international perspective. Cambridge University Press.

37. Penelas-Leguía A, Galera-Casquet C, Galan-Ladero M, Valero-Amaro V (2012) Marketing Solidario. El Marketing en las Organizaciones No Lucrativas. Pirámide
38. Quintanilla I, Berenguer G, Díaz R (1988) Problemas y desafíos del marketing social. Esic Market, 61: 137–151
39. Martinez J (2020) Chapter 12. Teaching and learning quality of life in urban studies: a mixed-methods approach with walking interviews. In: Tonon G (ed) Teaching quality of life indifferent domains, Social indicators research series, vol 79: pp 209–230 Springer, Switzerland

M. Mercedes Galan-Ladero is an Associate Professor (Prof. Contratado Doctor) in the Department of Business Management and Sociology, at the University of Extremadura (Spain), where she teaches Marketing courses in the Faculty of Economics and Business Sciences. She also has extensive international teaching experience.

She is currently engaged in innovative research in the areas of Social Marketing, Cause-Related Marketing, Corporate Social Responsibility, Nonprofit Marketing, and Fair Trade, as well as consumer behavior, ethnocentrism, local food products and their internationalization.

Her research has been published in national and international journals, such as *Journal of Cleaner Production, Journal of Retailing and Consumer Services, International Journal of Nonprofit Voluntary Sector Marketing, International Review on Public and Nonprofit Marketing, Economics & Sociology, Journal of Security and Sustainability Issues, International Journal of Bank Marketing, Food Quality and Preference, Agribusiness. An International Journal, Spanish Journal of Marketing—ESIC, ...* She presents her research regularly at various national and international conferences (AIMPN/IAPNM, AEMARK, EMAC, ...).

She has completed, as co-editor and/or co-author, different books and book chapters for Springer, Piramide, and Delta, among others.

She is currently the coordinator of the Red Iberoamericana de Investigación en Desarrollo Sostenible (the Ibero-American Network for Research in Sustainable Development)—RIIDS . https://riids.auip.org/

3 Leveraging Choice Architecture in Social Marketing to Promote Good Health

Beatriz Casais, Ana Maria Soares, and Mona El-Badry

> *Any attempt to influence people's judgment, choices, or behaviour can be deemed a nudge if it predictably impacts behaviour, as altering behaviour does not always imply changing minds.*
>
> Lehner et al. [1]

Abstract

Social marketing tools have been important in obtaining changes in citizens' attitudes and behaviours, especially in health-related issues. Governments and non-governmental organizations around the world have made use of social marketing towards this end. Choice architecture is a policy design strategy derived from behavioural economics that aims to obtain automatic responses from citizens. Its use in social marketing may have the forms of nudges and shoves. This chapter explores the assumptions of choice architecture in social marketing to overcome social constraints and promote good health for the citizens. Considering that access to good health is challenging, particularly in developing countries, due to the problems of citizens' literacy, accessibility to health care, and misunderstanding of healthy habits, choice architecture can be a useful social marketing tool to obtain citizens' responses to incorporating healthy habits.

B. Casais (✉) · A. M. Soares
School of Economics, Management, and Political Science, iBMS – Centre for Research in Business, Markets & Society, CICS.NOVA.UMinho, University of Minho, Braga, Portugal
e-mail: bcasais@eeg.uminho.pt; amsoares@eeg.uminho.pt

M. El-Badry
Arab Academy for Science, Technology & Maritime Transport (AAST), Giza, Egypt

B. Casais (ed.), *Integrated Science to Achieve Sustainable Development Goals*, Integrated Science 37, https://doi.org/10.1007/978-3-031-88777-2_3

Graphical Abstract

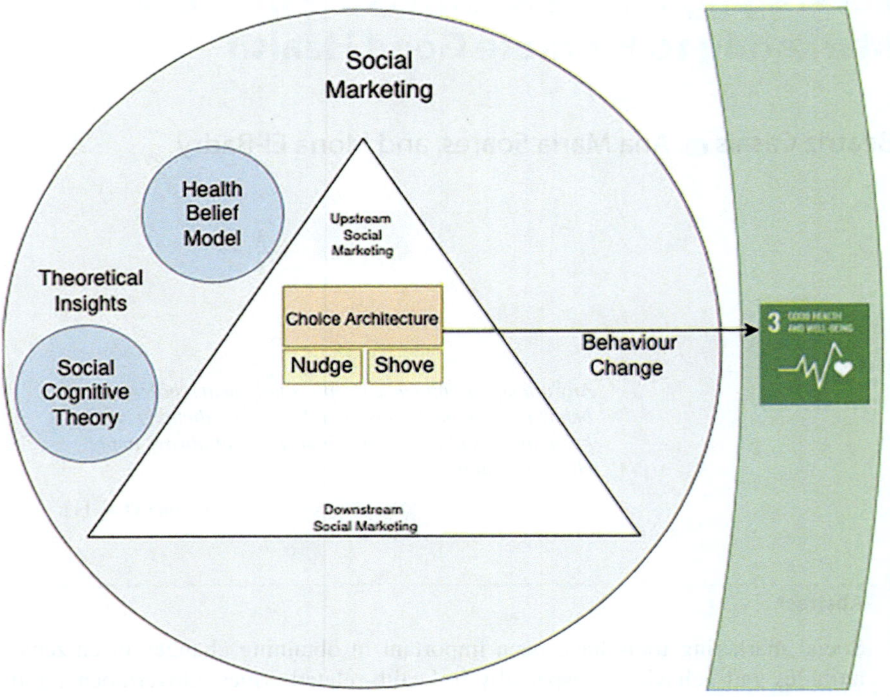

Source: Authors

Keywords

Behavioural change · Health promotion · Public health · Upstream intervention · Nudge · Shove

1 Introduction

Improving citizens' quality of life, especially the most vulnerable, is a fundamental goal for any society [2]. Achieving good health and well-being is the third Sustainable Development Goal (SDG) of the Agenda 2030, involving challenges regarding universal health coverage as a global health priority aiming to provide access to essential health services without financial hardship [3]. The concept of universal health coverage has evolved into health service responses and financial protection, but despite advancements, significant disparities persist within and between countries [4].

However, both health policies and individual behaviours are crucial in improving health and reducing inequalities [5]. Citizens' health behaviour change is an important driver of a healthy society [6], although challenging due to factors of social determinants and the disconnect between knowledge and action [7]. There are different approaches that can be used for behavioural change, of which social marketing stands out by offering policy makers tools for influencing attitudes, beliefs, and behaviours by leveraging principles from commercial marketing to empower citizens to social and behavioural change [8, 9]. Social marketing can be used to design community interventions to decrease or remove dangerous and unhealthy factors [10] as well as understand the direction of appeals most effective in social marketing communications [11].

Encouraging healthy behaviours requires a thorough understanding of the mechanisms that drive voluntary changes in behaviour on both individual and societal levels. Two important theories in the context of health are the Health Belief Model (HBM) and the Social Cognitive Theory (SCT), or social learning theory (SLT). The HBM is one of the first theories developed to explain the change process in health behaviour. This theory is built on the idea of choice based on individuals' perception of the outcome [12]. The SCT, on the other hand, holds that expectancies and incentives determine behaviour [13].

Social marketing has been successfully applied in various health contexts, including stress reduction, smoking cessation, clinical screenings, dietary changes, and physical activity. It has also proven effective in mitigating epidemics [14]. Although relevant in all societies, social marketing is crucial in developing countries due to the lack of community involvement in health practices [15]. This problem highlights that to obtain good health from a behaviour change response, there is also a need for an alignment with other SDGs, such as access to education and poverty reduction for example.

The community's social, economic, and environmental contexts are crucial to improve health protection [16]. Government intervention should provide the necessary infrastructures for proper health standards and promote effective social marketing campaigns [15]. Choice architecture is an approach that emerged from behavioural economics [17] that reflects on how choices are presented, influencing how the decision-maker chooses [18]. Choice architecture implies the creation of nudges and shoves to alter behaviours [19].

This chapter reviews the main theories that sustain social marketing interventions in health, such as the health belief model and the social cognitive theory. It explains the applicability of social marketing actions at different levels—upstream and downstream. Finally, the chapter explains the power of choice architecture in health social marketing interventions to obtain automatic healthy habits from the citizens. However, social marketing designers should overcome the ethical issues that choice architecture raises, for example, by combining other interventions [20].

2 Global Challenges to Achieve Good Health and Well-Being

While progress has been made in expanding access to healthcare, significant disparities remain globally. Financial constraints, geographical barriers, and inequitable distribution of healthcare resources continue to hinder access for many individuals and communities. Universal health coverage aims to provide everyone access to quality, affordable healthcare services without financial hardship [3]. However, developing healthcare systems demands substantial investments in infrastructure, human resources, and technology, which represent a significant challenge for many countries. Establishing and maintaining effective universal social and healthcare protection is complex and costly, particularly in developing countries [4]. Moreover, ensuring equitable access to these mechanisms for all members of society remains a significant challenge. These challenges highlight the complexity of achieving good health for all. Addressing these issues requires a response from different stakeholders working together to create a healthier and more equitable world [21].

Achieving good health requires a multi-faceted approach that includes promoting individual behaviour change. Healthy lifestyles play a crucial role in preventing disease and promoting well-being. However, encouraging and supporting healthy behaviours can be challenging. Socioeconomic factors, cultural norms, and access to food and safety can influence individual health choices [6, 7]. Addressing these underlying social determinants of health is crucial for promoting healthy behaviours and achieving population-level health goals.

3 Health Belief Model for Social Marketing in Public Health

Social marketing is a technique to achieve behaviour changes and favorably impact people's health and well-being. Research shows that several social marketing programs have been effective in promoting public health. Most programs emphasize healthier eating choices, decreased sugar-filled drinks and high-fat dairy products, and a shift in behaviour among schoolchildren, teenagers, and their parents [22].

Biomedical interventions alone are insufficient to guarantee better health. Social, economic, and political factors significantly influence health [23]. To be most effective, public health and health-promotion interventions should adopt an ecological perspective, considering not only individual factors but also interpersonal, organizational, and environmental influences on health behaviour [24].

Behavioural change models are crucial for influencing behaviour because they provide a framework for identifying the root causes of behaviour, a critical step in developing effective interventions [25]. Effective behaviour change interventions often draw upon various theories and models, including the social cognitive theory (SCT), the health belief model, the theory of planned behaviour, and the social-ecological model. These theories provide a comprehensive framework for understanding the factors influencing health behaviours and offer specific strategies to promote behaviour change.

Social Cognitive Theory (SCT) is a theoretical framework of the various psychological and social factors influencing human actions [13]. SCT emphasizes the reciprocal interaction between personal factors, environment, and behaviour and builds upon the premise that individual behaviour is shaped by learning by observing others in the social environment. As such, SCT emphasizes the human capability for learning, adaptation and seld-regulation [26].

SCT has been applied to various domains, including career counseling, health behaviour change, and education and is particularly helpful in understanding and modifying health-related behaviours, such as alcohol and drug use.

The Health Belief Model (HBM) is another valuable theory for researchers and practitioners in health-related fields which provides a useful framework for designing and evaluating interventions to promote behaviour change [23]. This model offers a detailed understanding of individual behaviour toward health-related issues by focusing on individual perceptions of health risks and behaviours. Social psychologists first proposed the HBM to explain why many individuals do not engage in health prevention programs. The model was expanded to examine how individuals respond to symptoms and diagnosed illnesses, including their adherence to treatment plans.

The HBM emphasises the importance of raising awareness about the risks associated with certain health behaviours [27]. For example, in the context of COVID-19, this model has a direct application [14], showing that interventions that emphasize the severity of the illness and the potential consequences of not taking preventative measures may be more effective in motivating behaviour change than interventions that focus solely on the benefits of such measures [28]. The HBM has also been applied to explain and predict exercise behaviour [29].

The Health Belief Model posits that individual health behaviours are influenced by their perceived value and likelihood of achieving a desired outcome. In the context of health, individuals' beliefs about their susceptibility to illness, the severity of potential consequences, and the perceived benefits and costs of preventive actions significantly impact their decisions to engage in health-promoting behaviours. Hence, these four factors play a significant role in influencing an individual's intention and behaviour [30]:

(a) Perceived susceptibility: refers to an individual's perceived susceptibility reflecting their belief about their likelihood of experiencing negative health outcomes.
(b) Attitude towards a specific health behaviour: individuals develop attitudes based on their beliefs, experiences and intentions regarding a particular health behaviour. They weigh the pros and cons of the behaviour before deciding whether to adopt it.
(c) Perceived norms: an individual's behaviour is influenced by perceived norms, which are shaped by their social and community environment. These norms can be descriptive (what others do) or injunctive (what others approve or disapprove of).
(d) Self-efficacy: reflects an individual's confidence in their ability to execute a specific behaviour successfully. It plays a crucial role in behaviour change, as individuals are likelier to engage in behaviours, believing they can successfully execute.

These four factors of the Health Belief Model collectively determine the success of mass media health campaigns. Mass media, particularly television and cinema, have a significant impact on shaping modern lifestyles. Due to their extensive reach and influence, policymakers can use these channels to influence people's health-related attitudes and behaviours [30].

The HBM's consideration of perceived benefits and barriers to health behaviour acknowledges that individuals may weigh the costs and benefits of engaging in a particular behaviour before deciding. This means that individuals need to perceive the risk of the health problem [31]. Interventions that address perceived barriers, such as access to resources or social support, may be more effective. In sum, the HBM posits that adopting health-promoting behaviours is more likely when individuals perceive themselves as vulnerable to a serious health problem, believe the behaviour will effectively reduce that risk, and perceive minimal barriers to adopting the behaviour [29].

3.1 Upstream and Downstream Social Marketing Approaches in Public Health

To be effective, social marketing requires a coordinated effort to address both upstream factors like environmental and policy changes and downstream factors related to individual behaviour change [32]. Upstream social marketing involves policymakers, educators, and the media, working to influence decision-making processes, while downstream approaches aim to change individual behaviour [33]. Upstream social marketing aims to shape the macro-level environment to encourage policy and solution adoption [34]. An example is advocating for sugar taxes to discourage the consumption of sugary drinks and promote healthier choices.

Downstream social marketing emphasizes the individual assigning the responsibility for change and targets individuals within their immediate social environment, such as family, school, or workplace [32]. However, the impacts on behaviour change are typically complicated to address effectively by microsocial marketing alone [35]. Tobacco cessation programs are an example of a downstream approach in the health field.

4 Health Impact Pyramid

Governments and civil society organizations are constantly working to understand better how and why people behave in the ways they do to develop and implement social interventions that have the best chance of assisting citizens in having a positive life experience. A 5-tier health impact pyramid has been proposed to describe the impact of different types of public health intervention. Public actions and interventions with the highest population impact are situated at the pyramid's base, requiring the least effort [36]. The elements of the pyramid are as follows:

- Socioeconomic Factors and Health: Socioeconomic factors like poverty, low education, and lack of access to sanitation significantly impact health outcomes. Although the exact mechanisms are not fully understood, these factors increase exposure to environmental hazards and correlate with higher risks for diseases like cardiovascular disease. Poverty also contributes to increased illness within society.
- Contextual Interventions for Health: Creating environments that make healthy choices the default option is crucial for promoting health. This includes policies encouraging physical activity, like walking and cycling and designing communities for better mobility. People respond differently to messages framed as gains or losses. While negative appeals can be effective, they can also lead to fear and disengagement if overused.
- Long-lasting Protective Interventions: valuable but often less impactful than population-level interventions due to the challenges of reaching individuals individually.
- Universal Health Coverage and Cardiovascular Disease: While interventions to prevent cardiovascular disease hold the most significant potential health impact, their effectiveness can be limited by factors such as lack of access, inconsistent adherence, and imperfect implementation.

The pyramid model prioritizes addressing socioeconomic determinants as the foundation for public health interventions, followed by interventions to improve the context for health, implement protective measures, and provide direct clinical care and health education. These programmes aim to avoid chronic diseases by changing the information environment and causing behaviour changes [37]. To effectively influence public health behaviours through mass media, campaigns must overcome the challenge of reaching fragmented audiences. This calls for an adequate communication strategy, involving well-crafted messages delivered widely and frequently to reach, be seen, heard, and retained by the target audience [38]. Given the often scarce resources available for social marketing initiatives, it is crucial to demonstrate their effectiveness to secure continued funding and support. Measuring outcomes helps to identify what works and what does not, allowing for continuous improvement and optimization of future campaigns. Moreover, assessing effectiveness is essential for building credibility and trust in social marketing. By demonstrating tangible results, social marketers can strengthen their case for the effectiveness of their interventions and obtain support from policymakers, funders, and the public [39].

4.1 Choice Architecture to Promote Health

Choice architecture involves designing decision-making environments to influence behaviour without subtly limiting choices or altering economic incentives [17]. Decision architecture was stated to reduce biases caused by restricted rationality. Choice architects must balance the desire to offer a wide range of options with the cognitive burden this places on decision-makers [18]. Limitations such as cognitive capacities, problem difficulty, and decision-making time may be addressed if choice architects guide individuals toward favourable options.

The tools of the choice architect include defaults, expecting error, giving feedback, understanding mappings, providing incentives and changing the order of choice defaults [17]; defaults refer to the fact that choice scenarios typically have a default option, which tends to be selected more frequently than alternatives [18]. Expecting error refers to anticipating where people may fail and providing information or guidance to prevent it. Giving feedback refers toallowing people to understand the outcomes of their decisions, while understanding mappings involves presenting information clearly in order to make it easy to understand. Providing incentives refers to motivating desirable behaviour through rewards, and changing the order of choice can affect the options people choose. Moreover, Johnson et al. [18] distinguish between tools used to structure the choice task, such as defaults and limited options, and those used to describe the choice options, such as information about the consequences of the options.

One example of the choice architecture approach encompasses using choice architecture principles by policymakers and healthcare providers to enhance the attractiveness and accessibility of breast screening for the target population [40]. By incorporating breast screening with other healthcare services, policymakers can enhance its perceived value and mitigate cognitive and logistical barriers that may hinder women from attending screening appointments [53]. Furthermore, extending breast screening services to rural areas and underserved locations enables policymakers to address health inequities and ensure equitable access to vital screening services for all women. Ultimately, applying choice architecture principles can contribute to a higher breast screening uptake and improved health outcomes for women [41].

4.2 Nudge and Shove

Research has investigated how choice architecture tools, such as defaults and sorting, influence behaviour. Adjustments to the choice design can lead to changes in consumers' decisions. These adjustments and manipulations are advantageous due to their cost-effectiveness [42].

French [43] proposed the Behavioural Forms Exchange Matrix, which includes four quadrants describing the exchange forms governments and public institutions can use in behavioural interventions. This matrix is a two-by-two conceptual framework based on the type of decision (conscious considered vs. Automatic/unconscious) and motivation to act (Incentive/reward vs. Desincentive/punishment). The model thus considers four types of exchange: Hug, Smack, Nudge, and Shove. The important two for this case are *Nudge* (gentle push in the right direction) by guiding people toward the right choices or better decisions; *Shove,* on the side of disincentives, to push someone forcefully (restriction of choice), more suited for passive choices [44]. Nudge and shove are interventions in choice design to guide individuals using psychological effects or to overcome them, by maintaining the freedom to choose. Nudging and shoving highlight the role of choice architecture in influencing human behaviour by modifying the environment to encourage better choices while preserving option of choice [45]. Nudge is any aspect of the decision environment "that alters people's behaviour predictably without forbidding any options or significantly changing their economic incentives" ([46], p. 125). Nudging involves indirectly changing people's behaviour by altering their environment and the circumstances surrounding their decisions [47]. So, a nudge means giving a positive choice to the individual in the external environment. The difference between nudge and shove is very slight: both give the choice, following the choice architecture concept, but shove gives a choice and penalties while nudge gives a choice without consequence, i.e., "nudge" means to push someone gently, and "shove" means to push someone forcefully. They still have the same benefit since nudge/shove activities have lower costs than traditional marketing approaches and can help policymakers improve societies with the available tools [16]. This distinction has significant practical implications for policy creation and implementation [44]. By focusing on enabling behaviours and decisions, nudges and shoves avoid attempting to change individual value systems or provide additional information [48]. Nudges are most appropriate for addressing routine behaviours and complex decisions that often exceed individuals' cognitive resources [1, 49].

The widespread use of nudges in marketing and policy circles reflects their low cost and significant impact [42]. Nudge theory provides a framework for understanding decision-making and designing choice architectures that encourage better choices [45], but is not a standalone solution. Nudges can influence both overall decision-making and the disparities in choices. Moseley & Stoker [50] consider nudging as an active exchange where people rationally assess the exchange, weighing the pros and cons of the benefits and costs compared to the traditional policy tools, including financial incentives, bans and mandates and, more recently, information campaigns. Hence, nudging helps improve decisions about health, wealth and happiness [51].

5 Ethical Concerns of Choice Architecture

While choice architecture can be a powerful tool for promoting positive behaviour change, it must be used ethically and responsibly. Choice architecture inherently influences decision-making by subtly guiding choices. There is a risk that nudges could be misused in a manipulative manner, raising concerns about individuals' autonomy and free will to make their own choices without undue influence [52].

It is fundamental to use Nudging in a way that is transparent, fair, and respectful of self dtermination. Nudges must be implemented in a fair and equitable way to empower informed choices for everyone, regardless of individual socioeconomic status, cultural background, or other relevant factors. Choice architecture must be used to empower individual agency and ability to make well-informed options rather than to manipulate them [20].

6 Conclusion

In conclusion, achieving good health and well-being for all, as outlined in the third Sustainable Development Goal, requires a multi-pronged approach. While universal health coverage and social security protection are crucial for enabling access to healthcare services, they are insufficient. Promoting healthy behaviours through interventions by using approaches such as social marketing is equally important. By leveraging evidence-based theorethical frameworks, such as the Health Belief Model, and developing effective social marketing campaigns, it is possible to empower individuals to make better decisions about their health. However, the success of such initiatives hinges on addressing the social determinants of health, including poverty, inequality, and access to education. Furthermore, collaboration between policymakers, healthcare providers, communities, and individuals is essential to create a supportive environment that fosters healthy lifestyles and promotes well-being for all. Upstream interventions, using the principles of behavioural economics and choice architecture allow designing forms of exchange that may be particularly effectivein influencing citizens' behaviours toward public health. This type of approach for behavioural change has lower costs, particularly in developing countries where communities have low health literacy, because automatic behaviours by default may lead to increased public health, notwithstanding ethical concerns regarding the application of choice architecture principles.

References

1. Lehner M, Mont O, Heiskanen E (2016) Nudging – a promising tool for sustainable consumption behaviour? J Clean Prod 134:166–177. https://doi.org/10.1016/j.jclepro.2015.11.086
2. Buheji M (2018) Behavioural economics trends in improving governments outcomes – much more than nudge. Am J Econ 8(3):163–173. https://doi.org/10.5923/j.economics.20180803.06
3. Kutzin J (2013) Health financing for universal coverage and health system performance: concepts and implications for policy. Bull World Health Organ 91:602–611
4. Mamdani M (2020) Universal health coverage: from aspirations to reality. Global Social Policy 20(2):242–246. https://doi.org/10.1177/1468018120922227
5. Pons-Vigués M, Diez È, Morrison J, Salas-Nicás S, Hoffmann R, Burstrom B et al (2014) Social and health policies or interventions to tackle health inequalities in European cities: a scoping review. BMC Public Health 14:1–12. https://doi.org/10.1186/1471-2458-14-198
6. Riekert KA, Ockene JK, Pbert L (eds) (2013) The handbook of health behaviour change. Springer Publishing Company. https://doi.org/10.1891/9780826142658
7. Kelly MP, Barker M (2016) Why is changing health-related behaviour so difficult? Public Health 136:109–116. https://doi.org/10.1016/j.puhe.2016.03.030
8. Dietrich T, Hurley E, Carins J, Kassirer J, Rundle-Thiele S, Palmatier RW et al (2022) 50 years of social marketing: seeding solutions for the future. Eur J Mark 56(5):1434–1463. https://doi.org/10.1108/EJM-06-2021-0447
9. Kamin T, Kubacki K, Atanasova S (2022) Empowerment in social marketing: systematic review and critical reflection. J Mark Manag 38(11–12):1104–1136. https://doi.org/10.1080/0267257X.2022.2078864

10. Akbar MB, Foote L, Lawson A, French J, Deshpande S, Lee NR (2022) The social marketing paradox: challenges and opportunities for the discipline. Int Rev Public Nonprofit Mark 19(2):367–389. https://doi.org/10.1007/s12208-021-00308-0
11. Casais B, Proença JF (2022) The use of positive and negative appeals in social advertising: a content analysis of television ads for preventing HIV/AIDS. Int Rev Public Nonprofit Mark 19(3):623–647. https://doi.org/10.1007/s12208-021-00318-y
12. Green EC, Murphy EM, Gryboski K (2020) The health belief model. In: The Wiley encyclopedia of health psychology. Wiley, pp 211–214. https://doi.org/10.1002/9781119057840.ch68
13. Bandura A (2001) Social cognitive theory: an agentic perspective. Annu Rev Psychol 52(1):1–26. https://doi.org/10.1146/annurev.psych.52.1.1
14. Casais B, Proença JF (2023) Social marketing contributions to mitigate global epidemics. In: Rezaei N (ed) Integrated science of global epidemics. Integrated science, vol 14. Springer, Cham, pp 347–360. https://doi.org/10.1007/978-3-031-17778-1_15
15. Schmidtke DJ, Kubacki K, Rundle-Thiele S (2021) A review of social marketing interventions in low- and middle-income countries (2010–2019). J Soc Mark 11(3):240–258. https://doi.org/10.1108/JSOCM-10-2020-0210
16. Wymer W (2015) Formulating effective social marketing and public health communication strategies. In: Wymer W (ed) Innovations in social marketing and public health communication. Applying quality of life research. Springer, Cham. https://doi.org/10.1007/978-3-319-19869-9_1
17. Thaler RH, Sustein CR, Balz JP (2013) Choice architecture. In: Shafir E (ed) The behavioural foundations of public policy. Princeton University Press, pp 428–439. https://doi.org/10.2307/j.ctv550cbm.31
18. Johnson EJ, Shu SB, Dellaert BGC, Fox C, Goldstein DG, Häubl G et al (2012) Beyond nudges: tools of a choice architecture. Mark Lett 23(2):487–504. https://doi.org/10.1007/s11002-012-9186-1
19. Landais LL, Damman OC, Schoonmade LJ, Timmermans DRM, Verhagen EALM, Jelsma JGM (2020) Choice architecture interventions to change physical activity and sedentary behaviour: a systematic review of effects on intention, behaviour and health outcomes during and after intervention. Int J Behav Nutr Phys Act 17(1). https://doi.org/10.1186/s12966-020-00942-7
20. Selinger E, Whyte K (2011) Is there a right way to nudge? The practice and ethics of choice architecture. Sociol Compass 5(10):923–935. https://doi.org/10.1111/j.1751-9020.2011.00413.x
21. Yovo E (2022) Challenges on the road to achieving the SDG 3.2 targets in resource-limited settings. Lancet Glob Health 10(2):e157–e158. https://doi.org/10.1016/S2214-109X(21)00597-0
22. Truong VD, Dong XD, Saunders SG, Pham Q, Nguyen H, Tran NA (2021) Measuring, evaluating, and documenting social marketing impact. J Soc Mark 11(3):259–277. https://doi.org/10.1108/JSOCM-11-2020-0224
23. Kumar S, Preetha GS (2012) Health promotion: an effective tool for global health. Indian J Community Med 37(1):5–12. https://doi.org/10.4103/0970-0218.94009
24. Glanz K, Bishop DB (2010) The role of behavioural science theory in development and implementation of public health interventions. Annu Rev Public Health 31:399–418. https://doi.org/10.1146/annurev.publhealth.012809.103604
25. Luca NR, Suggs LS (2013) Theory and model use in social marketing health interventions. J Health Commun 18(1):20–40. https://doi.org/10.1080/10810730.2012.688243
26. Luszczynska A, Schwarzer R (2020) Changing behaviour using social cognitive theory. In: Hagger MS, Cameron LD, Hamilton K, Hankonen N, Lintunen T (eds) The handbook of behaviour change. Cambridge handbooks in psychology. Cambridge University Press, pp 32–45. https://doi.org/10.1017/9781108677318.003
27. Chin JH, Mansori S (2019) Theory of planned behaviour and health belief model: females' intention on breast cancer screening. Cogent Psychol 6(1). https://doi.org/10.1080/23311908.2019.1647927

28. Suess C, Maddock J, Dogru T, Mody M, Lee S (2022) Using the health belief model to examine travelers' willingness to vaccinate and support for vaccination requirements prior to travel. Tour Manag 88(June 2021):104405. https://doi.org/10.1016/j.tourman.2021.104405
29. Sulat JS, Prabandari YS, Sanusi R, Hapsari ED, Santoso B (2018) The validity of health belief model variables in predicting behavioural change: a scoping review. Health Educ 118(6):499–512. https://doi.org/10.1108/HE-05-2018-0027
30. Fishbein M, Yzer MC (2003) Using theory to design effective health behaviour interventions. Commun Theory 13(2):164–183. https://doi.org/10.1111/j.1468-2885.2003.tb00287.x
31. Gaube S, Lermer E, Fischer P (2019) The concept of risk perception in health-related behaviour theory and behaviour change. In: Perceived safety: A multidisciplinary perspective. Springer International Publishing, pp 101–118. https://doi.org/10.1007/978-3-030-11456-5_7
32. Khajeh E, Dabestani R, Fathi S (2015) The role of upstream and downstream social marketing in electricity consumption management. Int J Bus Innov Res 9(3):311–328. https://doi.org/10.1504/IJBIR.2015.069138
33. Key TM, Czaplewski AJ (2017) Upstream social marketing strategy: an integrated marketing communications approach. Bus Horiz 60(3):325–333. https://doi.org/10.1016/j.bushor.2017.01.006
34. Kennedy A-M, Kemper JA, Parsons AG (2018) Upstream social marketing strategy. J Soc Mark 8(3):258–279. https://doi.org/10.1108/JSOCM-03-2017-0016
35. Wood M (2016) Social marketing for social change. Soc Mark Q 22(2):107–118. https://doi.org/10.1177/1524500416633429
36. Frieden TR (2010) A framework for public health action: the health impact pyramid. Am J Public Health 100(4):590–595. https://doi.org/10.2105/AJPH.2009.185652
37. Randolph W, Viswanath K (2004) Lessons learned from public health mass media campaigns: marketing health in a crowded media world. Annu Rev Public Health 25:419–437. https://doi.org/10.1146/annurev.publhealth.25.101802.123046
38. Burgess C, Wright AJ, Forster AS, Dodhia H, Miller J, Fuller F et al (2015) Influences on individuals' decisions to take up the offer of a health check: a qualitative study. Health Expect 18(6):2437–2448. https://doi.org/10.1111/hex.12212
39. Helmig B, Thaler J (2010) On the effectiveness of social marketing – what do we really know? J Nonprofit Publ Sect Market 22(4):264–287. https://doi.org/10.1080/10495140903566698
40. Quigley M (2013) Nudging for health: on public policy and designing choice architecture. Med Law Rev 21(4):588–621. https://doi.org/10.1093/medlaw/fwt022
41. Mills S, Sætra HS (2022) The autonomous choice architect. AI Soc 0123456789:583–595. https://doi.org/10.1007/s00146-022-01486-z
42. Benartzi S, Beshears J, Milkman KL, Sunstein CR, Thaler RH, Shankar M et al (2017) Should governments invest more in nudging? Psychol Sci 28(8):1041–1055. https://doi.org/10.1177/0956797617702501
43. French J (2011) Why nudging is not enough. J Soc Mark 1(2):154–162. https://doi.org/10.1108/20426761111141896
44. Mojašević AS, Nikolić L (2022) Nudge, shove, budge, sludge and administrative burden: terminological demarcation and practical implications. Facta Univ Ser Law Polit 1:083–096. https://doi.org/10.22190/FULP2102083M
45. Mele C, Russo Spena T, Kaartemo V, Marzullo ML (2021) Smart nudging: How cognitive technologies enable choice architectures for value co-creation. J Bus Res 129(March 2019):949–960. https://doi.org/10.1016/j.jbusres.2020.09.004
46. Hausman DM, Welch B (2010) Debate: to nudge or not to nudge*. J Polit Philos 18(1):123–136. https://doi.org/10.1111/j.1467-9760.2009.00351.x
47. Savigamin C, Mahakit N, Stithit S (2022) How to initiate fecal microbiota transplantation in developing countries using the behaviour economics concept of "choice architecture". Front Med 8(January):1–5. https://doi.org/10.3389/fmed.2021.746230
48. Oliver A (2018) Nudges, shoves and budges: behavioural economic policy frameworks. Int J Health Plann Manag 33(1):272–275. https://doi.org/10.1002/hpm.2419
49. Rachlin H (2015) Choice architecture: a review of why nudge: the politics of libertarian paternalism. J Expe Anal Behav 104(2):198–203. https://doi.org/10.1002/jeab.163

50. Moseley A, Stoker G (2013) Nudging citizens? Prospects and pitfalls confronting a new heuristic. Resour Conserv Recycl 79:4–10. https://doi.org/10.1016/j.resconrec.2013.04.008
51. Marchiori DR, Adriaanse MA, De Ridder DTD (2017) Unresolved questions in nudging research: putting the psychology back in nudging. Soc Personal Psychol Compass 11(1):e12297. https://doi.org/10.1111/spc3.12297
52. Loewenstein G, Chater N (2017) Putting nudges in perspective. Behav Public Policy 1(1):26–53. https://doi.org/10.1017/bpp.2016.7
53. Chan, D. N., & So, W. K. (2017). A systematic review of the factors influencing ethnic minority women's cervical cancer screening behavior: from intrapersonal to policy level. Cancer nursing, 40(6):E1–E30. https://doi.org/10.1097/NCC.0000000000000436

Beatriz Casais has a Ph.D. in Business and Management Studies from the University of Porto and a MSc in Marketing, with a bachelor's degree in communication sciences and a Post-Graduation in Health Communication. She is currently an Associate Professor at the University of Minho in the fields of Marketing and Strategy, a senior researcher at iBMS—Centre for Research in Business, Markets, and Society—and a board member of the European Social Marketing Association (ESMA). Her research focuses on social marketing and public health advertisement, digital marketing, and tourism marketing. She was social marketing manager at the Portuguese Ministry of Health, HIV/AIDS National Prevention Program. Beatriz Casais was vice-Dean of the School of Economics and Management of the University of Minho between 2020 and 2023, and head of the executive education unit—UminhoExec.

Ana Maria Soares is an Associate Professor with habilitation at the School of Economics and Management and Political Science and a member of CICS.NOVA.UMinho and iBMS, University of Minho, Portugal. She teaches several undergraduate, graduate, and doctoral courses in international marketing and strategy. Her latest research interests focus on different facets of consumer behavior, including voluntary simplicity, the impact of virtual assistant technologies, and social networks. Her work has been presented at international conferences and published in several peer-reviewed journals, including the International Journal of Consumer Studies, the Journal of Retailing and Consumer Services and Marketing Theory.

Mona El-Badry is lecture at the Arab Academy for Science, Technology & Maritime Transport (AAST), Egypt. She teaches Consumer Behaviors, Integrated Marketing, Service Marketing, Marketing Management and Advertising Management. Her research interest focuses on behavioural change in health and social marketing. She is currently finishing her doctoral thesis about Choice Architecture in Social Marketing.

Education for All as a Challenge in a Fragmented World

4

Naouel Abdellatif Mami

Education is the most powerful weapon which you can use to change the world.

– Nelson Mandela [1]

Abstract

Education for all is a fundamental human right and a key driver of sustainable development. However, global fragmentation, marked by inequality, social divisions and gender disparities, continues to undermine access to education. This article examines the challenges and efforts made in education in Algeria, focusing on its role in promoting education for all within the framework of the 2030 Sustainable Development Goals and Agenda 2063 of the African Union. This article explores Algeria's progress in expanding access to quality education, addressing barriers such as urban-rural divides, gender inequality, and social and cultural fragmentation, while aligning national policies with global and continental agendas. In addition, the article analyzes Algeria's contributions to regional educational, social and economic development through initiatives such as the Pan-African University, regional infrastructure projects, and youth empowerment and gender equality programs. The article calls for increased investments in inclusive education and regional cooperation to overcome obstacles and promote a prosperous, integrated and peaceful Africa and world, with Algeria as a major contributor to these efforts.

N. A. Mami (✉)
Mohamed Lamine Debaghine, Sétif 2 University, Sétif, Algeria
e-mail: n.abdellatif@univ-setif2.dz

B. Casais (ed.), *Integrated Science to Achieve Sustainable Development Goals*, Integrated Science 37, https://doi.org/10.1007/978-3-031-88777-2_4

Graphical Abstract

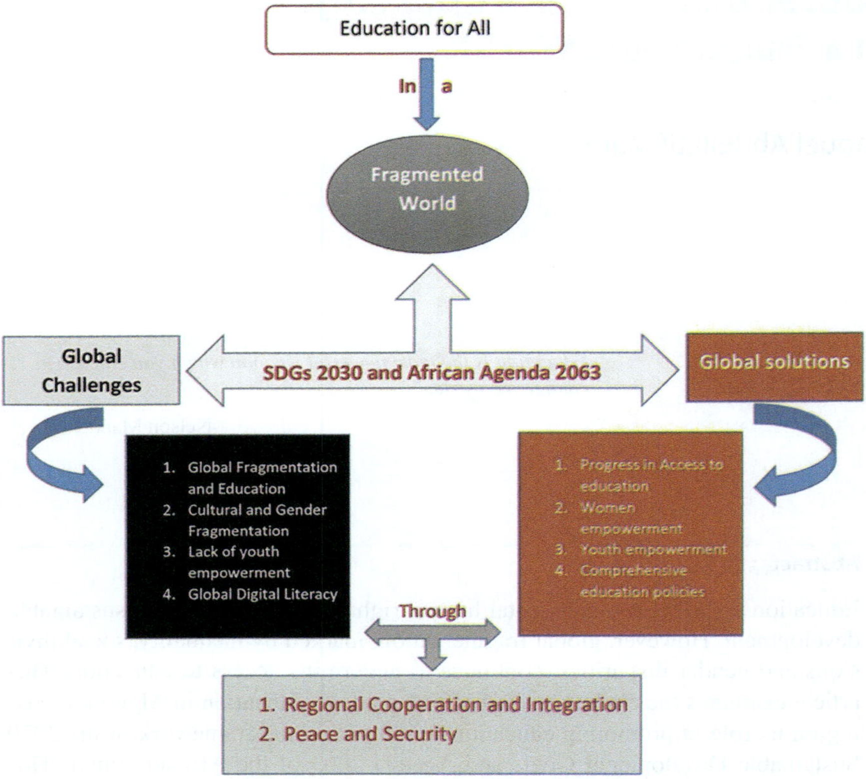

Source: Author

Keywords

Education for all · Sustainable development goals · Agenda 2063 · Social responsibilities · Access to education · Digitalization · Democratization of education. Gender equal opportunities

1 Introduction

Education is widely considered a cornerstone of human development, playing a vital role in addressing global inequality and promoting social and economic progress. As the world faces increasing fragmentation, manifested in economic disparities, cultural divides and unequal access to resources, it is becoming increasingly difficult to ensure that education is an effective driver of development. The 2030 Agenda for Sustainable Development, with its Sustainable Development Goal 4 on quality education, includes a clear commitment to providing equitable and inclusive education for all. [2] This goal recognizes that education is not only essential for empowering individuals, but also vital for addressing broader societal challenges such as poverty, inequality and climate change. At the continental level, the African Union's Agenda 2063 envisions a prosperous, integrated and peaceful Africa, underpinned by the achievement of quality education across the continent. Education, as set out in Aspiration 1 of Agenda 2063, is essential for achieving "high standards of living, good quality of life, good health and well-being for all" [3], making it a catalyst for sustainable development and social and economic transformation in Africa. In light of the challenges posed by fragmentation, the Sustainable Development Goals and Agenda 2063 highlight the role of education in overcoming barriers to development, promoting gender equality, and ensuring a sustainable and peaceful future for nations.

As a key player in Africa, Algeria is committed to respecting these global and continental frameworks, and aligning its national education policies with the goals set out in the Sustainable Development Goals and the African Agenda 2063. Through significant investments in education, infrastructure, and regional cooperation, and abiding to the African Youth Charter since 2006, [4] and to the Pan African Youth Declaration drafted in Oran, Algeria on November 4th, 2024 during the Pan African Youth Forum 2024 [5], Algeria is working to advance education in Africa by: Seeking to address its own educational challenges while contributing to broader development in Africa. This article examines Algeria's efforts to advance education, focusing on how these efforts align with the Sustainable Development Goals 2030 as well as Agenda 2063 of the African Union. It will explore Algeria's progress in improving access to education, particularly in rural areas, to address gender disparities and overcome social and cultural barriers, as well as its role in contributing to the educational, social, and economic development of the African continent.

2 Challenges Facing Education for All

2.1 Global Fragmentation and Education

It is very essential to understand that in this fragmented world, education for all becomes a challenge for everyone. Where inequalities, poverty and socio-economic disparities are widespread, the challenge becomes even harder to face worldwide. Following the UNESCO's world statistics of 2020, it is estimated that more than 258 million children and youth are out of school with the majority from disadvantaged backgrounds [6]. These disparities impede access to quality education, reinforce cycles of poverty and undermine the potential for social mobility. As outlined in Sustainable Development Goal 4 about Quality Education, ensuring inclusive, equitable and quality education is essential to breaking the cycle of persistent poverty. Yet, in a world deeply divided economically, socially and culturally, this goal remains elusive for many, especially in areas where inequalities are deeply entrenched. One of the most significant barriers to access to education is socio-economic inequality, which creates disparities in the quality and availability of education. For example, families living in poverty often do not have the resources to send their children to school, and even when children are enrolled, they do not always receive an education that meets global standards. As the World Bank [7] notes, children from low-income families often face challenges such as overcrowded classrooms, outdated curricula, and inadequate educational resources, which impact the quality of education they receive. As explained by Naouel Abdellatif Mami in her chapter about Citizenship Education in Post-conflict Contexts: The Case of Algeria [7], in many cases, these challenges are exacerbated by political instability or conflict, which can further disrupt education systems. Furthermore, the urban-rural divide exacerbates educational inequality. Children in rural areas often face significant barriers to education, such as long distances to school, lack of infrastructure, and limited access to qualified teachers. This gap is particularly pronounced in developing countries, where rural areas often receive fewer government resources and attention than urban centers as highlighted by the World Bank's report of 2020. As a result, children in rural areas are less likely to complete their primary and secondary education, perpetuating cycles of poverty and inequality.

2.2 Cultural and Gender Fragmentation

In addition to social, economic and regional disparities, cultural fragmentation remains a major barrier to access to education, especially for marginalized groups, including women, minorities and refugees. Gender disparities in education remain a critical issue worldwide, with girls often facing barriers such as societal expectations, early marriage and violence that prevent them from attending school. According to UNESCO [6], nearly one in five girls in developing countries are out of school due to these gender-related barriers [8]. In many societies, girls are expected to take on domestic responsibilities, limiting their ability to attend and complete school. In some cases, early marriage or cultural pressures can further reduce educational opportunities, reinforcing gender inequality in the long term.

In Algeria, in line with Aspiration 6 of Agenda 2063, which focuses on gender equality and women's empowerment, Algeria has implemented policies to promote girls' education and ensure gender parity in school enrollment. For example, Algeria has implemented various programs and initiatives to reduce girls' dropout rates and provide financial support to families to ensure that girls remain in school. Scholarly age of schooling is compulsory until 16 years old for both girls and boys. The Algerian government has also made significant strides in increasing women's representation in higher education, particularly in traditionally male-dominated fields such as science and engineering [3].

One of Algeria's most notable efforts to achieve gender equality in education and broader community participation is the quota system, among the first of its kind in Africa and the Arab world [36]. This policy has played an important role in promoting women's empowerment and ensuring their participation in politics and education. The introduction of gender quotas in Algeria reflects a proactive approach to addressing historical gender imbalances and promoting equitable representation of women in decision-making roles, thereby reinforcing the country's commitment to Sustainable Development Goal 5 (gender equality) and the ambition of Agenda 2063 [36, 37].

In politics, by the year 2000, Algeria became the first African country to institute a gender quota system in its national parliament, stipulating that at least 30% of parliamentary seats must be reserved for women. This historic decision marked a major turning point in Algeria's political landscape and served as a powerful tool to promote gender equality in public life. According to the Inter-Parliamentary Union (IPU) [9], Algeria's quota system has significantly increased the number of women in the country's parliament, with women now holding over 31% of parliamentary seats, a remarkable achievement that places Algeria among the leaders in women's representation in Africa. This policy has not only promoted political empowerment, but has also served as a model for other African countries seeking to increase women's participation in governance.

The gender quota system has also affected women's educational outcomes in Algeria. By ensuring women's representation in leadership positions, the policy has fostered a more inclusive environment for women's advancement in various sectors, including education. As noted by UNDP [10], the quota system has facilitated the development of policies that support women's education, including scholarships, mentoring programs, and initiatives to close the gender gap in higher education and vocational training. While challenges remain, particularly in rural areas, the quota system has played a critical role in promoting women's education in Algeria.

In addition, Algeria has made progress in addressing gender disparities in higher education by implementing policies that specifically target women's empowerment in academic institutions. For example, female enrollment in Algerian universities has increased dramatically reaching 60% of the total student population by 2024 [11], and women are increasingly represented in traditionally male-dominated fields, such as engineering and medicine. The quota system is also part of Algeria's broader commitment to gender equality and reflects the country's alignment with Agenda 2063, which emphasizes women's empowerment as a key element of Africa's development. This system has not only contributed to the empowerment of women in Algeria, but has also served as an important model for other African countries seeking to increase women's participation in education and governance, thereby contributing to broader social and economic development goals African Union [3].

Sustainable development goals also suggest including refugees and marginalized minority groups to whom barriers to accessing education are most pronounced. These groups often face not only socioeconomic deprivation, but also discrimination, exclusion from mainstream education systems, and displacement due to conflict. Refugees, in particular, may experience interruptions in their education due to lack of access to schools, legal barriers, or displacement-related trauma. In Algeria, which has welcomed refugees from neighboring countries such as Occidental Sahara, Syria and Mali, the government's efforts to integrate these displaced persons into the national education system have been commendable. Algeria has taken steps to integrate refugee children into public schools and provide them with the same educational opportunities as Algerian citizens. For example, the 2018 law allowed refugees to access free primary and secondary education [12]. However, challenges remain in ensuring that these children receive quality education that meets the standards set by the Sustainable Development Goals, particularly in terms of infrastructure, trained teachers, and provision of materials in refugee camps or underserved areas.

Refugee children often face significant language barriers, cultural differences, and psychological challenges that can hinder their ability to succeed in school, highlighting the need for targeted support programs to help them integrate effectively. As Mami [13] points out, gender and cultural fragmentation intersect with socio-economic factors to create multiple layers of disadvantage that prevent full access to education for all. Mami's research project about the creation of institutional capacities for the integration of refugees into Higher education "Ci-RES" [14] pinpoints to the need to a University—University and a University—Society Cooperation that reorganizes the organic and functional structure of the higher education institutions in order to provide an effective integration of refugees and to elaborate normative and institutional mechanisms favoring the integration of this category into higher education.

2.3 The Role of Youth in Algeria's Development: Empowerment and Policy Changes

In addition to the great strides made in women's empowerment and refugees' integration, youth have also become a priority in Algeria's development agenda. According to the Algerian National Office of Statistics (ONS) [15], nearly 70% of the population is under the age of 30, with a significant proportion, around 40%, falling within the 15–29 age group. Recognizing the importance of involving young people in shaping Algeria's future, the government has implemented various policies and institutional reforms aimed at empowering young people and providing them with the tools to actively participate in the nation's growth. These efforts are closely aligned with the Sustainable Development Goals, particularly Goal 4 (Quality Education), Goal 8 (Decent Work and Economic Growth), Goal 16 (Peace, Justice and Strong Institutions), and the African Union's Agenda 2063, which emphasizes the critical role of youth in driving social and economic transformation in Africa.

Education remains a key tool to address these challenges, with a focus on improving the quality and accessibility of education for young people. The Algerian Ministry of National Education (MNE) [16] reported that the secondary school enrollment rate is close to 94% and that female enrollment in higher education institutions is steadily increasing. (MESRS) [11]. As of 2024, women represent approximately 60% of university students in Algeria, reflecting the country's commitment to gender equality in education. (MESRS) [11]. The government has also implemented policies to encourage girls' education in disadvantaged areas, including scholarship programs aimed at changing community perceptions.

In response to the challenges facing youth, Algeria has taken significant steps to ensure youth participation in governance and policymaking. The Higher Youth Council was created by Presidential Decree No. 21-416 of 20 Rabie el Aouel 1443 corresponding to October 27, 2021, establishing its attributions, composition, organization and operation. This advisory body is placed under the President of the Republic and endowed with moral responsibility and financial autonomy [17]. Its missions mainly consist of formulating opinions, recommendations and proposals on issues relating to the needs of youth as well as their development in the economic, social, cultural and sporting fields. It also contributes to the promotion among youth of national values, practical awareness, civic spirit and social solidarity. It participates in the design, monitoring and evaluation of the national youth plan.

The establishment of the Supreme Youth Council in 2021 was a landmark initiative to ensure that young people have a formal platform to represent their interests and contribute to national policies. According to its president, Mustapha Hiddaoui who is since December 2024 Minister of Youth, the Supreme Youth Council has played an effective role in providing opportunities for young people to participate in discussions on key issues such as education reform, employment, and social inclusion. The Supreme Youth Council aims to ensure that young people are not just passive beneficiaries of policies, but active contributors to shaping the country's future.

In another move to prioritize youth development, on November 18th, 2024, following the Algerian reshuffle of members of the government, [19], Algeria separated the Ministry of Youth from the Ministry of Sports. This decision reflects the recognition that youth are placed at the heart of the political decision-making ladder and are not only limited to sports but also include education, employment, and social services portfolios. The Algerian Ministry of Youth (2024) is now focused on developing policies specifically aimed at improving youth livelihoods and opportunities. This restructuring is particularly important given the country's youthful demographic, as it allows for more targeted and strategic interventions that target the specific needs of youth and foster a stronger sense of participation in the nation's development.

Algeria's youth represent an immense wealth and a major challenge for the country's development. As Algeria strives to achieve the goals set out in SDG 4 (Quality Education), SDG 8 (Decent Work and Economic Growth), and SDG 16 (Peace, Justice, and Strong Institutions), it is imperative that the government continue to prioritize youth empowerment. Efforts such as the creation of the Higher Council for Youth, the restructuring of the Ministry of Youth, and programs to improve youth employment and education are crucial steps to ensure that Algerian youth have the opportunity to contribute to the nation's growth. By continuing to invest in education and employment, Algeria can unleash the full potential of its youth, who will be essential to achieving the Sustainable Development Goals and Agenda 2063.

2.4 Digital Literacy: A Strategic Priority for Algeria's Educational and Developmental Goals

Digital literacy is recognized as a critical factor in Algeria's quest for sustainable development, with specific alignment with the Sustainable Development Goals 2030 and Africa's Agenda 2063. As part of the 54 presidential commitments, particularly commitment 25 [19], President Abdelmadjid Tebboune has given high priority to the digitalization of all sectors, including education, Higher Education and Vocational and Professional education and training to enhance innovation, inclusion, and social and economic growth. By integrating digital skills into its education and development strategies, Algeria aims to empower its youth, reduce inequalities, and build a knowledge-based economy.

Integrating digital tools and skills into education systems is a cornerstone of global development strategies. For Algeria, digital literacy is a key means of achieving SDG 4, which focuses on providing quality education, and SDG 4.4, which focuses on equipping young people with skills adapted to the global digital economy [18]. Similarly, the first ambition of Agenda 2063 for Africa envisions a prosperous Africa driven by inclusive growth and sustainable development, with digital education playing a transformative role. In this context, Algeria's commitment to digitalization, as stipulated in the 54 Presidential Commitments, focuses on reducing the digital divide and promoting innovation in all sectors [19].

Digital literacy plays a critical role in bridging the gap between education and employment in an increasingly technology-driven world. By equipping young people with digital skills, Algeria not only promotes access to information and lifelong learning, but also prepares its workforce for high-growth sectors such as information technology, renewable energy, and e-commerce. Furthermore, Commitment 25 underlines the importance of digital transformation as a foundation for national and regional competitiveness [20]. This approach ensures that digital education is not limited to the classroom but is integrated into broader social and economic policies and initiatives.

Algeria has made significant progress in promoting digital literacy through various policies and programs targeting both students and teachers. Launched as a response to the Covid-19 pandemic and lately reinforced in 2022, the e-School initiative provides free online educational resources to students in disadvantaged and rural areas, demonstrating the government's commitment to reducing regional disparities in access to quality education [21]. This program, supported by international organizations such as UNICEF and UNESCO, embodies successful public-private partnerships in promoting educational goals.

In line with Commitment 25, the government also distributed more than 100,000 tablets and laptops to students from low-income families in 2023, as part of the National Digital Strategy 2025. This initiative addresses the challenges of digital accessibility and infrastructure gaps in rural areas. Additionally, collaborations with telecommunications providers such as Mobilis, Ooredoo and Djezzy have helped provide affordable internet packages to educational institutions, improving connectivity for students and teachers.

Despite these achievements, significant challenges remain. A report by the High Commission for Digitalization [22] indicates that the digital literacy rate among urban youth is 70%, while rural areas lag behind due to limited infrastructure and internet connectivity. Addressing these challenges is essential to achieving Sustainable Development Aspiration 6 of Agenda 2063, which calls for inclusive and equitable education.

The development of digital literacy in Algeria is hampered by several challenges. Many rural schools lack adequate infrastructure, including computer rooms and internet connectivity, leaving students without access to basic digital tools [21]. Limited opportunities for teacher training also compound the problem, as teachers are often ill-equipped to integrate digital technologies into their teaching methods.

In addition, social and cultural norms and lack of infrastructure disproportionately affect young women and girls [21]. report highlights that these barriers hinder progress towards gender parity in education, reinforce social and economic disparities, and limit opportunities for women in the digital economy [21].

The impact of digital literacy extends beyond education and affects broader social and economic outcomes. By equipping young people with digital skills, Algeria can address high levels of youth unemployment, which reached 30.78% in 2023 for individuals aged 15–24 [23]. Digital skills are essential for creating jobs in emerging sectors and fostering entrepreneurship, particularly in disadvantaged areas.

For Algeria to promote digital literacy and achieve its education and development goals, it must adopt a comprehensive and inclusive approach. Expanding digital infrastructure, especially in rural areas, is essential to bridge the urban-rural divide. Targeted teacher training programs should equip teachers with the skills to effectively integrate digital tools into their curricula. Strengthening public-private partnerships can provide the financial and technical resources needed to scale up digital literacy initiatives. Gender-responsive policies must also address the particular barriers that young women and girls face in accessing digital education and ensure equal opportunities for all.

Digital literacy is an educational goal and a key enabler for achieving sustainable development. Algeria's efforts, guided by the Sustainable Development Goals, Agenda 2063, and the 54 Presidential Commitments, demonstrate a clear commitment to building a digitally literate society capable of meeting the challenges of the twenty-first century. By addressing existing barriers and scaling up successful initiatives, Algeria can empower its youth, foster innovation, and contribute to a more inclusive and prosperous future. Continued investments and strategic partnerships will be essential to support these efforts and position Algeria as a regional leader in digital education.

3 Algeria's Education System: Achievements and Barriers

Education is a cornerstone of Algeria's development strategy, reflecting its commitment to the Sustainable Development Goals and the aspirations of Africa's Agenda 2063. While the country has made significant progress in improving access to education and addressing systemic barriers, challenges remain in ensuring quality, equity, and inclusion across all regions and demographic groups. This section examines the progress made, existing barriers, and systemic reforms needed to advance education.

3.1 Progress in Access to Education

Education in Algeria aims to promote social inclusion and equality of opportunity by providing free and compulsory education for all, including vulnerable groups, while removing barriers that may hinder their access to education. The government seeks to improve infrastructure, provide financial support for equitable education, and develop the skills of young people to enable them to contribute to society. The educational system also focuses on instilling national values and building a knowledge-based society through investment in science and technology. Furthermore, education promotes social cohesion and Algeria's commitment to international standards for sustainable and inclusive development.

Since independence, Algeria has made significant progress in its educational system by increasing the number of educational institutions and expanding literacy and vocational education programs [13]. The literacy rate rose from 10% in the 1960s to more than 81% in 2023, with the expansion of primary, middle, and secondary school networks. Reforms also included updating curricula in 2003 by introducing new subjects such as science and technology, and enhancing practical and technical skills. Digital technology was introduced into education and platforms for distance learning were developed after the COVID-19 pandemic. At the higher education level, the number of universities increased significantly to 115 institutions, with the strengthening of international cooperation in scientific research and innovation [11]. This progress has contributed to improving the quality of education and meeting the needs of the modern labor market.

The Algerian educational system is based on the principles of free and comprehensive education, and includes primary, middle and secondary education, in addition to vocational training. Since independence, free education has contributed to expanding access to literacy. The system also focuses on strengthening national identity through the teaching of Algerian history and culture, as well as Arabic, Berber and African affiliation [29]. In the 2024–2025 school year, Algeria has reached 11.7 million students distributed across 29,415 educational institutions, with 1.02 million supervisors [16]. Free textbooks cover 40% of students, and 1700 institutions are equipped with tablets to promote digitization [16]. In higher education, 115 universities receive about 1.8 million students, mainly distributed between science and technology (57%) and social sciences (43%), with 5120 foreign students. The country also invests in scientific research, with 42,000 researchers in 1800 laboratories [11]. Despite the regional challenges facing the system, it continues to focus on improving the quality of education and contributing to African development.

The Algerian educational system relies on a set of mechanisms to ensure universal and free education for all students up to the age of 16. According to Article 53 of the Algerian Constitution, [16], Education is free and compulsory from the age of 6–16, allowing all children to access education regardless of their family's economic status, with a primary enrollment rate of 98% in 2023, with preparatory classes being 100%. The government also provides financial support programs and school meals for low-income families. The system also includes national exams such as the Middle School Certificate (BEM) which qualifies for secondary education, with a success rate of 62% in 2024, as well as the Baccalaureate which qualifies for higher education with a success rate of around 58% [16] for the same academic year. Curriculum reforms have been introduced since 2003, with an emphasis on subjects such as programming, technology and environmental education, as well as partnerships with the private sector to develop practical skills. Teachers in higher education are trained based on their Baccalaureate results, with ongoing training programs and periodic evaluation of their performance, which seeks to improve the quality of education. These mechanisms aim to ensure comprehensive and quality education that contributes to the development of Algerian society and meets the needs of the labor market.

Algeria's advancement in access to education is largely due to the policies of free and compulsory education for children aged 6 to 16, as stipulated in the 1996 Education Law. The secondary school enrollment rate has also improved significantly, reaching 76% in 2023, up from 68% in 2010 [21]. These achievements are in line with the fourth goal of the Sustainable Development Goals (quality education) and the sixth aspiration of Agenda 2063, which focuses on inclusive and equitable education. In Higher Education, the year 2024 has witnessed the enrollment of more than One million and eight hundred thousand students according to the Ministry of Higher Education and Scientific Research [11].

From a political perspective, Algeria invests around 15% of its budget in education, reflecting its commitment to improving its quality and infrastructure. More than 1000 new schools have been built, primary school enrollment has reached 98% and literacy 81% [15]. In 2025, about 1645 billion dinars (12.3 billion dollars) are allocated to education, supporting priorities such as the opening of new teaching positions that reach 43,000, as well as investments in educational infrastructure and the introduction of computer equipment in schools [30]. Curricula are regularly updated and teachers are trained to enhance efficiency. Technology is integrated into education through the use of digital tools such as smart boards, and Algeria is strengthening cooperation with African countries through scholarships and student exchange programs [16].

The vocational training sector in Algeria plays a vital role in enhancing the employability of youth, the number of trained youth has reached 600,000 young people in 2023, focusing on areas such as industry, construction and information technology [31]. Through these programs, Algeria seeks to meet the needs of the labor market and reduce the unemployment rate among youth, contributing to the achievement of the 2030 Sustainable Development Goals and the Africa Agenda 2063. Algeria's efforts include expanding vocational training centers, especially in remote areas, and developing specialized training programs in vital areas such as renewable energy and sustainable agriculture. Algeria also cooperates with international organizations such as UNESCO and the International Labor Organization [31] to enhance the quality of vocational training programs and exchange expertise with other African countries. By engaging in such initiatives, Algeria aims to improve access to vocational education and enhance the skills of youth in line with the needs of the labor market, contributing to the economic and social development of the African continent and ensuring a better future for youth.

At the international level, Algeria endeavors to develop more South-South cooperation such as the Pan African University of Tlemcen initiative, which receives students from various African countries and offers training programs in vital areas such as water management and renewable energy [32]. Algeria also offers scholarship programs for African students from countries such as Mali and Niger, contributing to the promotion of higher education on the continent. Algeria has also signed several bilateral agreements to enhance cooperation in education and training, including the exchange of students and professors with countries such as Tunisia and Libya [16]. In addition, the country offers specialized training programs in areas such as sustainable agriculture and public health, and actively participates in discussions organized by the African Union to promote education [32]. These efforts seek to improve the educational capacities of African youth, contributing to the development of education and strengthening regional cooperation among African countries.

However, despite these considerable efforts deployed in Algeria, educational disparities remain. As a matter of fact, and in an attempt to reduce them, the government has launched several initiatives targeting marginalized populations. The National School Support Program provides free textbooks, meals, and transportation to more than 3 million pupils each year, with a focus on rural and low-income communities [24]. In addition, specialized programs targeting children with disabilities, such as inclusive classes and resource centers, have expanded in recent years. These initiatives reflect Algeria's commitment to leaving no child behind, in line with the spirit of Sustainable Development Goal 10 on reducing inequalities.

Moreover, and despite all the progress registered, deep disparities persist between urban and rural areas in Algeria's educational system. According to the World Bank report of 2023, 15% of schools are still lacking adequate facilities such as libraries, laboratories, and sanitation [25]. Access to internet as an essential for modern education, remains limited, with only 40% of rural schools having access compared to 90% in urban areas [20]. These disparities undermine efforts to ensure equitable education for all.

Significant challenges also remain in closing urban-rural gaps, and ensuring quality education for all. Strengthening infrastructure, expanding teacher training, and integrating technology into the curriculum are critical steps toward a more inclusive and equitable education. By addressing these challenges, Algeria can continue to build on its achievements and establish itself as a regional leader in education reforms.

3.2 Algeria's Role in Advancing Education and Development in Africa

Algeria's contributions to educational, social and economic development in Africa reflect its alignment with the Sustainable Development Goals and the African Union's Agenda 2063. As a key player in the African Union, Algeria actively participates in regional and continental initiatives, including those focused on sustainable development Goal 4 (Quality Education). Goal 5 (gender equality) and Ambition 1 of the African Agenda 2063 which consists in providing a high standard of living and quality of life for all citizens. Through its strategic policies and cooperation efforts, Algeria has made great strides in developing the educational sector and empowering young people, particularly in the context of regional cooperation and peacebuilding [34].

Algeria has also worked hard to align its national development strategies with the global objectives of the Sustainable Development Goals and the African Union's Agenda 2063. In this attempt, the country's focus on Sustainable Development Goal 4 is reflected in many initiatives towards improving access to education, promoting digital literacy and improving the quality of learning across Africa. At the continental level, Algeria contributes to Aspiration 1 of Agenda 2063, which envisions a prosperous and integrated Africa, as well as Aspiration 6, which focuses on youth-led development. The country's support for education across Africa is essential to addressing the continent's challenges of poverty reduction, economic integration and sustainable development.

Furthermore, Algeria plays a vital role in technical education, skills development, and vocational training across Africa. The country cooperates with African countries through joint programs aimed at improving workforce skills in sectors such as agriculture, health, ICT, and engineering. These initiatives are directly aligned with Sustainable Development Goal 8 (Decent Work and Economic Growth), aimed at equipping young Africans with the skills needed to succeed in the twenty-first century job market. For example, thousands of young Africans coming from 60 nationalities have benefited from scholarships at the Higher Education Institutions, preparing them for leadership roles in their country [26].

In Economy, Algeria has long supported Africa's economic integration through initiatives such as the African Continental Free Trade Area, which aims to promote intra-African trade and reduce trade barriers across the continent. Education plays a key role in this integration, preparing young people with the skills and knowledge needed to participate in the emerging African economy. Through cooperation with regional organizations and African countries, Algeria is helping to establish educational and commercial links that will strengthen economic growth and collective stability in Africa [33].

In terms of infrastructure development, the country has also invested heavily in regional access to education. It has supported projects aimed at improving school infrastructure and educational facilities in disadvantaged areas. These efforts are in line with Sustainable Development Goal 9, which calls for building resilient infrastructure, promoting inclusive industrialization, and fostering innovation. These political actions to contribute to regional infrastructure are an integral part of ensuring that quality education is accessible to all African children, regardless of their geographic location.

Another area in which Algeria has made significant progress is Youth empowerment through education. The creation of the Supreme Youth Council and the separation of the Ministry of Youth from the Ministry of Sports reflect Algeria's recognition of youth as a key pillar in achieving the African Agenda 2063 and the Sustainable Development Goals. The One Million next level, launched in Oran, in 2024 with the African Union confirms Algeria's commitment to providing education, skills development, and employment opportunities to one million young Africans. The initiative aims to provide young people with the tools to drive social and economic transformation in Africa [27].

However, it is undeniable that development in Africa can only be achieved if peace and security are ensured in the region. Algeria's role in peacebuilding on the African continent has long been effective in creating a stable environment for educational initiatives, particularly in conflict zones such as in the Sahel region. Algeria has actively supported regional peace efforts and played a major role in peacekeeping missions in Africa such as the efforts deployed in Mali and Lybia. Its commitment to Agenda 2063's Aspiration 4, which focuses on peace and security, ensures that education institutions and initiatives are protected from the devastating effects of conflict. Through diplomatic and peacebuilding efforts, the Algerian diplomacy has helped create the conditions for education to thrive in regions facing instability, thereby contributing to the broader goal of promoting peaceful and inclusive societies, as set out in Goal 16 about Peace, Justice, and Strong Institutions [26].

Despite these efforts, stability is still a strong concern in the region and the process of promoting sustainable peace faces major challenges. These challenges arise from internal and external factors that complicate the country's efforts to contribute to regional stability. These challenges are due to regional instability, geopolitical rivalries, the terrorist threat, and internal problems. Its ability to promote sustainable peace will depend not only on successfully addressing these challenges, but also on strengthening regional institutions and participating in multilateral cooperation efforts. As a key player in African diplomacy and peace efforts, Algeria will need to continue to address these challenges while balancing its domestic priorities and regional commitments. Ultimately, Algeria's peacebuilding efforts will require internal stability and regional cooperation to ensure peace and prosperity in Africa.

4 Addressing Solutions for Achieving Education for All

Achieving education for all remains a global priority, with education being a fundamental driver of sustainable development and social cohesion. However, one of the most significant challenges to achieving this goal is conflict. War and violence destabilize societies, disrupt educational systems, and displace millions of children, making access to education nearly impossible. Ongoing conflicts in regions such as Palestine and across the Middle East have clearly demonstrated how war exacerbates the challenges of providing quality education. These areas face major educational setbacks due to damaged infrastructure, displacement, and trauma caused by conflict. According to UNESCO [6], nearly one in five children worldwide are out of school due to violence or conflict, with the Middle East being a critical area of concern. For example, in Gaza, the destruction of schools and restrictions on movement have made access to education impossible, affecting the country's long-term development prospects.

Conflict zones not only disrupt the day-to-day functions of educational systems, but also limit the ability of young people to achieve their potential. Children in these regions grow up in unstable environments, where their education is often interrupted, leading to profound social and economic consequences, limiting future opportunities and hindering social mobility. In this context, promoting peace becomes crucial to advancing education, as educational systems cannot thrive in environments of violence and instability.

As we look to the future and explore possible solutions to conflict-driven education challenges, important strategies can be drawn from the experiences and initiatives discussed above. Algeria's role in supporting education in Africa, including through regional cooperation and initiatives, offers valuable lessons on how countries can work together to overcome education fragmentation. By investing in digital education, promoting inclusive policies, and strengthening regional cooperation, countries can begin to remove the barriers that prevent millions of children from accessing education.

4.1 Digital Education and Policy Reforms

The digital divide remains one of the greatest challenges facing education in both developed and developing countries. However, as Algeria's National Digital Strategy demonstrates, governments can overcome this barrier by investing in digital infrastructure that ensures access to education for rural and marginalized communities. The One Million Next Level initiative, which aims to empower young people through education, employment, and entrepreneurship, demonstrates how digital platforms can reach underserved communities, helping to bridge the urban-rural divide [35]. According to UNESCO [6], Algeria's efforts to introduce online learning platforms in remote areas have improved access to education, particularly for children previously excluded from traditional schools.

4.2 Comprehensive Education Policies

Educating marginalized groups, including girls, children with disabilities, and refugees, is essential to ensure that no one is left behind, as highlighted in Sustainable Development Goal 4. In Algeria, major steps have been taken to ensure gender parity in education. According to UNICEF (2020) report, [28] Algeria has achieved gender parity in school enrolment rates, with a 95% enrolment rate for girls in primary education. However, these successes need to be replicated across Africa and in conflict zones to ensure that marginalized groups, including those affected by displacement and poverty, and are not excluded from educational opportunities. To this end, policy reforms that make education accessible to these groups are essential. As stated in Aspiration 6 of Agenda 2063, the empowerment of women and children through education plays a crucial role in the socio-economic transformation of the continent.

4.3 Regional Cooperation and Integration

Algeria has long supported African education initiatives, such as the Pan-African University, designed to promote higher education, research and cooperation among African countries [38]. Through such initiatives, African countries can work together to create regional educational networks that facilitate cross-border educational exchanges and ensure that the continent's educational needs are met collaboratively. Algeria's role in promoting regional peacebuilding and educational cooperation can help mitigate the impact of regional conflicts on education and provide peaceful solutions that support access to education.

Considerable efforts are also made in the Higher Education sector where more than seven thousand African students are hosted at the level of Algerian universities to fulfill their higher Education degrees. More than 60 African nationalities are hosted at universities in Algeria [16] and an Alumni network is also developed that will help link the ties between the Algerian institutions and the African students once they are back to their countries. Furthermore, the Ministry of Higher Education has put in place a program called "Study in Algeria" that supports International students during their stay in the country and get the necessary facilities for quality education.

4.4 Building Peace and Stability

Peace is a prerequisite for good education. As the Palestinian conflicts and other crises in the Middle East have demonstrated, war not only disrupts daily life but also has a lasting impact on education. Promoting peace and stability in the region, such as mediation efforts in Mali, has provided a model for how countries can resolve conflicts without resorting to violence [38]. By promoting dialogue and creating peaceful environments, it is possible to build the foundation for the development of education in countries affected by conflict. This supports Goal 4 of Agenda 2063, which underlines the importance of peace, security and stability to achieve development goals in Africa.

5 Conclusion

This chapter has aimed to explore education for all as a challenge in a fragmented world, exploring the various obstacles, such as conflict, socio-economic disparities and regional fragmentation that hinder universal access to quality education. It highlighted the important role of education in achieving the Sustainable Development Goals 2030 and Agenda 2063, and more specifically how Algeria has positioned itself as a key player in promoting these goals across Africa. The country's efforts to promote SDG 4 for quality education and Agenda 2063's vision for a prosperous, integrated and peaceful Africa have demonstrated tangible progress, particularly in inclusive education, gender equality and regional cooperation.

Through initiatives such as the One Million Next Level program and being a host of the Pan African University, commitments to empowering African youth, promoting cross-border educational cooperation, and bridging the urban-rural divide have been achieved. These efforts have helped ensure that education reaches disadvantaged populations and promote regional unity and development.

But despite these developments, many challenges remain, including the effects of regional instability, conflict, and social inequality. As this chapter clearly shows, the impact of war, as in the Middle East and other conflict zones, remains a major obstacle to educational progress. It disrupts access to schools, prevents infrastructure development, and perpetuates social and economic disparities. In light of these challenges, the need for increased investment in education, policy reform, and commitment to regional cooperation is essential to overcome educational fragmentation and ensure access to quality education for all.

The call to action is clear. In order to remove barriers to education, it is essential to prioritize digital education, inclusive policies, and peacebuilding efforts. This comprehensive approach will ensure that marginalized groups, especially girls and youth, are not left behind in the educational journey. There is no doubt that education is the cornerstone of sustainable development, social cohesion, and economic empowerment. By focusing on inclusive education systems and creating stable environments, countries like Algeria can help lead the way in advancing Africa's development agenda.

The role of education in promoting a prosperous, integrated, and peaceful countries is of paramount importance. It equips individuals with the skills and knowledge to contribute to economic growth, reduce disparities, and promote unity across borders. As the world moves towards achieving the Sustainable Development Goals and the African Agenda 2063, it is essential that education remains at the heart of this vision. Only through cooperation, increased investment and continued commitment to inclusive and accessible education can we ensure a brighter and more inclusive future for all.

References

1. Mandela N (1990) Long walk to freedom: the autobiography of Nelson Mandela. Little, Brown
2. United Nations (UN) (2015) Transforming our world: the 2030 agenda for sustainable development. United Nations . https://sdgs.un.org/2030agenda
3. African Union (AU) (2013) Agenda 2063: the Africa we want. African Union. https://au.int/en/agenda2063
4. The African Youth Charter (2006) Chromeextension://efaidnbmnnnibpcajpcglclefindmkaj/https://au.int/sites/default/files/documents/30922-doc-african_youth_charter_english_0.pdf
5. Pan African Youth Forum Declaration (2024) https://fr.scribd.com/document/790383405/2024-Pan-African-Youth-Forum-Declaration
6. UNESCO (2020) Global education monitoring report: inequality in education. UNESCO. https://en.unesco.org/gem-report
7. World Bank (2020) Access to education in rural Algeria. World Bank
8. Abdellatif Mami N (2020) Citizenship education in post-conflict contexts: the case of Algeria. In: Akkari A, Maleq K (eds) Global citizenship education. Springer, Cham. https://doi.org/10.1007/978-3-030-44617-8_9
9. Inter-Parliamentary Union (IPU) (2020) Women in politics 2020: the impact of gender quotas in national parliaments. IPU. https://www.ipu.org/women-in-politics
10. UNDP (2022) Gender equality in Algeria: a focus on education and labor market integration. UNDP
11. Ministry of Higher Education and Scientific Research MESRS (2024) www.mesrs.dz
12. UNHCR (2018) Education and refugees in Algeria: access and integration. United Nations High Commissioner for Refugees. https://www.unhcr.org
13. Mami NA (2023) Educational challenges in Algeria: policies, gender, and access. J N Afr Stud 28(3):456–468
14. Ci-RES, The Creation of Institutional Capacities for the Integration of Refugees in Higher Education. www.ciresproject.eu. Last seen on 21/12/2024
15. Algerian National Office of Statistics (ONS) (2021) Youth employment and demographic trends in Algeria. ONS. https://www.ons.dz
16. Ministry of National Education. https://www.education.gov.dz/fr/
17. Le Haut Conseil National de la Jeunesse. https://www.mjs.gov.dz/index.php/fr/actualites-4/jeunesse/haut-conseil-national-de-la-jeunesse. Last seen on 21/12/2024
18. United Nations (2022) SDG progress report. https://www.un.org
19. Presidency of Algeria (2022) The Presidential 54 commitments: a blueprint for national development. https://www.presidency.gov.dz
20. Algerian National Agency for the Promotion of Digital Technologies (ANPT) (2023) Digital literacy and access in Algeria. https://www.anpt.dz
21. UNESCO (2023) Closing the gender gap in digital education: case studies from North Africa. https://www.unesco.org
22. Le Haut-Commissariat de la Numérisation. https://sondage.hcn.gov.dz/
23. ANEM (2023) Youth unemployment in Algeria: annual statistical report. https://www.anem.dz
24. Algerian Ministry of National Solidarity (2023) Inclusive education programs for vulnerable populations. https://www.solidarity.gov.dz
25. World Bank (2023) Algeria's rural development and education challenges. World Bank, Washington, DC
26. UNESCO (2024) Global education monitoring report: Africa. UNESCO, Paris
27. Algerian Ministry of Youth (2024) Strategic framework for youth empowerment. Government of Algeria, Algiers
28. UNICEF (2020) Education for all: the state of education in Algeria. UNICEF
29. Mami NA (2013) La diversité linguistique et culturelle dans le système éducatif algérien. Revue internationale d'éducation de Sèvres [En ligne], 63 | septembre 2013, mis en ligne le 01 septembre 2015, consulté le 21 décembre 2024. http://journals.openedition.org/ries/3473. https://doi.org/10.4000/ries.3473

30. Projet de loi de finances 2025 : Vision et préconisations du Conseil Scientifique de Jil Jadid. https://jiljadid.org/2024/10/30/projet-loi-finances-2025-algerie-defis-reformes/?lang=fr#:~:text=Environ%201%20645%20milliards%20de%20dinars%20%2812%2C3%20milliards,dans%20les%20infrastructures%20%C3%A9ducatives%20et%20l%E2%80%99introduction%20d%E2%80%99%C3%A9quipements%20infor. 30/10/2024
31. Ministère de l'Education et de la Formation Professionnelle https://webmfep.mfp.gov.dz/?playlist=3b65b62&video=ae72f3a
32. Pan African University Tlemcen, PAUWES. https://pau-au.africa/index.php?id=62
33. African Union (2018) Agreement establishing the African continental free trade area. African Union
34. African Union (2015) Agenda 2063: the Africa we want. African Union
35. ExpressDZ (2024) L'Algérie adhère à l'initiative « 1 million, prochain niveau » de l'Union africaine pour créer des opportunités d'emploi et de formation pour les jeunes africains. https://www.express-dz.com/2024/11/02/lalgerie-adhere-a-linitiative-1-million-prochain-niveau-de-lunion-africaine-pour-creer-des-opportunites-demploi-et-de-formation-pour-les-jeunes-africains/
36. Algerian Constitution (2016) Constitution of Algeria. Official Journal of the People's Democratic Republic of Algeria
37. Law No. 12-03 (2012) Law on quotas for women in elected assemblies. Official Journal of the People's Democratic Republic of Algeria
38. Algerian Ministry of Foreign Affairs (2013) Algeria's contribution to peace and stability in Africa. Algerian Ministry of Foreign Affairs. https://www.mfa.gov.dz/foreign-policy/multilateral-relations/algeria-african-union

Naouel Abdellatif Mami is Vice Rector of the External Relations and Cooperation at Mohamed Lamine Debaghine, Sétif 2 University. She is Full professor and detainer of a PhD in Psychopedagogy and Foreign Language Teaching and Learning. She followed her Post-Doctoral research at the university of Fribourg in Switzerland. She has been awarded "Youngest Professor in Algeria". She is also a Higher Education Reform Expert (HERE) for Algeria at the European Commission. She has a long experience in cooperation, international research and project development and management. She worked as expert from 2010 to 2014 for the Council of Europe coordinating two research projects, namely EDIR and ECUD. She is the coordinator of several research projects nationally and internationally such as ABDEM, Dire-MED, ESAGOV and PraNet and Ci-RES. She also has extensive experience in the Erasmus+ Programme. She is the initiator of the Erasmus+ Virtual Exchange pilot programme in Algeria. She has an interdisciplinary profile with an extensive para-academic experience. She touches to the questions related to Educational Psychology, education, internationalization, citizenship and global citizenship, human rights, intercultural dialogue, digitalization and IT in education, Artificial Intelligence in human sciences. She currently coordinates a n international research project on the development of mechanisms of social responsibility for the socio-ecological transition of the university. She has been the first Algerian personality awarded the Virtue and Conosceza Special "Mare Nostrum" award in Italy in 2022.

Ha, Made You Look! Rethinking Gender Representation in Marketing

5

Marisa R. Ferreira, José Nuno Teixeira, Emília Fernandes, and Regina Leite

We realize the importance of our voices only when we are silenced.

– Malala Yousafzai

Abstract

Addressing the issue of female under/misrepresentation in marketing approaches and aligning with goal five—achieve gender equality and empower all women and girls—within the framework of the sustainable objective goals from the United Nations, the present chapter provides a broader and more comprehensive framework of gender relations and its associated stereotypes within the realm of marketing. So, firstly, this chapter begins by conceptualizing and theorizing gender, followed by exploring gender inequalities and stereotypes. The second part discusses the media's role in shaping gender perceptions and highlights initiatives for gender equality. In the third part, we use examples from the automobile industry, a traditionally masculine sector, to briefly illustrate how gender discrimination was (re)produced in the marketing campaigns, and how are the automobile industry brands trying to promote gender equality and promote gender-responsive approaches. The chapters conclude with a reflection on female representation in marketing and suggestions for future research.

M. R. Ferreira (✉)
CIICESI, ESTG, Polytechnic of Porto, Porto, Portugal
e-mail: mferreira@estg.ipp.pt

J. N. Teixeira
Research Centre on Education (CIEd), University of Minho, Braga, Portugal

E. Fernandes · R. Leite
School of Economics, Management and Political Science, CICS.Nova/UMinho, University of Minho, Braga, Portugal
e-mail: mifernandes@eeg.uminho.pt; rleite@eeg.uminho.pt

B. Casais (ed.), *Integrated Science to Achieve Sustainable Development Goals*, Integrated Science 37, https://doi.org/10.1007/978-3-031-88777-2_5

Graphical Abstract

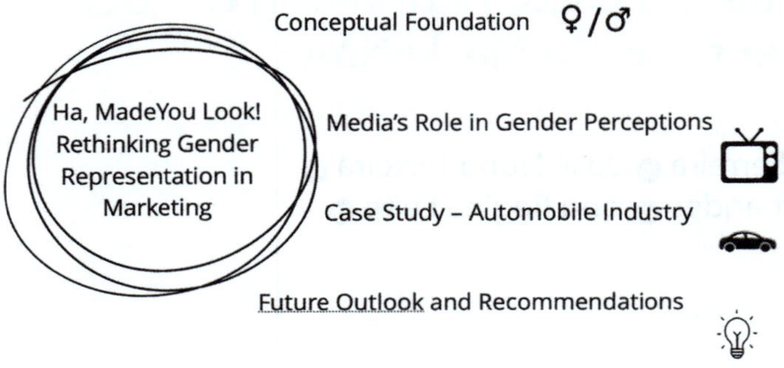

Source: Authors

Keywords

Gender · Marketing · Discrimination · Representation · SDG 5 · Female empowerment · Representation gaps · Automobile industry and social perceptions

1 Introduction

Historically, women have often been under/misrepresented in several sectors of the human and society life, with limited visibility and access to certain social and work roles due to gender discrimination and prejudice. Representation of women in marketing is a complex and multifaceted issue. Gender stereotypes persist through various dimensions, including beauty standards, societal expectations, and/or role representations.

Overall, in 2023 [77], gender parity in Europe (76.3%) exceeds that of North America (75%). Latin America and the Caribbean follow closely with 74.3% parity, Eurasia and Central Asia (69%), East Asia and the Pacific (68.8%). Sub-Saharan Africa ranks sixth at 68.2%, slightly below the global weighted average score of 68.3%. Southern Asia (63.4%) has overtaken the Middle East and North Africa (62.6%), making the latter the region furthest from gender parity in 2023. In education, in particular, we have seen that educational attainment among women is growing, considering the global parity score, with only 4.8% of the gender gap left to close [77]. Several studies [41, 57, 65] mention the prioritization and non-discrimination in education and scientific research, areas that can be seen as vehicles for societal gender emancipation.

However, the overall trajectory toward gender equality is slow and characterized by advances and setbacks, often revealing enduring gaps across various social and human life dimensions. The pursuit of global gender parity is delayed by systemic issues and socio-economic structural barriers that disproportionately impact women negatively [77], underscoring the need for sustained and targeted political and social interventions to achieve meaningful progress. In this context, gender equality is recognized as one of the United Nations Sustainable Development Goals, specifically SDG 5, which aims to "achieve gender equality and empower all women and girls." This chapter aligns with this global objective by analyzing the persistent gender disparities and exploring strategies to overcome them, thereby contributing to international efforts in favor of gender equality.

In the labor market, gender parity remains a significant challenge [24, 28] for individuals, organizations, and society. Although women have re-entered the labor force at higher rates than men, resulting in a slight improvement in gender parity in the workplace contexts, large gaps persist in work opportunities and resources, career progression, and leadership positions [26]. When analyzing average monthly earnings, it becomes evident that women lag behind, highlighting significant gender wage disparities. Women's average monthly salary is consistently lower, making them more susceptible to precarious employment situations than men [74]. Notably, this wage discrepancy increases with age, meaning that as age and professional careers advance, the wage gap between women and men widens [33].

While unique in its own ways, the marketing context is not exempt from the inequalities present in gender relations. It is often used as a strategic tool to reinforce gender norms and stereotypes. However, marketing also has the potential to challenge these norms and encourage new ways of understanding gender identity in relation to consumption and social marketing [49]. In this chapter, we aim to present a broader framework of gender relations and the associated stereotypes within this specific context.

This chapter initially conceptualizes and theorizes gender; then, the topic of gender inequalities and stereotypes will be addressed. In the second part of the chapter, we discuss the media's role in gender equality, focusing on perceptions of gender roles in society. To better understand these concepts, we briefly mention some initiatives for gender equality, in Sect. 3, including marketing examples that might influence perceptions of gender. The chapter concludes with a reflection on the understanding of women under/misrepresentation through marketing approaches. Building a sustainable future that effectively realizes human rights and ensures everyone's full participation is fundamental. With this chapter, we aim not only to raise awareness but also to provide insights into best practices aimed at promoting gender equality and women's empowerment in the marketing context.

2 Conceptualizing and Theorizing Gender

In the mid-1960s, the first references to gender appear in the scientific panorama, in the field of psychology [3]. Since then, the debate around gender has been ongoing globally, but with greater scope and relevance in developed countries [13]. Two major social and cultural transformations have historically and socially influenced the affirmation of the gender concept development. On one hand, the resurgence of feminist movements—which had temporarily suspended their activities due to the two major wars that ravaged the world—in a logic of (re)affirming the emancipatory role of women [34, 80]. And on the other hand—albeit on a small scale, due to the educational constraints to which women have been subjected throughout history—the access women to professions related to scientific fields [66].

For a long time, the theoretical perspective of gender conceptualization focused on a purely essentialist view [11], which was based on the idea that gender arose from a direct association with biological and anatomical sex, linearly and objectively predetermining an individual's gender identity [20]—and here Sigmund Freud's theory [30] assumed significant breadth and influence. The main argument of this theory was that the biological and physiological basis of each individual (e.g., chromosomes, sexual organs, and/or the hormonal system) was responsible for natural differences in behavior between men and women. This idea remained for centuries, although, more recently, lost some strength with the evolution and progress of science [60] towards new forms of social and human knowledge and, also, due to feminist movements [2, 3, 47]. Over time, particularly from the second half of the twentieth century, as a result of scientific and academic advances and various scientific studies, it was understood that individuals could exhibit a certain autonomy of psychological identity [3] and behaviorally dissociate from their biological sex [18, 44]. Consequently, the need to conceptualize and theorize gender from a different perspective increase. This theorization and conceptualization largely resulted from the questioning and insufficiency of arguments to clarify the inequalities between men and women merely supported by sex [2, 3].

Despite the intrinsic complexity of separating sex from gender [67], it was from this that the desire to show gender as a social and cultural construction emerged. Gender is neither the result of sex nor as apparently fixed as sex [12], if we consider Simone de Beauvoir's work "The Second Sex," we find a famous quote, "one is not born, but rather becomes, a woman" ([29], pp. 283). Following this more sociological line of thought, we can better understand the dimension that considers gender as a social and cultural construction. So, the concepts of sex and gender are distinguished, assigning them different analytical perspectives and domains [60], with this differentiation being of fundamental importance [30]. This rupture and distinction between biological sex, seen as 'destiny,' and gender, as a 'cultural construct' [12], allowed for a differentiated understanding of individuals as social beings influenced by cultural experiences. In other words, it is suggested that gender is a social and cultural construct, not depending exclusively on biology, which pushed the debate about sex and gender even further.

The conception of gender is presented as a set of social and cultural acquisitions integrated through the construction of a psychological identity associated with notions, concepts, and characteristics of socially constructed femininity and masculinity. These two concepts (masculinity and femininity) are not immutable and universal, as they differ based on cultural, religious, spatial, and historical specificities. Therefore, this concept is mainly circumscribed to the cultural domain of individuals [30, 61] based on social interactions with others [32, 76, 78]. Gender becomes then a social and interactional practice, where the gendered self is always in a process of becoming constrained by the disciplinary discourses of what it means to be a woman/feminine or man/masculine [12].

From this conceptualization of gender as a sociocultural construct, it is understood that there are no universal, standardized, and absolute determinations about the behaviors of men and women, assumed and based exclusively on biological determination [38, 71]. Therefore, despite the apparent similarity in meaning that the terms 'sex' and 'gender' may present, they are conceptually dissimilar. Their inappropriate use, disregarding their epistemological values and limits, can lead to an incorrect conceptual understanding of the phenomenon under study [17]. It is important to have in mind that, whenever we undertake a social analysis of the understanding of genders, it is important that they are not approached as opposites (like a binary system) [69]. The social analysis of this matter requires a lens that allows us to understand gender as a system of meanings dependent on the social context of individuals.

Feminist movements, starting in the 1960s, were a true catalyst for advancing gender studies. In countries such as the United States and Great Britain, women organized socially to establish university courses, ensuring their presence within academia to facilitate reflections underlying feminist studies 'women's studies' [12].

2.1 Gender Inequalities and Stereotypes

Historically, women seem to have always been in a position of inferiority compared to men, with their expectations primarily confined to the domestic sphere [63], being intensely disadvantaged professionally and socially. These social conceptions regarding women have hindered their progress in many areas of life, including the workforce [13, 58]. Today, living in a contemporary society involves various ways of experiencing femininity and masculinity. If we consider that its construction is based on cultural and contextual aspects, any analysis that can be made or interpreted about the characteristics of men and women becomes complex, dynamic, and varied [22, 59]. However, despite the evolution of time and the way society is viewed and experienced, there are still many stereotypes associated with gender that place women at a disadvantage.

The conception of a stereotype is understood, from the perspective of various authors [6, 39], as a set of characteristics, attributes, and beliefs widely established in society that are believed to be more characteristic of a certain social group. The construction of stereotypes can, on one hand, assume a more positive perspective where the focus is on understanding and organizing the multiplicity of behaviors; or, on the other hand, a more negative matrix if we direct these behaviors or attributes towards generalized forms and discriminatory judgments and prejudice [56, 59, 79]. The understanding of stereotypes in the field of gender analysis [2, 32] incorporates a strong normative power, often transcending the merely descriptive logic and acting in a more prescriptive and deterministic logic of what should be the behaviors of men and women [40].

At the origin of gender stereotypes, there is a strong relationship with bodily, biological, and physical appearance that seeks to associate men and women with perceived innate abilities and certain places and/or occupations in society [19, 52]. Thus, inequality can be understood as the social interpretation of these differences, and here we have, once again, a relationship between sex, which refers to biological and anatomical issues, and, on the other hand, gender, which focuses on social construction.

Another dimension presented in the literature as a justification for asymmetries is the experiences and contexts of the individuals who create and reproduce them. It is believed that indicators of social and economic class, as well as the social and geographic contexts of origin, immediately influence gender perceptions [74]. Still from the author's perspective, these aspects reinforce a strong marginalization of women in various social and community contexts, such as education, work and access to leadership positions.

The insertion of women into the workforce continues to register significant inequalities and gender differences that result from horizontal and vertical segregation between women and men [24, 26, 62]. Although there has been an increase in women, due to the evolution of time and changes in organizational dynamics, certain professions, labor occupations, and leadership roles are still considered typically male occupations [36, 46, 53].

From the perspective of management and assuming management and leadership positions, there continues to be a highly stereotyped view of women occupying these roles [7, 21, 51], with women being less represented in these positions. This conditionality is based on highly stereotyped conceptions of men and women. In general terms, women are thought of as more fragile, indecisive, and passive, while, in contrast, masculinity is more associated with independence, decision-making ability, and assertiveness. These gender representations penalize the ascension of women to leadership positions [25, 68]. Some studies, [4, 53] point out that aspects such as competitiveness, productivity, and many of the logics associated with management and the labor market are mainly presented as a male domain, suggesting the possibility of incompatibility between femininity and leadership.

Two ways that reveal how management and leadership positions are constructed through an ideal of masculinity are access to power and time usage. Both are related to an ideal worker who is totally available to work and from whom the personal and family dimension is occluded. In this regard, women are generally more limited in their ability to establish networks on an informal level (participation in dinners, networking, and discussion groups) and in their training (mentoring, participation in capacity-building and development programs) [50]. If we understand that these activities often occur outside of working hours and contribute significantly to women's ascension to power, women are disadvantaged [69]. The primary reason for this is the restriction of time resulting from the unequal segregation of time use related to domestic tasks, motherhood, and unpaid work. This influences access to management roles and constitutes a barrier to remaining in leadership positions [9, 27, 53].

The pursuit of effective and full gender equality thus becomes fundamental if we consider that the increasing presence of women and their recognition in various spheres of society has not been accompanied by due recognition of their rights and duties as legitimate subjects. These gender representations can result in adverse generalizations about the posture and role of gender assumed by the individual, reflecting in the way society, in general, perceives its various domains: political, economic, labor, personal, and family [45, 66].

In the research that has been developed, subordinated to gender studies, a transdisciplinary approach has been adopted. Thus, gender and the social and discursive representations we make of it result from social and power processes, and it is through these processes that we construct ourselves and others as gender subjects. As such, it is relevant to understand how a disciplinary power as it is marketing contributes to gender relations and fosters gender (ine)quality.

3 Media's Role in Gender Equality: Is Marketing for or Against It?

Gender roles in marketing have been a subject of significant scholarly interest. The way media represents women and men influences societal perceptions, as some studies have shown that media, including advertising and television, plays a crucial role in shaping attitudes and stereotypes related to gender roles [5, 14, 43]. These portrayals can have long-lasting effects on individuals, impacting body image, self-esteem, and/or behavior [15], replicating stereotypical images of masculinity and femininity that can lead to the internalization of conservative gender roles [40, 64]. Moreover, media images often emphasize unrealistic beauty standards, affecting both women and men, eventually leading to body dissatisfaction and gender-based insecurities [10, 35].

Considering marketing practices, advertising has been crucial to shaping the perceptions of gender roles [55]. It can both reinforce traditional notions of gender relations and challenge them [70]. However, despite some changes, male and female roles in advertising have remained largely unchanged, reflecting a tacit acceptance of mainly normative masculinities and femininities [29]. Advertisers often rely on stereotypical images of gender roles, potentially perpetuating societal expectations [43], highlighting patriarchal gender roles and traditional family values, and reflecting cultural norms and expectations [42]. Has we can see in Fig. 5.1, in 2021–2022, in a report that analyzed 10.000 ads, women were highly represented in family roles.

It is not surprising to confirm that advertising often portrays women mainly as sexualized figures or caregivers while men are shown as breadwinners or leaders. These stereotypes can limit women's opportunities, reinforce gender inequality and create barriers for women to access work market and business opportunities [8, 41]. So, the representation of gender in advertising can have direct effects on individuals, such as affecting confidence and career progression [54].

However, it is also important to mention that advertisements play a significant role in shaping and changing consumer behavior. While female stereotypes dominate the industry, there is a growing emergence of non-stereotypical gender representations in advertising [5]. Even though women are under-represented and

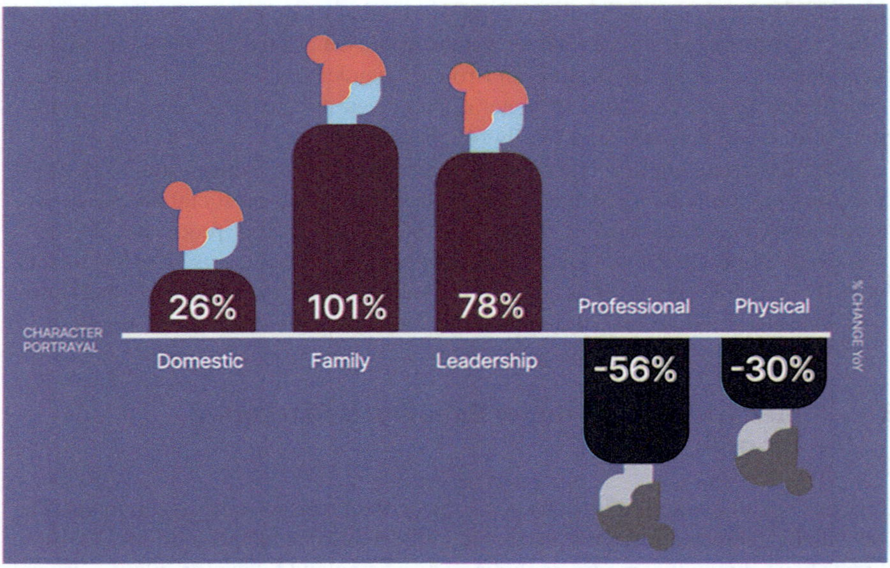

Fig. 5.1 Women's roles in ads, 2021–2022. (Source: [16], pp. 6. https://learn.creativex.com/gender-in-advertising-report-2023)

stereotyped [16], we can see a slow change in women's portrayal in advertising, trying to move away from passive, more frequently in domestic and family roles representations to more active, independent, and sexually empowered representations [31]. Despite these changes, the marketing industry is still a long way from true gender equity and continues to perpetuate traditional gender roles and stereotypical representations [75, 81].

Femvertising, a blend of "feminism" and "advertising," refers to marketing campaigns that use feminist themes and messages to promote products or brands, and it can enhance brand perception by aligning a company with progressive values, particularly those related to gender equality [5, 48, 72]. Some consumers may develop a stronger connection with brands they perceive as advocates for women's rights and empowerment. This can lead to increased brand loyalty and positive word-of-mouth promotion.

In summary, media has immense power to shape societal attitudes [14] and, simultaneously, the responsibility to promote balanced and diverse representations. Promoting positive representations and challenging stereotypes can contribute significantly to achieving gender equality. Media can challenge norms by portraying strong, independent female characters and promoting gender equality.

4 Initiatives for Gender Equality: Marketing Examples That Might Influence Perceptions of Gender

Gender stereotypes in advertising, through media and marketing tools, negatively impact both women and men, leading to higher levels of ad reactance and negative brand-related effects across both genders. Although consumers react negatively to stereotyping across genders, this perspective has received significantly less research attention [1]. As such, marketers and consumers can benefit from adopting a more mindful and critical approach to the portrayals of gender used in advertising, trying to highlight more egalitarian and emancipatory roles [37]. We therefore present some examples that illustrate how media and marketing tools might influence perceptions of gender. We have chosen the car industry, a traditionally male-dominated sector since it can be an important illustration of gender equality initiatives.

Brands can contribute to a more inclusive world by avoiding harmful stereotypes and promoting positive portrayals of both genders. Many automotive brands, like Ford (Fig. 5.2)[1] or Audi (Fig. 5.3),[2] have developed campaigns for the International Women's Day as follows:

In recognition of International Women's Day, Ford Motor Company is celebrating the significant role that women have played in the development of the modern automobile by launching the video "The Ford Explorer Men's Only Edition." Audi's #DriveTheChange is an initiative that mentions gender-related stereotypes in a video launched on International Women's Day. In Audi's campaign, we can see a tentative fight against the stereotypes related to the association of femininity with passivity, indecisiveness, and fragility. However, despite their impactful messaging, these campaigns are confined to a specific temporal event—International Women's Day—thereby risking the reinforcement of the same patriarchal logics they aim to challenge, which, while impactful, may not achieve sustained change without ongoing efforts. Thus, while Ford and Audi contribute to an important dialogue, the transient nature of such campaigns may fail to disrupt the deep-rooted gender stereotypes that hinder women's career progression to top management positions and leadership opportunities. Research indicates that one-time interventions are often insufficient to alter deeply ingrained societal norms and behaviors. So, a wider framework and role models are needed since they can more effectively change attitudes and behaviors towards gender equality [73].

While these campaigns raise important awareness, they should be part of a broader, sustained effort to challenge and dismantle harmful stereotypes effectively and gradually change societal gendered representations. In recent years, the automotive industry, has developed campaigns with the aim of challenging traditional gender roles and stereotypes and promoting gender equality.

---

[1] As illustrated in Figure 5.2, Ford's 'Women's History Month - ad from 2023' website can be found at the following link: https://www.ford.com/explorermensonlyedition

[2] As illustrated in Figure 5.3, Audi's 'Campaign for the International Women's Day— Audi—#DriveTheChange ad from 2021 can be found at the following link: https://www.youtube.com/watch?v=UgEmnGyoXxU

Fig. 5.2 Ford—Women's History Month—ad from 2023. (Source: Ford Official Website, 2024)

Audi's 2017 campaign—Daughter—featured a young girl racing against boys in a go-kart race, challenging traditional gender roles by showing that girls can compete and excel in areas typically dominated by boys. The campaign shows how gender role stereotypes stay in advertising, frequently strengthening outdated societal norms, which is supported by the literature [55, 70]. Additionally, the campaign's message that abilities and interests are not defined by gender, echoing results from literature [7, 21, 51] that stress the unfavorable effects of gender inequalities and stereotypes on societal progress.

Mercedes 2021 Campaign—The Reinvention of "Pretty"—the campaign reconceptualize the notion of "pretty" to integrate qualities like strength, resilience, confidence, and intelligence, differing from traditional meanings, dismantling gender inequalities and stereotypes by challenging conventional beauty norms [23, 36]. By presenting women who break the pattern and show these traits, the campaign confronts conventional beauty standards and endorses a more inclusive and empowering picture of women. The campaign supports the results of Aruna and Gunasundari [5], that highlights the importance of inclusive marketing strategies in redefining gender roles, and such proposals can disrupt implanted stereotypes by exhibiting diverse exemplifications in media [42].

Fig. 5.3 Audi—#DriveTheChange ad from 2021. (Source: Audi India official YouTube channel, 2024)

Peugeot 2023 Campaign—Girls Like Cars Too—the brand intends to show that driving and the interest for cars are not exclusive of a certain gender. The campaign intends to present a sensitive case study, by focusing topics like gender inequalities and stereotypes, showing that the automotive excitement is not exclusive of male. By highlighting female drivers and enthusiasts, the brand not only challenges conventional gender roles but also aligns with Creativex [16] in promoting more diverse and representative marketing practices, and showcasing women as fervent supporters of cars, challenging the traditional stereotype, giving a critical role to marketing, redesigning gender roles and supporting inclusivity [9].

These campaigns—of Audi, Mercedes and Peugeot—were deliberately selected from different geographies, in order to show diverse cultural backgrounds, reveal that the issue of gender stereotypes is a worldwide challenge. By emphasizing campaigns from many regions, these cases showcase how different brands, from diverse parts of the world, are acknowledging the need to address gender equality, regardless of cultural or geographical dissimilarities. This variety not only highlights the universal significance of the discussion about gender equity but also shows how different markets are engaging with this topic in innovative and impactful ways.

The mentioned campaigns highlight that interests, abilities, and strengths are not dictated by gender, aiming to deconstruct risky stereotypes. By showing more energetic and conscious representations of women, these campaigns contribute to a wider common effort to nurture gender inclusivity and equality. In all of them, we see that brands use a more consistent, sustained and strategic methodologies. These examples from the car industry show how media and marketing can successfully take attention ("Ha, Made You Look!") and use that attention to challenge and reconsider conventional gender roles. By focusing in universal inequalities, leveraging social marketing for gender-equality programs, and fostering gender-responsive tactics, these campaigns illustrate the importance of rethinking gender representation in marketing. They emphasize the potential for marketing to be a tool for social change, beyond mere intermittent works, boosting a more uninterrupted and consequential commitment to gender equality.

5 Conclusion

The investigation of gender representation in marketing, particularly within conventionally male-dominated sectors like the automotive industry, emphasizes a serious connection among gender inequalities, societal norms, and corporate responsibility. Within a more traditional framework, across time, marketing was not always very progressive, and many times stressed a more conventional and frequently stereotypical representations of women, underlining social structures, hierarchies and dynamics that creates boundaries to women's involvement and participation in many dimensions of the society. Nevertheless, through this chapter, we present several progressive and inclusive examples of gender representation, that illustrate important changes in corporate strategies and societal expectations. The examples, represented by the Mercedes, Peugeot and Audi campaigns, show that some brands are trying to fight long-standing gender stereotypes by emphasizing women's roles and experiences, mainly in industries where their presence has traditionally been minimized. Although these examples are extremely important and meaningful, is important to underline that unregular interventions are insufficient, so, brands should consider go beyond sporadic approaches and work on more continuous, sustainable and meaningful changes.

In this chapter, we consider that there is an assiduous underrepresentation and misrepresentation of women in marketing and the workplace. Despite worldwide efforts to reach gender equality, the embedded stereotypes last, and shape societal expectations and media representations. These misrepresentations constraint women's access to management, and particularly leadership roles and delay their complete participation and involvement in public and professional life. The chapter's analysis of gender-responsive marketing emphasizes how media and marketing campaigns can act as influential tools to challenge these stereotypes. We recognize that progress has been made, although the installed patriarchal norms within several sectors and industries are deeply rooted and shows that more efforts are needed, in order to achieve a more meaningful and real gender equality.

According to the United Nations' Sustainable Development Goal 5, at the current rate, it will take more than hundred years to achieve equal representation in leadership in the workplace. Marketing practices can have an important effect on it, and so, must change in order to suggest more equitable and egalitarian gender dynamics. At the same time, brands should implement strategies that help to prevent misrepresentations of gender, and actively fight against gender stereotypes. The campaigns, from the automotive industry, presented in this chapter shows how brands and corporations are answering to these challenges by implementing gender-sensitive marketing practices. It is important to note that the impacts of these campaigns strongly depend on their consistency and regularity, as well as the existing corporate culture. Facing the intricacy of gender representation involves a multidisciplinary approach, mixing visions from sociology, psychology, economics, and management, amid other fields.

Lastly, this chapter highlights the need for more research, underlining the interconnections between gender representation and marketing, not forgetting the importance of considering multidisciplinary approaches. Is important to mention that the world is evolving and changing every day, and the questions related to diversity, equity, and inclusion are central to this development. So, academics, researchers and practitioners must continue assessing the impact of marketing campaigns on gender norms and stereotypes. Future research must explore how dissimilar sectors, approach these subjects and pinpoint best practices for supporting gender-responsive marketing. Generally, we can say that the achievement of gender equality is highly dependent on the support that human rights and gender equality gets from the society, from the collective commitment, including the marketing industry.

Acknowledgements Authors extends special thanks to António José Ferreira for inspiring their interest in gender representation in the automotive industry.

Marisa R. Ferreira gratefully acknowledge financial support from FCT—Fundação para a Ciência e Tecnologia (Portugal), national funding through project UIDB/04728/2020.

References

1. Åkestam N, Rosengren S, Dahlén M, Liljedal KT, Berg H (2021) Gender stereotypes in advertising have negative cross-gender effects. Eur J Mark 55(13):63–93. https://doi.org/10.1108/EJM-02-2019-0125
2. Amâncio L (1992) As assimetrias nas Representações de Género. Revista Crítica Das Ciências Sociais 34(Fevereiro):9–22
3. Amâncio L (2001) O Género na Psicologia: uma História de Desencontros e Rupturas. Psicologia *XV*(1):9–26
4. Amâncio L, Santos MH (2021) Gender equality and modernity in Portugal. An analysis on the obstacles to gender equality in highly qualified professions. Soc Sci 10(5). https://doi.org/10.3390/socsci10050162
5. Aruna M, Gunasundari K (2022) Empowering of feminine in Indian advertisements. Int J Comput Commun Inf 4(1):11–22. https://doi.org/10.34256/ijcci2212
6. Ashmore RD, Sewell AD (1998) Sex/gender and the individual. In: Barone DF, Hersen M, Van Hasselt VB (eds) Advanced personality. Springer, pp 377–408. https://doi.org/10.1007/978-1-4419-8580-4_16
7. Athanasopoulou A, Moss-Cowan A, Smets M, Morris T (2018) Claiming the corner office: female CEO careers and implications for leadership development. Hum Resour Manag 57(2):617–639. https://doi.org/10.1002/hrm.21887

8. Auriol E, Friebel G, Weinberger A, Wilhelm S (2022) Underrepresentation of women in the economics profession more pronounced in the United States compared to heterogeneous Europe. Proc Natl Acad Sci 119(16):e2118853119. https://doi.org/10.1073/pnas.2118853119
9. Badman S (2022) Gender imbalance in the genetic counseling profession: an Australasian perspective. J Genet Couns 31(1):291–295. https://doi.org/10.1002/jgc4.1453
10. Blond A (2008) Impacts of exposure to images of ideal bodies on male body dissatisfaction: a review. Body Image 5(3):244–250. https://doi.org/10.1016/j.bodyim.2008.02.003
11. Brinkman B, Rabenstein K, Rosén L, Zimmerman T (2014) Children's gender identity development: the dynamic negotiation process between conformity and authenticity. Youth Soc 46(6):835–852. https://doi.org/10.1177/0044118X12455025
12. Butler J (1990) Gender trouble – feminism and the subversion of identity. Routledge
13. Cech EA (2016) Mechanism or myth?: family plans and the reproduction of occupational gender segregation. Gend Soc 30(2):265–288. https://doi.org/10.1177/0891243215608798
14. Collins RL (2011) Content analysis of gender roles in media: where are we now and where should we go? Sex Roles 64(3):290–298. https://doi.org/10.1007/s11199-010-9929-5
15. Coyne SM, Linder JR, Rasmussen EE, Nelson DA, Birkbeck V (2016) Pretty as a princess: longitudinal effects of engagement with Disney princesses on gender stereotypes, body esteem, and prosocial behavior in children. Child Dev 87(6):1909–1925. https://doi.org/10.1111/cdev.12569
16. Creativex (2023) Gender in advertising 2023 report
17. Davidson K, Trudeau K, Roosmalen E, Stewart M, Kirkland S (2007) Gender as a health determinant and implications for health education. Perspective 33(6):731–743. https://doi.org/10.1177/1090198106288043
18. de Breij S, Huisman M, Boot CRL, Deeg DJH (2022) Sex and gender differences in depressive symptoms in older workers: the role of working conditions. BMC Public Health 22(1):1–11. https://doi.org/10.1186/s12889-022-13416-1
19. Deaux K, Lewis LL (1984) Structure of gender stereotypes: interrelationships among components and gender label. J Pers Soc Psychol 46(5):991–1004. https://doi.org/10.1037/0022-3514.46.5.991
20. Delphy C (1993) Rethinking sex and gender. Women's Stud Int Forum 16(1):1–9. https://doi.org/10.1016/0277-5395(93)90076-L
21. Druskat, V. U. (1994). Gender and leadership style: transformational and transactional leadership in the Roman Catholic Church. In The leadership quarterly (Vol. 5, 2 pp. 99–119) https://doi.org/10.1016/1048-9843(94)90023-X
22. Ellemers N (2018) Gender stereotypes. Annu Rev Psychol 69:275–298. https://doi.org/10.1146/annurev-psych-122216-011719
23. Ellemers N, De Gilder D, Haslam SA (2004) Motivating individuals and groups at work: a social identity perspective on leadership and group performance. Acad Manag Rev 29(3):459–478
24. Erhel C, Guergoat-Larivière M (2013) Labor market regimes, family policies, and women's behavior in the EU. Fem Econ 19(4):76–109. https://doi.org/10.1080/13545701.2013.842649
25. Fagenson EA, Burke WW (1990) The activities of organization development practitioners at the turn of the decade of the 1990s a study of their predictions. Group Organ Stud 15(4):366–380
26. Fana M, Villani D, Bisello M (2023) Gender gaps in power and control within jobs. Soc Econ Rev 21(3):1343–1367. https://doi.org/10.1093/ser/mwac062
27. Faniko K, Ellemers N, Derks B (2021) The Queen bee phenomenon in academia 15 years after: does it still exist, and if so, why? Br J Soc Psychol 60(2):383–399. https://doi.org/10.1111/bjso.12408
28. Farsia L (2024) Ensuring equal opportunity: promoting gender equality in workplace. J Engl Lang Educ 4(June):21–28
29. Gentry J, Harrison R (2010) Is advertising a barrier to male movement toward gender change? Mark Theory 10(1):74–96. https://doi.org/10.1177/1470593109355246
30. Giddens A (2008) Sociologia (6ª edição). Fundação Calouste Gulbenkian
31. Gill R (2008) Empowerment/sexism: figuring female sexual agency in contemporary advertising. Fem Psychol 18(1):35–60. https://doi.org/10.1177/0959353507084950

32. Golombok S, Fivush R (1994) Gender development. Cambridge University Press. https://books.google.pt/books?id=CSgcZVmGBGcC
33. Gomes M, Martinho AL (2022) Social vulnerability as the intersection of tangible and intangible variables: a proposal from an inductive approach. Rev Nac de Adm 12(2):25–42
34. Gómez AMA, Restrepo AG (2022) Los trabajos de cuidado no remunerados de las mujeres campesinas, desde la óptica del papel emancipatorio de los derechos humanos y los feminismos. Revista Controversia 219:211–245
35. Grabe S, Ward LM, Hyde JS (2008) The role of the media in body image concerns among women: a meta-analysis of experimental and correlational studies. Psychol Bull 134(3):460–476. https://doi.org/10.1037/0033-2909.134.3.460
36. da Grangeiro R et al (2023) Women in leadership positions in universities: are they really queen bees? Manag Res Rev 46(5):739–754. https://doi.org/10.1108/MRR-03-2021-0239
37. Grau SL, Zotos YC (2016) Gender stereotypes in advertising: a review of current research. Int J Advert 35(5):761–770. https://doi.org/10.1080/02650487.2016.1203556
38. Harrison WC (2006) The shadow and the substance – the sex/gender debate. In: Davis K, Evans M, Lorber J (eds) Handbook of gender and women's studies. Sage, p 513. https://doi.org/10.4135/9781848608023.n3
39. Haslam SA, Oakes PJ (1994) Stereotyping and social reality. Wiley
40. Heilman ME (2001) Description and prescription: how gender stereotypes prevent women's ascent up the organizational ladder. J Soc Issues 57(4):657–674. https://doi.org/10.1111/0022-4537.00234
41. Ilie C, Monfort A, Fornes G, Cardoza G (2021) Promoting female entrepreneurship: the impact of gender gap beliefs and perceptions. SAGE Open 11(2). https://doi.org/10.1177/21582440211018468
42. Karamullaoglu N, Sandikci O (2020) Western influences in Turkish advertising. J Hist Res Mark 12(1):127–150. https://doi.org/10.1108/JHRM-10-2018-0050
43. Kim K, Lowry DT (2005) Television commercials as a lagging social indicator: gender role stereotypes in Korean television advertising. Sex Roles 53(11–12):901–910. https://doi.org/10.1007/s11199-005-8307-1
44. Lagro-Janssen T (2007) Sex, gender and health: developments in research. Eur J Women's Stud 14(1):9–20. https://doi.org/10.1177/1350506807072314
45. Lam M (2004) The perception of inequalities: a gender case study. Sociology 38(1):5–23. https://doi.org/10.1177/0038038504039355
46. Lämsä AM, Vehkaperä M, Puttonen T, Pesonen HL (2008) Effect of business education on women and men students' attitudes on corporate responsibility in society. J Bus Ethics 82(1):45–58. https://doi.org/10.1007/s10551-007-9561-7
47. Laurol G (2016) The relevance of feminist epistemology and feminist ethics. Athene Noctua: Undergraduate Philos J 4(4)
48. Lima AM, Casais B (2021) Consumer reactions towards femvertising : a netnographic study. Corp Commun Int J 26(3):605–621. https://doi.org/10.1108/CCIJ-02-2021-0018
49. Maclaran P, Chatzidakis A (2022) Gendered marketing. Edward Elgar
50. Maheshwari G (2023) A review of literature on women's leadership in higher education in developed countries and in Vietnam: barriers and enablers. Educ Manag Adm Leadersh 51(5):1067–1086. https://doi.org/10.1177/17411432211021418
51. Mareque M, de Prada E, Pino Juste M (2022) Aspiring and inspiring: the role of women in educational leadership. Gender Manag Int J 37:1009–1025. https://doi.org/10.1108/GM-07-2021-0221
52. Mavin S, Grandy G (2013) Doing gender well and differently in dirty work: the case of exotic dancing. Gend Work Organ 20(3):232–251. https://doi.org/10.1111/j.1468-0432.2011.00567.x
53. Meister A, Sinclair A, Jehn KA (2017) Identities under scrutiny: how women leaders navigate feeling misidentified at work. Leadersh Q 28(5):672–690. https://doi.org/10.1016/j.leaqua.2017.01.009
54. Mengel F, Sauermann J, Zölitz U (2019) Gender bias in teaching evaluations. J Eur Econ Assoc 17(2):535–566. https://doi.org/10.1093/jeea/jvx057

55. Middleton K, Turnbull S, de Oliveira MJ (2020) Female role portrayals in Brazilian advertising: are outdated cultural stereotypes preventing change? Int J Advert 39(5):679–698. https://doi.org/10.1080/02650487.2019.1658428
56. Morrison Z, Bourke M, Kelley C (2005) "Stop making it such a big issue": perceptions and experiences of gender inequality by undergraduates at a British University. Women's Stud Int Forum 28(2–3):150–162. https://doi.org/10.1016/j.wsif.2005.04.020
57. Nash M, Moore R (2019) 'I was completely oblivious to gender': an exploration of how women in STEMM navigate leadership in a neoliberal, post-feminist context. J Gend Stud 28(4):449–461. https://doi.org/10.1080/09589236.2018.1504758
58. Ndobo A (2013) Discourse and attitudes on occupational aspirations and the issue of gender equality: what are the effects of perceived gender asymmetry and prescribed gender role? Rev Eur de Psychol Appl 63(4):231–241. https://doi.org/10.1016/j.erap.2013.02.003
59. Neff KD, Cooper CE, Woodruff AL (2007) Children's and adolescents' developing perceptions of gender inequality. Soc Dev 16(4):682–699. https://doi.org/10.1111/j.1467-9507.2007.00411.x
60. Nye RA (2005) Locating masculinity: some recent work on men. Signs J Women Cult Soc 30(3):1937–1962. https://doi.org/10.1086/426799
61. Oakley A (1972) Sex, gender and society. Temple Smith. https://books.google.pt/books?id=BhKOQAAACAAJ
62. Ourahmoune N, Jurdi HE (2022) Marketing and the missing feminisms. In: Maclaran P, Stevens L, Kravets O (eds) The Routledge companion to marketing and feminism, 1st edn. Routledge, p 11
63. Perrot M (2008) Mi historia de las mujeres. Fondo de Cultura Económica
64. Reilly MO, Talbot A, Harrington D (2023) Adolescent perspectives on gendered ideologies in physical activity within schools: Refleections on a female-focused intervention. Fem Psychol 33(2):175–196. https://doi.org/10.1177/09593535221109040
65. Sakhiyya Z, Locke K (2019) Empowerment vs. meritocracy discourses in Indonesian public universities: the case of female leaders. Asian J Women's Stud 25(2):198–216. https://doi.org/10.1080/12259276.2019.1610210
66. Santos MH, Amâncio L (2016) Gender inequalities in highly qualified professions: a social psychological analysis. J Soc Polit Psychol 4(1):427–443. https://doi.org/10.5964/jspp.v4i1.487
67. Sapolsky RM (1997) The trouble with Testosterone: and Other Essays on the Biology of the Human *Predicament*. Scribner. https://books.google.pt/books?id=b-jaAAAAMAAJ
68. Schein V (1975) The relationship between sex role stereotypes and requisite management characteristics among female managers. J Appl Psychol 60(3):340–344. https://doi.org/10.1037/h0076637
69. Schouten MJ (2011) Uma Sociologia do Género. In Húmus. Húmus – Universidade do Minho
70. Schroeder JE, Zwick D (2004) Mirrors of masculinity: representation and identity in advertising images. Consum Mark Cult 7(1):21–52. https://doi.org/10.1080/1025386042000212383
71. Scott JW (1986) Gender: a useful category of historical analysis. Am Hist Rev 91(5):1053–1075. https://doi.org/10.4324/9780203966105-16
72. Sterbenk Y, Champlin S, Windels K, Shelton S (2022) Is Femvertising the new greenwashing? Examining corporate commitment to gender equality. J Bus Ethics 177(3):491–505. https://doi.org/10.1007/s10551-021-04755-x
73. Stewart R, Wright B, Smith L, Roberts S, Russell N (2021) Gendered stereotypes and norms: a systematic review of interventions designed to shift attitudes and behaviour. Heliyon 7(4):e06660. https://doi.org/10.1016/j.heliyon.2021.e06660
74. Torres A et al (2018) Igualdade de Género ao Longo da Vida. Anal Biochem 11(1)
75. Ward LM, Grower P (2020) Media and the development of gender role stereotypes. Annu Rev Dev Psychol 2(1):177–199. https://doi.org/10.1146/annurev-devpsych-051120-010630
76. West C, Zimmerman DH (1987) Doing Gender. Gend Soc 1(2):125–151. https://www.gla.ac.uk/0t4/crcees/files/summerschool/readings/WestZimmerman_1987_DoingGender.pdf

77. World Economic Forum (2023) Global gender gap report. In World economic forum. https://www3.weforum.org/docs/WEF_GGGR_2023.pdf
78. Wymer W (2012) Gender differences in social support in the decision to volunteer. Int Rev Public Nonprofit Mark 9(1):19–26
79. Yaish M, Stier H (2009) Gender inequality in job authority: a cross-national comparison of 26 countries. Work Occup 36(4):343–366. https://doi.org/10.1177/0730888409349751
80. Zayadin R, Zucchella A, Anand A (2022) Exploring the emancipatory role of entrepreneurship in a developing context. Int J Entrep Behav Res 28(2):527–547. https://doi.org/10.1108/IJEBR-08-2021-0642
81. Zotos Y, Grau S, Taylor CR (eds) (2018) Current research on gender issues in advertising, 1st edn. Routledge

Marisa R. Ferreira has a PhD in Business Sciences from University of Porto. She is an associate professor and head of the MSc in Nonprofit Management at ESTG-IPP. At the moment, she is the Vice-Dean at ESTG-IPP, in charge of Internationalization, Knowledge Transfer and Sustainability.

Participates in several pedagogical and scientific conferences, national and international, being that the primary focus of the research is nonprofit management and marketing, as well as corporate social responsibility and social innovation.

She is member of the Centre for Quality Assessment in Higher Education (SKVC)—Lithuanian quality assurance agency, as international expert; adviser and examiner of several master's and PhD's theses; and invited lecturer in numerous international programs, spanning countries like Slovenia, Germany, Lithuania, Kosovo, Algeria, Italy, Austria, Greece, and many others.

José Nuno Teixeira is studying for a PhD in Educational Sciences, specialising in Sociology of Education and Educational Policy. He works in the field of the Social Sciences of Education and his current research interests are in the areas of gender equality, leadership, higher education and professional integration. He is currently a Research Fellow, collaborating with the Education Research Centre at the University of Minho. He has also actively participated in research projects and in organising committees for national and international events.

Emília Fernandes is an assistant professor of organizational behaviour and human resource management (HRM) at the School of Economics and Management at the University of Minho in Portugal. Her research has been published in both national and international journals and books. Currently, her research interests focus on work discrimination, diversity management, feminist theory, HRM, and professional identities.

Regina Leite is an Assistant Professor in Organizational Behavior and Human Resource Management at the University of Minho, School of Economics and Management, and an integrated researcher at CICS.NOVA.UMinho—Interdisciplinary Centre of Social Sciences. Her current research interests include gender issues, sexual harassment, and privacy in the workplace. She is a co-author of articles and book chapters in the areas of organizational behavior and human resource management, having participated in several conferences and other national and international scientific meetings. Her research findings have been presented at national and international conferences and published in academic journals and book chapters.

Closing the Water-Use Loop in Households Through the Lens of Behavioural Economics

6

Lígia M. Costa Pinto and Catarina Silva Gonçalves

Never doubt that a small group of thoughtful, committed citizens can change the world; indeed, it's the only thing that ever has.

– Margaret Mead

Abstract

Global challenges such as climate change, water scarcity and increasing urbanisation will put increasing pressure on access to water. Although agriculture is the primary consumer of drinking water, the domestic sector also plays an important role, especially in urban areas. In households, strategies based on circular economy principles to change consumer behaviour must be implemented to reduce water consumption. Behavioural economics can provide tools to help change behaviour in favor of water saving. This chapter discusses how behavioural economics can support adopting circular economy practices in the domestic sector to save water by analyzing different practical cases.

L. M. C. Pinto (✉)
iBMS – Center for Research in Business, Markets & Society, University of Minho, Braga, Portugal

School of Economics and Management, University of Minho, Braga, Portugal
e-mail: pintol@eeg.uminho.pt

C. S. Gonçalves
School of Economics and Management, University of Minho, Braga, Portugal
e-mail: d8243@eeg.uminho.pt

B. Casais (ed.), *Integrated Science to Achieve Sustainable Development Goals*, Integrated Science 37, https://doi.org/10.1007/978-3-031-88777-2_6

Graphical Abstract

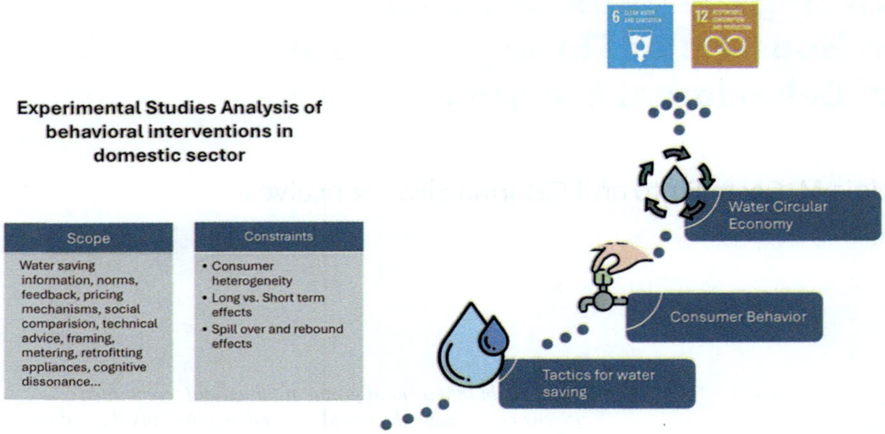

Source: Authors

Keywords

Circular economy · Consumer behaviour · Domestic sector · Water savings · Strategies · Case studies

1 Introduction

The world faces surmountable resource availability challenges. According to the Flash Eurobarometer on EU challenges and priorities (July 2024), the third most crucial challenges in the EU are environmental issues and climate change (after the war in Ukraine and Irregular migration). However, these are ranked first in terms of what should be the priority of EU policy. Regarding Environmental issues, Eurobarometer results from May 2024 reveal that a circular economy and restoring nature are the most effective ways to tackle environmental problems. Going deeper into EU citizens' opinions on water issues, 78% agree that the EU should propose additional measures to address water-related problems, notably pollution, overconsumption, and wasting water.

To increase water-saving behaviour and tackle water-related problems, along side regulation, economic environmental policy instruments are applied: taxes, subsidies, and permit markets being the most common. However, their efficacy and efficiency have been questioned, as economic agents sometimes seem to behave inconsistently with the predictions of economic theory. Behavioural biases, such as the use of heuristics, social norms, or inertia, among others, have explained these inconsistencies.

Behavioural economics can provide tools to help change behaviour in favour of water saving. Focusing on domestic sector strategies based on circular economy principles could be implemented to reduce water consumption and increase its efficiency. This chapter discusses how behavioural economics can help promote the adoption of circular economy strategies at the household level to save water, by analysing different practical cases.

2 Behavioural Economics and Environment

Behavioural Economics (BE) has received significant attention among economists in recent years, notably when Daniel Kahneman, a psychologist and one of the founders of behavioural economics, won the Nobel Prize in Economics in 2002. In 2017, Richard Thaler also won the Nobel Prize in Economics for his contributions to the discipline, particularly for his work on nudge theory. Drawing on insights from economics and psychology, BE challenges some of the assumptions of *homo economicus* by suggesting that people are motivated not only by selfish interests but also by altruism and perceptions of justice; that the social context influences them; and that they have cognitive limitations that lead them to make decisions that are not considered rational [1]. Studies have shown that people are time inconsistent, their decisions depend on framing and reference points, they use heuristics to solve complex problems, and emotions influence their choices [2]. Other biases influence individuals' decisions, such as present bias, the tendency to undervalue future outcomes compared to immediate ones, inertia, and risk aversion [3].

In particular, In the environmental field, people in some instances go beyond economic self-interest and tend to cooperate (e.g., in climate change negotiations, in concerns about social norms related to recycling and water and energy conservation, and in the management of common goods through community-based solutions) [1]. Often, environmental issues are in the realm of public and common goods (e.g., fish stocks, rainforests, freshwater, and clean air), where decision-making involves weighing individual costs against (potential) collective benefits [4]. In this context, the design of effective environmental policies that take account of the common good is particularly relevant.

Command and control policies (e.g. regulations) and economic instruments (e.g. environmental taxes) have been used in environmental policy to condition citizens' behaviour towards pro-environmental choices and actions. Other information tools, such as labeling or awareness-raising campaigns, can contribute to more informed decisions. However, information and awareness alone are insufficient to change behaviour, as other factors condition individual behaviour effectively. Park [5] identifies three areas that should be considered when designing behaviour change interventions: (i) context, (ii) unconscious processes, and (iii) values, attitudes, beliefs, and behaviours.

(i) Contextual forces

Individual behaviour is shaped by cultural, political, economic, physical, and social contexts. If a new context is cheaper, more convenient, and socially acceptable, interventions may be more successful than those focusing only on attitudes and beliefs. Some examples of contextual forces include interpersonal influences, community expectations, advertising, government regulations, monetary incentives and costs, physical barriers, technology and built environment constraints, public policy, and others [6]. In this case, behavioural interventions are not enough to target the behaviour of individuals; they must target the socio-technical structures that encourage unsustainable behaviour.

(ii) Non-conscious processes

Mental activity operates through two systems—one is slow, reflective, conscious, and deliberative, resembling rational choice. Still, our rationality is constrained by limited information, and the other is driven by intuition, where the choice is fast and automatic, based on habits, emotions, and heuristics. [7]. These quick and frugal processes are mostly knee-jerk responses to signals from our social and physical environment, leaving us highly vulnerable to external influences. They also leave us vulnerable to predictable errors of judgment or cognitive biases as we trade accuracy for cognitive efficiency. Therefore, it is necessary to consider these automatic processes to design strategies that are more effective in changing behaviour.

(iii) Attitudes, norms, beliefs and values

Today, environmental issues are increasingly on the political agenda, and environmental awareness is becoming more widespread. People are expressing a growing interest and concern in buying more sustainable, biodegradable, and environmentally friendly products. However, studies consistently show a gap between consumer intentions and their actions—the so-called green attitude-behaviour gap [8].

Park [5] identifies two categories to explain this gap:

- ***The tension between pro-environmental values and self-interest,*** that is, the concern for economic well-being and convenience, often goes beyond the integrity to maintain the environmental concern for the planet;
- ***Psychological and practical barriers undermine consumer intentions*** due to a lack of knowledge or options, the need to invest, or other factors related to cognitive biases such as risk aversion and inertia.

The theory of Planned Behaviour (TPB) can be used to explain the green gap phenomenon. This theory suggests that attitude is one of the most important determinants of behaviour, and intentions influence the relationship between attitude and behaviour[8]. It has been applied in several studies on environmental behaviour (use of alternative transport, recycling, water saving, energy saving, low carbon consumption, etc.) [9].

In addition to TPB, other theories have been used to understand pro-environmental and pro-social behaviour:

- The **Value-Belief-Norm Theory** posits that individuals develop pro-environmental attitudes when they feel a moral obligation to protect themselves, society, or the ecosystem. This model suggests that personal values shape general environmental beliefs that make individuals aware of the environmental consequences of their actions and take responsibility, thereby activating a moral obligation (personal norms) that leads to pro-environmental behaviour [6];
- The **Moral norm-activation theory of altruism** suggests that three antecedents—awareness of consequences, attribution of responsibility, and personal norms—drive pro-social behaviour, making it suitable for studying pro-environmental behaviour such as recycling and energy conservation. The theory posits that awareness of harmful consequences and personal responsibility activate personal norms, which then guide actions to prevent harm, with the likelihood of action increasing as the intensity of awareness and attribution of responsibility increases, depending on the content of an individual's norms that prescribe such actions [10];
- **ABC Theory state**s that behaviour (B) depends on attitudes (A) and contextual factors (C). This formulation of the 'ABC theory' implies that when the context does not favour the behaviour (because is more challenging, costly or time-consuming) it becomes less dependent on attitudes. [11] .

Practical strategies to promote pro-environmental behaviour should consider individual issues (motivations, decision-making processes, habits, emotions, attitudes, and awareness) and the socio-economic context, including policies, the built environment, social norms, and incentives [6].

Some studies show that intrinsic motivation can be undermined by introducing monetary incentives, i.e., paying an environmental tax can make people feel that they have a 'right to pollute' because they are paying for it. Thus, economic instruments such as environmental taxes alone may not lead to behavioural change and may even exacerbate the situation [1].

Recently, policymakers have focused on researching changes to the low-cost choice architecture that do not change the available options or economic incentives, known as nudges. These interventions are designed to harness the influence of social norms, change the default option, and, for example, reveal the savings achieved over time to address current biases [4].

3 Circular Economy

The circular economy is currently popular in academic, business, and political agendas [12]. This concept was built from different schools of thought, such as industrial ecology [13], biomicricy [14] cradle-to-cradle [15], performance economy [16], blue economy [17], among others. The term was first used by Pearce & Turner [18], who described how, in economics, natural resources are inputs to production and consumption activities, and waste is an output of these activities. This study was based on studies of Boulding [19], who described the economy as a closed system in which materials circulate in such a way as to avoid waste, which is considered necessary for the sustainability of the planet.

The circular economy is seen as a model that allows economic growth to be decoupled from environmental impacts. It is emerging as an alternative to the linear economic model based on 'extract-produce-discard.' Through the adoption of clean production processes and eco-design, the implementation of appropriate policies, and the cooperation of different actors in society, the circular economy should contribute to more sustainable development.[20].

On an economic level, the circular economy can contribute to reducing energy dependency, creating new business models, and promoting innovation; on an environmental level, the circular economy should contribute to reducing the extraction of raw materials and improving environmental quality. On a social level, the circular economy should create new jobs, a fairer tax structure, and welfare benefits due to the ecological benefits. However, the environmental and economic benefits are usually emphasised, while the social benefits are not prioritised [12, 21].

One of the most cited definitions is that of the Ellen MacArthur Foundation, which refers to the economy as 'an industrial system that is restorative and regenerative by intention and design. It replaces the concept of 'end of life' with restoration, moves towards the use of renewable energy, eliminates the use of toxic chemicals that make reuse difficult, and aims to eliminate waste through the highest quality design of materials, products, systems, and, within that, business models' [22], p. 7.

The circular economy has received attention from local, national, and international policymakers. In 2020, the European Union launched the new Circular Economy Action Plan. This plan includes initiatives for the entire life cycle of products—from design and production processes to consumption and waste prevention—to extend the useful life of resources in the economy [23]. Although the circular economy is applied to the entire life cycle of products, the following section focuses on the consumption dimension, as consumers have an essential role in reinforcing sustainability through purchasing and using products and services [20].

3.1 Circular Economy and Consumer Behaviour

To succeed, circular economy practices and products require changes in consumers' decisions, which depend on their preferences and external factors such as income, prices, and context. Consumption decisions can be divided into three stages: (1) pre-purchase or antecedents, including search, comparison, etc.; (2) purchase or decisions: decision and actual purchase; and (3) post-purchase or outcomes: use, shared-use, repair, recycle and upcycle [24].

Promoting consumers' responsibility is of the utmost importance to enhance the market viability of circular business models, namely implementing a sharing economy and moving from a product-based economy to a service base. Following

Vidal-Ayuso et al. [25] results, the antecedents to purchase or the pre-purchase phase can be explained by the theory of planned behaviour, which comprises the attitudes, subjective norms, and perceived control behaviour explaining the intention to buy. The antecedent phase starts with need recognition, followed by a search process and evaluation of alternatives. Need recognition can be affected by internal factors (e.g., personal identity) or external factors (such as marketing and information). Information on the product/service's characteristics is key for informed choices and awareness of the environmental dimensions affecting purchase intention. In addition, social norms may affect purchase intention by generating pressure to adopt or change some behaviour patterns [26]. Change in social norms may be facilitated or face barriers the local culture creates.

Consumer behaviour changes are more likely to occur if the consumer perceives a significant effect of his behaviour changes on the state of affairs (the feedback). Another internal factor affecting purchase intention is self-identity, mainly green self-identity [27], which refers to the consumer's identification with the "typical" green behaviour. Consumers with stronger green self-identities are expected to be more likely to adopt circular purchases. According to Magnier et al. [28], sustainable products (which can be circular) tend to activate a moral evaluation in consumers, making them very aware of the environment.

Consumer awareness, in addition to information through labeling, is also an instrument for raising consumers' responsibility. Awareness changes through education and information [25], namely on the product's origin, production process, and materials used. Education, labeling, and packaging [29] can develop links between producers' information and consumers, providing the channels for consumers' preference change and enhancing market acceptance [30].

After creating the need, consumers start the search process, culminating with the purchase after evaluating the alternatives. The search process depends crucially on consumers' information and the information supplied to them in the form, for example, of labels on the product's ingredients, production process, and/or impact on the environment.

Following the search, consumers evaluate the alternatives. In this phase, consumers' perceptions regarding the expected quality, experience, and safety of the product/service are the focal point, in addition to the financial risk that might be involved. In this regard, reducing the uncertainty involving these factors is the key.

The decision is the last phase of consumers' purchase intention. It may involve choosing different, more circular products or demanding a behaviour change so the consumer becomes an agent in the circular loop. It may even require consumers to be active members in creating or improving loops for others, with no direct individual benefit. Examples of less demanding changes are decisions to buy products that can be repaired [31]; the next level is decisions such as extending the lifetime of products such as repairing [32] and sharing [33]. In the same vein, consumers' willingness to participate in circular business models (1) may also vary with the degree of involvement required; we should expect that take-back behaviour relying on ownership is more straightforward to adopt than product lease associated with responsibility or Pay-per-use associated with payment structures.

Following the decision to purchase, the outcome is the last phase. In this phase, consumers experience the good/service and compare its performance with their expectations. A successful experience eventually translates into repeated purchases and/or word-of-mouth. According to Vidal-Ayuso et al. [25], this is the least-studied phase.

In addition to information and knowledge, innovation is key for implementing circular economy business models, particularly in product design, reverse logistics, and process design. One barrier often associated with innovation is that it is rarely developed in collaboration with consumers, and it is mainly concerned with system efficiency, such as improving resource efficiency.

For some consumers, circular economy products and services can be designated as ethical consumption. "Ethical consumption is a desirable behavioural practice to modify existing non-sustainable consumption practices that have degraded Nature, putting future resource availability at risk" [34], p. 1. For Carrington et al. [35], ethical consumption is a social movement. Davies and Gutsche [36], analyzing the motivations for mainstream ethical consumption, conclude that peer pressure is the primary driver of ethical consumption, while information processing and values are found not relevant, providing support for Carrington et al. [35] proposal. So far, as circular products/services are seen as ethical goods by consumers, it is relevant to attain this characteristic when designing policies. A contrasting result was found by Freestone and McGoldrick [37], who concluded that motivations for ethical consumption depend on the consumer's level of awareness and concern. The link between the circular economy and the water sector is explored in the next section.

3.2 Water Circular Economy in Households

The circular economy is mainly applied to waste management and various industrial sectors such as manufacturing, construction, and fashion. In recent years, however, it has also received increasing attention in the field of water management [38] due to the growing problem of water scarcity and the imbalance between the ever-increasing demand for water and its availability [39].

Water is essential for life and economic development. It is vital to produce food and electricity for various industries, transport, and tourism [40]. Water also has the particularity of being considered as a service (e.g., water supply, cooling and heating of buildings), a source of energy (e.g., hydroelectric and thermal energy), and a carrier of materials (e.g., chemicals, nutrients) [41].

Like other resources, water is traditionally managed in a linear 'extract-use-discharge' model. At an urban level, water is extracted, treated to meet drinking water quality standards and distributed to consumers via a centralised network. This drinking water can be used for different purposes, and, after use, it is sent to the sewerage network and to a wastewater treatment plant where it is treated and then discharged into the natural environment (sea, rivers...). Rainwater is collected via a drainage network and discharged untreated into a watercourse. In some older systems, the sewage and rainwater networks may be combined in the same pipe [42].

Table 6.1 Strategies of circular economy for water sector

Rethink		
Decreasing	Optimising	Retaining
Avoid	Reuse	Store
Reduce	Recycle	Recover
Replace	Cascading	

Source: Own elaboration based on Morseletto et al. [43]

However, there are many inefficiencies in this linear system. Given the challenges outlined above, investing in a circular model that allows resources to be conserved is necessary. Morseletto et al. [43], p. 1465 define circular water management as «*an economic framework for reducing, preserving and optimising the use of water through waste avoidance, efficient utilisation and quality retention while ensuring environmental protection and conservation*».

The authors define nine circular economy strategies for the water sector, which, except Rethink, can be divided into three categories: Decreasing (Avoid, Reduce, Replace), Optimising (Reuse, Recycle, Cascading), and Retaining (Store and Recover) (Table 6.1).

To summarise, **Rethink** refers to a cross-cutting strategy to restructure practices, processes, policies, infrastructure and technologies to increase the circularity of the sector; **Avoid** refers to strategies to avoid the use of water, such as vacuum flush toilets; **Reduce** refers to strategies to reduce water consumption compared to baseline, such as the use of showers that mix air into the water jet; **Replace** refers to strategies to replace water with other materials that are also circular, such as replacing drinking water with rainwater for irrigation; **Reuse** refers to the use of used water that has not undergone any treatment so that it is of the same or lower quality but sufficient for its intended purpose, such as using water from washing food to water indoor plants; **Recycle** refers to strategies that make it possible to use used water that has undergone treatment for the same or a different purpose, for example the installation of grey water treatment systems in homes for reuse; **Cascading** may combine different strategies (reuse, recycling, recovery) and refers to the sequential use of water for various purposes; **Store** refers to strategies that may complement others (reuse, recycling and cascading) and involves the transfer of water to a reservoir where it becomes available for future use; and **Recover** refers to the extraction of valuable materials contained in wastewater and sludge (e.g. chemical elements, organic matter) or the extraction of water from wastewater and sludge. Or from biogas for energy recovery [43].

The transition to a circular economy model in the water sector must occur in different sectors—agriculture, industry, the public sector, commerce, and services... In this chapter, we focus on the residential sector. Households have an excellent potential for reducing consumption. They can be an opportunity to test some strategies for developing water-saving habits that can be transferred to other contexts, particularly the workplace. Domestic water consumption is the fastest-growing sector (more than 80 percent over the next 25 years) [44]. By 2050, two-thirds of the world's population will live in cities, increasing pressure on water systems [38]. Urban areas are, therefore, particularly vulnerable to global water challenges and climate change.

The application of the circular water economy in households should include strategies to reduce water consumption from the traditional supply system while maintaining water safety and consumer comfort [45].

Water is used directly in households for several basic purposes: drinking, hygiene, sanitation, and cooking. To meet these basic needs, (Gleick [46] defined a reference value of 50 liters/person/day. However, other uses may be included to maintain the comfort and well-being associated with higher well-being standards, such as housecleaning, cars, water-related sports, and recreational activities such as spas, swimming pools, or gardening. For [47], the reference value for essential water consumption to maintain a healthy urban lifestyle is 92 liters/person/day, although this includes some restrictions on daily activities.

In the context of the European Union, reference values for domestic water consumption from the public supply system, the average consumption per inhabitant is between 40 and 50 m^3, i.e., between 110 and 137 l/day/person [48]. As a result, there is some scope for reducing consumption compared to the reference values.

However, household consumption can vary depending on several factors, including the number of occupants, age, occupation, household income level, the presence of a swimming pool and garden area, the presence of young people, cultural preferences, and others [47, 49, 50]. All these factors must be considered to determine the best strategies for reducing household water consumption.

The following section analyzes and discusses some case studies about how consumer behaviour contributes to a circular economy.

4 Applications of Behavioural Economics on Water Circular Economy

Although behavioural interventions are not the mainstream of water consumption management policies, several applications exist, varying by the instrument used and the specific constraints of each application.

The most common forms of intervention in literature are based on providing information through various channels, on diverse topics, and in varied formats. For example, it is common to find examples of interventions consisting of providing information on consumption and equipment performance or "normal" consumption with comparable households, pro-social behavioural appeals, technical advice on saving water, and drought conditions.

The literature has also examined the influence of the context of application on the results of behavioural interventions. In particular, the effects of meteorological conditions, spillover effects, socio-economic conditions, household size, tariff structure, and long-term versus short-term effects.

Koop et al. [51] present an empirical literature review and identify eight behavioural influencing tactics for promoting household water-saving behaviour.

To structure the debate on these tactics, the authors distinguish three ways of processing information: reflexive, semi-reflexive, and automatic. The reflexive route is the conscious process based on rational arguments, experience, and knowledge to develop attitudes. The automatic route relates to decisions that are made automatically from intuition.,. Because these pathways do not operate in isolation and some tactics may require a combination of the two, the authors identify a semi-reflective pathway.

The authors identified 52 articles on field experiences of water-saving behaviour, from which they identified eight tactics. They present a summary table of the tactics, principles, and their effectiveness (Table 6.2):

From this literature review, the authors concluded that most studies were conducted in developed countries experiencing water stress. The first studies on the subject focused on the reflexive pathway, while studies exploring the semi-reflexive processing pathway are more recent. Studies on the automatic path are less common in domestic water conservation but have increased in recent years. Some studies refer to experiments that combine several tactics, suggesting that the appropriate integration of different tactics can increase their effectiveness in influencing behaviour.

Table 6.2 Tactics, principals in water saving field experiments

Category	Tactic	Description
Reflective	Awareness	Dissemination of information through behaviour change campaigns. Although these alone may not be sufficient to achieve water savings in the long term, they can be effective in the short term, particularly if targeted at high users and less informed households.
	Self-confidence	Increase people's confidence in their ability to adopt the desired behaviour. The use short and practical tips, guides and concrete examples of how to save water improves water-saving habits.
Semi-reflexive	Norms	Patterns of behaviour used for comparison with the social environment. Consistent reinforcement of these messages can promote sustainable water use in the long term.
	Framing	Selecting and highlighting specific elements to influence interpretation by exploiting unconscious biases in how information is processed. Messages framed in suggestive ways, focusing on immediate effects or intrinsic motivation tend to be more effective.
	Tailoring	Personalised messages increase recipient engagement. Highlighting discrepancies between attitudes and behaviours creates discomfort, which can motivate water savings. Real-time information encourages short-term water savings.
Automatic	Emotional shortcuts	Evoke emotions to influence people's responses to messages, even if they are unrelated. Positive emotions can promote cooperation and trust, while humour can reduce resistance.
	Priming	Exposure to a stimulus, can influence how a person responds in the future. Primes can guide goal-directed thinking and behaviour without a person's conscious awareness.
	Nudging	The choice architecture that influences people's behaviour without restricting their choices. The idea is to make it easier to choose the 'better' option.

Source: Koop et al. [51]

Although the authors show that many studies appear to demonstrate the effectiveness of different tactics, they also point out what may be their limitations:

- Many experiments are subject to the 'Hawthorne effect,' which means that participants may behave differently because they know they are being watched;
- Many water conservation campaigns are a response to extreme events, such as droughts. These campaigns have short-term results, but once the extreme event has passed, consumption patterns return to baseline;
- Studies of automatic or semi-reflexive tactics focus on the individual impact of these tactics, which are introduced in a short intervention or by sending one-off messages.

For a more in-depth look at the strategies that individual consumers can use to increase water savings, the same authors point to the need for more studies and experiments that use different tactics together. In particular, they suggest that tactics related to the automatic processing system can be combined to reinforce more traditional approaches so that the effects of reducing water consumption are sustained over time.

An alternative organization of the literature on water-saving field experiments regarding the mechanisms used and the efficacy constraints is presented in Table 6.3.

The results of the reviewed articles point to widespread intervention types and efficacy. Interventions encompassing technical advice, appeal to pro-social preferences, and social comparison have significant short- and long-term effects (after 4–6 years), although the effect decays over time. These effects tend to be stronger for more prominent and wealthier consumers [56, 57, 72, 74]; however, this result is not consensual [49, 76].

Moreover, according to the studies reviewed, information alone does not decrease water consumption compared to other communication approaches, such as those appealing to social norms and personal and social identity [59, 70]. Moreover, information framing has been shown to affect different individuals' decisions, from a loss framework [59] to national security versus individual security [63], normative versus restrictive frames [60, 61], short-term versus long-term temporal frames [62].

One often-mentioned determinant for the success of behavioural initiatives is the feedback provided to the decision-makers on the effect of their actions. Studies have analysed support for this claim when combined with a cognitive dissonance effect [1, 71]. Moreover, the effectiveness of the feedback varies [69] with the individuals' characteristics, namely the household size [54, 66]. Feedback is increasingly associated with using smart meters and other digital tools. Results show various degrees of effectiveness of these devices [49, 62, 65].

One interesting effect associated with behavioural interventions is possible spillover effects, which affect communities not targeted by the campaign. Jaime Torres and Carlsson [77] found significant effects for Colombia, which aligns with results previously obtained in developed countries. Additionally, increases in water efficiency and a consequent decrease in water consumption can be accompanied by a

Table 6.3 Summary table of experimental studies by scope and constraints

Scope	References
Water saving information, norms and feedback information (through meters)	Fielding et al. [49]
Information leaflets, norms	Kurz et al. [52]
Pricing mechanism and information provision	Lu et al. [53], Goette et al. [54], Tijs et al. [55]
Social comparison and feedback	Brent et al. [56]
Technical advice, prosocial information and social comparison	Ferraro and Price [57], Brent et al. [56]
Normative Information	Schultz et al. [58]
Information framing	Hahn et al. [59], Jaeger and Schultz [60], Katz et al. [61], Zhuang et al. [62], Benedict and Hussein [63], Howarth and Butler [64]
Metering	Davies et al. [65]
Metering and advice	Tom et al. [66]
Retrofitting appliances	Suero et al. [67]
Cognitive dissonance and feedback	Aitken et al. [68]
Feedback	Otaki et al. [69]
Social norms and personal knowledge	Seyranian et al. [70], Fan et al. [71]
Constraints	
Consumer heterogeneity	Ferraro and Miranda [72], Ferraro and Price [57], Singha et al. [73], Brick et al. [74], Fan et al. [71]
Long versus short term effects	Bernedo et al. [75], Ferraro and Price [57], Ferraro et al. [76], Fielding et al. [49]
Spill over and rebound effects	Jaime Torres and Carlsson [77], Brent et al. [56]

Source: Own elaboration

rebound effect (or boomerang) due to the rise in consumption, given that they are now more efficient. The evidence suggests the insignificance of this effect [56].

The combination of price and behavioural policies was examined by Lu et al. [53] concluding that there may be complementarity between the two policies.

5 Conclusions

As water scarcity becomes more significant and households become more aware, its use can easily be associated with ethical consumption. As such, the decision process is regulated by more than just the price, and the role of behavioural interventions becomes increasingly essential.

As the case studies reviewed illustrate, behavioural interventions in household demand for water have explored several biases in individual decision-making, from the framing of information provision to the use of intelligent water meters to the provision of information on social norms, among others.

Results show that, in general, the interventions successfully change water use behaviour. However, the effect varies with the type of intervention, the household's characteristics, and the application's context. Moreover, there is no consensus regarding the persistence of these effects in the long term. The results also stress the role of economic incentives, mainly when focusing on non-essential water consumption.

Notwithstanding, the number of case studies, their scale, geographical scope, and context of application are limited, and the scope for new field experiments is vast. Crucial would be the replication of previous successful applications under different conditions.

References

1. Carlsson F, Johansson-Stenman O (2012) Behavioural economics and environmental policy. Ann Rev Resour Econ 4:75–99. https://doi.org/10.1146/annurev-resource-110811-114547
2. Dellavigna S (2009) Psychology and economics: evidence from the field. J Econ Lit 47(2):315–372. https://doi.org/10.1257/jel.47.2.315
3. Schubert C (2017) Green nudges: do they work? Are they ethical? Ecol Econ 132:329–342. https://doi.org/10.1016/j.ecolecon.2016.11.009
4. Homar AR, Cvelbar LK (2021) The effects of framing on environmental decisions: A systematic literature review. Ecol Econ 183:106950. https://doi.org/10.1016/j.ecolecon.2021.106950
5. Park T (2020) Behavioural insights for conservation and sustainability. In: Conservation research, policy and practice. Cambridge University Press, pp 293–308. https://doi.org/10.1017/9781108638210.018
6. Stern PC (2000) Toward a coherent theory of environmentally significant behaviour. J Soc Issues 56(3):407–424
7. Kahneman D (2011) Thinking, fast and slow. Macmillan
8. ElHaffar G, Durif F, Dubé L (2020) Towards closing the attitude-intention-behaviour gap in green consumption: a narrative review of the literature and an overview of future research directions. J Clean Prod 275:122556. https://doi.org/10.1016/j.jclepro.2020.122556
9. Yuriev A, Dahmen M, Paillé P, Boiral O, Guillaumie L (2020) Pro-environmental behaviours through the lens of the theory of planned behaviour: a scoping review. Resour Conserv Recycl 155:104660. https://doi.org/10.1016/j.resconrec.2019.104660
10. Schwartz SH (1977) Normative influences on altruism. In: Advances in experimental social psychology, vol 10. Academic, pp 221–279. https://doi.org/10.1016/S0065-2601(08)60358-5
11. Guagnano GA, Stern PC, Dietz T (1995) Influences on attitude-behaviour relationships: a natural experiment with curbside recycling. Environ Behav 27(5):699–718. https://doi.org/10.1177/0013916595275005
12. Geissdoerfer M, Savaget P, Bocken NMP, Hultink EJ (2017) The circular economy – a new sustainability paradigm? J Clean Prod 143:757–768. https://doi.org/10.1016/j.jclepro.2016.12.048
13. Frosch RA, Gallopoulos NE (1989) Strategies for manufacturing. Sci Am 261(3):144–153. http://www.jstor.org/stable/24987406
14. Benyus J (1997) Biomimicry: innovation inspired by nature, Morrow
15. McDonough W, Braungart M (2002) Cradle to cradle: remaking the way we make things, 1st edn. North Point Press
16. Stahel W (2006) The performance economy. Springer
17. Pauli G (2010) The blue economy: 10 years, 100 innovations , 100 million jobs. Paradigm Publications
18. Pearce D, Turner K (1990) Economics of natural resources and the environment. Johns Hopkins
19. Boulding KE (1966) The economics of the coming spaceship earth. In: Environmental quality in a growing economy. Resources for the Future/Johns Hopkins University Press, MD, pp 3–14

20. Ghisellini P, Cialani C, Ulgiati S (2016) A review on circular economy: the expected transition to a balanced interplay of environmental and economic systems. J Clean Prod 114:11–32. https://doi.org/10.1016/j.jclepro.2015.09.007
21. Chaves C, Pinto L, Valente M (2023) Economia do Ambiente: Conceitos e desenvolvimentos. Almedina
22. Ellen MacArthur Foundation (2013) Towards the circular economy: economic and business rationale for an accelerated transition
23. European Commission. (2020) Communication from the Commission to the European Parliament, the Council, the European Economic and Social Committee and the Committee of the Regions, A New Circular Economy Action Plan. For a Cleaner and More Competitive Europe, COM(2020) 98 final. European Commission: Belgium. https://eur-lex.Europa.eu/legal-content/EN/TXT/?uri=CELEX%3A52020DC0098
24. Liang T-P, Huang J-S (1998) An empirical study on consumer acceptance of products in electronic markets: a transaction cost model. Decis Support Syst 24(1):29–43
25. Vidal-Ayuso F, Akhmedova A, Jaca C (2023) The circular economy and consumer behaviour: literature review and research directions. J Clean Prod 418:137824. https://doi.org/10.1016/j.jclepro.2023.137824
26. Singhal D, Jena SK, Tripathy S (2019) Factors influencing the purchase intention of consumers towards remanufactured products: a systematic review and meta-analysis. Int J Prod Res 57(23):7289–7299. https://doi.org/10.1080/00207543.2019.1598590
27. Oliver J, Rosen D (2010) Applying the environmental propensity framework: A segmented approach to hybrid electric vehicle marketing strategies. J Mark Theory Pract 18(4):377–393. https://doi.org/10.2753/MTP1069-6679180405
28. Magnier L, Mugge R, Schoormans J (2019) Turning ocean garbage into products – consumers' evaluations of products made of recycled ocean plastic. J Clean Prod 215:84–98. https://doi.org/10.1016/j.jclepro.2018.12.246
29. Gåvertsson I, Milios L, Dalhammar C (2020) Quality labelling for re-used ICT equipment to support consumer choice in the circular economy. J Consum Policy 43(2):353–377. https://doi.org/10.1007/s10603-018-9397-9
30. Confente I, Scarpi D, Russo I (2020) Marketing a new generation of bio-plastics products for a circular economy: the role of green self-identity, self-congruity, and perceived value. J Bus Res 112:431–439. https://doi.org/10.1016/j.jbusres.2019.10.030
31. Laitala K, Klepp IG, Haugrønning V, Throne-Holst H, Strandbakken P (2021) Increasing repair of household appliances, mobile phones and clothing: experiences from consumers and the repair industry. J Clean Prod 282:125349. https://doi.org/10.1016/j.jclepro.2020.125349
32. Mak V, Terryn E (2020) Circular economy and consumer protection: the consumer as a citizen and the limits of empowerment through consumer law. J Consum Policy 43(1):227–248. https://doi.org/10.1007/s10603-019-09435-y
33. Mathews JA (2021) Schumpeterian economic dynamics of greening: propagation of green eco-platforms. In: Innovation, catch-up and sustainable development: a schumpeterian perspective. Springer International Publishing, Cham, pp 339–361. https://doi.org/10.1007/978-3-030-84931-3_14
34. Arman S, Mark-Herbert C (2024) Ethical consumption: a review and research agenda. Int J Consum Stud 48(5):e13079
35. Carrington MJ, Neville BA, Whitwell GJ (2014) Lost in translation: exploring the ethical consumer intention-behaviour gap. J Bus Res 67(1):2759–2767. https://doi.org/10.1016/j.jbusres.2012.09.022
36. Davies IA, Gutsche S (2016) Consumer motivations for mainstream "ethical" consumption. Eur J Mark 50(7–8):1326–1347. https://doi.org/10.1108/EJM-11-2015-0795
37. Freestone OM, McGoldrick PJ (2008) Motivations of the ethical consumer. J Bus Ethics 79(4):445–467. https://doi.org/10.1007/s10551-007-9409-1
38. Delgado A, Rodriguez DJ, Amadei CA, Makino M (2024) Water in Circular Economy and Resilience (WICER) Framework. Util Policy 87:101604. https://doi.org/10.1016/j.jup.2023.101604

39. Koseoglu-Imer DY, Oral HV, Coutinho Calheiros CS, Krzeminski P, Güçlü S, Pereira SA, Surmacz-Górska J, Plaza E, Samaras P, Binder PM, van Hullebusch ED, Devolli A (2023) Current challenges and future perspectives for the full circular economy of water in European countries. J Environ Manag 345:118627. https://doi.org/10.1016/j.jenvman.2023.118627
40. Fernandes E, Cunha Marques R (2023) Review of water reuse from a circular economy perspective. Water 15(5):848. https://doi.org/10.3390/w15050848
41. Tahir S, Steichen T, Shuoler M (2018) Water and circular economy: a white paper
42. McCarton L, O'Hogain S, Nasr A (2022) NBS for resilient cities and communities – how understanding the micro components of domestic water consumption can provide multiple water uses to facilitate a transition to a circular economy of water. Nature-Based Solutions 2:100028. https://doi.org/10.1016/j.nbsj.2022.100028
43. Morseletto P, Mooren CE, Munaretto S (2022) Circular economy of water: definition, strategies and challenges. Circ Econ Sustain 2(4):1463–1477. https://doi.org/10.1007/s43615-022-00165-x
44. Smol M, Adam C, Preisner M (2020) Circular economy model framework in the European water and wastewater sector. J Mater Cycles Waste Manag 22(3):682–697. https://doi.org/10.1007/s10163-019-00960-z
45. Bąk J, Żaba T (2024) Towards reducing the consumption of drinking water in buildings as part of the circular economy model: strengths–weaknesses–opportunities–threats analysis and perspectives for implementation. Energies 17(6):1444. https://doi.org/10.3390/en17061444
46. Gleick PH (1996) Basic water requirements for human activities: meeting basic needs. Water Int 21(2):83–92. https://doi.org/10.1080/02508069608686494
47. Crouch ML, Jacobs HE, Speight VL (2021) Defining domestic water consumption based on personal water use activities. Aqua Water Infrastruct Ecosyst Soc 70(7):1002–1011. https://doi.org/10.2166/aqua.2021.056
48. European Commission (2024 August 23) Water statistics. water uses. https://Ec.Europa.Eu/Eurostat/Statistics-Explained/Index.Php?Title=Water_statistics#Water_uses
49. Fielding KS, Russell S, Spinks A, Mankad A (2012) Determinants of household water conservation: the role of demographic, infrastructure, behaviour, and psychosocial variables. Water Resour Res 48(10). https://doi.org/10.1029/2012WR012398
50. Grespan A, Garcia J, Brikalski MP, Henning E, Kalbusch A (2022) Assessment of water consumption in households using statistical analysis and regression trees. Sustain Cities Soc 87:104186. https://doi.org/10.1016/j.scs.2022.104186
51. Koop SHA, Van Dorssen AJ, Brouwer S (2019) Enhancing domestic water conservation behaviour: A review of empirical studies on influencing tactics. J Environ Manag 247:867–876. https://doi.org/10.1016/j.jenvman.2019.06.126
52. Kurz T, Donaghue N, Walker I (2005) Utilizing a social-ecological framework to promote water and energy conservation: a field experiment. J Appl Soc Psychol 35(6):1281–1300
53. Lu L, Deller D, Hviid M (2019) Price and behavioural signals to encourage household water conservation: implications for the UK. Water Resour Manag 33(2):475–491. https://doi.org/10.1007/s11269-018-2133-z
54. Goette L, Leong C, Qian N (2019) Motivating household water conservation: a field experiment in Singapore. PLoS One 14(3):e0211891. https://doi.org/10.1371/journal.pone.0211891
55. Tijs MS, Karremans JC, Veling H, de Lange MA, van Meegeren P, Lion R (2017) Saving water to save the environment: contrasting the effectiveness of environmental and monetary appeals in a residential water saving intervention. Soc Influ 12(2–3):69–79. https://doi.org/10.1080/15534510.2017.1333967
56. Brent DA, Cook JH, Olsen S (2015) Social comparisons, household water use, and participation in utility conservation programs: evidence from three randomized trials. J Assoc Environ Resour Econ 2(4):597–627. https://doi.org/10.1086/683427
57. Ferraro PJ, Price MK (2013) Using nonpecuniary strategies to influence behaviour: evidence from a large-scale field experiment. Rev Econ Stat 95(1):64–73. https://doi.org/10.1162/REST_a_00344

58. Schultz PW, Messina A, Tronu G, Limas EF, Gupta R, Estrada M (2016) Personalized normative feedback and the moderating role of personal norms: a field experiment to reduce residential water consumption. Environ Behav 48(5):686–710. https://doi.org/10.1177/0013916514553835
59. Hahn R, Metcalfe RD, Novgorodsky D, Price MK (2016) The behaviouralist as policy designer: the need to test multiple treatments to meet multiple targets. http://www.nber.org/papers/w22886
60. Jaeger CM, Schultz PW (2017) Coupling social norms and commitments: testing the underdetected nature of social influence. J Environ Psychol 51:199–208. https://doi.org/10.1016/j.jenvp.2017.03.015
61. Katz D, Kronrod A, Grinstein A, Nisan U (2018) Still waters run deep: comparing assertive and suggestive language in water conservation campaigns. Water (Switzerland) 10(3):275. https://doi.org/10.3390/w10030275
62. Zhuang J, Lapinski MK, Peng W (2018) Crafting messages to promote water conservation: using time-framed messages to boost conservation actions in the United States and China. J Appl Soc Psychol 48(5):248–256. https://doi.org/10.1111/jasp.12509
63. Benedict S, Hussein H (2019) An analysis of water awareness campaign messaging in the case of Jordan: water conservation for state security. Water (Switzerland) 11(6):1156. https://doi.org/10.3390/w11061156
64. Howarth D, Butler S (2004) Communicating water conservation: how can the public be engaged? Water Sci Technol Water Supply 4(3):33–44. https://iwaponline.com/ws/article-pdf/4/3/33/417354/33.pdf
65. Davies K, Doolan C, Van Den Honert R, Shi R (2014) Water-saving impacts of smart meter technology: an empirical 5 year, whole-of-community study in Sydney, Australia. Water Resour Res 50(9):7348–7358. https://doi.org/10.1002/2014WR015812
66. Tom G, Tauchus G, Williams J, Tong S (2011) The role of communicative feedback in successful water conservation programs. Appl Environ Educ Commun 10(2):80–90. https://doi.org/10.1080/1533015X.2011.575632
67. Suero FJ, Mayer PW, Rosenberg DE (2012) Estimating and verifying United States households' potential to conserve water. J Water Resour Plan Manag 138(3):299–306. https://doi.org/10.1061/(asce)wr.1943-5452.0000182
68. Aitken CK, Mcmahon TA, Wearing AJ, Finlayson BL (1994) Residential water use: predicting and reducing consumption. J Appl Soc Psychol 24(2):136–158
69. Otaki Y, Ueda K, Sakura O (2017) Effects of feedback about community water consumption on residential water conservation. J Clean Prod 143:719–730. https://doi.org/10.1016/j.jclepro.2016.12.051
70. Seyranian V, Sinatra GM, Polikoff MS (2015) Comparing communication strategies for reducing residential water consumption. J Environ Psychol 41:81–90. https://doi.org/10.1016/j.jenvp.2014.11.009
71. Fan L, Wang F, Liu G, Yang X, Qin W (2014) Public perception of water consumption and its effects on water conservation behaviour. Water (Switzerland) 6(6):1771–1784. https://doi.org/10.3390/w6061771
72. Ferraro PJ, Miranda JJ (2013) Heterogeneous treatment effects and mechanisms in information-based environmental policies: Evidence from a large-scale field experiment. Resour Energy Econ 35(3):356–379. https://doi.org/10.1016/j.reseneeco.2013.04.001
73. Singha B, Karmaker SC, Eljamal O (2023) Quantifying the direct and indirect effect of socio-psychological and behavioural factors on residential water conservation behaviour and consumption in Japan. Resour Conserv Recycl 190:106816. https://doi.org/10.1016/j.resconrec.2022.106816
74. Brick K, De Martino S, Visser M (2023) Behavioural nudges for water conservation in unequal settings: experimental evidence from Cape Town. J Environ Econ Manag 121:102852. https://doi.org/10.1016/j.jeem.2023.102852

75. Bernedo M, Ferraro PJ, Price M (2014) The persistent impacts of norm-based messaging and their implications for water conservation. J Consum Policy 37(3):437–452. https://doi.org/10.1007/s10603-014-9266-0
76. Ferraro PJ, Miranda JJ, Price MK (2011) The persistence of treatment effects with norm-based policy instruments: evidence from a randomized environmental policy experiment. Am Econ Rev 101(3):318–322. https://doi.org/10.1257/aer.101.3.318
77. Jaime Torres MM, Carlsson F (2018) Direct and spillover effects of a social information campaign on residential water-savings. J Environ Econ Manag 92:222–243. https://doi.org/10.1016/j.jeem.2018.08.005

Lígia M. Costa Pinto holds a PhD in Economics from the University of South Carolina, USA. She's a full member of the Research Centre on Business, Economics and Society at the University of Minho (iBMS). She has developed research and teaching activities at the University of Minho since 1992, but also at the University of Porto, the University of Central Florida, the University of California-Riverside, the Catholic University of Mozambique (Beira), and the National University of Timor Leste. Her research develops in the field of applied microeconomics. She applies behavioral and experimental economics methodologies in environmental economics, health economics, and consumer behavior.

Catarina Silva Gonçalves holds a Master's in Environmental Engineering from the Faculty of Engineering and a Master's in Environmental Economics and Management from the Faculty of Economics at the University of Porto. She has professional experience in logistics and quality and has worked in project management in non-profit organisations for the last 5 years. Since 2018, she has collaborated with the School of Economics and Management of the University of Minho as a guest lecturer in Economics of the Environment and Natural Resources. She is also currently working as a project manager in a business association in the field of circular economy. Her areas of interest are environmental economics, education for sustainable development, and circular economy.

Human Capital at the Crossroads of Sustainability: Integrating Key Trends in HRM with the Sustainable Development Goals

7

Helena Martins and Sandrina B. Moreira

> *The greatest threat to our planet is the belief that someone else will save it.*
>
> — Robert Swan.

Abstract

This chapter presents a literature review on the intersection of human capital research trends and their impact on the United Nations Sustainable Development Goals (SDGs). By examining ten major research tendencies including remote work, diversity, equity and inclusion, mental health, talent acquisition, continuous learning, team dynamics and interpersonal relationships, generational shifts, crisis management, and digital transformation within Human Resource Management (HRM), we identify the current focal points in managing human capital. These trends reflect the contemporary concerns and strategies of HRM and play a crucial role in achieving the SDGs of the UN 2030 Agenda. This exploration delineates how each identified human capital trend contributes to or challenges the accomplishment of specific SDGs, emphasizing the need for HRM to align its strategies with these global goals. The findings underscore the importance of integrating SDG considerations into the core of HRM

H. Martins (✉)
RESILIENCE, ESCE – Instituto Politécnico de Setúbal, Setúbal, Portugal

CEOS.PP, ISCAP, P.Porto, Porto, Portugal

Nova SBE, Carcavelos, Portugal

S. B. Moreira
RESILIENCE, ESCE – Instituto Politécnico de Setúbal, Setúbal, Portugal

BRU-IUL, Instituto Universitário de Lisboa, Lisbon, Portugal
e-mail: sandrina.moreira@esce.ips.pt

B. Casais (ed.), *Integrated Science to Achieve Sustainable Development Goals*, Integrated Science 37, https://doi.org/10.1007/978-3-031-88777-2_7

decision-making processes. Our work enriches both academic literature and management practices by highlighting the pivotal role of human capital management in advancing toward the SDGs and advocating for a strategic alignment with the UN 2030 Agenda. This chapter maps the relationship between HRM trends and SDGs and promotes awareness and action towards incorporating sustainability goals in human capital strategies.

Graphical Abstract

Ten major trends found in the present work's literature review. (Source: Authors)

Keywords

Human capital management · Organizational sustainability · Sustainable development · Impact reporting · Innovation in human resources · Digital transformation · Diversity and inclusion · Green human resources Mangament · Mental health and Well-being · Remote work

1 Introduction

In 2015, the United Nations General Assembly unanimously adopted the 2030 Agenda for Sustainable Development, which includes 17 Sustainable Development Goals (SDGs) aimed at addressing global challenges such as poverty, inequality, climate change, environmental degradation, peace, and justice. The SDGs build on the Millennium Development Goals (MDGs) by providing a more comprehensive framework that applies to both developed and developing countries, with specific targets and indicators for measuring progress.

The concept of sustainable development integrates economic, social, and environmental dimensions, focusing on meeting the current generation's needs without compromising future generations' ability to meet theirs []. This principle, rooted in the 1987 Brundtland Report, emphasizes prudent management of non-renewable resources and attention to renewable sources, adding social cohesion to the pillars of sustainable development. Within this framework, the role of organizations in implementing sustainability strategies has become increasingly prominent, guided by Elkington's triple bottom line: economic, social, and environmental sustainability.

Human Capital Management (HCM), also known as Human Resource Management (HRM), involves a wide range of activities aimed at optimizing an organization's workforce. Monitoring emerging trends in HRM is crucial for researchers and practitioners to filter information, predict future trends, and create effective strategies. Understanding these trends helps in addressing contemporary concerns and shaping future HR strategies.

This chapter reviews HRM research trends and their impact on the UN SDGs, identifying ten major research tendencies that reflect current focal points in managing human capital.

The methodology involved analyzing the most relevant and highly cited articles on HRM between January 1, 2019, and December 31, 2023. These articles were categorized into specific themes based on their titles, abstracts, and keywords to determine the major HR trends and their relationship with the SDGs.

Aligning HR practices with the SDGs ensures that organizations contribute positively to broader economic, societal, and environmental goals. This alignment enhances organizational performance by fostering a more engaged, motivated, and productive workforce. For example, implementing green HRM practices can reduce carbon footprints, contributing to SDG 13 (Climate Action). Continuous learning and development opportunities support SDG 4 (Quality Education), while inclusive HR policies promote diversity and equal opportunities, aligning with SDG 5 (Gender Equality). Additionally, promoting fair, safe, and empowering workplaces directly supports SDG 8 (Decent Work and Economic Growth), and workplace wellness programs align with SDG 3 (Good Health and Well-being).

By integrating SDGs into HRM practices, organizations support global goals and enhance their effectiveness and resilience. This dual benefit underscores the importance of aligning HR strategies with the SDGs, positioning organizations as key players in the global effort towards sustainable development.

2 The Main Trends and Their Relationship with SDGs

Each trend or topic is explored in its own section with the following structure: identification of the trend, key aspects and definitions, contextualization, main implications and practices, and potential links with the UN SDGs.

2.1 Remote Work

Remote work has surged, particularly during the COVID-19 pandemic, leading to significant changes in HRM practices. Hybrid work models, blending in-office and remote work, enable organizations to optimize resource use while accommodating employee preferences, impacting "people, productivity, and the planet" (McPhail et al. [57], p. 154). This shift has disrupted organizational routines, posing challenges in balancing employee well-being with company performance [14].

The pandemic-induced transition to remote work caused postponed performance evaluations, weakening feedback mechanisms and psychological safety [2]. Increased virtual communication initially led to productivity declines due to more frequent meetings and longer workdays [34]. Despite adaptations restoring pre-pandemic productivity levels [11], issues like "Zoom fatigue" and disconnection persist [].

The concept of a four-day work week gained traction, promising benefits for morale and productivity but also risking increased performance pressures without a strategic shift [23, 88]. Organizations must adapt to better manage talent attraction and retention, mitigating the global "great resignation."

While remote work enhances work-life balance and reduces commuting time [69], it challenges employee engagement, collaboration, and organizational agility [6]. The feasibility of remote work depends on job tasks and HRM practices, with non-routine tasks and performance-based management being more conducive [46]. HRM strategies must evolve to support remote workers, emphasizing technology orientation, leadership, and organizational culture [6]. However, remote work may not suit all job types and could reinforce gender biases [10].

Additional challenges include the digital divide, data security, and maintaining corporate culture, necessitating equitable and inclusive HR policies [24]. From a strategic perspective, remote and hybrid work models require HR professionals to develop new competencies, including digital literacy and remote workforce management. Moreover, HR strategies must increasingly address mental health, offering support systems tailored to the unique stresses of remote work [32].

This shift aligns with several Sustainable Development Goals (SDGs). It addresses immediate health and safety needs (SDG 3), reduces inequality (SDG 10), promotes decent work and economic growth (SDG 8), and supports sustainable cities and communities (SDG 11) [53]. Hybrid models can lower carbon footprints by reducing the need for physical office space and daily commutes, supporting SDG 13 (Climate Action) [36].

Remote work democratizes employment opportunities, making jobs accessible to diverse populations, including those in rural or underserved areas, supporting SDG 10 [17]. It offers flexibility beneficial for women, helping to close gender gaps in the workplace (SDG 5). Additionally, remote work drives innovation in digital tools and infrastructure, aligning with SDG 9 (Industry, Innovation, and Infrastructure).

Remote and hybrid work models present significant opportunities to align HRM practices with Sustainable Development Goals. By addressing the challenges and leveraging the benefits of these models, organizations can enhance operational efficiency, support employee well-being, and contribute to a more sustainable and equitable global economy. This transition, driven by strategic HRM, requires ongoing adaptation and innovation to fully realize the potential of remote work in advancing the SDGs.

2.2 Diversity, Equity, and Inclusion (DEI)

The integration of diversity, equity, and inclusion (DEI) principles in HRM is increasingly recognized not merely as a moral imperative but as a strategic asset. In the current age of globalization and demographic shifts, the ability to harness a wide range of human experiences and perspectives is crucial for addressing complex business challenges and fostering innovation [7]. DEI is evolving from compliance concerns to strategic imperatives, enhancing innovation, creativity, and problem-solving in workplaces [40].

Contrary to conventional wisdom that inaccurately pits diversity against competence, DEI enriches competence by encompassing technical skills, emotional intelligence, creativity, and strategic thinking. Diverse teams bring multifaceted experiences and cultural competencies that foster nuanced understanding and innovative solutions to emerging problems. Effective DEI strategies are vital for creating workplaces that comply with legal standards and excel in employee engagement and satisfaction. This involves developing inclusive policies, rigorous training programs, equitable recruitment practices, and transparent promotion processes to ensure equal opportunities for all employees [29].

Organizations with comprehensive diversity and equality management systems (DEMS) often outperform peers in talent acquisition and financial outcomes [47]. HRM practices aligned with DEI initiatives, such as tailored recruitment, training, and performance management, leverage a diverse workforce to its full potential. However, challenges such as communication barriers, stereotypes, and resistance to change persist [40]. Overcoming these requires persistent effort, clear communication about DEI benefits, and commitment from senior leadership [42].

DEI practices directly influence several Sustainable Development Goals (SDGs). Promoting inclusive work environments contributes to building more equitable societies, aligning with SDG 8 (Decent Work and Economic Growth) and SDG 10 (Reduced Inequalities). Additionally, DEI practices align with SDG 5 (Gender Equality) by ensuring women and other underrepresented groups have equal access to opportunities and resources. Transparent promotion processes and equitable policies help build trust and integrity, foundational to strong and just institutions, supporting SDG 16 (Peace, Justice, and Strong Institutions).

The integration of DEI into HRM practices is not merely a trend but a strategic imperative that enhances organizational resilience and competitiveness. Effective DEI strategies involve creating inclusive cultures, equitable recruitment practices, and transparent promotion processes. Despite challenges, the persistent effort and commitment from senior leadership can foster an inclusive organizational culture, leveraging diversity for greater innovation and problem-solving. As HR leaders navigate the complexities of the modern workplace, DEI will undoubtedly play a critical role in shaping sustainable organizational practices. By aligning HRM practices with DEI principles, organizations can contribute significantly to achieving the SDGs, fostering a more equitable and sustainable global economy.

2.3 Mental Health and Well-being

The contemporary discourse on HRM increasingly emphasizes mental health and well-being as pivotal elements within organizational settings. The intrinsic link between employee well-being and organizational productivity underscores the need for strategic HR interventions that prioritize mental health as a core aspect of workplace culture. Mental health in the workplace encompasses emotional, psychological, and social well-being, influencing how individuals handle stress, relate to others, and make decisions. Therefore, well-being at work is not merely about physical health but also about promoting environments that foster mental resilience and job satisfaction [37].

Organizations benefit from well-being initiatives through enhanced engagement, reduced absenteeism, and lower turnover rates [43]. Effective HR practices integrate health and safety programs, employee assistance programs, and work-life balance initiatives [64]. Such outcomes contribute to a positive organizational culture, bolster productivity, and improve financial performance. Well-being programs also mitigate the risk of occupational burnout, which has been linked to significant psychological and physical health issues, impacting organizational costs and workforce stability [73].

Effective HR practices that support mental health and well-being are becoming increasingly comprehensive and multifaceted. Initiatives such as Health and Safety Programs are being implemented to address both physical and mental health risks, reflecting a holistic approach to employee wellness. Additionally, Employee Assistance Programs (EAPs) provide confidential counseling services, assisting employees with both personal and work-related challenges. Work-life balance is another critical area, with initiatives promoting flexible work schedules and remote work options to help employees balance their professional and personal lives [64]. In response to the demands of high-stress industries, particularly healthcare, HR professionals are adopting strategies that include employee assistance programs, stress management initiatives, and mental health awareness campaigns. Moreover, contemporary HR practices are evolving to incorporate personalized well-being programs that leverage technology and data analytics, offering tailored solutions to enhance employee health [19]. These integrated strategies exemplify the dynamic nature of HR's role in fostering an environment supportive of mental health and well-being.

The push towards evidence-based management in HR underscores the importance of grounding well-being initiatives in robust research. Utilizing data to inform wellness programs ensures that interventions are tailored to meet the specific needs of the workforce, thereby enhancing their effectiveness [59].

The trend of prioritizing mental health and well-being in HRM aligns with several Sustainable Development Goals (SDGs). It directly supports SDG 3 (Good Health and Well-Being) by reducing the prevalence of occupational burnout and associated health issues. Expected outcomes of reduced absenteeism and lower turnover rates also enhance productivity, contributing to economic growth (SDG 8). Additionally, promoting well-being for all at all ages (SDG 10) aligns with broader sustainable development objectives.

Incorporating mental health and well-being into HRM practices is not just a trend; it is a strategic necessity that boosts organizational resilience and competitiveness. Organizations that proactively engage in well-being initiatives see myriad benefits, including enhanced employee engagement, reduced absenteeism, and lower turnover rates. Effective HR practices that support mental health integrate comprehensive approaches, including health and safety programs, employee assistance programs, and work-life balance initiatives. These practices align with several SDGs, promoting well-being, reducing inequalities, and fostering economic growth. As HR leaders continue to navigate the complexities of the modern workplace, the focus on mental health and well-being will undoubtedly play a critical role in shaping sustainable organizational practices. Embracing this approach ensures that organizations remain resilient, competitive, and capable of fostering a thriving workforce.

2.4 Talent Acquisition

The landscape of talent acquisition has become increasingly complex and challenging for organizations. Rapid technological changes, evolving workforce expectations, and the residual effects of the COVID-19 pandemic have significantly reshaped talent acquisition strategies [22]. Factors such as demographic shifts, heightened demand for skilled labor, and changing employee preferences, particularly a desire for flexible work arrangements and meaningful engagement, have made talent acquisition tougher [56]. Trends like the "Great Attrition" or "Quiet Quitting" highlight a critical shift in worker engagement, where employees seek deeper connections and purpose in their roles [21].

Organizations must adopt dynamic talent attraction strategies that go beyond traditional recruitment methods. This involves creating tailored Employee Value Propositions (EVPs) that resonate with diverse employee segments and address their specific career aspirations and needs [21]. Employer branding has emerged as a pivotal element of talent attraction. A strong employer brand that communicates a company's values, culture, and commitment to employee development can attract a wider pool of candidates [56].

Adopting advanced technologies is crucial for streamlining recruitment processes and enhancing the candidate experience. Technologies facilitating virtual interviews, digital onboarding, and remote collaboration can expand the talent pool by enabling companies to tap into global talent resources effectively [21]. HR analytics also play a vital role in improving talent acquisition strategies by enabling data-driven decision-making [75, 90].

By ensuring that talent acquisition strategies are aligned with decent work principles, organizations can contribute to sustainable economic growth (SDG 8). The focus on inclusivity and flexibility within talent acquisition strategies supports SDG 10 (Reduced Inequalities). Using advanced technologies not only streamlines recruitment but also fosters innovation within HR practices (SDG 9). Moreover, by highlighting education through lifelong learning and skill enhancement, employees ensure they are equipped with the necessary competencies to thrive in a rapidly changing work environment (SDG 4).

The evolving landscape of talent acquisition demands that organizations adapt to changing workforce dynamics and anticipate future trends in employee behavior and preferences. By understanding and implementing strategic HR practices that prioritize the personal and professional needs of potential employees, companies can successfully navigate the complexities of modern talent acquisition. These strategies not only enhance organizational competitiveness but also contribute to broader sustainable development goals. Embracing tailored EVPs, leveraging advanced technologies, and fostering an inclusive employer brand are essential for attracting and retaining top talent in today's dynamic environment.

2.5 Continuous Learning

Continuous learning is essential for both personal and professional development, especially in today's rapidly evolving job market. As technological advancements and globalization reshape industries, the demand for new skills and competencies grows. Continuous learning enables individuals to stay relevant and competitive by adapting to these changes and enhancing their abilities [76]. The shift towards a knowledge-based economy underscores the importance of continuous learning as a strategic priority for organizations seeking to maintain a skilled and adaptable workforce [86].

HRM plays a vital role in fostering a learning culture within organizations. Strategic HRM aligns learning activities with business objectives, leading to improved performance and profitability [44, 48]. Digital HRM transforms traditional training into personalized, self-paced learning journeys, empowering employees to take responsibility for their development [80]. Self-directed learning is essential for productivity and leadership development, requiring HRM to create a supportive learning environment [55, 91].

Organizations must prioritize ongoing learning and development opportunities to enhance workforce capabilities and adapt to changing market demands. This involves not only traditional training programs but also innovative approaches such as digital skills workshops, emotional intelligence training, and experiential learning methodologies [35]. Integrating social and emotional learning and fostering cognitive agility are also crucial for developing a well-rounded and resilient workforce. Addressing foundational learning gaps through targeted intervention programs can ensure all employees have the essential skills needed for their roles [65].

Continuous learning directly supports SDG 4 (Quality Education), which aims to ensure inclusive and equitable quality education and promote lifelong learning opportunities for all. By fostering a culture of continuous learning, organizations contribute to this goal by providing employees with ongoing opportunities to develop and enhance their skills. This not only supports individual career growth but also drives organizational innovation and competitiveness, aligning with broader sustainable development objectives.

Organizations prioritizing ongoing learning help create a skilled and adaptable workforce, essential for maintaining economic productivity and growth (SDG 8). Promoting creative problem-solving and innovation to encourage cognitive agility also drives technological and process innovations (SDG 9). Additionally, promoting social and emotional intelligence fosters mental well-being and reduces workplace stress, contributing to employees' overall health and happiness (SDG 3).

Continuous learning is a key component of modern HRM practices, crucial for adapting to the rapidly changing professional landscape. Organizations can prioritize lifelong learning opportunities to ensure their workforce remains skilled, adaptable, and resilient. This aligns with SDG 4's goal of promoting quality education and lifelong learning for all. Implementing comprehensive learning and development strategies, including digital skills enhancement, emotional intelligence training, cognitive agility development, and addressing foundational learning gaps, will enable organizations to thrive in a dynamic and competitive environment.

2.6 Team Dynamics and Interpersonal Relationships

Team dynamics and interpersonal relationships are pivotal in enhancing the effectiveness of Human Resource Management (HRM) within organizations. These elements are crucial for fostering a harmonious work environment and enhancing employee collaboration, which are key to achieving organizational goals. Effective teamwork positively impacts organizational innovation, especially when supported by high-quality HRM systems [27]. Interpersonal skills and emotional intelligence are vital for managers to handle social challenges and implement change [12].

Team dynamics encompass the behavioral relationships and interactions among team members, critically influencing an organization's performance. Effective team dynamics facilitate a cooperative atmosphere that significantly boosts productivity and creativity. Aligning individual behaviors and interactions within teams contributes to achieving common organizational goals [9]. Interpersonal relationships within the workplace are equally critical, impacting job satisfaction and employee retention. HRM strategies that foster positive interpersonal relationships improve communication and conflict resolution, enhancing overall morale and workforce engagement [20].

Organizations must implement strategic HRM practices to optimize team dynamics that encourage effective communication, conflict management, and role clarity among team members [15]. These practices are essential for cultivating a collaborative, flexible work environment where innovation can thrive. However, developing effective team dynamics and interpersonal relationships presents challenges, including managing diverse personalities and overcoming communication barriers. Organizations must proactively identify and address these issues to prevent them from undermining team cohesion and productivity [4].

Effective team dynamics and interpersonal relationships within organizations align with several SDGs. By creating a harmonious work environment that promotes effective communication and conflict resolution, team dynamics can reduce workplace stress and improve mental health, contributing to overall employee well-being (SDG 3). Enhanced productivity and creativity from well-managed team dynamics support SDG 8 (Decent Work and Economic Growth). Furthermore, effective team dynamics and interpersonal relationships foster collaboration and partnerships, essential for achieving SDG 17 (Partnerships for the Goals).

Team dynamics and interpersonal relationships are fundamental components of HRM that directly influence organizational success. By strategically enhancing these elements, companies can improve their HR practices and achieve a competitive advantage in the marketplace. The ongoing development and maintenance of healthy team dynamics and interpersonal relationships not only support HR objectives but also contribute to the overall stability and growth of the organization. Through these efforts, organizations can foster environments that are conducive to innovation, employee satisfaction, and sustainable development.

2.7 Generational Shifts

Generational shifts significantly influence recruitment strategies and workplace culture, requiring HR practices to evolve [5, 92]. These shifts present both challenges and opportunities for HRM, impacting everything from recruitment strategies to organizational culture. As Baby Boomers retire and Generations X, Y (Millennials), and Z establish themselves in the workplace, HR practices must adapt to address each generation's unique characteristics and expectations.

Workplace generational differences have become a significant focus for HRM research and practice. Each generation brings distinct values, work ethics, and communication styles. Baby Boomers are known for their strong work ethic and loyalty, Generation X values independence and work-life balance, Millennials prioritize meaningful work and flexibility, and Generation Z seeks innovation, technological integration, and social responsibility [5], 92. Recognizing and leveraging these traits can enhance both individual and organizational performance.

Managing generational diversity involves creating flexible work environments and fostering mutual respect through mentoring programs [45]. HR professionals must develop strategies that cater to diverse needs while promoting inclusivity. For instance, older generations may appreciate traditional communication methods and hierarchical structures, while younger generations thrive in collaborative, tech-savvy environments [45, 50].

One of the primary challenges in managing generational diversity is the potential for misunderstandings and conflicts arising from differing values and communication styles. HR managers must facilitate understanding and cooperation among generational cohorts to harness their strengths rather than let these differences lead to workplace discord [30]. Organizations can turn generational diversity into a competitive advantage by fostering a culture of learning and mutual respect. Initiatives like mentoring programs, where older employees share their knowledge and experience with younger employees, and vice versa, can lead to innovative solutions and a more dynamic workplace [62].

Understanding and integrating generational shifts in the workplace can ensure inclusive and sustainable economic growth by adapting to changing workforce needs. This trend supports several SDGs. Promoting work-life balance and flexibility, values particularly important to Generations X and Millennials, supports SDG 3 (Good Health and Well-being). Furthermore, generational shifts in the workforce directly support SDG 8 (Decent Work and Economic Growth) by creating adaptable and inclusive work environments. Promoting equal opportunities and reducing workplace disparities aligns with SDG 10 (Reduced Inequalities). Additionally, younger generations, particularly Generation Z, drive organizations to adopt new technologies and practices, aligning with SDG 9 (Industry, Innovation, and Infrastructure).

Generational shifts necessitate adaptive HR strategies that recognize the unique attributes of each generation while aligning these characteristics with organizational goals. By understanding and integrating these shifts, HRM can contribute to sustainable development goals such as decent work and economic growth, reduced inequalities, and sustainable cities and communities. This approach creates more inclusive and effective workplaces, ensuring organizations remain competitive and resilient in a rapidly changing global landscape.

2.8 Crisis Management

Crisis management is critical to organizational resilience, particularly in response to climate change, pandemics, and global disruptions. The increasing frequency and severity of these crises highlight the need for robust strategies to ensure organizations can continue operations during adverse conditions and recover swiftly from setbacks. The COVID-19 pandemic exemplified the necessity for agile and effective crisis management practices [39]. The pandemic disrupted established organizational routines and created a complex environment for managers and HRM practitioners to find innovative solutions to sustain business continuity and support employees [14, 18].

Effective crisis management involves a combination of preparedness, response, recovery, and mitigation strategies. Preparedness includes developing comprehensive plans and conducting regular training and simulations to ensure all employees are aware of their roles during a crisis. Response strategies focus on immediate actions to protect lives and assets, while recovery efforts aim to restore normal operations as quickly as possible. Mitigation involves implementing measures to reduce the impact of future crises, such as investing in resilient infrastructure and adopting sustainable practices [1]. HR plays a vital role in crisis planning, training, and employee welfare during crises [74]. HRM systems that provide distinctive, consistent, and consensual information help employees navigate crises more effectively. Effective leadership and HRM practices are essential for maintaining employee and organizational performance during crises [38].

Human Resource Development (HRD) can contribute significantly to crisis management by aligning strategic HRD focus with organizational crisis efforts [41, 84]. HRD interventions can support crisis management processes and build organizational crisis management capabilities [89]. Proactive crisis management, including well-executed human development initiatives, is crucial for reducing vulnerability to crises, particularly in the tourism industry [68]. HR crisis management involves comprehensive planning, diagnostics, and implementation of strategies to address organizational challenges [51].

Key practices in crisis management include thorough risk assessments to identify potential threats, clear communication channels, regular training and simulations, investing in resilient infrastructure, and continuously evaluating and improving crisis management strategies [39]. The COVID-19 crisis underscored the importance of strategic HRM in crisis management. Organizations must align their HR practices with crisis management strategies to support employees effectively and sustain business operations. Enhancing organizational resilience through innovative HRM practices can help absorb and face disturbances that threaten survival [63].

Effective crisis management practices contribute to multiple SDGs. For SDG 13 (Climate Action), they enhance resilience and reduce the vulnerability of communities and organizations to climate-related hazards. For SDG 16 (Peace, Justice, and Strong Institutions), strong institutional responses and transparent communication during crises promote peace and justice, ensuring that organizations and communities can recover and thrive post-crisis. SDG 4 (Quality Education) is supported through ongoing education, regular training, and simulations that enhance the skills and preparedness of employees for future crises. Finally, effective crisis management under SDG 9 (Industry, Innovation, and Infrastructure) promotes long-term sustainability and innovation by investing in resilient infrastructure and adopting sustainable practices to minimize the impact of crises.

Crisis management is essential to organizational resilience, enabling businesses to withstand and recover from various disruptions. Organizations can enhance their preparedness and response capabilities by adopting comprehensive risk assessment, planning, and mitigation strategies. This ensures business continuity and aligns with global efforts to promote sustainability and resilience as outlined in the SDGs, particularly SDG 13 and SDG 16. The integration of HRM and crisis management is vital for creating resilient organizations capable of thriving in an uncertain global landscape.

2.9 Digital Transformation

HRM is undergoing a profound transformation driven by digital technologies. Accelerated by the COVID-19 pandemic, this shift has significantly increased the integration of digital tools within HR processes, emphasizing the growing role of information technologies in shaping modern HR practices. Digital transformation is reshaping HRM in various sectors, including education [60]. This transformation impacts HR practices such as recruitment, performance management, and employee development [28]. HRM plays a critical role in successful digital transformation by focusing on people factors and developing appropriate strategies [70, 79].

The advent of algorithmic HRM and digital management systems represents a crucial evolution in HR practices. The use of artificial intelligence (AI) in decision-making processes and the implementation of electronic human resource management (e-HRM) systems are at the forefront of this transformation. These technologies enhance organizational efficiency by supporting data-driven decision-making and reducing the environmental impact of HR operations [7]. Key aspects of HRM digital transformation include improving digital competencies, cultural and leadership changes, organizational restructuring, and effective communication [33].

While the digital transformation offers numerous advantages, it also presents challenges, including ethical concerns and the need for clear terminological definitions. The application of AI in HR, although promising, remains underutilized in many organizations, highlighting a gap in understanding its full potential [16]. Additionally, the disparity in terminology such as 'digitalization,' 'digital transformation,' and 'digital disruption' adds complexity to academic and practical understandings of these changes.

For HR professionals, adapting to digital transformation involves more than just implementing new technologies; it requires a strategic overhaul of HR functions to align with digital advancements. This includes developing IT competencies among HR professionals and leveraging e-HRM systems that promote sustainability and improve performance [13]. The integration of sustainable e-HRM practices is essential for the long-term success of digital strategies in HR. These practices support operational needs and contribute to broader environmental and economic goals by enhancing organizational performance and sustainability [7].

The digital transformation in HRM can drive innovation and support the development of sustainable industrial infrastructure, aligning with SDG 9 (Industry, Innovation, and Infrastructure). Moreover, the adoption of digital tools and e-HRM systems enhances organizational efficiency, leading to increased productivity and economic growth, aligning with SDG 8 (Decent Work and Economic Growth). The shift from paper-based processes to e-HRM promotes sustainable resource use and more environmentally responsible practices, supporting SDG 12 (Responsible Consumption and Production). Furthermore, by investing in education to enhance the digital literacy of employees, the digital transformation of HRM aligns with SDG 4 (Quality Education).

Digital transformation in HRM is reshaping how organizations manage their human resources. HR professionals must stay abreast of technological advancements and integrate them effectively into their strategic plans. As HR continues to evolve in response to digital technologies, the role of HR professionals will increasingly focus on managing the intersection of technology, strategy, and human resource development. This integration supports operational needs and aligns with global efforts to promote sustainability and resilience, particularly in achieving SDGs 4, 8, 9, and 12.

2.10 Green Human Resource Management

Green Human Resource Management (Green HRM) integrates environmental management into HR practices, promoting sustainability [71]. This approach is pivotal for modern organizations striving to balance economic success with ecological responsibility. Green HRM involves strategic recruitment, development, and retention practices that enhance organizational performance while ensuring environmental sustainability. By fostering a workforce that is environmentally conscious and skilled in sustainable practices, organizations can promote eco-friendly behaviors and resource conservation throughout their operations [25, 87].

Green HRM encompasses environmentally-friendly HR practices and knowledge capital preservation [52]. These practices span the entire employee lifecycle, from recruitment to exit. Implementing Green HRM can reduce costs, increase efficiency, and improve employee management [3]. By adopting sustainable practices internally and considering the broader impacts of their technological choices, organizations can reduce their carbon footprint, attract environmentally conscious talent, and enhance their reputation [87]. Key strategies include selecting environmentally friendly technologies and optimizing AI usage to minimize energy consumption. Additionally, HR policies should promote environmental awareness and encourage practices such as digital minimalism to reduce the ecological footprint of technology use in HR processes [54].

Despite its benefits, implementing Green HRM faces challenges such as resistance to change within traditional HR practices and the need for continuous education on environmental issues for all employees. Overcoming these challenges requires a strategic approach, including substantial initial investments and efforts to align HR practices with environmental goals [77, 78].

Green HRM directly supports several Sustainable Development Goals (SDGs). Promoting sustainable business practices and responsible consumption aligns with SDG 12 (Responsible Consumption and Production). Efforts to combat climate change through sustainable operations and strategies contribute to SDG 13 (Climate Action). Specifically, adopting practices that reduce carbon footprints and optimize energy usage aligns with SDG 7 (Affordable and Clean Energy). Moreover, by fostering a workforce knowledgeable in environmental issues and skilled in sustainable practices, Green HRM contributes to SDG 4 (Quality Education). Finally, ensuring that economic growth does not come at the expense of environmental health aligns with SDG 8 (Decent Work and Economic Growth).

Green HRM integrates environmental sustainability into HR practices, playing a crucial role in driving organizational sustainability. By embedding environmental goals into HR practices, organizations can significantly reduce their ecological impact while fostering a culture of sustainability. The strategic implementation of Green HRM can lead to substantial benefits, including reduced carbon footprints, enhanced corporate reputation, and compliance with environmental regulations. However, the adoption of high-energy-consuming technologies like AI poses new challenges that require innovative solutions to align with the principles of Green HRM. Overall, Green HRM supports operational needs and aligns with global efforts to promote sustainability and resilience as outlined in the SDGs, particularly SDGs 4, 7, 8, 12, and 13.

3 Holistic Perspective

The Sustainable Development Goals (SDGs) are interlinked, with advancements in one area impacting others positively or negatively [8, 31]. Aligning HR policies with the SDGs offers organizations a comprehensive framework for managing human capital efficiently and responsibly, addressing key social and environmental issues, and enhancing employee satisfaction and retention [82]. By integrating sustainable practices into HR strategies, companies can focus on profit while maximizing economic value through positive societal and environmental contributions (see Fig. 7.1).

In this work, some SDGs are more frequently reflected in HRM practices than others. Although most SDGs are addressed, there are gaps in addressing SDG 1 (No Poverty), SDG 2 (Zero Hunger), SDG 6 (Clean Water and Sanitation), SDG 14 (Life Below Water), and SDG 15 (Life on Land) in developed countries' HRM practices. The lack of focus on SDGs 1 and 2 may reflect the context of developed countries where these issues are less pressing. However, HRM practices aligned with SDG 8

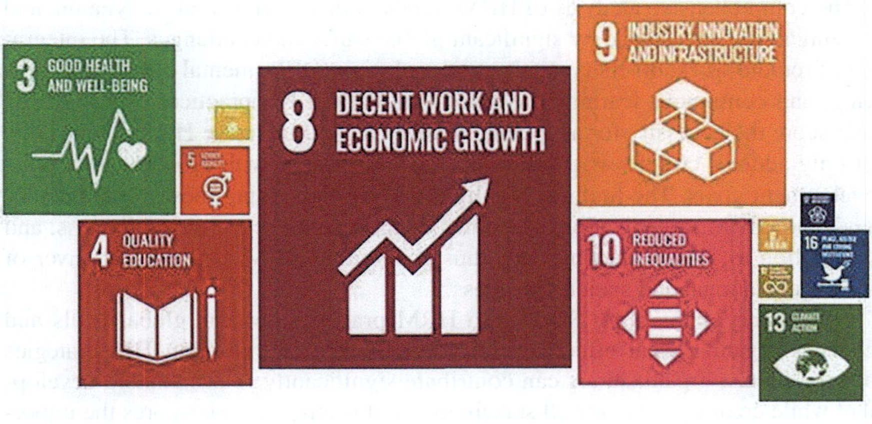

Fig. 7.1 Graphic Depiction of the frequency of each SDG's in the trends identified by this chapter. (Source: Authos)

(Decent Work and Economic Growth) in developing countries can also contribute to reducing poverty and hunger, indicating a broader impact of HRM on these goals. Future research should include perspectives from professionals in developing contexts to explore these relationships further.

The SDGs encourage organizations to adopt economically viable, socially, and environmentally responsible practices [26]. This alignment helps companies identify and address sustainability weaknesses. For HR professionals involved in impact, ESG (Environmental, Social, and Governance), or sustainability reporting, this chapter offers insights into identifying and addressing gaps in current SDG strategies, facilitating the alignment of organizational strategies with social responsibility.

The relationship between SDGs and ESG is intrinsic, driving organizations towards sustainable and responsible practices. Understanding this relationship is crucial for HR professionals as it highlights the company's role in creating value for shareholders, stakeholders, and society. This holistic value creation approach is central to sustainable development, influencing corporate marketing strategies to emphasize transparency and avoid greenwashing [49].

HRM advances the SDGs by promoting sustainability through policies and practices. Despite the SDGs' broad scope, there is a significant gap in their emphasis on mental health. SDG 3 primarily targets physical health and general well-being, with minimal focus on mental health. This oversight is concerning given mental health's profound impact on quality of life, productivity, and societal participation. Addressing this gap could lead to more focused policies, funding, and programs aimed at mental health, fostering a holistic approach to global health and development.

HR professionals and organizations offer unique perspectives that should be included in shaping social responsibility, policy, and legislation. As businesses navigate complex issues, they can influence and be influenced by the SDGs, creating a symbiotic relationship that drives both corporate success and global sustainability.

The comprehensive analysis of HRM trends in this work reveals a dynamic and evolving landscape shaped by significant global shifts and challenges. The integration of remote work, diversity, equity, and inclusion (DEI), mental health and well-being, and continuous learning are pivotal in modern HR practices. These trends underscore the necessity for adaptable, innovative, and inclusive HR strategies that not only address current workforce needs but also align with broader sustainable development goals. The findings highlight that by embedding these contemporary trends into HRM, organizations can enhance their resilience, competitiveness, and contribution to global sustainability, thus positioning HRM as a critical driver of both organizational and societal progress.

In summary, integrating SDGs into HRM practices benefits global goals and enhances organizational effectiveness and resilience. By aligning HR strategies with the SDGs, organizations can contribute significantly to sustainable development while creating value for all stakeholders. This chapter underscores the importance of this alignment and provides a roadmap for HR professionals to effectively navigate the intersection of human capital management and sustainable development.

4 Conclusion

This chapter has shown that integrating key trends in HRM with the SDGs significantly enhances organizational effectiveness and contributes to global sustainability efforts. Aligning HR strategies with the SDGs allows organizations to address contemporary challenges, foster innovation, and build more resilient workplaces. The necessity of incorporating sustainability goals into human capital strategies is highlighted, promoting awareness and action towards sustainable development within HRM.

The SDGs are intrinsically linked to HCM through various goals directly related to workforce management and development. Conversely, HCM drives the organizational changes needed to meet the SDGs. By integrating sustainability into HR strategies, organizations can enhance their economic, social, and environmental impact. For instance, implementing green HRM practices contributes to SDG 13 (Climate Action) by reducing carbon footprints through remote work, reduced energy consumption, and sustainable commuting options. HCM advances SDG 4 (Quality Education) by providing continuous learning and development opportunities, enhancing workforce skills and supporting inclusive quality education for all.

SDG 8 (Decent Work and Economic Growth) aligns with HCM practices that create fair, safe, and empowering workplaces, promoting sustained, inclusive, and sustainable economic growth. Similarly, SDG 5 (Gender Equality) aims for gender equality and empowerment, which aligns with inclusive HR policies that promote diversity and equal opportunities. SDG 3 (Good Health and Well-being) underscores ensuring healthy lives and well-being, supported through workplace wellness programs and health benefits.

Integrating SDGs into Human Capital Management supports global goals and enhances organizational effectiveness by promoting responsible and sustainable HR practices. This dual benefit underscores the importance of aligning HR strategies with the SDGs, positioning organizations as key players in the global effort towards sustainable development.

"Aligning human resource strategies with the Sustainable Development Goals unlocks the potential for a future where economic growth and social progress go hand in hand."

References

1. Agrawal S, De Smet A, Lacroix S, Reich A (2020) To emerge stronger from the covid-19 crisis, companies should start reskilling their workforces now. McKinsey & Company. https://www.mckinsey.com/capabilities/people-and-organizational-performance/our-insights/to-emerge-stronger-from-the-covid-19-crisis-companies-should-start-reskilling-their-workforces-now
2. Aguinis H, Burgi-Tian J (2021) Talent management challenges during COVID-19 and beyond: performance management to the rescue. BRQ Bus Res Q 24(3):233–240. https://doi.org/10.1177/23409444211009528
3. Ahuja D (2015) Green HRM: management of people through commitment towards environmental sustainability. Int J Res Finance Marketing 5:50–54

4. Alberti TF, Abegg I, Costa MRJ, Titton M (2014) Dinâmicas de grupo orientadas pelas atividades de estudo: desenvolvimento de habilidades e competências na educação profissional. Revista Brasileira de Estudos Pedagógicos 95:346–362
5. Alferjany M, Alias R (2020) Generational differences in values and attitudes within the workplace. Psychol Educ 57(9):1496–1503
6. Arunprasad P, Dey C, Jebli F, Manimuthu A, El Hathat Z (2022) Exploring the remote work challenges in the era of COVID-19 pandemic: review and application model. Benchmarking: Int J
7. Bag S, Dhamija P, Pretorius JHC, Chowdhury AH, Giannakis M (2022) Sustainable electronic human resource management systems and firm performance: an empirical study. Int J Manpow 43(1):32–51. https://doi.org/10.1108/IJM-02-2021-0099
8. Barbier EB, Burgess JC (2022) Sustainable development goal indicators: analyzing trade-offs and complementarities. World Dev 122:295–305. https://doi.org/10.1016/j.worlddev.2019.05.026
9. de Brito Barros M, Formiga NS, de Vasconcelos CRM (2021) Uma reflexão teórica sobre a confiança nas relações interpessoais em ambientes organizacionais. Pesquisa, Sociedade e Desenvolvimento 10(5):1–13. https://doi.org/10.33448/rsd-v10i5.15299
10. Best SJ (2021) The future of work: remote work in the emerging new normal. The business and management. Review
11. Bloom N (2020) How working from home works out. Stanford Institute for Economic Policy Research. https://api.includere.co/uploads/Stanford%20Research-How%20working%20from%20home%20works%20out%20-%20June%202020.pdf
12. Bolman LG, Deal TE (2017) Interpersonal and group dynamics. Wiley
13. Bondarouk T, Parry E, Furtmueller E (2017) Electronic HRM: four decades of research on adoption and consequences. Int J Hum Resour Manag 28(1):98–131. https://doi.org/10.1080/09585192.2016.1245672
14. Bose S, Shams S, Ali MJ, Mihret D (2022) COVID-19 impact, sustainability performance and firm value: international evidence. Account Finance 62(1):597–643. https://doi.org/10.1111/acfi.12801
15. Chen S, Fan Y, Zhang G, Zhang Y (2019) Collectivism-oriented human resource management on team creativity: effects of interpersonal harmony and human resource management strength. Int J Hum Resour Manag 32(18):3805–3832. https://doi.org/10.1080/09585192.2019.1640765
16. Cheng MM, Hackett RD (2021) A critical review of algorithms in HRM: definition, theory, and practice. Hum Resour Manag Rev 31(1):100698. https://doi.org/10.1016/j.hrmr.2019.100698
17. Choudhury P (2020) Our work-from-anywhere future. Harv Bus Rev 98(6):58–67
18. Collings DG, McMackin J, Nyberg AJ, Wright PM (2021) Strategic human resource management and COVID-19: emerging challenges and research opportunities. J Manag Stud 58(5):1378–1382. https://doi.org/10.1111/joms.12695
19. Daraojimba RE, Elufioye OA, Ndubuisi NL, Awonuga KF, Omolara L, Asuzu OF (2024) Reviewing employee Well-being and mental health initiatives in contemporary HR practices. Int J Sci Res Archive
20. de Oliveira D, Carrara K, Souza C (2022) Developing positive interpersonal relationships at work: a systematic review. Int J Workplace Health Manag 15(1):58–80. https://doi.org/10.1108/IJWHM-05-2021-0094
21. De Smet A, Dowling B, Hancock B, Schaninger B (2021) 'Great attrietion' or 'great attraction'? The choice is yours. McKinsey & Company. https://www.mckinsey.com/capabilities/people-and-organizational-performance/our-insights/great-attrition-or-great-attraction-the-choice-is-yours
22. De Smet A, Dowling B, Hancock B, Schaninger B (2022) The great attrition is making hiring harder. Are you searching the right talent pools? McKinsey & Company. https://www.mckinsey.com/capabilities/people-and-organizational-performance/our-insights/the-great-attrition-is-making-hiring-harder-are-you-searching-the-right-talent-pools

23. Delaney H, Casey C (2022) The promise of a four-day week? A critical appraisal of a management-led initiative. Employee Relations: Int J 44(1):176–190. https://doi.org/10.1108/ER-02-2021-005
24. Donnelly R, Johns J (2021) Recontextualizing remote work and its management in the digital economy: an integrated framework for theory and practice. Int J Hum Resour Manag 32(1):84–105. https://doi.org/10.1080/09585192.2020.1828343
25. Dutta S (2014) Greening people: A strategic dimension. ZENITH Int J Multidiscipl Res 4(1):110–118
26. Elkington J (2018) 25 years ago I coined the phrase 'triple bottom line.' Here's why it's time to rethink it. Harv Bus Rev 25:2–7
27. Fay D, Shipton H, West MA, Patterson M (2015) Teamwork and organizational innovation: the moderating role of the HRM context. Creat Innov Manag 24(2):261–277. https://doi.org/10.1111/caim.12100
28. Fenech R, Baguant P, Ivanov D (2019) The changing role of human resource management in an era of digital transformation. J Manag Inform Decision Sci 22:166
29. Ferreira LL, Maciel PD, de Coleti JC, Macedo KG (2022) Departamento de diversidade, equidade e inclusão: uma nova tendência empresarial. E-Acadêmica 3(3):e5933374. https://doi.org/10.52076/eacad-v3i3.374
30. Flach R, Pinheiro S, Klunk A, Dill O, Flach D (2022) Multigenerational work market: A study on the specifics and perceptions of generations. Revista Conexão 10:67–101
31. Fonseca LM, Domingues JP, Dima AM (2020) Mapping the sustainable development goals relationships. Sustain For 12(8):3359. https://doi.org/10.3390/su12083359
32. Ford D, Storey MA, Zimmermann T, Bird C, Jaffe S, Maddila C, Nagappan N, Xie T (2021) A tale of two cities: software developers working from home during the COVID-19 pandemic. IEEE Trans Softw Eng 47(9):1–14. https://doi.org/10.1109/TSE.2021.3095145
33. Gadzali SS, Gazalin J, Sutrisno S, Prasetya YB, Almaududi Ausat AM (2023) Human resource management strategy in organisational digital transformation. Jurnal Minfo Polgan 6(1):20–36
34. Gibbs M, Mengel F, Siemroth C (2023) Work from home and productivity: evidence from personnel and analytics data on information technology professionals. J Political Econ Microecon 1(1):7–41. https://doi.org/10.1086/721803
35. Goel S, Kovács-Ondrejkovic O (2023) Reskilling for a rapidly changing world. Boston Consulting Group. https://www.bcg.com/publications/2023/reskilling-workforce-for-future
36. Gratton L (2021) Four principles for making hybrid work effective. MIT Sloan Manag Rev 62(2):11A–16A
37. Guimarães JVF, de Neto ENS (2021) Bem estar e satisfação no trabalho: Uma revisão da literatura atual. Revista Científica do UniRios 5(1):279–301
38. Hakim G a, Bastian BL, Ayanian MS, Sarkis N (2022) Leadership and human resource management during crisis. Arab Economic and Business Journal 14(2):Article 4. https://doi.org/10.38039/2214-4625.1016
39. Hamouche S (2021) Human resource management and the COVID-19 crisis: implications, challenges, opportunities, and future organizational directions. J Manag Organ 29(5):799–814. https://doi.org/10.1017/jmo.2021.15
40. Hossain MI (2023) Managing diversity through human resource management: a USA perspective and conceptual framework. Archives of Business Research 11(1):40–59
41. Hutchins HM, Wang J (2008) Organizational crisis management and human resource development: a review of the literature and implications to HRD research and practice. Adv Dev Hum Resour 10(3):310–330. https://doi.org/10.1177/1523422308316450
42. Iqbal N, Ahmad M, Allen MMC (2019) Unveiling the relationship between e-HRM, impersonal trust and employee productivity. Manag Res Rev 42(7):879–899. https://doi.org/10.1108/MRR-02-2018-0094
43. Johnson A, Dey S, Nguyen H, Growth M, Joyce S, Tan L, Glozier N, Harvey SB (2020) A review and agenda for examining how technology-driven changes at work will impact workplace mental health and employee Well-being. Aust J Manag 45(3):402–424. https://doi.org/10.1177/0312896220922292

44. Jørgensen F, Laugen BT, Boer H (2007) Human resource management for continuous improvement. J Manuf Technol Manag 18(4):433–447. https://doi.org/10.1108/17410380710743796
45. Junqueira MH (2020) The impacts of different generations on talent management. Revista Científica Semana Académica 199(1):1–19
46. Kawaguchi D, Motegi H (2021) Who can work from home? The roles of job tasks and HRM practices. Journal Japanese Int Econ 62:101162. https://doi.org/10.1016/j.jjie.2021.101162
47. Konrad AM, Yang Y, Maurer CC (2016) Antecedents and outcomes of diversity and equality management systems: an integrated institutional agency and strategic human resource management approach. Hum Resour Manag 55(1):83–107. https://doi.org/10.1002/hrm.21659
48. Kramar R (2007) Strategic human resource management: A broadening horizon? Asia Pac J Hum Resour 45(3):311–318. https://doi.org/10.1177/1038411107082272
49. Lashitew AA (2021) Corporate uptake of the sustainable development goals: mere greenwashing or an advent of institutional change? J Int Bus Policy 4(1):184–200. https://doi.org/10.1057/s42214-020-00097-x
50. Lirio A, Gallon S, Costa C (2020) Perceptions of work-life quality across different generations. Gestão Regionalidade 36(107):201–220. https://doi.org/10.13037/gr.vol36n107.5185
51. Lositska T, Bieliaieva N (2020) HR crisis management at trade enterprises. ERN: Human Resources Developing Economies (Topic)
52. Mandip G (2012) Green HRM: people management commitment to environmental sustainability. Int J Marketing Human Resource Manag 3(1):1–8
53. Martins H, Maritsa E, Rodrigues E (2022) Where are you going, work from anywhere?: the challenges of remote work before and after the COVID-19 pandemic. In: Figueiredo P, Tomé E, Rouco J (eds) Handbook of research on challenges for human resource management in the COVID-19 era, pp 62–82). IGI Global. https://doi.org/10.4018/978-1-7998-8114-9.ch004
54. Mascaranhas A (2019) Sustainable human resource management and social and environmental responsibility. RAE-Revista de Administração de Empresas 59(5):353–364. https://doi.org/10.1590/s0034-759020190505
55. Maurer TJ (2002) Employee learning and development orientation: toward an integrative model of involvement in continuous learning. Hum Resour Dev Rev 1(1):9–44. https://doi.org/10.1177/1523422302001001002
56. McConnell M, Schaninger B (2019) Are we long—or short—on talent? McKinsey & Company. https://www.mckinsey.com/capabilities/people-and-organizational-performance/our-insights/are-we-long-or-short-on-talent
57. McPhail R, Chan XW, May R, Wilkinson A (2024) Post-COVID remote working and its impact on people, productivity, and the planet: an exploratory scoping review. Int J Hum Resour Manag 35(1):154–182. https://doi.org/10.1080/09585192.2023.2221385
58. Mensah J (2019) Sustainable development: meaning, history, principles, pillars, and implications for human action: literature review. Cogent Soc Sci 5(1):1653531. https://doi.org/10.1080/23311886.2019.1653531
59. Methley AM, Campbell S, Chew-Graham C, McNally R, Cheraghi-Sohi S (2014) PICO, PICOS and SPIDER: A comparison study of specificity and sensitivity in three search tools for qualitative systematic reviews. BMC Health Serv Res 14(1):579. https://doi.org/10.1186/s12913-014-0579-0
60. Moh Saifudin M, Rindanigsih I (2024) Transformation of human resource management in education in the digital era. Int J Multidiscipl 6(1):1–9
61. Moreira SB, Crespo N (2012) Economia do desenvolvimento: Das abordagens tradicionais aos novos conceitos de desenvolvimento. Rev Econ 38(2):25–50. https://doi.org/10.5380/re.v38i2.29899
62. Nascimento C (2021) The challenges in managing people from different generations in the workplace. Revista Científica Multidisciplinar Núcleo do Conhecimento 6(14):20–30
63. Ngoc SD, Luc Tra D, Thi Huynh HM, Nguyen HHT, O'Mahony B (2021) Enhancing resilience in the COVID-19 crisis: lessons from human resource management practices in Vietnam. Curr Issue Tour 24(10):1321–1338. https://doi.org/10.1080/13683500.2020.1863930

64. Nunes AL d PF, Martins GG, Mendonça J d M (2021) A retenção de talentos e o novo normal de recursos humanos. Id on Line Revista de Psicologia 15(58):391–409. https://doi.org/10.14295/idonline.v15i58.3335
65. Olsen C (2020) The assumptions underlying the foundation skills gap. LinkedIn. https://www.linkedin.com/pulse/assumptions-underlying-foundation-skills-gap-corey-olsen/
66. Ozili PK (2022) Sustainability and sustainable development research around the world. Managing Global Trans 20(3):259–293. https://doi.org/10.26493/1854-6935.20.259-293
67. Payne A, Phillips N (2010) Development. Polity Press, Cambridge
68. Pforr C, Hosie P (2008) Crisis management in tourism: preparing for recovery. J Travel Tour Mark 23(2–4):249–264. https://doi.org/10.1300/J073v23n02_19
69. Rahman MH, Rahman SM (2021) Impact of remote working on human resource management: the role of IT in the COVID-19 era. Asian J Econ Business Accoun 21(4):1–13. https://doi.org/10.9734/ajeba/2021/v21i430382
70. Rajeev Joshi P (2022) Importance of people and HRM in the digital transformation. Proc Int Conf Indus Eng Operations Manag 2022(1):1–10
71. Ren S, Tang G, Jackson SE (2017) Green human resource management research in emergence: a review and future directions. Asia Pac J Manag 35(3):769–803. https://doi.org/10.1007/s10490-017-9532-1
72. Sachs JD (2012) From millennium development goals to sustainable development goals. Lancet 379(9832):2206–2211. https://doi.org/10.1016/S0140-6736(12)60685-0
73. Salas-Vallina A, Alegre J, López-Cabrales Á (2021) The challenge of increasing employees' Well-being through work engagement. Pers Rev 50(1):267–282. https://doi.org/10.1108/PR-07-2019-0389
74. Seif Athamneh S (2018) HR planning for crisis management. In: Cavico RY, Mujtaba B, Seif S (eds) Human resource planning for the 21st century. IntechOpen, pp 213–230. https://doi.org/10.5772/intechopen.72240
75. Sharma SP (2024) Impact of HR analytics for talent acquisition in identifying quality resources. Int J Innov Res Eng Manag 11(1):45–51
76. Sims RR (2020) Human resource management: contemporary issues, challenges, and opportunities. IAP
77. Singh D, Pandey A (2020) Green HRM: an organizational commitment. JIMS8M: J Indian Manag Strategy 25(1):14–18. https://doi.org/10.5958/0973-9343.2020.00003.2
78. Singh H, Hassan MF, Ram S (2022) Green HRM: a new outlook to safeguard environment. J Environ Manag 287:112302. https://doi.org/10.1016/j.jenvman.2021.112302
79. Susanto E, Bagus IG, Darma KA, Suparsana IM, Ugiantara MB, Made GA, Herawan A, Widana GA, Idea S (2024) Pengembangan strategi manajemen sumber daya manusia dalam transformasi digital untuk meningkatkan kinerja perusahaan. Syntax Idea 9(1):1–12
80. Tran T (2023) How does digital HRM transform training to learning in organizations? J Econ Finance Manag Stud 6(1):1–7. https://doi.org/10.47191/jefms/v6-i1-01
81. Tseng ML, Wu KJ, Lim MK, Wong WP (2009) Assessing the drivers of green performance in the context of green supply chain management. J Clean Prod 17(12):1251–1263. https://doi.org/10.1016/j.jclepro.2009.04.009
82. Ulrich D, Allen J, Brockbank W, Younger J, Nyman M (2021) HR transformation: building human resources from the outside in. McGraw-Hill Education
83. United Nations (2024) Take action for the sustainable development goals. United Nations. https://www.un.org/sustainabledevelopment/sustainable-development-goals/
84. Wang J, Hutchins HM, Garavan TN (2009) Exploring the strategic role of human resource development in organizational crisis management. Hum Resour Dev Rev 8(1):22–53. https://doi.org/10.1177/1534484308330018
85. WCED - World Commission on Environment and Development (1987) Our common future. Oxford University Press, New York
86. World Economic Forum (2023) The future of jobs report 2023. World Economic Forum. https://www.weforum.org/reports/the-future-of-jobs-report-2023

87. Yin Q (2023) The impact of green human resource management on organizational performance. Frontiers Business Econ Manag 5(1):1–9. https://doi.org/10.3389/fbuse.2023.1018239
88. Zilber A (2022) Four-day work week pilot set to kick off in UK. The New York Post. https://nypost.com/2022/01/18/four-day-work-week-pilot-set-to-kick-off-in-uk/
89. Zulkarnaini NA, Shaari R, Sarip A (2019) Crisis management and human resource development: towards research agenda. Int Conf Appl Human Factors Ergon 1(1):1001–1009
90. Vadithe RN, Kesari B (2023) Human resource analytics on talent acquisition: A systematic review. J Dev Econ Manag Res Stud 10(18):30–39
91. Guglielmino LM, Guglielmino PJ (2008) Productivity in the workplace: The role of self-directed learning and the implications for human resource management. Int J Hum Resour Dev Manag 8(4):293–305. https://doi.org/10.1504/IJHRDM.2008.019541
92. Rathi S, Kumar P (2023) The mediating role of job satisfaction between work-life balance and employee retention. In: Dave S, Sainy M, Sharma D, Singh A (eds) Climate change management and social innovations for sustainable global organization (pp 241–262). IGI Global. https://doi.org/10.4018/978-1-6684-9503-2.ch016

Helena Martins is a professor at the Instituto Politécnico de Setúbal where she coordinates the Bachelor's program in HRM, teaches Organizational Communication and Research Methodologies, and serves as subcoordinator of the RESILIENCE Research Center. She leads the Beyond Sustainability Trends Blended Intensive Program, addressing sustainability in organizations through a project-based learning and design thinking methodology. At the Nova School of Business and Economics, she teaches in executive programs and supervises Masters' projects. She holds a PhD in Management from the University of Porto and an MSc in Work, Organizational, and Personnel Psychology through an Erasmus Mundus program at Coimbra (Portugal) and Valencia (Spain).

With a strong focus on sustainability Helena's work emphasizes soft skills such as communication, emotional intelligence, and leadership in fostering resilience and effective decision-making during crises like economic disruptions, pandemics, and climate challenges.

Sandrina B. Moreira Sandrina Berthault Moreira research and teaching interests have focused on sustainable development | regional development and sustainability; circular economy | measurement and applications (including design thinking). Some recent work in these areas are: (i) Key-researcher on E3UDRES2 Research Centre of Excellence on Business Modeling for Managing Sustainability in a Circular and Climate Neutral Economy: Creating opportunities for Smart and Sustainable Regions, funded by Erasmus+ (2023–2027); (ii) Principal investigator at EULAC for Energy Transition: Research Infrastructure Cooperation for Energy Transition between Europe and Latin-American and the Caribbean Countries, funded by Horizon 2020 (Jan/2024-Dec/2025); (iii) Trainer for the National Energy Agency (ADENE, Portugal) on Environmental, Social and Governance (ESG) Factors and Circular Economy in Organizations (since 2023); (iv) Guest editor of the 2023 special issue of the journal *Energies* (Q1) 'Sustainability and Circular Economy Applied to Energy, Entrepreneurship and Environmental Management'.

8 Decent Work and Sustainable Economic Growth—A European Perspective

João Cerejeira and Sílvia Sousa

> *The right to decent work for all, family rights and all human rights be respected in the life of each company, for every worker, and guaranteed by the social policies of each country.*
>
> Pope Francis in the Economy of Francesco

Abstract

The chapter explores the concept of decent work and its role in inclusive economic growth, integrating these concepts into European policies, using Portugal as a case study to assess the impact of national policies on achieving these goals. The International Labour Organization defines decent work as work that combines job creation, social protection, labour rights and social dialogue with gender equality. The United Nations' 2030 Agenda for Sustainable Development, through Sustainable Development Goal 8 (SDG 8), underscores the importance of sustainable economic growth combined with productive and decent work, recognising that economic growth alone does not guarantee the creation of quality jobs. Thus, inclusive growth, driven by policies that value fair wages and work conditions, is essential to improving social well-being. In Europe, policies such as the European Pillar of Social Rights (EPSR) reinforce the focus on quality jobs, but economic crises and inequalities threaten social contracts. In Portugal, the SDGs and the EPSR were translated into the Agenda for Decent Work and the Valorisation of Youth in the Labour Market. The country's post-crisis economic recovery was accompanied by export growth, an increase in the minimum wage, and policies aimed at reducing job insecurity and improving work-life balance. Despite Portugal's progress in the labour market, the country still faces challenges in converging with the European average regarding productivity and

J. Cerejeira (✉) · S. Sousa
EEG, University of Minho, Braga, Portugal
e-mail: joao.cerejeira@eeg.uminho.pt; ssousa@eeg.uminho.pt

B. Casais (ed.), *Integrated Science to Achieve Sustainable Development Goals*, Integrated Science 37, https://doi.org/10.1007/978-3-031-88777-2_8

investment. In conclusion, the chapter highlights the crucial role of decent work in fostering social well-being and inclusion. While challenges remain, the coexistence of decent work and sustainable economic growth remains a critical ambition for the future.

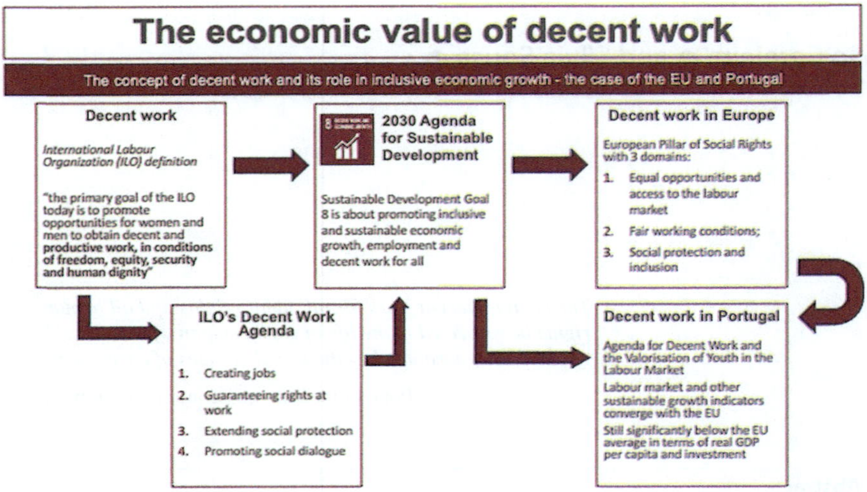

Keywords

Decent work · Quality jobs · Inclusive growth · Sustainable growth · European pillar of social rights · SDG · Social dialogue · Social protection · Fair wages

1 Introduction

Since the eighteenth century, particularly with the advent of the Industrial Revolution and the rise of capitalism, work has become a central aspect of people's lives and of the organization of societies. Paid work now takes up most of the time and energy of many individuals; a person's profession often dictates their salary, influences their social interactions and shapes their self-image. Additionally, societies are structured around paid work: the education system is designed to prepare young people for the workforce and time schedules are organized according to working hours. In contemporary societies, work plays a crucial role both individually and collectively. While the realm of work has become separate from other life spheres — such as family, community, and leisure — it continues to impact these areas significantly. Thus, work is not only the primary income source for most citizens but also a means of socialization. Production of goods and services always involves a division of labour and, therefore, interdependence between several workers, where each worker depends on the work of the others to perform their duties and satisfy their needs [15]. The work environment is, hence, important and needs to be addressed in developing and developed countries, independently of their specificities.

The importance of working conditions led to the establishment of concepts such as job quality or decent work, which are crucial for analysing the impact of working conditions or workers' rights on economic growth [13]. Global policy decision-makers have placed these issues at the centre of their priorities, with important strategic commitments being adopted across the globe, such as the Decent Work Agenda, coexisting with broader commitments, such as the Agenda for Sustainable Development.

The present analysis addresses the importance of decent work and inclusive growth, emphasizing that employment is not only a source of income but also vital for well-being, dignity, and social inclusion. It underscores the need for policies that create quality jobs, reduce inequality and ensure adequate working conditions for all. Focusing on the EU, the analysis tries to understand how these concepts were included in the main strategic documents, becoming an inexorable commitment across Europe. A closer look at the Portuguese, motivated by the country's specificities concerning the 2009 economic crisis, proposes evaluating the instruments implemented and the success attained. The conclusion draws on the possibility and the nature of a relationship between decent work and sustainable economic growth.

2 Decent Work and Inclusive Growth

For most people, employment is the primary source of income and the most significant factor affecting living standards. A job alone may not provide enough economic security, especially in cases of low pay. Therefore, generating a sufficient income through work is essential. Research from both quantitative and qualitative studies consistently shows that increasing income from work is the main factor in reducing poverty. This can occur through moving from a low-paying job to a higher-paying job or earning more within the same job. A higher income enables individuals to consume more goods and services, improving their overall quality of life.

The impact of employment on an individual's standard of living is multifaceted. It involves not only the provision of income but also enhancements to life satisfaction and personal well-being. Having a job can provide a sense of dignity by meeting family needs, fostering a professional identity and contributing to an improved social status. Furthermore, employment offers a sense of purpose and fulfillment and essential opportunities for social interaction. As a result, employed individuals typically experience higher levels of life satisfaction than those unemployed.

While there is a general consensus on the importance of working conditions for employee's well-being, establishing objective and universally applicable minimum standards for job quality is challenging. The challenge is not only the definition of a good job or the quality of work and employment but also how to measure those concepts. These vary according to the units of analysis and the extent of the domains included.[1]

[1] See Green [11] for a deep analysis of the concepts in the context of decent work.

Table 8.1 Strategic objectives of the ILO's Decent Work Agenda

1. Creating jobs	Foster an economy that generates opportunities for investment, entrepreneurship, skills development, job creation, and sustainable livelihoods.
2. Guaranteeing rights at work	Ensure recognition and respect for workers' rights. It is essential that all workers, particularly those who are disadvantaged or in poverty, have representation, participation, and laws that serve their interests.
3. Extending social protection	Promote inclusion and productivity by providing men and women with safe working conditions, adequate time off, and consideration for family and social values. This objective also ensures adequate compensation for lost or reduced income and access to necessary health care.
4. Promoting social dialogue	Involve strong and independent workers' and employers' organizations to enhance productivity, prevent workplace disputes, and build cohesive societies.

Source: ILO [14]

The aspiration for higher wages and enhancements in all areas of work and employment that contribute to well-being has become a primary goal for international organizations and several national governments. The International Labour Organization (ILO), a branch of the United Nations, declared that "decent work" was "... the most widespread need, shared by people, families and communities in every society, and at all levels of development ..." and went on to announce that "the primary goal of the ILO today is to promote opportunities for women and men to obtain decent and productive work, in conditions of freedom, equity, security and human dignity" [ILO 13, p.3]. The ILO has developed an agenda (the Decent Work Agenda (DWA)) for the work community, looking at job creation, rights at work, social protection and social dialogue, with gender equality as a crosscutting objective. The Decent Work Agenda is structured around four strategic objectives, presented in Table 8.1.

The concept of "decent work" is the most comprehensive, encompassing jobs, workers, the labour market and other society-level features and became a central focus in policy discussions following the agreement by the Heads of State at the United Nations, in 2015, on the 2030 Agenda for Sustainable Development [21], which succeeded the Millennium Development Goals. The UN Sustainable Development Goals 2030 (SDGs) include a specific goal on employment promotion and decent work, namely the Sustainable Development Goal 8 (SDG 8), which aims to "promote sustained, inclusive, and sustainable economic growth, full and productive employment, and decent work for all" [21].

The SDG 8 highlights the importance of linking employment with economic growth. This dual emphasis acknowledges both their interconnection and the reality that growth alone does not guarantee adequate employment opportunities. According to SDG 8, adequate employment encompasses both quantitative and qualitative dimensions. Specifically, employment should be: (i) "full," ensuring that anyone in the workforce willing to work has access to job opportunities; (ii) "productive", meaning that income from work is adequate to lift workers and their dependents above the poverty line; and (iii) "decent," reflecting the ILO's concept of decent work, which states that working conditions are grounded in four pillars (Table 8.1). Employment-related targets are not limited to SDG 8 but are also incorporated into many other SDGs. Moreover, several overarching principles of the SDGs implementation will have an impact on employment promotion interventions (see European Commission: Directorate-General for International Cooperation and Development [10], p. 2:17).

Inclusive growth refers to "... people's ability to participate in and benefit from wealth and job creation ..." (European Commission [9], p. 7). Based on the above definitions, inclusive growth is intrinsically linked to employment. Employment acts as the main transmission mechanism between economic growth and improving living standards for society (rather than focusing primarily on, for example, income redistribution). This transmission mechanism, of course, can only be effective if large parts of society have access to it, i.e., if there is widespread participation in the labour market and, ideally, no one is excluded against their will. The concept of inclusive growth is thus intrinsically linked to two other key objectives: equality (or reduced inequality) and social justice. In addition to promoting the existence of jobs, inclusiveness and "healthy" levels of inequality require systems that protect people from shocks and unethical working conditions and assist them in their transition or reintegration to work, as well as adopting redistributive policies (e.g. social assistance transfers) [5]. This is the role of labour regulation and policies, as well as of social protection systems.

The link between employment and inclusive growth depends on the ability of the economic system to increase a supply of "good jobs", as defined by Rodrik and coauthors as "... jobs that provide a middle-class living standard, a sufficiently high wage, good benefits, reasonable levels of personal autonomy, adequate economic security, and career ladders ..." (Rodrick and Sabel [20], p. 825). These authors also report a decrease in the share of jobs for medium-skill occupations, as well as rising spatial inequality, declining job stability, greater self-reported economic insecurity, and declining middle-class income shares [3, 8, 16].

The failure to generate good jobs has significant economic, social, and political costs. First, the polarization of the labour market, with the decline of middle-wage jobs and the increase of low- and high-wage jobs, leads to a lower spread of innovation from the more advanced sectors and firms to the rest of the economy through the creation of more productive jobs in the middle of the skill distribution, that may be related to the slowdown in U.S. and Europe aggregate productivity. Second, the scarcity of good jobs is linked to social problems such as family restructuring, dependency and crime, where communities affected by middle-class job losses suffer from social problems such as unemployment, male mortality, and the rise of single-parent families. Third, the scarcity of good jobs leads to the rise of populist movements and political polarization. Rodrik [18] points out that these negative costs associated with the lack of good jobs are externalities that private employers have no incentive to consider. This justifies the need for industrial policies that actively promote the creation of good jobs, similar to the traditional argument for industrial policies based on technological, learning and national security externalities.

Rodrik [18] proposes a comprehensive industrial policy strategy focused on the productive sector of the economy, aiming to increase the availability of "good jobs" by combining skill training programs with support for firms [20], improving the demand side of the labour market as well as the supply side. Good jobs require good firms, and vice versa. Active labour market policies aimed at enhancing skills and employability must expand to include partnerships with firms that explicitly focus on creating good jobs [19]. Industrial and regional policies, which currently emphasize tax incentives and investment subsidies, should shift toward providing tailored business services and amenities to maximize job creation [4]. Innovation policies have to be restructured to encourage the development of labour-friendly technologies [1], and international economic policies should support the upholding of robust domestic labour and social standards.

3 Decent Work in Europe

From a European perspective, it is relevant to go back to the beginning of the current century and to the Lisbon Strategy, an action and development plan set out by the European Council in Lisbon, in March 2000 for the following decade. The strategy aimed at making the European Union "... the most competitive and dynamic knowledge-based economy in the world capable of sustainable economic growth with more and better jobs and greater social cohesion ...",[2] by 2010. This strategy highlighted the importance of social policy within the European context and emphasized the need to promote innovation and to invest in jobs not only in terms of the number (more) but also in terms of the quality (better) on the basis of economic growth and competitiveness. By 2010, most of its goals were not achieved, a failure for which the 2008 economic crisis has contributed decisively. It has been succeeded by the Europe 2020 strategy, another 10-year plan designed to help recover Europe from the crisis and to regain the confidence of the Europeans in the European project. It aimed at "smart, sustainable, inclusive growth"[3] with greater coordination of national and European policy. The idea of better jobs is implicit in its main targets, particularly those related to promoting the reduction of school dropouts and the rise of the proportion of adults with higher education while also promoting the rise of employment rates.

As mentioned, the final years of the Lisbon Strategy were highly affected by the economic crisis which end up influencing deeply at least the first half of the implementation of the Europe 2020 strategy. In fact, in 2013 and 2014, the ILO published several studies on the challenges faced by the European countries most affected by the international financial and economic crisis triggered in 2007 and the subsequent crisis in the Eurozone, which began in 2009. At the time, there was widespread concern about the drastic drop in the number and the quality of jobs. The ILO supports the targets of the Europe 2020 strategy, vigorously advocating the importance

[2] https://www.consilium.europa.eu/uedocs/cms_data/docs/pressdata/en/ec/00100-r1.en0.htm

[3] https://ec.europa.eu/eu2020/pdf/COMPLET%20EN%20BARROSO%20%20%20007%20-%20Europe%202020%20-%20EN%20version.pdf

of global economic policies, which promote economic recovery focused on investment, employment and social protection, together with macroeconomic policy, to achieve job creation and equitable growth.

One year later, in 2015, the UN adopted the 2030 Agenda for Sustainable Development, establishing 17 SDGs built upon the Millennium Development Goals (MDGs), which were in force between 2000 and 2015. This new Agenda, alongside continuing development priorities such as education, sets out a wide range of economic, social and environmental objectives. The European Union countries commit to this 2030 Agenda and to its full implementation, implying, among other dimensions, "to create conditions for sustainable, inclusive and sustained economic growth, shared prosperity and decent work for all".[4] This later commitment is in line with the targets of the Europe 2020 strategy, broadening the concept of better jobs to decent work, as mentioned in the previous section.

In fact, the dimensions present in the SDG 8 find additional support in the European Pillar of Social Rights (EPSR),[5] adopted at the Gothenburg Social Summit in 2017 and reaffirmed at the Porto Social Summit in 2021 [7]. The EPSR aims to increase the employment rate of people aged 20 to 64 to at least 78% and to reduce the proportion of young people aged 15 to 29 who are neither employed nor in education or training to less than 9% by 2030. This structural document for the European Union's social policies is developed around three domains: equal opportunities and access to the labour market; fair working conditions; and social protection and inclusion.

Within the first domain, the focus is on education, training and lifelong learning; equality between men and women; equal opportunities; and active support for employment. The second domain deals with: secure and adaptable employment; wages; information on employment conditions and protection in the event of dismissal; social dialogue and worker protection; work-life balance; and a healthy, safe and well-adapted work environment and data protection.

Two years after the Porto Social Summit, the European Parliament approved a Resolution on a Roadmap for a Social Europe, which aimed to reinforce the call for social rights to play a central role in future European policies, highlighting social objectives that promote collective bargaining, respect for workers' rights and the assurance of better working conditions, following the perception that the implementation of the EPSR was falling short of the expectations [7].

There is growing concern about the sustainability of Europe's social contracts, which protect citizens from socioeconomic risks. These contracts are based on an inclusive growth model characterized by a more egalitarian revenue generation and distribution approach. However, in the last decade, the consequences of the European debt crises, the economic disruption caused by the Covid-19 pandemic, the surge of inflation and the Ukraine war have put significant strain on this model. Governments have reduced social spending, resulting in higher inequality, while many citizens remain worried about potential further declines. More broadly, median income

[4] https://sdgs.un.org/2030agenda

[5] https://op.europa.eu/webpub/empl/european-pillar-of-social-rights/downloads/KE0921008ENN.pdf

growth in Europe has lagged behind its long-term trend. This economic stagnation has driven many citizens to support non-mainstream political parties and express resistance to increased migration. Consequently, trust in institutions—both national and EU-level among member states' citizens—has also diminished [2].

The McKinsey Global Institute research in 2018 identified six global trends that are coming of age at the same time that put upward pressure on inequality [6]. These trends are the following: (i) ageing demographics; (ii) digital technology, automation, and artificial intelligence (AI); (iii) increased global competition; (iv) migration; (v) climate change and pollution; and (vi)shifting geopolitics. The ultimate impact of these megatrends on inclusive growth will depend on how actively European policymakers respond to them, either to seize positive opportunities or to mitigate potential negative effects. However, as noted by Pissarides and Bughin [17], even with the implementation of necessary policies, rising inequality in Europe seems inevitable due to concurrent forces. For example, digital technology and AI are likely to exert downward pressure on wages for routine jobs while rewarding higher-skilled workers with wage premiums. Similarly, the transition to a circular economy could disproportionately impact certain sectors, such as manufacturing, more than others. These challenges must be addressed without exception, and the most effective—and essential—response involves investing in skills, creating new models of workforce participation, and fostering innovation. Only through these measures can Europe achieve inclusive growth in the medium term.

To assert the importance of SDG 8, which aims at promoting sustained, inclusive, and sustainable economic growth, full and productive employment, and decent work for all, in Europe, the analysis focuses on a specific country, namely Portugal. The idea is to offer a quantitative approach to its performance compared to the European Union's, alongside a description of the country's context as well as the identification of a selection of policy measures that were designed and implemented to serve that specific SDG.

4 The Portuguese Case

Among the European Union countries, Portugal was one of most affected by the economic crisis, requiring the intervention of international organizations through a financial assistance program. However, while other countries affected by the crisis barely managed to benefit from the recovery in economic growth in Europe by the end of the last decade, Portugal was considered an interesting case due to the rapid recovery of its economy and labour market, without compromising workers' rights [12]. The evidence points to the creation of almost half a million new jobs since the beginning of the recovery and an average economic growth of 2%—and with an increasing trend—in the second half of the last decade. However, it is the way in which these results were achieved that makes the Portuguese case special. Factual evidence from the experiences of other countries demonstrates that fiscal consolidation alone cannot recover a declining economy. Instead, when countries move beyond the application of fiscal consolidation policies, strong and inclusive growth based on universal principles of decent work is possible. Portugal's recovery was based on solid export performance, business reforms and structural changes introduced over two decades, from the mid-nineties, and an increase in domestic demand based on income support measures and minimum wage increases in those later years (ILO,2018). Increasing workers' income is not only good for workers—as it reduces their risk of poverty—but also has a cumulative positive effect on the whole economy. Furthermore, the ILO's analyses of Portugal's recovery suggest that the easing of the labour market through legislation aimed at weakening collective bargaining and reducing employment protections—which was a condition of the financial assistance program—did little to contribute to the economic recovery. In fact, there seem to be positive effects resulting from the return of collective bargaining and a stronger focus on the creation of permanent and well-protected jobs in the country since 2015. Portugal has demonstrated that the adoption of measures aimed at promoting employment-oriented policies and protecting social cohesion, policies aligned with SDG 8 and the EPSR, helped speed the recovery [12].

In Portugal, the SDGs and the EPSR were translated into the Agenda for Decent Work and the Valorization of Youth in the Labour Market, presented in 2021, and transformed into Portuguese law in 2023.[6] The Agenda for Decent Work results from the analysis of the current economic circumstances and the work context, as well as a negative assessment of the results of a more liberalizing trend that has been present in recent decades.

The Agenda for Decent Works was then developed around the following set of objectives: to combat precariousness and to promote the valorization of wages; to value young people in the labour market; to promote a better professional, personal and family balance and to promote equality in the labour market between men and women; to promote collective bargaining and workers participation; and to strengthen monitoring mechanisms of legal compliance.

To accomplish these objectives, a set of measures was designed and started to be implemented to fight precariousness and support young workers, combat unjustified temporary work, and protect the platform and domestic workers. Concerns about situations of discrimination are addressed through the clarification that the right to equal access to employment and at the workplace also applies in the case of decision-making based on algorithms or other artificial intelligence systems, as well as concerns about the information provided to workers.

In the context of promoting better professional, personal and family balance and equality in the labour market between men and women, changes concerning parental leave, sick leave and family support were introduced, as well as measures recognizing a set of rights for the informal caregivers.

Finally, regarding promoting collective bargaining and worker participation, new measures were designed to create incentives for both firms and workers to be involved in social dialogue. The Agenda for Decent Work is, therefore, a crucial instrument to implement SDG 8 and the EPSR in Portugal.

[6] Law 13/2023, April 3.

Table 8.2 Eurostat SDG indicators for SDG 8

SDG / Sub-theme	Indicator	Unit
Sustainable economic growth	Real GDP per capita	EUR per capita, chain-linked volumes (2010)
	Investment share of GDP	% of GDP
	Material footprint	Tonnes per capita
Employment	Employment rate	% of population aged 20 to 64
	Long-term unemployment rate	% of population in the labour force
	Young people neither in employment nor in education and training (NEET)	% of population aged 15 to 29
	Gender gap for being outside the labour force due to caring responsibilities	Percentage points, persons aged 20 to 64
Decent work	Fatal accidents at work	Number per 100,000 workers
	In-work at-risk-of-poverty rate	% of population aged 18 or over

Source: Eurostat, Sustainable development in the European Union: monitoring report on progress towards the SDGs in an EU context—2024 edition. Available at: https://ec.europa.eu/eurostat/en/web/products-flagship-publications/w/ks-05-24-071

Since 2017, Eurostat has prepared annual reports monitoring the progress towards the SDGs in the EU context. These reports present an objective assessment of whether the EU — according to the selected indicators — has progressed towards the SDGs over the past 15-year period based on the official EU SDG indicator set.[7] Monitoring SDG 8 in an EU context involves looking into trends in the areas of sustainable economic growth, employment and decent work. The set of the leading indicators to monitor the SDG 8 is presented in Table 8.2.

To evaluate Portugal's performance in this matter, the above set of indicators was analysed and compared to the European Union's.

Portugal tends to perform well concerning the employment rate, either in absolute terms or compared to the EU. Recalling the objective for the employment rate in the Europe 2020 strategy (75%), the Portuguese data shows a very positive performance (and trend) of this indicator (see Fig. 8.1).

Analysing other labour market indicators, such as the long-term unemployment rate (see Fig. 8.2) or the proportion of young people neither in employment nor in education and training (NEET) (see Fig. 8.3), it is possible to gain an idea of the dynamics of the labour market and the level of attractiveness. Despite showing a positive trend with a reduction in the long-term unemployment rate, Portugal still has a higher proportion of long-term unemployed individuals in the labor market compared to the EU. Additionally, the decrease in this percentage has not been as significant as it has been in the EU.

[7] See: https://ec.europa.eu/eurostat/web/sdi/database

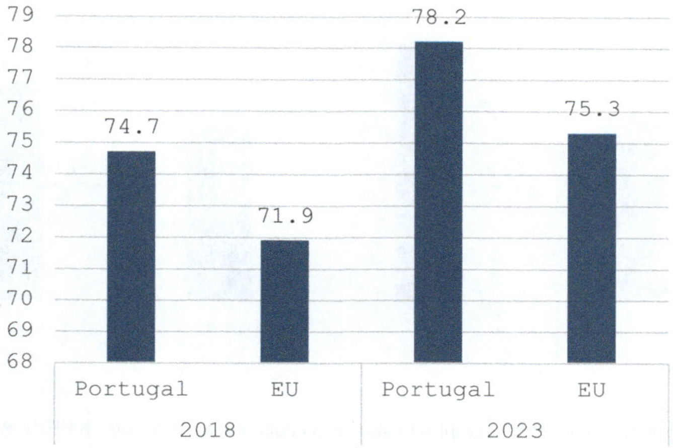

Fig. 8.1 Employment rate, Portugal and EU, 2018 and 2023. (Note: Employment rate = % of population employed aged 20 to 64. Source: Eurostat, EU SDG indicators (data extracted on 29 April 2024). Available at: https://ec.europa.eu/eurostat/web/sdi/database)

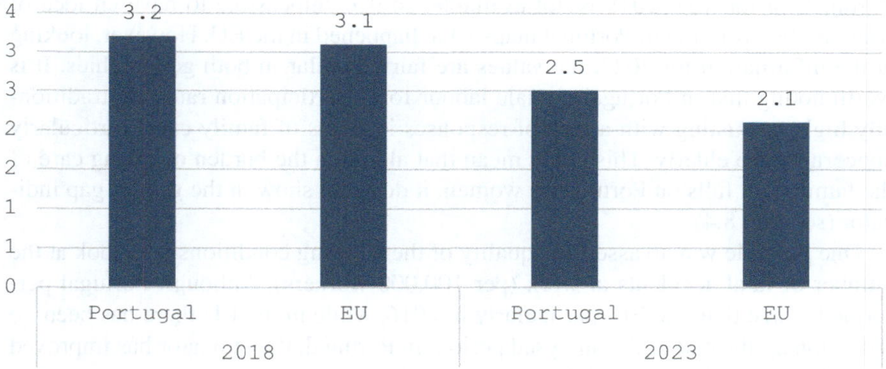

Fig. 8.2 Long-term unemployment rate, Portugal and EU, 2018 and 2023. (Note: Long-term unemployment rate = % of long-term unemployed population in the labour force. Source: Eurostat, EU SDG indicators (data extracted on 29 April 2024). Available at: https://ec.europa.eu/eurostat/web/sdi/database)

As to what concerns the proportion of the population NEET aged 15 to 29, again, the evolution is positively translated in reducing this indicator, now with Portugal showing a better performance than the EU. The extension of the age of compulsory education to 18 years old, or until the conclusion of upper secondary education (ISCED 3), by Law No 85/2009, 27 August, might have contributed to this result.

Promoting equality in the labour market between men and women goes beyond equal pay. The fact that the burden of caring for the family falls mainly on women

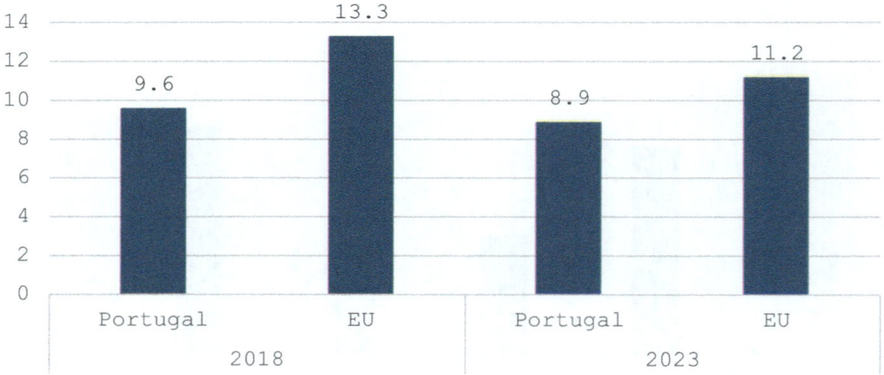

Fig. 8.3 Young people neither in employment nor in education and training (NEET), Portugal and EU, 2018 and 2023. (Note: Young people neither in employment nor in education and training (NEET) = % of population aged 15 to 29 neither in employment nor in education and training (NEET). Source: Eurostat, EU SDG indicators (data extracted on 29 April 2024). Available at: https://ec.europa.eu/eurostat/web/sdi/database)

also contributes to higher inequalities in this domain. Unfortunately, data for Portugal for the year 2018 is not available, so it is impossible to have an idea of whether the evolution in Portugal maps what happened in the EU. However, looking at the information for 2023, the values are fairly similar in both geographies. It is worth noting that in Portugal, female labour force participation rates are traditionally high, coexisting with a lack of responses in terms of family care, particularly concerning the elderly. This could mean that although the burden of taking care of the family still falls on Portuguese women, it does not show in the gender gap indicator (see Fig. 8.4).

One possible way to assert the quality of the working conditions is to look at the number of fatal accidents at work (per 100,000 workers). Although Portugal performed worse than the EU, particularly in 2016, while in the EU there has been no reduction by the end of the analysed period, in Portugal, the indicator has improved strongly, converging to the EU average (see Fig. 8.5).

The workers' income, deriving from participating in the labour market, should be enough to offer a decent life and level of well-being. Nevertheless, there is evidence of an employed population in Europe whose labour income does not allow individuals to meet their needs. To measure this phenomenon, data on being in work and at risk of poverty is analysed for the population aged 18 or over (see Fig. 8.6).

According to the data for 2017 and 2022, there is an improvement in the workers' living conditions, particularly in the EU, where the indicator decreased by 1 p.p. whereas in Portugal it only decreased by 0.5 p.p.. In 2022, still more than one-tenth of the Portuguese working population was at risk of poverty.

In Portugal, the commitment to SDG 8 and decent work is present in the Portuguese Agenda for Decent Work with a strong focus on young workers. In general, looking at the selected labour market indicators, the Portuguese performance is

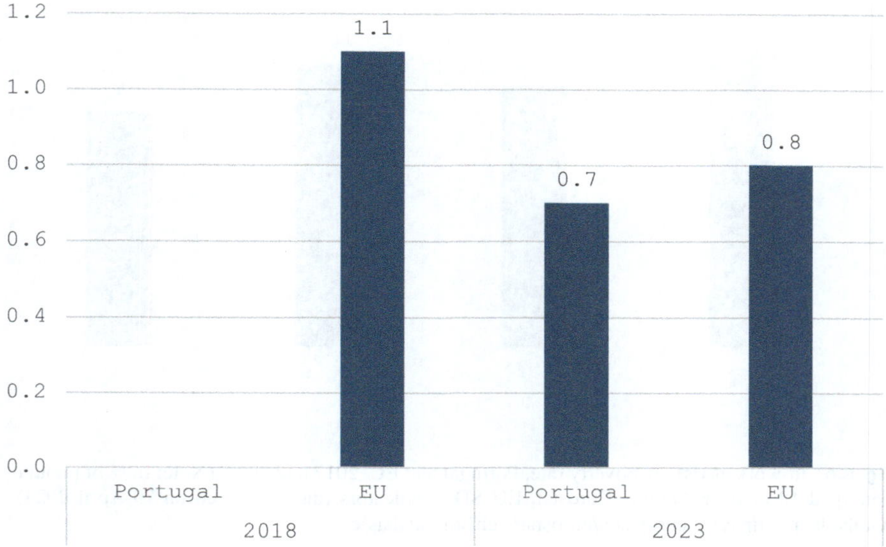

Fig. 8.4 Gender gap for being outside the labour force due to caring responsibilities, Portugal and EU, 2018 and 2023. (Note: In percentage points, persons aged 20 to 64. Data for Portugal is not available for the year 2018. Source: Eurostat, EU SDG indicators (data extracted on 29 April 2024). Available at: https://ec.europa.eu/eurostat/web/sdi/database)

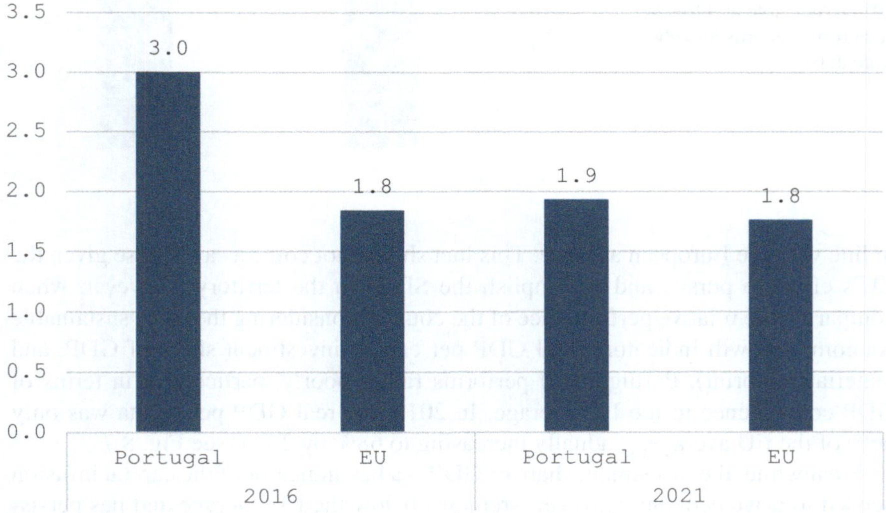

Fig. 8.5 Fatal accidents at work, Portugal and EU, 2016 and 2021. (Note: Number of fatal accidents at work per 100,000 workers. Source: Eurostat, EU SDG indicators (data extracted on 29 April 2024). Available at: https://ec.europa.eu/eurostat/web/sdi/database)

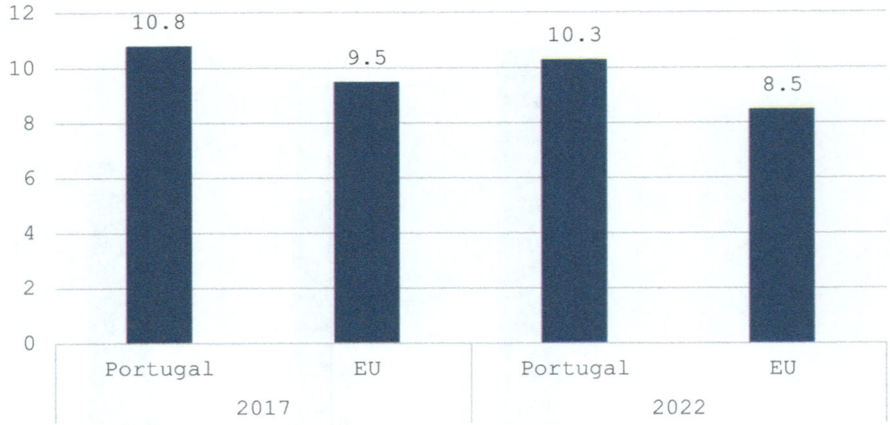

Fig. 8.6 In-work at-risk-of-poverty rate, Portugal and EU, 2017 and 2022. (Note: In % of population aged 18 or over. Source: Eurostat, EU SDG indicators (data extracted on 29 April 2024). Available at: https://ec.europa.eu/eurostat/web/sdi/databas)e

Fig. 8.7 Real GDP per capita in Portugal (EU27 = 100), 2018 and 2023. (Source: Eurostat, EU SDG indicators (data extracted on 29 April 2024). Available at: https://ec.europa.eu/eurostat/web/sdi/database)

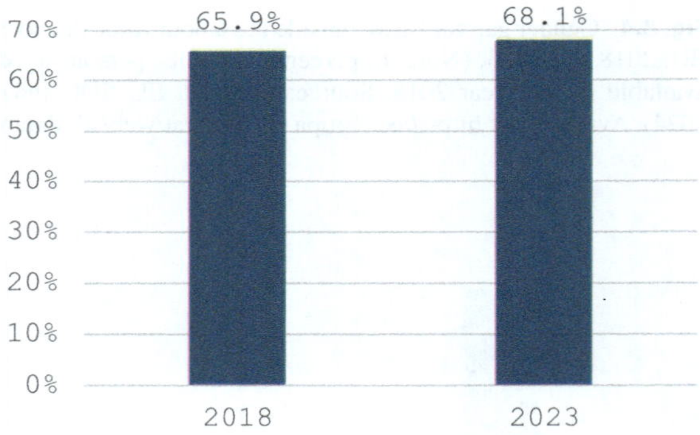

in line with the European average. This fact should not come as a surprise given the EU's effort to pursue and accomplish the SDGs in the territory. However, when comparing the relative performance of the country considering the three sustainable economic growth indicators (real GDP per capita; investment share of GDP; and material footprint), Portugal still performs rather poorly, particularly in terms of GDP convergence to the EU average. In 2018, the real GDP per capita was only 66% of the EU average, gradually increasing to 68% by 2023 (see Fig. 8.7).

Meanwhile, the investment share of GDP—a key indicator of the capital infusion needed to drive economic growth—remains below the EU average and has persistently stayed below 20% (see Fig. 8.8).

The material footprint, which measures the total amount of raw materials extracted to produce the goods and services consumed by Portugal's residents, exceeds the EU average (see Fig. 8.9). However, the gap has narrowed, decreasing from 2.7 to 2.0 tonnes per capita. Differences in material footprints between

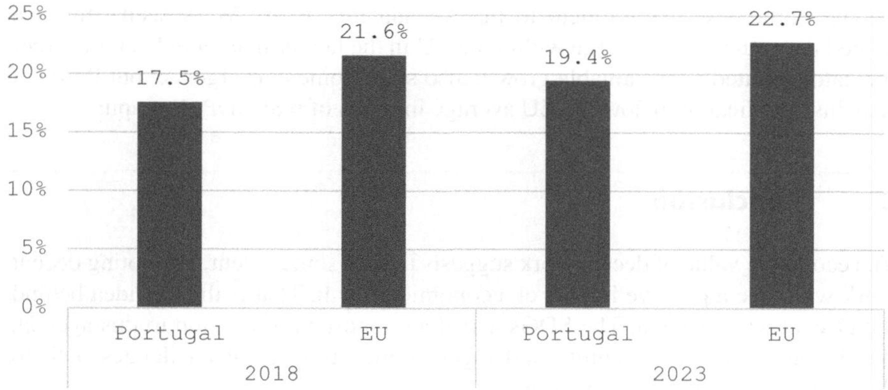

Fig. 8.8 Investment share of GDP, Portugal and EU, 2018 and 2023. (Source: Eurostat, EU SDG indicators (data extracted on 29 April 2024). Available at: https://ec.europa.eu/eurostat/web/sdi/database

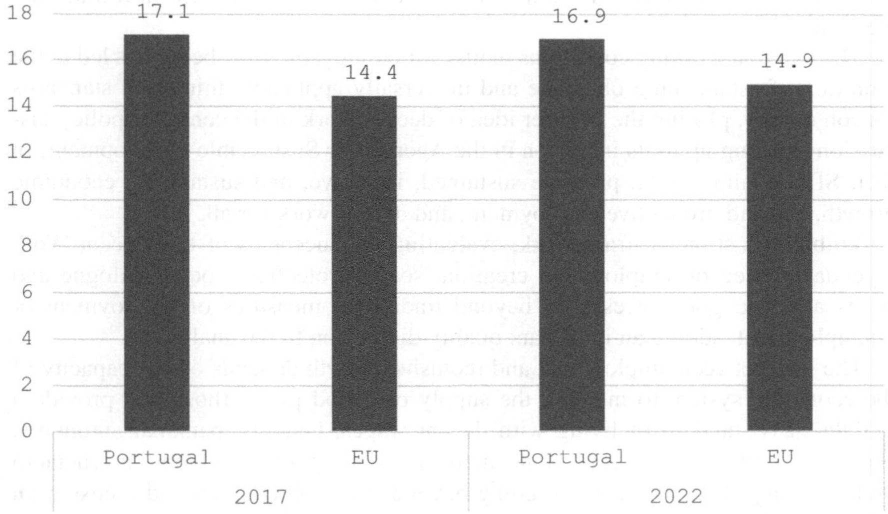

Fig. 8.9 Material footprint (tonnes per capita), Portugal and EU, 2017 and 2022. (Note: The material footprint—also referred to as raw material consumption (RMC) - represents the total amount of raw materials extracted needed to produce goods and services consumed by residents of Portugal or the EU. Source: Eurostat, EU SDG indicators (data extracted on 29 April 2024). Available at: https://ec.europa.eu/eurostat/web/sdi/database)

countries are complex to explain, as they depend on factors such as the structure and efficiency of the economy and citizens' consumption patterns. Portugal's higher material footprint might reflect a lower circular material use rate than the EU average.

The Portuguese commitment to the Agenda for Decent Work seems to have helped the country to converge within the EU in the labour market indicators. Other indicators related to sustainable growth also show some convergence, but Portugal remains significantly below the EU average in terms of real GDP per capita.

5 Conclusion

The economic value of decent work suggests that, to some extent, promoting decent work will have a positive impact on economic growth. That is the key idea behind the Decent work agenda. The SDGs added an important dimension to this agenda, the dimension of sustainability and together they pose great challenges both to developing and developed countries.

The relevance of work goes beyond being the primary source of income for most people. Labour market participation is an important means of socialization and being employed is associated with a variety of non-material benefits, e.g., enhanced self-esteem. It is well established that higher income levels enable individuals to consume more and, therefore, improve their overall quality of life in a multifaceted way.

The fact that working conditions matter for employees' well-being has led to the ambition of establishing objective and universally applicable minimum standards for job quality, placing the broader idea of decent work in the centre of policy discussions leading up to its inclusion in the Agenda for Sustainable Development. In fact, SDG 8 aims to "... promote sustained, inclusive, and sustainable economic growth, full and productive employment, and decent work for all."

Within this strategic framework, evaluating the successes of the Decent Work Agenda focused on employment creation, social protection, social dialogue and rights at work, goes necessarily beyond traditional measures of employment or unemployment, adding an important quality dimension to the analysis.

The link between employment and inclusive growth depends on the capacity of the economic system to increase the supply of "good jobs"- those that provide a middle-class standard of living with decent wages, benefits, personal autonomy, economic security and career advancement. The concept of "good jobs" is crucial to understanding the importance of going beyond mere job creation and focusing on job quality. The negative consequences of the lack of good jobs include the polarization of the labour market, social problems such as family breakdown, and the rise of populism and political polarization.

In Europe, the dimensions present in the SDG 8 find additional support in the European Pillar of Social Rights (EPSR).[8] This structural document for the European Union's social policies is developed around three domains: equal opportunities and access to the labour market; fair working conditions; and social protection and inclusion.

[8] https://op.europa.eu/webpub/empl/european-pillar-of-social-rights/downloads/KE0921008ENN.pdf

Among the European Union countries, Portugal was one of the most affected by the economic crisis and was considered an interesting case due to the rapid recovery of its economy and labour market without compromising workers' rights [12]. A country where the SDGs and the EPSR were translated into the Agenda for Decent Work and the Valorization of Youth in the Labour Market and then transformed into Portuguese law.

The Portuguese commitment to the Agenda for Decent Work seems to have helped the country to converge within the EU in the main labour market indicators. Other indicators related to sustainable growth also show some convergence, but Portugal remains significantly below the EU average in terms of GDP per capita.

Nevertheless, the complexity of the relationship between decent work and sustainable economic growth cannot shadow the importance of the coexistence of both—a great challenge, but a crucial ambition.

References

1. Aemoglu D, Restrepo P (2020) The wrong kind of AI? Artificial intelligence and the future of labour demand. Camb J Reg Econ Soc 13(1):25–35
2. Algan Y, Guriev S, Papaioannou E, Passari E (2017) The European trust crisis and the rise of populism. Brook Pap Econ Act 2017(2):309–400
3. Autor DH, Dorn D (2013) The growth of low-skill service jobs and the polarization of the US labor market. Am Econ Rev 103(5):1553–1597
4. Bartik TJ (2019) Making sense of incentives: taming business incentives to promote prosperity, WEfocus Series. W.E. Upjohn Institute for Employment Research
5. Berg J (2015) Labour market institutions: the building blocks of just societies. In: Berg J (ed) Labour markets, institutions and inequality. Edward Elgar Publishing, pp 1–36
6. Bughin J, Mischke J, Tacke T, Hazan E, Sjatil PE (2018) Testing the resilience of Europe's inclusive growth model. McKinsey Global Institute
7. EAPN Portugal (2023) Agenda do Trabalho Digno. https://www.eapn.pt/wp-content/uploads/2023/12/Documento-_-Agenda-do-trabalho-Digno_-final.pdf
8. Eurofound (2017) Income inequalities and employment patterns in Europe before and after the great recession. Publications Office of the European Union, Luxembourg
9. European Commission (2011) Increasing the impact of EU development policy: an agenda for change. Communication, COM(2011) 637 final. European Commission, Brussels
10. European Commission: Directorate-General for International Cooperation and Development (2017) Promoting employment and decent work in development cooperation. In: Volume 1, Concepts and foundations. Publications Office. https://data.europa.eu/doi/10.2841/335227
11. Green F (2021) Decent work and the quality of work and employment. In: Zimmermann KF (ed) Handbook of labor, human resources and population economics. Springer Cham, pp 1–39
12. ILO (2018) Trabalho Digno em Portugal 2008–2018—Da crise à recuperação. https://www.ilo.org/sites/default/files/wcmsp5/groups/public/@dgreports/@dcomm/@publ/documents/publication/wcms_647524.pdf
13. International Labour Organization (1999) Decent work: report of the director-general at 87th session
14. International Labour Organization (2013) Mainstreaming decent work in European Commission development cooperation - toolkit: guidance on monitoring employment and decent work in developing countries. ILO, Geneva
15. Lopes H, Cerejeira J (2023) Economia do Trabalho—Mercados e Instituições, Almedina
16. OECD (2019) The future of work: OECD employment outlook 2019. OECD Publishing, Paris

17. Pissarides C, Bughin J (2019) Testing the resilience of Europe's inclusive growth model. VoxEU Column. https://cepr.org/voxeu/columns/testing-resilience-europes-inclusive-growth-model
18. Rodrik D (2022) An industrial policy for good jobs. Hamilton Project—Policy proposal. Brookings Institution, Washington, DC
19. Rodrik D, Sabel C (2020) Building a good jobs economy. Harvard Kennedy School, John F. Kennedy School of Government, Cambridge
20. Rodrik D, Stantcheva S (2021) Fixing capitalism's good jobs problem. Oxf Rev Econ Policy 37(4):824–837
21. UN (United Nations) (2015) Transforming our world: the 2030 agenda for sustainable development. General Assembly Resolution A/RES/70/1

João Cerejeira holds a PhD in Economics at the European University Institute (Florence). He is currently an Assistant Professor at the School of Economics, Management, and Political Science at the University of Minho and a member of the Center for Research in Economics and Management (NIPE), and a research affiliate of the Centre for Research in Higher Education Policies (CIPES). His main research areas are labour and education economics and program evaluation. His advising experience includes policy-oriented reports on the economic impact of climate change, impacts of cultural events, or evaluation of labour market policies for the Portuguese Government and for the International Labour Organization (ILO), as well as for private companies and non-profit organizations. He has published in referred journal articles and several chapters and books.

Sílvia Sousa is an Assistant Professor at the School of Economics, Management, and Political Science at the University of Minho and a member of the Center for Research in Economics and Management (NIPE). She holds a PhD in Economics from the European University Institute, Florence, and teaches and researches in Labour Economics, Social Economics and Social Policy. She has published articles in scientific journals, such as the International Journal of Management and Education, Economic Analysis and Policy, and Economics and Politics, being the author and co-author of book chapters. She participated in research projects financed by external entities, such as the Foundation for Science and Technology, Portugal, and in consultancy activities for mainly Portuguese public institutions.

Developing Sustainable Business Models for the Fashion Industry: A Comprehensive Value Perspective

9

Isabela Casares Araújo
and José Carlos M. Rodrigues de Pinho

Abstract

The fashion industry is undergoing a significant transformation driven by sustainability demands and regulatory changes prompted by environmental concerns such as resource depletion, pollution, and unethical labor practices. Addressing these challenges requires the industry to adopt sustainable business models that integrate economic, social, and environmental considerations. This chapter investigates the development and implementation of Sustainable Business Models within the fashion industry, emphasizing their potential to align with the rising consumer demand for ethical practices and drive long-term success.

The research proposes a comprehensive 3D SBM framework that examines value from creation, capture, and delivery perspectives. Drawing on data from various stakeholders in the fashion industry, focusing on Portugal, the study provides insights applicable across different contexts. It highlights a network perspective on value within the broader ecosystem in which businesses operate. The study underscores the critical role of SBMs in transforming the fashion industry by addressing sustainability challenges and meeting regulatory and societal demands. The proposed Ecosystemic Business Model emerges as a versatile

I. C. Araújo
School of Economics, Management and Political Science, University of Minho, Braga, Portugal
e-mail: pg39698@alunos.uminho.pt

J. C. M. R. Pinho (✉)
School of Economics, Management and Political Science, University of Minho, Braga, Portugal

iBMS – Center for Research in Business, Markets & Society, University of Minho, Braga, Portugal
e-mail: jcpinho@eeg.uminho.pt

B. Casais (ed.), *Integrated Science to Achieve Sustainable Development Goals*, Integrated Science 37, https://doi.org/10.1007/978-3-031-88777-2_9

framework adaptable to various industry contexts, promoting long-term success, resilience, and innovation. This approach ensures the sustainable growth of fashion companies and enhances their competitive edge in an increasingly conscious market landscape.

Keywords

Sustainable business model · Economic · Social · And environmental pillars · Creation · Capture and delivery of value · Sustainable value · Social value · Environmental value · Economic value · Fashion industry

1 Introduction

The quest for viable and Sustainable Business Models (SBMs) in the fashion industry has become urgent in a landscape marked by increasing environmental and social awareness. Traditional Business Models (BMs) have historically prioritized economic viability at the expense of environmental and social concerns [4, 36], perpetuating unsustainable practices [23, 31]. The prevalent "take-make-dispose" approach has emphasized economic value while neglecting broader impacts. However, integrating sustainability principles into BMs has become crucial to address global challenges [3, 38].

In response to these challenges, the concept of SBMs emerges (Nidumolu et al. 2009, as cited in [15]), redefining the traditional logic of BMs by prioritizing not only profitability but also positive social and environmental impacts [17, 31]. The transition to an SBM represents a necessary adaptation and an opportunity for companies to gain long-term competitive advantage, generating value for all stakeholders [19, 59].

This chapter explores the development and implementation of SBMs in the fashion industry, a sector characterized by significant environmental impacts, high waste, and low resource efficiency. Rapid production cycles, low ethical standards, and unfair labor practices have compounded these issues, highlighting the need for models that incorporate social and environmental dimensions [23, 55, 56]. Growing consumer demand, particularly from younger generations (GenZ), for ethical and sustainable practices is driving change [16, 55]. The emergence of "sustainable fashion" emphasizes holistic design and production approaches aimed at mitigating environmental harm, promoting economic well-being, and enhancing social equity [20, 22]. However, challenges remain in measuring progress and implementing circular economy strategies [56, 63].

SBMs provide a means to address these challenges by integrating social, environmental, and economic dimensions, securing long-term success for companies and creating value for all stakeholders. Thus, this research aims to address the following research questions: **RQ1:** From a value perspective (creation, delivery, and capture), what are the implications of adopting sustainable business models that integrate the economic, social, and environmental aspects of the business? **RQ2:** How can designing and visualizing a Business Model facilitate the communication and implementation of sustainable practices within the fashion industry?

By elucidating the multifaceted impacts of SBMs on value capture, creation, and delivery, this research seeks to inform strategic decision-makers about the relevant factors for success in a fashion business model. The proposed 3D framework addresses these challenges and provides fashion companies with a roadmap for designing and implementing sustainable business models. Adapting new BMs is essential to address challenges and seize emerging opportunities in the fashion industry. The chapter proceeds by presenting its conceptual foundation, methodology, and implications for theory and practice.

2 Literature Review

9.2.1 Achieving Value: The Business Models Perspective

The concept of "Business Model" was first introduced in 1957, leading to a wide-ranging discourse, although no unified definition has emerged [1, 11, 24, 49]. BMs are typically seen as multidimensional constructs that illustrate how companies create, deliver, and capture value through interactions with customers, resources, and stakeholders [24]. While BMs differ from strategy, focusing on interlinked activities that determine a company's operations [2], success depends on understanding their interaction within a sector and their ability to create value for stakeholders [11]. A "good" BM generates more revenue than costs, fosters innovation, and builds stakeholder trust [18, 51]. Evaluating a BM's viability requires strong knowledge of market conditions and strategic synergies [33, 54]. The dynamic nature of BMs requires a holistic understanding of their functions and value propositions [7]. The success of a BM depends on its adaptability to market changes and environmental contingencies [36].

> *value is what buyers are willing to pay, and superior value stems from offering lower prices than competitors for equivalent benefits or providing unique benefits that more than offset a higher price.* ([39], ***p. 3***)

The evolving discourse on BMs highlights the significance of value creation, delivery, and capture mechanisms [1, 9, 14]. Value creation involves addressing customer needs and innovating to discover new opportunities [8, 49], requiring coordination of resources and capabilities [40]. Value delivery ensures that customer expectations are met through effective relationship management [49]. Businesses capture value by exploring new markets and revenue streams, such as Airbnb's commission-based model [6, 8]. Business model innovation (BMI) emerges as a critical factor, enabling companies to explore new value creation and capture methods [6, 8], shifting from traditional, manufacturing-based models to more collaborative, network-oriented ones [30].

2.2 Integrating Economic, Environmental, and Social Pillars in the Sustainable Business Model

Traditional business models have predominantly focused on profit, often neglecting sustainability [25]. In recent years, however, there has been growing recognition that businesses must balance economic, social, and environmental impacts to promote sustainability [15, 63]. The need to adopt more sustainable practices calls for a holistic approach that integrates all dimensions of sustainability. However, barriers such as short-termism and rigid organizational structures hinder this integration [5]. To successfully implement SBMs, companies must align economic, environmental, and social objectives and adopt an ecosystem perspective, including all stakeholders in the value chain [12].

2.3 Innovative Business Models and Integration of Sustainability

Business models are evolving in response to market shifts and environmental challenges, with traditional models increasingly seen as unsustainable [19, 42]. The rise of BMIs represents a shift towards sustainability, where innovation helps businesses adapt to environmental changes and societal needs [23]. BMIs, particularly in SBMs, focus on reducing negative environmental and social impacts while creating economic value [31]. These models consider all stages of the product life cycle, ensuring long-term success through sustainable strategies [25, 32]. Aligning SBMs with global sustainability goals, such as the UN's SDGs, ensures long-term viability and a positive societal impact [21, 41]. Policy frameworks, like the EU's Circular Economy Action Plan, promote sustainable product design and circular business models [58]. Denicolai et al. [12] stress that SBMs succeed when they adopt an ecosystem approach, considering all stakeholders in the value chain, which helps businesses achieve long-term resilience. Rising consumer demand, especially from younger generations, also drives companies to integrate sustainability into their models [10]. This shift reflects a changing entrepreneurial mindset where sustainability and innovation are key to long-term success.

2.4 Integrating Social Concerns into Business Models

Successfully adopting SBMs requires overcoming internal resistance and aligning sustainability initiatives with financial performance metrics [10]. Integrating social concerns is critical to creating value beyond profits and addressing societal needs. Companies that effectively merge social, environmental, and economic values gain a competitive edge and strengthen their resilience in dynamic markets [5]. Social entrepreneurship (SE) principles and social innovation are increasingly being adopted by companies to address environmental degradation and social inequality [37]. Unlike traditional enterprises, social businesses focus on fulfilling social missions through commercial ventures [46], generating social value through interactions among various stakeholders [43, 44]. SE introduces new value to society by addressing specific social issues, functioning as a form of social transformation [27, 48]. These ventures combine social and commercial missions to create value for society, individuals, and the business [45]. While social value creation is important, financial returns remain essential, requiring new business models to innovate and generate value aggregation [24].

In summary, this section highlights the evolution of business models to address modern challenges, emphasizing the need for sustainability and innovation. It underscores the importance of integrating social, environmental, and economic concerns into business models to create value that benefits both companies and society. Innovative business models demonstrate how companies can balance competitive advantage with positive social and environmental impact, emphasizing the growing importance of sustainability in today's business landscape.

3 The Fashion Industry: Exploring New Areas Within the Business Model

Integrating social, environmental, and economic dimensions into the fashion business model is essential for creating and delivering value. This involves adopting sustainable sourcing, ethical labor standards, and minimizing carbon footprints, which attract environmentally conscious consumers. Communicating these practices transparently to customers helps reinforce the brand's commitment to social and environmental responsibility. Value capture in this context is derived from positive environmental and societal impacts. The fashion industry's increasing focus on these dimensions is key to adopting sustainable practices that align with both business goals and consumer expectations [34].

3.1 The Need for Sustainable Business Models in the Fashion Industry

As society evolves, existing business models in the fashion industry are becoming unsustainable [19, 42]. Todeschini et al. [50] provide insights into trends and drivers for innovative and sustainable business models in the fashion industry, identifying opportunities and challenges that will inform current research development (see Table 9.1).

The following table provides an overview of critical areas that must be addressed in the fashion industry's shift towards sustainability. It captures the complexity of integrating sustainable practices across different industry dimensions and emphasizes the need for innovative solutions and collaborative efforts.

Given the fashion industry's significant environmental impact, researchers are focusing on SBMs that address both social and environmental concerns [31]. These models aim to tackle environmental challenges and shape the industry's future by

Table 9.1 Summary of emerging trends, opportunities, and challenges in the fashion industry by Todeschini et al. [50]

Trends	**Consumer awareness**: changes in consumer habits and preferences with a focus on sustainability, driving the creation of alternatives to fast fashion.
	Emphasis on sustainability strategies: (**1**) Circular Economy; (**2**) Upcycling; (**3**) Recycling; (**4**) Vegan Production; (**5**) Transparent Communication about Working Conditions; (**6**) Fair Trade; (**7**) Sharing Economy and Collaborative Consumption; (**8**) Consumption of Second-hand Products
	Technological innovation: (**1**) Sustainable Raw Materials (e.g., organic cotton, hemp, bamboo, lyocell, and recycled fibers); (**2**) Zero Waste (minimizing material waste in clothing production); (**3**) Wearables (incorporation of technology into clothing)
Opportunities	**Corporate social responsibility:** Fairtrade, local supply chain.
	Service-based business models: The goal is to reduce production quantities and create new strategies that promote a new life for existing products.
	Utilizing consumers as "volunteers" in the business model: Incorporating strategies for upcycling and selling second-hand products.
Challenges	**Rethinking the design and production stage:** Decisions at this stage affect the product and the company's impact/benefit at various levels. This stage can address multiple dimensions, including natural dyeing methods, organic raw materials, zero-waste production, and slow fashion.
	Educating consumers for conscious consumption
	Consumer expectations regarding sustainability
	Aligning values along the supply chain: By sharing the same sustainable values along the supply chain, it is possible to develop collaborative relationships and build stakeholder commitments (e.g., for sharing capabilities, resources, and knowledge).

Source: Produced by the authors

integrating consumer behavior, sustainable design, and emerging technologies such as Industry 4.0 [29]. However, profit-driven models that focus on short-term consumer desires often hinder sustainable progress [51].

Shifting business paradigms towards sustainability requires aligning with market trends and adopting four key approaches in SBM design: (**1.**) A sustainable value proposition; (**2.**) Value creation; (**3.**) Value delivery; (**4.**) The simultaneous consideration of social, environmental, and economic benefits [31].

A major barrier to SBM adoption is the focus on short-term financial goals and rigid organizational structures, which prevent effective integration of sustainability into business models [5]. Overcoming these challenges requires cultivating supportive organizational cultures, investing in long-term sustainability, and fostering collaborative innovation. Adapting to consumer expectations and regulatory frameworks is essential for remaining competitive in the evolving global economy [5].

Consumer demand, particularly from younger generations like Gen Z, is a key driver of sustainable practices in the fashion industry. These consumers increasingly expect brands to demonstrate transparency, ethical practices, and environmental responsibility [55]. This demand pushes fashion companies to adopt SBMs to stay competitive.

Table 9.2 Contributions from literature studies on business model (BM) innovations, including their components

Study	Study type	Key features
Kozlowski et al. [22]	Tool development for sustainable fashion design	Introduces the reDesign Canvas tool for sustainable fashion design. Based on extensive literature review on SBM, SMEs, circular economy, and sustainable fashion. Focuses on consumer engagement and sustainable business behavior change. Framework consists of 12 essential components for building sustainable fashion brands.
Plé et al. (66)	Analysis of customer integration in BM	Introduces the Customer-Integrated Business Models (CIBM). Explores customers as resources in BM. Identifies different types of customer inputs and participation in value creation. Highlights the importance of aligning organizational and customer concerns.
Joyce and Paquin [20]	Triple layered BM canvas for sustainability	Introduces the Triple Layered Business Model Canvas (TLBMC). Focuses on economic, environmental, and social dimensions separately. Provides a visual framework for evaluating and integrating value creation across layers. Facilitates a holistic understanding of organizational value creation.
Evans et al. [13]	Unified perspective on sustainable BMs	Presents the BM as a sustainable value flow system. - Emphasizes economic, social, and environmental values in BM. Identifies challenges in stakeholder behavior and impact assessment. Proposes five key propositions for sustainable BM innovation.
Biloslavo et al. [4]	Value triangle BM model	Introduces the BM Value Triangle (BMVT) for co-creating value within a business ecosystem (Value Proposition Creation and Delivery Value Capture). Emphasizes circularity and societal integration in value creation. Depicts value creation as a network involving various stakeholders. Provides a visual representation of value creation through triangular components.

Source: Produced by the authors

Regulations also play a crucial role. Initiatives like the EU's Circular Economy Action Plan aim to make sustainable products the norm by promoting circular business models and sustainable product design [58]. These regulatory frameworks are pressuring companies to rethink their business models in line with new standards and consumer expectations.

The following Table 9.2 summarizes studies on BMI, providing insights into the various facets and components that will inform the development of SBMs in this research.

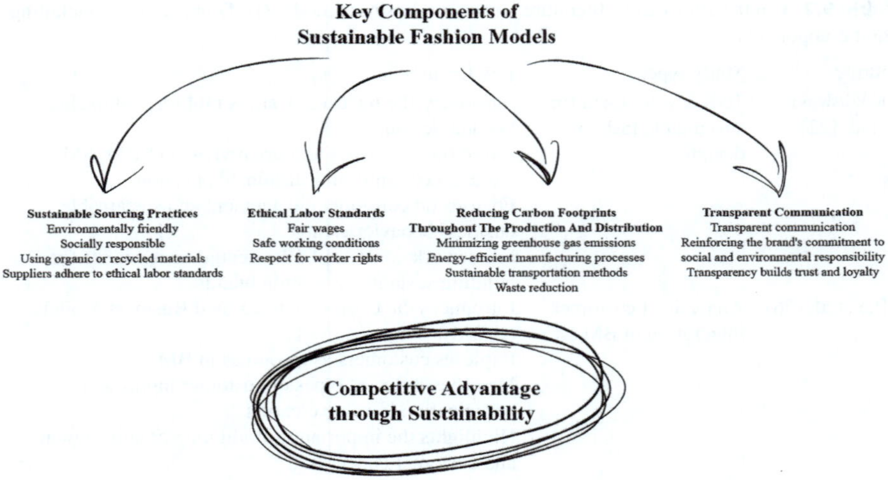

Fig. 9.1 Key components of sustainable fashion models. (Source: Produced by the authors)

To sum up, this section highlights the pressing need for sustainable business models in the fashion industry. It examines the industry's significant environmental impact and consumers' rising expectations for more responsible practices. The key components of sustainable fashion models, as illustrated in Fig. 9.1, emphasize practices such as sustainable sourcing, ethical labor standards, reducing carbon footprints, and transparent communication. These elements collectively provide businesses with a competitive advantage through sustainability, addressing both environmental and social concerns.

The section explores the potential benefits and challenges of transitioning to sustainability-focused models, emphasizing the importance of innovation in embedding sustainability throughout the value chain. We conclude that by aligning business strategies with sustainable principles, companies can not only mitigate environmental and social risks but also secure their long-term growth and competitiveness in the market. The following section delves into the evolution of the fashion industry, exploring key shifts and trends that have shaped its current landscape and the growing integration of sustainability in business practices.

4 Consumerist Model: The Evolution of the Fashion Industry

The fashion industry has undergone significant transformations since its shift from luxury goods to mass production, as described by Lipovetsky in 1987. This evolution, which spurred the rise of fast fashion, has been linked to environmental degradation, labor exploitation, and climate change [61]. Despite these challenges, fashion continues to play a critical societal role by enriching lives with beauty, driving economic growth, and fostering industrial development [23]. Historically, fashion has symbolized Western modernity and individualism, often prioritizing novelty and short-lived products [26].

Traditionally operating under a linear "take-make-waste" model, the industry prioritized economic growth over environmental and social concerns. However, growing awareness of its negative impacts has prompted a reevaluation of these practices [6]. While technological advancements and evolving consumer tastes have historically driven shorter product life cycles, current consumer demand emphasizes purpose, longevity, and accessibility in fashion items [55].

To address environmental and social challenges, the fashion industry is adopting SBMs, which emphasize a holistic ecosystem perspective. These models engage all stakeholders, including suppliers, consumers, and regulators, to create sustainable value across the entire value chain [4, 12]. However, transitioning to SBMs presents challenges such as balancing sustainability with financial goals, overcoming internal resistance, and rethinking supply chains to incorporate circular economy principles [10].

Recent developments, including forthcoming European Union regulations in 2024 targeting product design and marketing, underscore the need for industry-wide innovation and adaptation [57]. Rising consumer demand for ethical practices has further driven initiatives like sustainable fashion and the Fashion Pact, encouraging companies to align with ethical and environmental values [56, 64]. Social awareness has also motivated brands to adopt ethical business practices, support social causes, and respect human rights [23].

In summary, the fashion industry is in a transformative phase marked by digitization, sustainability demands and changing consumer preferences. The shift toward SBMs, underpinned by innovation and regulatory compliance, is essential for navigating these challenges and ensuring the industry's sustainable future [57].

5 Methodology

This study employs a qualitative research approach to explore sustainable BMs in the fashion industry, as qualitative methods are well-suited for understanding complex social phenomena [31]. The research is guided by two key questions: (1) the implications of sustainable BMs on value creation, delivery, and capture while addressing economic, social, and environmental aspects; and (2) how the design and visualization of BMs can facilitate communication and implementation of sustainable practices in the fashion sector. The study adopts Yin's [53] multiple-case study method to compare firms and extract theoretical insights for building a sustainable BM framework.

5.1 Sampling

The study employs a non-probabilistic convenience sampling approach, prioritizing accessibility and resource efficiency [28]. To ensure diversity, firms were selected based on size and sustainability practices. In total, 22 entities participated (17 Portuguese and 5 foreign firms) meeting criteria for sustainability orientation and an online presence. Respondents were selected for their relevance to the study's objectives, ensuring representation across the demographic spectrum [28].

5.2 Data Collection Methods

Following established practices (e.g., [20, 22]), data were gathered through qualitative interviews, participant observations, and document analysis. This approach aligns with Wilson's [52] emphasis on collecting rich data for theory construction. Interviews with industry professionals lasted approximately 45 min and included open-ended questions to explore their perspectives on sustainability-driven BM innovation.

Recognizing the tacit nature of knowledge surrounding BMs, the study collaborated with experts to uncover organizational dynamics and sustainability practices. Techniques such as triangulation, combining data from interviews, internal documents, annual reports, and online sources, were employed to enhance validity and reliability [53]. Ethical considerations were rigorously upheld, with participants providing informed consent and assurance that their data would be used exclusively for research purposes [28].

6 Findings & Data Analysis

This chapter identifies key elements embedded in BMs and marketing strategies of sustainable fashion businesses, based on insights from industry professionals. These findings inform the development of a model addressing the economic, social, and environmental aspects of sustainability, organized by research question.

RQ1: *From a value perspective (creation, delivery, and capture), what are the implications of adopting sustainable business models that contemplate the economic, social, and environmental aspects of the business?*

To address this RQ1, the following Research Answers (RAs) emerge from the interviews.

RA 1.1 Building Trust in the Value Network Through Economic, Social, and Environmental Relationships

Sustainable BMs rely on trustworthy relationships within the value network, characterized by shared values, ethical practices, and collaboration with stakeholders such as suppliers and communities. These relationships support organizational goals and enhance resilience by fostering loyalty and mutual benefit (see the frequency of words in Fig. 9.2). For instance, interviewees expressed the importance of these relationships with statements such as:

Fig. 9.2 Most frequently used words by interviewees in reference to the concept of Brand Community. (Source: Produced by the authors)

> *Having a close and respectful relationship (…) I highly value proximity and trust with suppliers. After all, they are crucial pillars for my company.* ***(Interviewee 11)***

> *Thezse partnerships have lasted for years. It's almost like a family.* ***(Interviewee 12)***

> *We always work with the same sole supplier, (…) it's a win-win situation for both parties.* ***(Interviewee 7)***

RA1.2 The Interplay of Social, Economic, and Environmental Relationships in Driving Business Success

A sustainable BM requires integrating social, economic, and environmental considerations. This holistic approach strengthens stakeholder relationships and aligns actions with broader sustainability objectives. Clear understanding of these values helps businesses make strategic decisions that contribute to long-term success.

Fig. 9.3 Most frequently used words by interviewees in reference to the concept of Brand Society. (Source: Produced by the authors)

NVivo analysis (see Fig. 9.3) identified "*For*" as particularly significant, indicating relationships established with specific environmental or societal goals.

RA1.3 Industry Insights on Balancing Sustainability Dimensions in Business Models

Industry professionals emphasize the need for balance among economic, social, and environmental pillars. Examples include the adoption of circular economy practices, ethical sourcing, and consumer engagement initiatives, which align these dimensions while driving innovation and brand success.

> *Effectively, I believe it's all three (economic, social, and environmental) that dictate the success of a brand aiming to enter the market.* (**Interviewee 3**)

> *I think all three have their balanced weight among them.* (**Interviewee 15**)

> *I think it's a balance (...) we will make every effort to maintain this... this concept (...) Economic balance is very important, as is the balance of location choice.* ***(Interviewee 7)***

> *I think the ideal is for these aspects to act simultaneously. (...) they all have to be on the scale. (...) Exactly, and I can't say which one is more relevant.* ***(Interviewee 5)***

These insights highlight the professionals' views on integrating all three sustainability dimensions, economic, social, and environmental, within business models, which is verified with Fig. 9.4.

RA1.4 Enhancing Value Through Data Control and Impact Management
Monitoring and reporting sustainability impacts are vital for strategic planning and stakeholder communication. Detailed reports are becoming essential for communicating sustainable practices to consumers and reflecting on the Value Network. Businesses increasingly track their environmental and social footprints alongside economic contributions, enabling a deeper understanding of their value chain and ecosystem influence.

Fig. 9.4 Most frequently used words by interviewees in reference to the brand pillars. (Source: Produced by the authors)

Impact and Benefit

The interviewed entities show a growing awareness of their impact on environmental, social, and economic dimensions, even if not all measure it with specific metrics (for additional data on the perception of "impact," see Annex A). Most have a general understanding of their environmental footprint, which informs them of sustainable practices. Economically, many prioritize supporting local industries and job creation (see Fig. 9.5).

Benefits are often seen as outcomes rather than predefined objectives, with some brands linking them to local contributions like industrial development (for additional data on the perception of "benefit," see Annex B). Increasingly, businesses monitor their impact and benefits across financial, environmental, and social dimensions. Financial returns are viewed as essential for driving innovation and supporting sustainability initiatives. Continuous tracking and reporting of impact and benefits are becoming central to future management and communication strategies.

To conclude, the findings culminate in a model illustrating how businesses create, deliver, and capture value through sustainability:

Fig. 9.5 Most frequently used words by interviewees regarding their analysis of action returns and strategies. (Source: Produced by the authors)

Value Creation: Embedding sustainable practices into production, fostering stakeholder trust, and aligning actions with environmental and social goals.
Value Delivery: Leveraging collaborative networks and transparent communication to align brand identity with sustainability values.
Value Capture: Achieving economic benefits, community development, and environmental stewardship through measurable impact and ongoing innovation.

This networked approach underscores the interconnected nature of the fashion industry and the role of collaboration in driving sustainable transformation. Integrating these dimensions ensures long-term profitability and societal relevance while aligning business practices with pressing global challenges.

7 Visualizing Sustainable Business Models: A Strategic Tool for the Fashion Industry

To address the second research question (RQ2), this section explores how BMs' design can be a powerful tool in advancing sustainability. It is important to note that this analysis is based on insights from interviews and critical analysis of different BM frameworks. Furthermore, the following proposal exemplifies how each element of the model organizes itself visually with the level of value of the company and how managers can organize their actions and think cognitively. RQ2 is the following: How can the design and visualization of a Business Model facilitate the communication and implementation of sustainable practices within the fashion industry?

To address this RQ2, the following dimensions emerge from our analysis.

Response Answer (RA) 2.1: Enhancing Stakeholder Engagement Through Narrative Visualization
Creating a visual BM is crucial for communicating complex concepts and engaging stakeholders. Narrative visualization, which combines storytelling with data visualization, enhances the understanding of intricate information and promotes reader engagement. This method proves particularly useful for addressing sustainability within the fashion industry. By visualizing how sustainable practices are embedded into business processes, the BM is a powerful communication tool supporting sustainability efforts (see Fig. 9.6: The ecosystem BM).

RA 2.2: The Ecosystemic Business Model – A Visual Framework for Sustainable Value
The proposed BM, The Ecosystemic Business Model (EBM), in this research conceptualizes the fashion industry as an "ecosystem," where each entity influences others, creating interdependent relationships [4, 62]. This ecosystem model integrates a sustainability perspective across economic, social, and environmental aspects. The BM's holistic approach aligns business actions with societal and

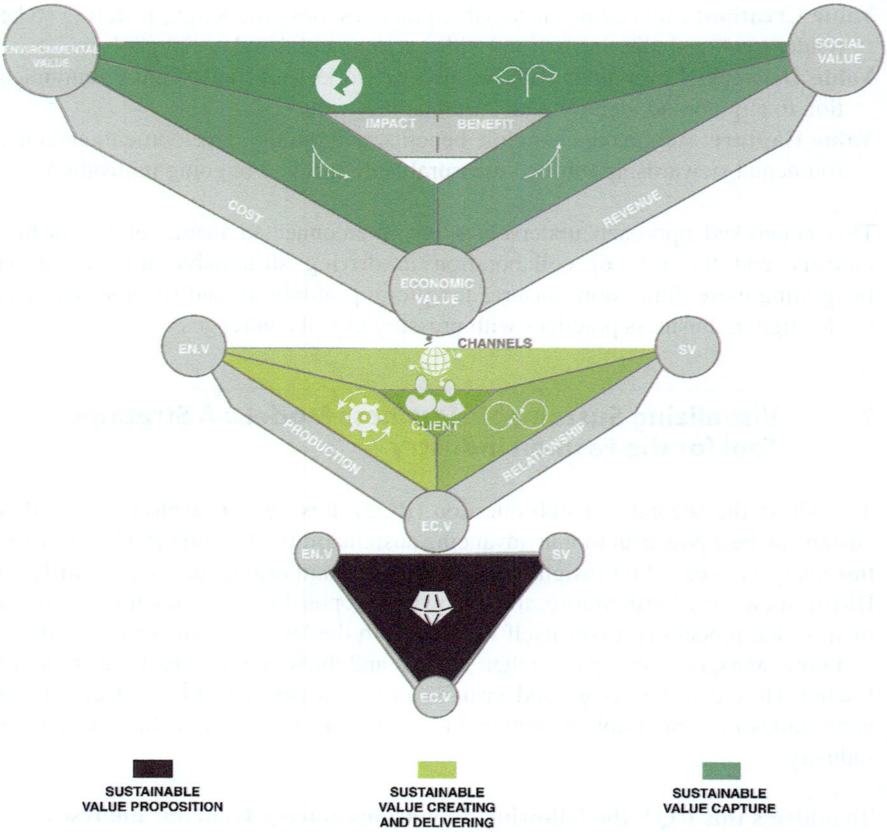

Fig. 9.6 The ecosystemic business model (EBM), 3D framework representation. (Source: Produced by the authors)

environmental goals by fostering a circular flow of value, exemplified by the principles of the circular economy. This framework (see Fig. 9.7) captures value and ensures that sustainable practices are embedded within the overall business structure [13].

RA 2.3: Structuring Sustainable Business Models Using Visual Design Principles

The 3D EBM framework model features a unique visual structure, a multi-layered inverted triangular pyramid, that organizes the business into three key levels: value proposition (foundation), value creation and delivery, and value capture (see Fig. 9.8). This structure promotes continuous communication across all elements, encouraging circular thinking that is fundamental to sustainability. The use of visual design principles like Gestalt's Proximity, Common Region, and Closure further enhances clarity by grouping and enclosing related business components, making the relationships between them intuitive and easy to perceive [47, 35]. Unlike

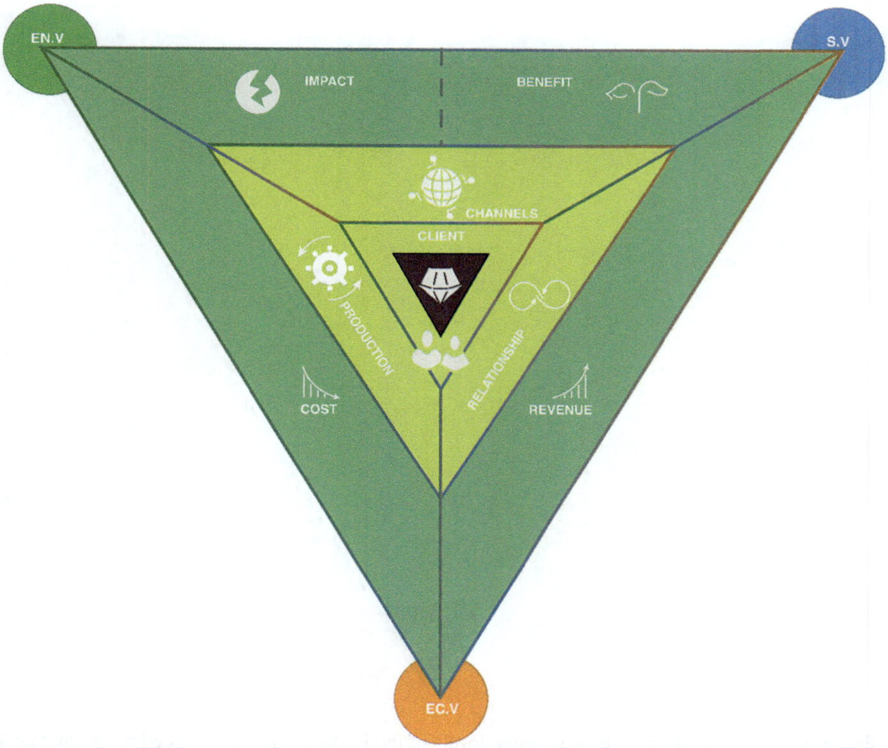

Fig. 9.7 Top view of the Ecosystemic Business Model (EBM), 3D framework representation. (Source: Produced by the authors)

traditional models, the EBM, uses an inverted triangular pyramid structure to depict hierarchical levels and continuous communication among elements, thereby enhancing visual understanding and promoting circular thinking. This design not only enhances visual understanding but also promotes circular thinking, which is integral to sustainable business practices.

RA 2.4: Horizontal and Vertical Coherence of Value Flows

The EBM facilitates a comprehensive understanding of value creation, delivery, and capture through horizontal and vertical coherence. Horizontally, it explores how value can exist through horizontal coherence within each operational level, where domains/components individually address economic, environmental, and social value [20]. Vertically, it shows how value flows up and down the hierarchy, connecting decisions and actions across different levels. The proposed value moves with organizational decisions, with its interconnected and interdependent components across levels to establish essential relationships for the entity. This coherence supports integrating sustainable practices, ensuring alignment between sustainability goals and business operations [20] (see Fig. 9.9).

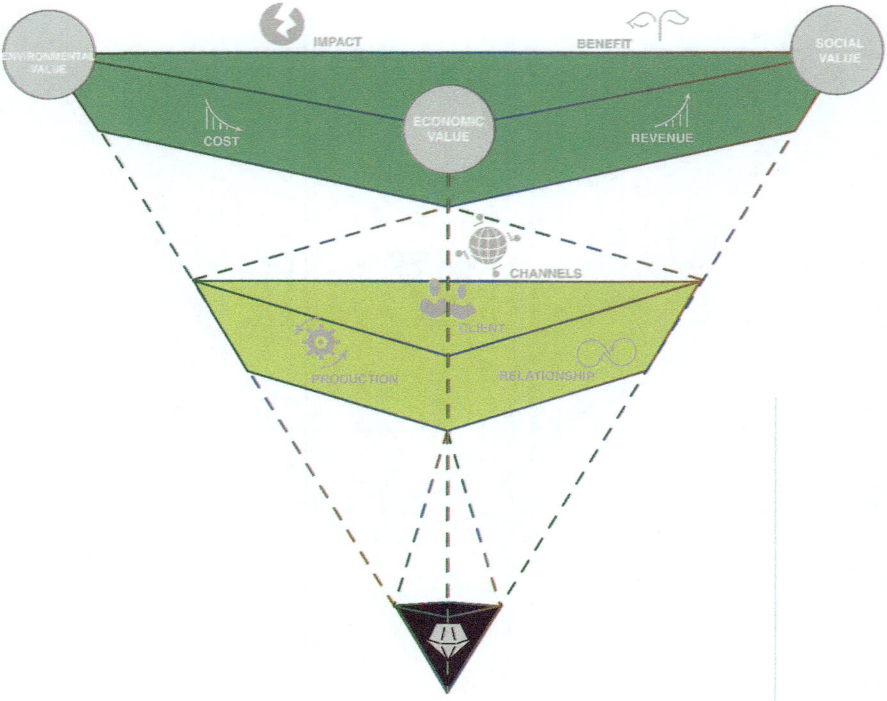

Fig. 9.8 Stratified representation of value levels of the EBM. (Source: Produced by the authors)

RA 2.5: Competitive Advantage through Sustainable Business Models

Integrating sustainability into the BM positions companies to differentiate themselves in the competitive market. As ethical consumption gains importance among consumers, brands that communicate their commitment to sustainability enjoy a competitive edge. Sustainable practices mitigate environmental impacts and promote long-term economic and social benefits. Thus, the BM enhances a company's ability to generate stakeholder value while contributing to broader environmental and societal well-being.

RA 2.6: Practical Implementation of Sustainability through Visual and Narrative Design

By transforming complex sustainability concepts into visually intuitive models, the EBM aids in the practical implementation of sustainability. The visual narrative design fosters stakeholder engagement and understanding, ensuring that sustainable practices are communicated clearly and implemented cohesively across the business and its value chain. This approach highlights how visual tools are crucial in translating sustainability from conceptual strategies to actionable business practices, contributing to the broader goal of integrating sustainable practices into the core of business operations.

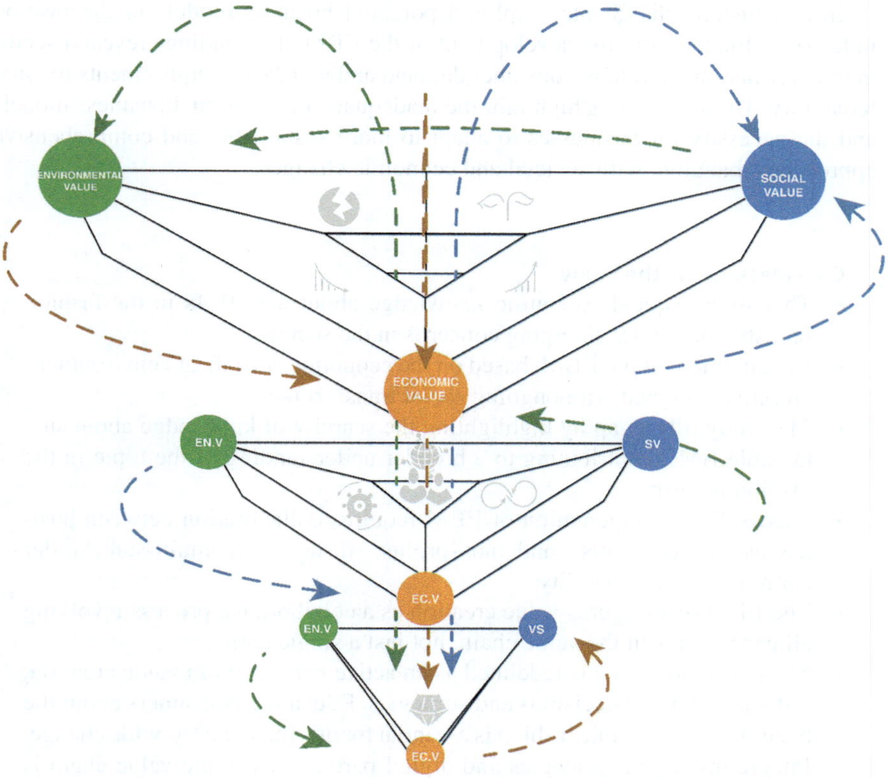

Fig. 9.9 Simulation of value flows within the value pyramid structure of the EBM. (Source: Produced by the authors)

In conclusion, the design and visualization of a BM effectively bridge the gap between conceptual sustainability and practical implementation. The EBM through its narrative visualization approach, enables businesses to communicate and implement sustainable practices within the fashion industry. By transforming sustainability into an accessible and actionable framework, the EBM empowers stakeholders to make informed decisions and ensures that sustainability is embedded into the core of the business strategy. The EBM's design fosters a shared vision among all participants, ensuring that sustainable practices are communicated effectively and implemented cohesively across the organization and its value chain.

8 Conclusion

It is not the most intellectual of the species that survives; it is not the strongest that survives; but the species that survives is the one that is able to best adapt and adjust to the changing environment in which it finds itself. (Darwin's Origin of Species).

In conclusion, this chapter explored potential business models in the fashion industry, culminating in the development of the EBM. The findings reveal a sector in transformation, driven by consumer demand and legislative requirements for sustainability. These pressures highlight the inadequacy of traditional business models and the necessity for businesses to adapt to more sustainable and comprehensive approaches that align with societal and economic changes.

Core Messages of the Study

- This study expands scientific knowledge about new BMs in the fashion industry, driven by emerging concerns in the sector.
- Development of the EBM, based on the economic, social, and environmental pillars, aligned with ongoing social transformation.
- The study fills a gap by highlighting the scarcity of knowledge about sustainable BMs, contributing to a broader understanding of the topic in the fashion industry.
- Successful implementation of EBM requires collaboration between businesses, governments, and non-profits, fostering a multi-stakeholder approach to sustainability.
- The EBM reconfigures value creation as a collaborative process involving all participants in the value chain, not just a single entity.
- The consumer's role is redefined as an active participant in value creation, influencing brand decisions and strategies. Educating consumers about the benefits of sustainable fashion is essential for driving industry-wide change.
- Integrating digital strategies and digital participants in the value chain is crucial, particularly with the rapid growth of e-commerce and social media. Leveraging platform digital tools enables fashion companies to enhance transparency, engage consumers, and streamline sustainable practices.
- Digital tools and technological innovations are crucial in supporting adopting sustainable practices in the fashion industry.
- The EBM offers users flexibility, allowing strategies to be adapted and adjusted to the company's ecosystem needs, promoting sustainable value creation.
- The findings provide actionable strategies for fashion industry practitioners and policymakers to implement sustainable business models effectively.
- This study has the potential to guide fashion industry professionals in creating long-term sustainable success, considering multiple levels of economic, social, and environmental return.

Future Studies and Limitations

- **Case Studies**: Incorporating real-world examples or case studies would help clarify the practical implications and effectiveness of the EBM.
- **Measurement and Evaluation:** Developing specific metrics to assess sustainable value capture, including financial, environmental, and social dimensions, would offer a deeper understanding of the model's impact.
- **Luxury vs. Fast Fashion:** Exploring how luxury fashion brands and fast fashion retailers apply the EBM could highlight sector-specific adaptations.
- **Scalability and Adaptability:** Investigating how the EBM can be adjusted to fit various business sizes, market segments, and geographic locations would enhance its flexibility and applicability.
- **Implementation Challenges:** Examining potential risks and challenges organizations face when adopting the EBM could provide insights into its practical limitations.
- **Risk Management:** Research could also focus on developing strategies for risk identification, assessment, and mitigation within the EBM framework.

Annexes

Annex A. Empirical Analysis of Perception of "Impact"

Understanding "impact"	Empirical analysis
They do not control the impact	*"we have no way to fully control our impact"* ***INT [9]***
For society and the environment	*"The environmental impact that our brand may have on society and the environment. (...) we are very aware of this and we have been trying to minimize it... (...) A fashion company always has this impact"* ***INT [5]***
Resulting from production	*"Our clothes are made with 96% less water than conventional clothes and we save 80% on land use. (...) measures the reduction in CO2, energy consumption, and water use with every sale (...) we control our impact by choosing partners that already have the same values and work to a high standard"* ***INT [10]*** *"(...) if a person has to buy a new piece of clothing after 1 or 2 years, the waste will be much greater (...) water consumption (...) our ideal is to have premium raw materials that (...) can last what we say is a lifetime."* ***INT [13]*** ***(...)***
Resulting from the product	*"(...) materials that have an impact in terms of CO2 emissions (...) already reduced (...) we want the product's end-of-life impact to also be minimized. (...) we have some shoes that are biodegradable (...) I know that when I make shoes from recycled bottles, I use an average of 6 to 8 recycled bottles. That's a metric (...)"* ***INT [18]*** *"large companies like Nike, Adidas (...) mostly produce in Asia, we try to reduce our environmental footprint (...) promoting the Portuguese business fabric."* ***INT [1]***

Understanding "impact"	Empirical analysis
Distribution	*"(...) an associated issue that has to do with the fact that for the pieces to reach us, there always has to be transportation (...) the issue of transport (...) the means are not as "green" (...) they are not so clean"* ***INT [19]***
What drives the project	*"how can I make a contribution that can have a positive impact, not only on the image of a sector but also on the economy and the environment in general"* ***INT [2]*** *"Especially in creating some local impact as well."* ***INT [7]***

Source: Produced by the authors

Annex B. Empirical Analysis of Perception of "Benefit"

Understanding "benefit"	Empirical analysis
Clients	"I think the benefits include having customers who feel satisfied and confident when wearing one of our pieces (...) that piece will last for many years" **INT [9]**
Environmental value	*"Linen is one of the materials we use the most (...) an amazing fiber in terms of soil recovery and the CO2 it absorbs (...)"* ***INT [14]*** *"One of the greatest benefits our business has is (...) not needing to produce, there is no need to consume natural resources..."* ***INT [19]***
Social value	*"(...) it is really about knowing that help reaches those women, that we made a difference in their lives (...) we know, for example, when we make a product donation, we know it will go to X number of people"* ***INT [17]*** *"we also share with local businesses (...) we have to understand if what we are producing brings greater benefit to society and the world (...)"* ***INT [3]***
Creating sustainability	*"We would love to be able to make sustainable clothing more affordable (...) We also work with renewable resources wherever we can"* ***INT [10]*** *"the leathers are biodegradable (...) the leathers come from the food industry cattle (...) we are using a product that is from another industry (...)"* ***INT [4]*** *"as a responsible company... we want (...) the best for our planet and society, and therefore we are constantly looking for alternatives that are more beneficial for everyone."* ***INT [6]***
Product quality	*"quality brings greater durability, and with that, people don't mind paying a price slightly above average, knowing that in the long run, it will bring benefits"* ***INT [15]***

Source: Produced by the authors

References

1. Amit R, Zott C (2001) Value creation in e-business. Strateg Manag J 22(6–7). https://doi.org/10.1002/smj.187
2. Amit R, Zott C (2012) Creating value through business model innovation. MIT Sloan Manag Rev 53

3. Barth H, Ulvenblad PO, Ulvenblad P (2017) Towards a conceptual framework of sustainable business model innovation in the agri-food sector: a systematic literature review. https://doi.org/10.3390/su9091620
4. Biloslavo R, Bagnoli C, Edgar D (2018) An eco-critical perspective on business models: the value triangle as an approach to closing the sustainability gap. J Clean Prod 174. https://doi.org/10.1016/j.jclepro.2017.10.281
5. Bocken NMP, Geradts THJ (2020) Barriers and drivers to sustainable business model innovation: organization design and dynamic capabilities. Long Range Plan 53(4):101950. https://doi.org/10.1016/j.lrp.2019.101950
6. Bocken NMP, de Pauw I, Bakker C, van der Grinten B (2014) Product design and business model strategies for a circular economy. J Ind Prod Eng 31(4):276–291. https://doi.org/10.1080/21681015.2014.883905
7. Casadesus-Masanell R, Ricart JE (2011) How to design a winning business model. Harv Bus Rev 89(1–2)
8. Chesbrough H (2007) Business model innovation: it's not just about technology anymore. Strateg Leadersh 35(6). https://doi.org/10.1108/10878570710833714
9. Chesbrough H, Rosenbloom RS (2002) The role of the business model in capturing value from innovation: Evidence from Xerox Corporation's technology spin-off companies. Ind Corp Chang 11(3). https://doi.org/10.1093/icc/11.3.529
10. Ciulli F, Kolk A (2023) International business, digital technologies, and sustainable development: connecting the dots. J World Bus 58:101445. https://doi.org/10.1016/j.jwb.2023.101445
11. DaSilva CM, Trkman P (2014) Business model: what it is and what it is not. Long Range Plan 47(6). https://doi.org/10.1016/j.lrp.2013.08.004
12. Denicolai S, Zucchella A, Magnani G (2021) Internationalization, digitalization, and sustainability: are SMEs ready? A survey on synergies and substituting effects among growth paths. Tech Forecasting Soc Chang 166:120650. https://doi.org/10.1016/j.techfore.2021.120650
13. Evans S, Vladimirova D, Holgado M, Van Fossen K, Yang M, Silva EA, Barlow CY (2017) Business model innovation for sustainability: towards a unified perspective for creation of sustainable business models. Bus Strateg Environ 26(5). https://doi.org/10.1002/bse.1939
14. Foss NJ, Saebi T (2018) Business models and business model innovation: between wicked and paradigmatic problems. Long Range Plan 51(1). https://doi.org/10.1016/j.lrp.2017.07.006
15. Garay L, Font X, Corrons A (2019) Sustainability-oriented innovation in tourism: an analysis based on the decomposed theory of planned behavior. J Travel Res 58(4). https://doi.org/10.1177/0047287518771215
16. Gazzola P, Pavione E, Pezzetti R, Grechi D (2020) Trends in the fashion industry: the perception of sustainability and circular economy: a gender/generation quantitative approach. Sustain For 12(7):2809. https://doi.org/10.3390/su12072809
17. Geissdoerfer M, Vladimirova D, Evans S (2018) Sustainable business model innovation: a review. J Clean Prod 198. https://doi.org/10.1016/j.jclepro.2018.06.240
18. Ghezzi A, Cortimiglia MN, Frank AG (2015) Strategy and business model design in dynamic telecommunications industries: a study on Italian mobile network operators. Technol Forecast Soc Chang 90(PA). https://doi.org/10.1016/j.techfore.2014.09.006
19. Jin BE, Shin DC (2020) Changing the game to compete: innovations in the fashion retail industry from the disruptive business model. Bus Horiz 63(3). https://doi.org/10.1016/j.bushor.2020.01.004
20. Joyce A, Paquin RL (2016) The triple layered business model canvas: a tool to design more sustainable business models. J Clean Prod 135. https://doi.org/10.1016/j.jclepro.2016.06.067
21. Kent D (2020) The role of SBMs in achieving the United Nations' Sustainable Development Goals. Bus Strateg Dev 3(4):423–433
22. Kozlowski A, Searcy C, Bardecki M (2018) The reDesign canvas: fashion design as a tool for sustainability. J Clean Prod 183:194–207. https://doi.org/10.1016/j.jclepro.2018.02.014
23. Lee Y-J (2012) Orgdot: a fashion and social enterprise in South Korea. J Glob Fash Market 3(1). https://doi.org/10.1080/20932685.2012.10593106

24. Li F (2020) The digital transformation of business models in the creative industries: a holistic framework and emerging trends. Technovation:92–93. https://doi.org/10.1016/j.technovation.2017.12.004
25. Linder M, Williander M (2017) Circular business model innovation: INHERENT uncertainties. Bus Strateg Environ 26(2):182–196. https://doi.org/10.1002/bse.1906
26. Lipovetsky G (1987) O Império do Efémero: a moda e seu destino nas sociedades modernas
27. Lubberink R (2019) Social entrepreneurship and sustainable development. In: Social entrepreneurship and sustainable development, pp 25–40. https://doi.org/10.4324/9781003042396-3
28. Malhotra NK, Nunan D, Birks DF (2017) Marketing research – an applied approach. In: The marketing book, 5th edn. https://doi.org/10.4324/9781315890005
29. Marques L, Pimenta M, Dias A (2020) Emerging technologies and business models in Industry 4.0. Int J Prod Econ 219:103–113
30. Nenonen S, Storbacka K (2010) Business model design: an analysis of the five key components. Int J Prod Econ 122(2):281–293. https://doi.org/10.1016/j.ijpe.2009.11.008
31. Nosratabadi S, Mosavi A, Shamshirband S, Zavadskas EK, Rakotonirainy A, Chau KW (2019) Sustainable business models: a review. Sustainability 11. https://doi.org/10.3390/su11061663
32. Nußholz JLK (2017) Circular business models: defining a concept and framing an emerging research field. Sustain For 9(10):1810. https://doi.org/10.3390/su9101810
33. Osterwalder A (2004) The business model ontology: a proposition in a design science approach. Doctoral Dissertation, Université de Lausanne. Faculté Des Hautes Études Commerciales
34. Pal R, Sandberg E (2017) Sustainability in the fashion supply chain: global practices and strategies. J Bus Res 75:162–170
35. Palmer SE (1992) Common region: a new principle of perceptual grouping. Cogn Psychol 24(3):436–447
36. Pateli AG, Giaglis GM (2004) A research framework for analysing eBusiness models. Eur J Inf Syst 13. https://doi.org/10.1057/palgrave.ejis.3000513
37. Phillips W, Lee H, Ghobadian A, O'Regan N, James P (2015) Social innovation and social entrepreneurship: a systematic review. Group Org Manag 40(3). https://doi.org/10.1177/1059601114560063
38. Pieroni MPP, McAloone TC, Pigosso DCA (2019) Business model innovation for circular economy and sustainability: a review of approaches. J Clean Prod 215:198–216. https://doi.org/10.1016/j.jclepro.2019.01.036
39. Porter ME (1985) Competitive advantage: creating and sustaining superior performance. Free Press
40. Rangaswamy A, Moch N, Felten C, Bruggen G, Wieringa J, Wirtz J (2020) The role of marketing in digital business platforms. J Interact Mark 51:72–90
41. Reichel J (2017) New business models: Research results and exemplary case studies. Humanit Soc Sci Q. https://doi.org/10.7862/rz.2017.hss.13
42. Richter M (2013) Business model innovation for sustainable energy: German utilities and renewable energy. Energy Policy 62:1226–1237. https://doi.org/10.1016/j.enpol.2013.05.038
43. Roh TH (2016) The sharing economy: business cases of social enterprises using collaborative networks. Procedia Comput Sci 91:502–511. https://doi.org/10.1016/j.procs.2016.07.012
44. Saebi T, Foss NJ, Linder S (2019) Social entrepreneurship research: past achievements and future promises. J Manag 45(1):70–95. https://doi.org/10.1177/0149206318793196
45. Seelos C, Mair J (2007) Profitable business models and market creation in the context of deep poverty: a strategic view. Acad Manag Perspect 21. https://doi.org/10.5465/AMP.2007.27895339
46. Smith WK, Gonin M, Besharov ML (2013) Managing social-business tensions: a review and research agenda for social enterprise. Bus Ethics Q 23(3):407–442. https://doi.org/10.5840/beq201323327

47. Stephen Few's work (2006) Applying Gestalt principles to improve data visualization
48. Tanimoto K (2008) A conceptual framework of social entrepreneurship and social innovation cluster : a preliminary study. Hitotsubashi J Commerce Manag 42(1)
49. Teece DJ (2010) Business models, business strategy and innovation. Long Range Plan 43(2–3). https://doi.org/10.1016/j.lrp.2009.07.003
50. Todeschini BV, Cortimiglia MN, Callegaro-de-Menezes D, Ghezzi A (2017) Innovative and sustainable business models in the fashion industry: entrepreneurial drivers, opportunities, and challenges. Bus Horiz 60(6):759–770. https://doi.org/10.1016/j.bushor.2017.07.003
51. Upward A, Jones P (2016) An ontology for strongly sustainable business models: defining an enterprise framework compatible with natural and social science. Organ Environ 29(1):97–123. https://doi.org/10.1177/1086026615592933
52. Wilson J (2010) Essentials of business research: a guide to doing your research project. Glob Bus Rev. https://doi.org/10.1177/097215091101200211
53. Yin RK (2003) Case study research: design and methods, 3rd edn. Sage
54. Zott C, Amit R, Massa L (2011) The business model: recent developments and future research. J Manag 37(4):1019–1042. https://doi.org/10.1177/0149206311406265

Other Sources Consulted

55. BoF-McKinsey (2019) The state of fashion 2020: Navigating uncertainty. https://www.mckinsey.com/industries/retail/our-insights/state-of-fashion-archive
56. BoF-McKinsey (2020) The state of fashion 2021: in search of promise in perilous times. https://www.mckinsey.com/industries/retail/our-insights/state-of-fashion-archive
57. BoF-McKinsey (2023) The state of fashion 2024: Riding out the storm. https://www.mckinsey.com/industries/retail/our-insights/state-of-fashion
58. European Commission (2020) Circular economy action plan. https://environment.ec.europa.eu/strategy/circular-economy-action-plan_en
59. Kent S (2020a) Fashion's growth-focused business model is not sustainable. What's the solution? Business of Fashion. https://www.businessoffashion.com/articles/professional/fashions-growth-focused-business-model-is-not-sustainable-whats-the-solution
60. Kent S (2020b) Fashion's sustainability goals threatened by the crisis. Business of Fashion. https://www.businessoffashion.com/articles/professional/can-fashions-sustainability-drive-survive-the-covid-19-crisis
61. Kent S (2020c) The sustainability goals Chanel, Kering and H&M could all agree on. Business of Fashion. https://www.businessoffashion.com/articles/professional/the-fashion-pact-sustainability-targets-chanel-kering-and-hm
62. Neves J (2020) Farfetch's José Neves: the future of luxury is online. VOGUE BUSINESS website: https://www.voguebusiness.com/companies/farfetchs-jose-neves-future-of-luxury-is-online-vogue-business-podcast
63. Pact, The Fashion Pact (2020) About The fashion pact. https://thefashionpact.org/?lang=en
64. Paraíso A (2020) Marroquinaria, Luxo e Sustentabilidade. CTCP QUALIFIC Webinars, 21 de Outubro 2020 17.00h
65. Patagonia (2020) Worn Wear: our commitment to environmental responsibility. Patagonia website: https://www.patagonia.com/our-responsibility-programs.html
66. Plé L, Lecocq X, Angot J (2010) Customer-integrated business models: A theoretical framework management 13(4):226. https://doi.org/10.3917/mana.134.0226

Isabela Casares Araújo holds a Master's in Marketing and Strategy from the University of Minho and is an experienced fashion design professional. She has worked with national and international fashion brands, focusing on design conceptualization, product development, and collaboration with industry stakeholders. Her research interests include digital innovation, sustainable business models, and adapting to Gen Z consumer demands. Isabela has presented at various conferences on sustainable fashion and technology's role in the industry's evolution, positioning her as a strategic thinker in the field.

José Carlos M. Rodrigues de Pinho * (Ph.D., Warwick University) is a full Professor with an affiliation in Marketing at the School of Economics and Management, University of Minho. He has a vast number of peer-reviewed publications, including the Journal of World Business, Journal of Business Research, International Journal of Project Management, and International Marketing Review, among others. He has also been actively involved in several International Projects, particularly with Portuguese-speaking countries, published in many International Conference Proceedings, as a reviewer for several international conferences and journals, and as Chair, Track Chair, and Co-Chair for International Conferences.

The Longevity Revolution: Challenges and Opportunities for an Inclusive Ageing Society

10

Oscar Ribeiro and Lia Araújo

> *We have the tools to take advantage of this exceptional demographic shift. But it will require nothing less than a total transformation of both the personal experience of aging and of cultural attitudes.*
>
> – Robert Butler (in The Longevity Revolution).

Abstract

The global population of those aged 65 and over is increasing drastically, and by 2050 this number is expected to exceed 1.5 billion. This "longevity revolution", driven by public health advances, medical science, and social development, presents challenges and opportunities for societies worldwide. The purpose of this chapter is to discuss a selection of such challenges and opportunities, bearing in mind the importance of improving older adults' social inclusion through intergenerational cooperation. Rooted in the frameworks of active and healthy ageing and their connection to advanced longevity, it explores how the unprecedented rise in life expectancy drives current demographic shifts, focusing on the impact of ageing on health and disability. The chapter underscores the principle of "leaving no one behind" while addressing specific challenges and vulnerabilities faced by distinct subgroups within the older population, such as the oldest old, older

O. Ribeiro (✉)
RISE-Health, Department of Education and Psychology, University of Aveiro, Aveiro, Portugal
e-mail: oribeiro@ua.pt

L. Araújo
RISE-Health, Department of Education and Psychology, University of Aveiro, Aveiro, Portugal

RISE-Health, School of Education, Polytechnic Institute of Viseu, Viseu, Portugal
e-mail: liajaraujo@esev.ipv.pt

B. Casais (ed.), *Integrated Science to Achieve Sustainable Development Goals*, Integrated Science 37, https://doi.org/10.1007/978-3-031-88777-2_10

women, and older informal caregivers. It ends outlining key efforts needed to create an inclusive society for all and examining key connections between ageing and the UN Sustainable Development Goals.

Graphical Abstract

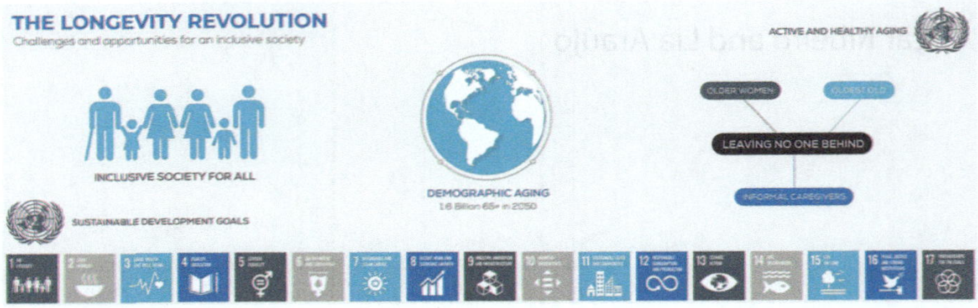

Source: Authors

Keywords

Longevity · Active and Healthy Ageing · Disability · Inclusion · SDGs

1 Introduction

Ageing and longevity are topics of increasing global interest, as life expectancy rises and societies need to adapt to the needs and opportunities presented by ageing populations. Despite widely recognized regional variations, particularly when considering high-income vs lower-income nations and gaps between genders, the number of older adults worldwide is increasing in an unprecedented rate. Globally, in 2021, approximately 761 million people were aged 65 or older, a figure expected to exceed 1.5 billion by 2050 [1]. According to the most recent UN's World Population Prospects, by the late 2070s that age group is projected to reach 2.2 billion, surpassing the number of children [2]. In addition, the report also projects that there will be 265 million persons aged 80 years or older, more than the number of infants.

Particularly in the European Union (EU), and according to available data from EUROSTAT, on 1 January 2023 the population was estimated at 448.8 million people, with more than one-fifth (21.3%) being aged 65+. The share of those aged 80+ not only increased from 3.7% to 6.0% between 2003 and 2023, as it is projected to have a two-and-a-half-fold increase between 2023 and 2100, from 6.0% to 15.3% [3]. The relative significance of the very old is growing at a faster pace than any other age segment of the EU's population. Individuals who are currently in their 70s, 80s and even 90s are benefiting from growing longevity, and this can be observed in the proportion of centenarians (people aged 100+), a subgroup that has been expressively rising over the last decades, with projections being made on a growth from close to 106,000 in 2018 to more than half a million by 2050 [4].

As the global population of older adults grows, societies are experiencing shifts in various sectors, from healthcare and the economy to urban planning and social support systems. Such shifts and challenges made the actual debate about longevity move from simply considering the length of life to the quality of remaining life, emphasizing the role politics, communities, families, and individuals have on dealing with the consequences of demographic ageing.

But enhancing the quality of the additional years one may expect to live brings along the need for rethinking societal roles, retirement, social and healthcare systems, and intergenerational dynamics. It also highlights the need for recognizing the situation of those in more vulnerable conditions, such as individuals who currently belong to the oldest-old subgroups and did not expect to reach such advances ages (and therefore probably not preparing themselves for a long life journey), and those who may be facing supplementary challenges, as it the case of older women (most likely to be poor and living alone), and older adults who provide some sort of support to a dependent family member (either and/or both to a partner, a child, of even to an exceptionally old parent)—to name a few.

The World Social Report 2023 [1] emphasizes that population ageing, along with the policies designed to address this significant global trend, can be leveraged to fulfill the commitment of "leaving no one behind" of the United Nations' 2030 Agenda for Sustainable Development [5]. In fact, the UN' Agenda has called for policies that promote health, well-being, and security for people of all ages, aligning ageing issues with global development goals. In that sense, countries are being ranked based on how prepared they are for the challenges of an ageing population (e.g., Active Ageing Index; Global AgeWatch Insights; Ageing Society Index), with robust healthcare services, social support, and age-inclusive policies, among other global components, being of crucial value. A country's policy and preparedness for an ageing world is assumed to be crucial to fostering an inclusive society where all individuals, regardless of their age, can thrive.

In 2021 the Green Paper on Ageing was launched to promote broad policy debates focusing on the challenges and opportunities of longevity considering the UN 2030 Agenda for Sustainable Development and UN Decade for Healthy Ageing [6]. Policy frameworks addressing critical areas such as healthcare access, pension sustainability, employment opportunities for older workers, and the creation of age-friendly environments are ought to ensure economic stability, reduce intergenerational inequalities, and promote social cohesion by enabling older adults to actively participate in society. Preparing for societal ageing requires therefore addressing more than just economic concerns and the provision of quality, affordable healthcare services; it is also essential to consider how different generations, with deferent expectations and roles, can coexist and help each other.

This chapter starts by outlining the active and healthy ageing frameworks and their interconnection with the phenomenon of "longevity revolution" we are currently facing, highlighting some of its challenges. Due to the pivotal role of the unprecedented increase in life expectancy in such a demographic change, a reflection on how the ageing process affects health and disability and on the importance of "healthy life expectancy" as a more comprehensive indicator is then presented. The chapter continues with stressing how the guiding principle of "leaving no one behind" must target specific challenges and vulnerabilities. This is made by reflecting about distinct subgroups of the current cohort of older generations and by presenting a selection of required efforts to attain an inclusive society for all. The chapter ends by exposing how the UN Sustainable Development Goals relate to ageing.

2 Active and Healthy Ageing and the Longevity Revolution

Globally, healthy and active ageing involve adopting healthy lifestyle choices throughout life, including balanced nutrition, regular physical activity, and active social engagement [6]. Although of potential combination, the terms active and healthy point to different aspects.

As a concept, "active ageing" emerged in the 1990s reflecting a growing awareness of the need for a significant paradigm shift about ageing [7]; it subsequently appeared as a policy framework that was articulated by the WHO [8], quickly gaining recognition as the foremost global policy approach to addressing population ageing. The term emphasizes the continued participation of older adults in societal, economic, and cultural activities, as well as the ability to maintain independence and autonomy; it also focuses on optimizing opportunities for health, participation, and security to enhance the quality of life as people age [9]. For years, active ageing remained the most globally recognized, widely implemented, and comprehensive policy framework, offering a holistic approach to support individuals across all stages of life [7, 10]. By complementing the II World Assembly on Ageing, the WHO report outlined a wide-ranging and innovative roadmap for health policy, serving as a source of inspiration and guidance for policy development and driving a significant number of scientific studies throughout the world [11]. In its most recent version, which acknowledges the ongoing demographic revolution and the need for abandoning the existing notions of old age and retirement, the active aging framework integrates the three original pillars of active ageing (participation, security, and health) adding a fourth one—lifelong learning [12].

In what refers to "healthy ageing", it is a broad concept that underpins active ageing by focusing on maintaining physical, mental, and social well-being throughout life [13]. It is defined as "the process of developing and maintaining the functional ability that enables well-being in older age" (p. 13) [14] and includes three key elements: (i) functional ability, which refers to maintaining the capacity to do what one values and is determined by intrinsic capacity (i.e., the combination of all the individual's physical and mental capacities); (ii) the environment in which one lives (including, in a broad sense, physical, social and policy environments); and (iii) the interactions among them [13, 14]. Healthy ageing is framed as a process of aligning individuals' intrinsic capacities with supportive environments. The approach assumes that individuals with chronic conditions can thrive when their surroundings are adapted to meet their needs and emphasizes the importance of transforming global environments to promote inclusion and reduce inequalities. The assumed life-course approach recognizes the prevailing inequalities among older adults, emphasizing that these disparities result from the cumulative effects of advantages and disadvantages experienced throughout life. The healthy ageing framework outlined a plan entitled the "Decade of Healthy Ageing 2020–2030" [13] declared by the UN General Assembly in December 2020, which consists of 10 years of collaborative actions across sectors and stakeholders to improve the lives of older people, their families and the communities in which they live [13]. As in the case of active ageing, along with constituting a policy roadmap, the framework, particularly the "Decade of Healthy Ageing", has also attracted large scientific interest [15] and debate [16].

The concepts of active ageing, healthy ageing, and the longevity revolution (globally referring to the unprecedented increase in life expectancy worldwide) are deeply interconnected. The longevity revolution requires proactive policies that promote active and healthy ageing across the life course, foster age-friendly environments to support independence, quality of life and well-being, encourage sustainable systems for healthcare, social protection, and intergenerational equity, and invest in research and innovation to address ageing-related challenges and opportunities. Within such interconnection, a set of key challenges can be expected: (i) those referring to healthcare system strain due to an increased demand for healthcare services, specially for chronic diseases associated with ageing, and to rising costs in supporting the health needs of older adults; (ii) financial and pension sustainability due to the support of about 20–30 years of post-retirement and the concurrent need for longer working lives; (iii) increased risk of poverty in old age since without adequate financial support systems, older adults may face economic insecurity, namely those who cannot rely on family or personal savings and have to deal with chronic conditions that configure increased health expenditures; (iv) changing family structure and care dynamics as smaller families mean fewer potential caregivers for older generations, increased burden on informal caregivers and the need for affordable long-term and community-based care solutions, including assisted living and home-based care; (v) increased risk of emotional and social loneliness related to the lack of opportunities for social interaction and aggravated by a potential shortage of mental health services tailored to older adults; (vi) age-appropriate housing and community planning that, on the one hand, face the rising demand for accessible, affordable and safe housing for older adults (including options for ageing in place, assisted living and co-housing communities) and, on the other hand, assure urban and rural areas alike with thoughtful planning that incorporates age-friendly public spaces, transport and healthcare access to support older adults' mobility and independence; (vii) workforce adaptation with age-friendly workplace policies, the offering of lifelong learning opportunities for skill development and/or re-skilling that allow for a continuous contribution to the economy and to the maintenance of a purpose and identity; and (viii) reimage of retirement as a period of potential contribution to society and self-growth.

3 Living Longer With(out) Disease and Disability

From the multitude of challenges that come with advancing age, an incontrovertible one refers to health and disability and its management. Currently, there are three main theories on how the ageing process affects health and disability in populations over time. Gruenberg [17], in the "expansion of morbidity" theory, posited that as life expectancy increases, the total amount of time individuals live with chronic illnesses or disabilities also increases. Fries [18], on the other hand, hypothesized that as life expectancy increases, the period individuals live with chronic illness, disability, or morbidity can be reduced into a shorter duration near the end of life. According to this theory, "compression of morbidity" occurs if the age at first appearance of ageing manifestations and chronic disease symptoms increases more rapidly than life expectancy. I.e., the average onset age of a marker of morbidity (first heart attack, first dyspnea from emphysema, first disability from osteoarthritis, first memory loss of a certain magnitude) can increase more rapidly than does life expectancy from the same age [19]. A third theoretical possibility has been proposed by Manton [20], who combined elements of both the compression and expansion hypotheses. According to the "dynamic equilibrium" theory, mortality reductions are the result of diminutions in the rate of chronic disease progression, leading to a decrease in the life span with serious illness or disability proportion, and an increase in the proportion with moderate disability or less severe illness. As new and more robust databases become available, this third theory has been gaining more evidence, suggesting that diseases are less disabling due to medical advancements, even if they last longer [21]. One consequence of the "dynamic equilibrium" scenario is that the impact of population ageing on demand for disability support services may be partially offset by a redistribution of demand from more to less intensive forms of support. Thus, while the expected duration of support required may increase, the average level of support required may decrease [22].

Defined as the average number of years that a person can expect to live in "full health" by considering years lived in less than full health due to disease and/or injury [23], healthy life expectancy is a more comprehensive metric when compared to life expectancy as it combines length and quality of life into a single measure [24]. This indicator has significantly increased in the last decades, but it's progression was significantly lower that life expectancy, meaning that people are living longer but that these added years are not necessarily lived with quality of life [25]. For instance, in 2019, the global/worldwide life expectancy at birth, for both sexes, was of 73.3 years, whereas the healthy life expectancy was of 63.7 years (Table 10.1). A difference of 9.6 years means that, on average, one can expect to live until 73.3 years old, but that from 63.7 years old onwards, years will be lived with health and functional constrains [26].

Table 10.1 Life expectancy vs. healthy life expectancy at birth

	Life expectancy at birth			Healthy life expectancy at birth		
	Total	Men	Women	Total	Men	Women
Global	73.3	70.8	75.9	63.7	62.5	64.9
High-income	80.9	78.4	83.3	69.8	68.7	70.9
Low-income	65.1	63	67.2	56.7	55.7	57.7
Europe	78.2	75.1	81.3	68.3	66.6	70.0
Africa	64.5	62.4	66.6	56	55.0	57.1

Adapted from WHO [26]

The difference between life expectancy and healthy life expectancy is influenced by a variety of factors, such as healthcare resources, economic development, and educational attainment [27]. As shown by the last available data from the WHO, when considering just high-income countries, we can observe that life expectancy has already surpassed the 80-year barrier, while the healthy life expectancy is below 70 years old [26]. In low-income countries, there is a lower life expectancy (65.1) and healthy life expectancy (56.7), with a difference between both indicators of 8.4 years. Specifically for Europe, this difference is even higher: the average life expectancy in 2019 was of 78.2 years old and the healthy life expectancy was of 64.5, exposing a difference of 13.7 years. In Africa, the life expectancy was 64.5 years old, and the healthy life expectancy was 56, meaning that an African person, in average, can expect to live a period of 8.5 years without full health and functional capacity [26].

An important feature of these indicators is the observed sex difference. Men tend to globally present lower values on both life expectancy and healthy life expectancy, but the difference between indicators is higher for women, which means that women live longer and have a longer period with morbidity. Globally, according to WHO's report [26], life expectancy was of 70.8 for men and 75.9 years for women (difference of 5.1) and healthy life expectancy was of 62.5 for men and 64.9 for women (difference of 2.4). The same trend is observed in high-income countries, where women can expect to live 4.9 years longer than men—but while men can expect to a period of morbidity of 9.7 years, for women that period is of 12.4 years. This trend can also be observed in low-income countries, as women have a difference between life expectancy and healthy life expectancy of 9.5 years, whereas this difference in men is of 7.3 years.

Within the National Academy of Medicine Global Roadmap for Healthy Longevity [28] the presented data provide a realistic vision of what is happening in terms of human life extension: improved living conditions have significantly increased the number of years lived worldwide, but there is still a part of those years that are lived with health and functional difficulties. Such a difference has important impacts on individual and societal dimensions, but also in health care provision. Improving functioning across the life course demands a shift from the orientation of health systems that are focused on mortality and morbidity towards the inclusion of functioning as a third indicator of health [29].

4 "Leaving No One Behind"

To consider the burdens of an aged society, along with maximizing the possible social benefits of individuals who live longer lives, we must also ensure their genuine inclusion regardless of any health or functional constraint. It is well recognized that the proportion of older adults who face daily life challenges and exhibit vulnerabilities increases with age due to the physical, cognitive, emotional, and social changes that often accompany ageing, and that life-course inequalities have an important impact on the way people experience advanced age. Acknowledging this makes it necessary to ensure the availability of effective systems of old-age support.

Presently, there is a wide-ranging number of initiatives that in pursuing inclusive societies for people of all ages put the rights and well-being of older persons at the center. The UN [1, 5] make the relevance of such initiatives very clear with their message of "leaving no one behind", calling for policies and interventions that can positively influence the future direction of inequality as populations continue to live longer, and manage the challenges and capitalize the opportunities that population ageing brings.

In the current cohort of older generations there are various conditions that increase one's vulnerability and needs. Usually, it is in the interrelationship of different factors, such as diseases and disability with lower social support and economical status, where the most complex and impactful situations arise [30]. We need therefore to look at specific subgroups whose societal relevance and/or numeric expression have been rising and constitute undeniable ageing challenges. This is the case, among several subgroups, of those individuals outliving the average life span (oldest old and centenarians), of those considered to be in a more vulnerable situation (older women), and of those caring for relatives in an age in which they are more commonly expected to be taken cared for (older informal carers).

4.1 Oldest Old and Centenarians

Specific studies of the oldest old (typically those aged 85+), and particularly of those reaching and outliving 100 years of age, have been showing that in very advanced age it is common to have mobility and sensorial impairment and some kind of disease that leads to high need for formal and informal support [31]. While heterogeneity is higher when compared to younger old populations, several studies have been suggesting that extreme longevity often comes with significant impairments. In relation to cognitive conditions, for instance, dementia was found to be highly prevalent among centenarians and near centenarians, with estimates of 53.2% in women and 45.5% in men, according to a recent meta-analysis review [32]. As for the physical conditions of centenarians, a Portuguese study on the frailty phenotype showed that only 4% were classified as "robust," whereas 36% were classified as "prefrail" and the great majority (60%) as "frail" [33]. Aligned with this, a study with Danish centenarians had already found that there were few healthy centenarians: the prevalence of chronic conditions was of 72% for cardiovascular disease,

54% for osteoarthritis, 52% for hypertension, 51% for dementia, and 28% for ischemic heart disease [34].

Along with health constraints and reduced functional capacity levels, centenarians also face the consequences of the continuous reduction of their social network, since most are widowers, lost several family members and friends, and become lonely survivors of an entire generation [35]. Also, the oldest old are commonly forced to quit activities they love due to physical, sensorial, cognitive and functional impairments. Even in Japan, that is considered a culture in which older adults are very respected and socially valued, only 7% of the centenarians were reported to take an active part in nonfamily group activities [36].

Economical resources are an additional concern since many individuals may be living well beyond the years for which their economic resources were expected to last [37]. Although there is scarce evidence regarding economic resources about centenarians, it is known that the wealth tends to decline with age after 65, reaching its lowest in the oldest old [31]. Some evidence has informed that almost 20% of centenarians have presented their economic resources to be insufficient, not having enough money for meet emergencies whereby needing financial assistance [37]. It is therefore not surprising that income inadequacy has been found to be associated with clinically significant anxiety in that age group [38].

Overall, the oldest old face unique challenges that demand targeted policy responses. Key issues include ensuring access to quality long-term care services, addressing financial insecurity and inadequate pensions, and mitigating healthcare disparities by supporting geriatric care and chronic disease management [39]. Policies must also promote age-friendly environments to reduce social isolation and improve mobility, while recognizing the need for caregiver support and workforce training in elder care. Lastly, fostering inclusion and combating ageism are essential to upholding the dignity and rights of the oldest old.

4.2 Older Women

Despite the advances and efforts in gender equality, there are still significant discrepancies between women and men, with a powerful impact on the health and well-being of older adults and with enormous consequences to the wider society [12]. Women have longer life expectancies than men, but that doesn't mean they live better. In fact, as it has already been shown, the difference between life expectancy and healthy life expectancy is higher for women. This is because a higher proportion of older women tend to report having suffered from a long-standing illness or health problem.

According to the WHO [8], there are several life course events that increase women's vulnerability to poor health in older age. These include restrictions on education at all levels, low incomes and inequitable access to decent work due to gender-discrimination in the labor force, caregiving responsibilities associated with mothering, grand mothering and looking after one's spouse and older parents, domestic violence, widowhood, and cultural traditions and attitudes that limit access to health care. The accumulation of the effects caused by these situations, related to both sex (biology) and gender (social roles), influence health risks, health-seeking behavior, and health outcomes, as well as the relationship with health care systems, including access and treatments [40].

Older women tend also to report more loneliness than male peers, so that this subjective feeling is a topic of concern related to wellbeing. Loneliness in women is associated with important problems such as higher risk of cardiovascular disease [41] and poorer physical and mental quality of life [42]. At economic and social levels, women are more vulnerable for having lower pensions and higher isolation rates. Older women generally have lower incomes than male counterparts, largely due to the cumulative effects of gender disparities in lifetime earnings, pension accumulation, and employment patterns. Illustratively, in Europe, the gender gap in pensions was of 35.7% in 2017, with a wide variation from 2.6% in Estonia to 46.1% in Malta [43]. As for living arrangements, in 2018, the share of older women living in households composed of a single person was 40.2% across the EU-27, while the share for older men living alone was 21.8% [44].

Overall, older women face distinct policy challenges due to a lifetime of gender disparities and longer life expectancy. They are more likely to experience financial insecurity due to lower lifetime earnings, limited pension benefits, and extended caregiving roles. Policies must therefore address these economic inequalities by ensuring equitable access to retirement benefits, prioritizing gender-specific care needs, and strengthening social support systems to mitigate potential caregiving burdens [2]. By facing higher risks of chronic illnesses and disability, older women also require access to affordable and gender-sensitive healthcare. Inclusive housing, community support programs, and efforts to combat ageism and gender bias are critical to improving their quality of life.

4.3 Older Caregivers

The longevity phenomenon highlights the global decline in the oldest-old support ratio (defined as the number of individuals aged 50–74 divided by those aged 85 and older—often the age group with need of more assistance), which is projected to decrease from 32.0 in 2005 to 12.5 by 2050 [45]; but it also puts in evidence the increasing number of older adults who are assuming themselves the role of caregivers. As population ages, the number of individuals over 65 assuming such a role has been augmenting, with an UK report noting an expressive 35% increase since 2001 [55]. According to the US National Alliance for Caregiving, the typical older caregiver is "a 78.9-year-old white female who cares for one adult, often a 77.1-year-old close relative (spouse, adult child, or sibling), who needs assistance due to a long-term physical condition" (p. 1); it is also often a sole, unpaid care provider [46].

While the experiences of older caregivers (progressively defined as those aged 75+) have been reported to be generally aligned with what is already known for other adult caregivers [47], evidence suggests they are disproportionately tasked with providing intensive care to relatives, often over many years, while receiving minimal support and recognition from care agencies [48]. It has also been noted that they may perceive the caregiving role as more natural and less demanding than younger caregivers, with many resisting to identify themselves as carers. Such a reluctance may inhibit them from recognizing the impact of caregiving on their own health and well-being or seeking help. It has also been noted a high prevalence of long-term health problems or disabilities, and that long-term caregiving is linked to declines in quality of life and life satisfaction, an increased risk of depression for both men and women, and negative socio-emotional effects after caregiving ends [55]. Additionally, older caregivers' unique support needs remain poorly understood [47], with only recent attention being directed toward them as a significant area of research [39, 49].

Overall, older caregivers face significant challenges that require targeted policy support. Many juggle caregiving responsibilities while managing their own health issues, leading to physical and emotional strain. Financial insecurity is common, as caregiving often limits retirement savings. Policies should therefore provide financial assistance and ensure access to respite care and mental health services. Training programs and resources may also help older caregivers navigate complex medical and caregiving tasks [49]. Recognizing and supporting the dual role of older caregivers as both providers and recipients of care in ageing populations is currently of utmost importance. Until policies and services are better aligned with the priorities of this growing subgroup of caregivers, they are likely to remain marginalized and unsupported.

5 An Inclusive Society for All Ages

As the increasing number of older adults reshapes the social and economic landscape, acknowledging and addressing the challenges societies face to create inclusive systems that support all generations, and their inter-relations, is an important goal to achieve. Changing cultural perceptions of ageing and promoting the inclusion of older adults is pivotal for achieving so. Combatting ageism requires raising awareness about the contributions of older adults and ensuring that policies promote age equity and inclusion in all areas—from healthcare and employment to media representation [50]. This will help to create a more supportive environment for the ageing population and encourage mutual respect between generations; furthermore, it will potentially strengthen communities and stimulate a society that is prepared for ageing by simultaneously accommodating the needs of older adults and valuing and encouraging their contributions.

Through a holistic approach that includes adequate healthcare services, financial stability, social connectivity, and respect for diversity, societies can better prepare for the future and create a sense of belonging and purpose for people of all ages. This is to be achieved through a wide-ranging number of initiatives that incorporate the promotion of age-friendly infrastructures, the enhancement of healthcare and support services, the promotion of lifelong learning and senior employment opportunities, the building of social connections and reduction of isolation, the leveraging of technology for independence and safety, the provision of financial security, and a global combat to ageism that acknowledges older adults' true value. Table 10.2

Table 10.2 Policy components aiming to address the promotion of an inclusive society for all ages

Age-friendly infrastructures
Accessible public spaces: Creating age-friendly cities involves designing public spaces with ramps, elevators, wide walkways, and easily readable signage, making it easier for older adults with mobility challenges to navigate.
Public transport: Affordable, reliable, and accessible public transportation is essential, particularly as some seniors may no longer be able to drive.
Housing options: Support for diverse housing solutions, such as accessible apartments, assisted living communities, and shared housing, can help older adults age in place.
Healthcare and support services
Preventive healthcare: A focus on preventive care and early interventions can help older adults maintain their health and independence longer.
Long-term care systems: Robust systems of long-term care those who require regular assistance with daily activities, including support for caregivers and end-of-life care.
Mental health services: Addressing the mental health needs of older adults, including emotional conditions related to depression, anxiety, and loneliness, is crucial as they may experience social isolation and lack of purpose in life.
Lifelong learning and employment
Education and skill-building: Offering education programs for older adults, including health, financial and digital literacy, helps older adults to stay connected and engage with modern society.
Flexible Employment Opportunities: Allowing older adults to stay in the workforce if they choose, with options like part-time roles, flexible hours, and remote work, helps them contribute their skills and experience while ensuring financial security.
Social connection
Community programs: Community centers, recreational clubs, and intergenerational programs provide spaces for socialization and community building, which is vital for mental health and well-being; they also contribute to diminishing loneliness and social isolation.
Intergenerational initiatives: Programs that encourage interaction between generations, such as mentorship opportunities or school partnerships, foster mutual respect and understanding across age groups.
Volunteering and lifelong learning: Engagement in volunteering and lifelong learning opportunities can promote social connections and a sense of personal growth and social worth.
Technology
Assistive technologies: Innovations such as remote health monitoring, voice-assisted devices, and emergency alert systems can support independent living.
Digital inclusion: Ensuring that older adults have access to digital tools and training prevents technological exclusion and allows them to stay connected with family, friends, and essential services.
Financial security
Pensions and social security: A sustainable pension system and fair retirement benefits ensure that older adults do not face financial hardship as they age.
Accessible financial education: Educating seniors on managing finances, understanding scams, and planning for retirement is crucial for their economic independence.
Ageism
Awareness campaigns: Public awareness campaigns that challenge stereotypes and promote the value of older adults can reduce ageism and foster a more respectful society.
Inclusive policies: Government and workplace policies should explicitly include age as a dimension of diversity and anti-discrimination protections.

Source: Authors

provides a non-exhaustive overview of policy components aiming to address the promotion of an inclusive society for all ages.

An inclusive society that is prepared for an ageing population is one that anticipates and actively supports the needs, rights, and contributions of its older members. It is also a society that pursues equitable access to resources, meaningful engagement in social and economic life, and the preservation of dignity for all age groups.

6 Addressing the SDGs in Older Populations

As previously exposed, the UN's Decade of Healthy Ageing (2021–2030) [13, 14] aims to create multisectoral changes that align healthy ageing with the UN' Sustainable Development Goals (SDGs). While ageing isn't explicitly a standalone goal, the SDGs promote inclusive development that encompasses people of all ages, including older adults. Such an inclusive approach is in fact key to a truly sustainable and equitable world for everyone, regardless of age. But addressing the SDGs with a focus on older populations requires tailored initiatives that consider the unique challenges and needs of ageing communities.

A recent review intending to summarize the efforts made to directly address the SGDs in older adults in community settings prior to the "Decade of Healthy Ageing" [51] revealed that initiatives targeting older adults were mentioned under 12 different SDGs, being SDG1 (*No Poverty*), SDG3 (*Good Health and Well-being*), SDG10 (*Reduced Inequalities*) and SDG11 (*Sustainable Cities and Communities*) the more often discussed; conversely, limited examples of actions under SGDs 2 (*Zero Hunger*), 4 (*Quality Education*), 5 (*Gender Equality*) and 17 (*Partnerships for the Goals*) were found. Paired with this review, a recent report published by the WHO [30] made it clear that to make older people visible in the SDG's monitoring framework and indicators, a closer examination is required of the kinds and types of data collection mechanisms and methods to measure each SDG indicator relevant for older persons. This would necessarily include closely examining existing levels of disaggregation, analysis and dissemination. According to the report, reliable age-disaggregated data is essential to identify and address the specific challenges faced by older people within each SDG. Such disaggregation is ought to be by at least 5-year age and sex groups to age 90 and over and analyzed for differences among other socioeconomic and demographic characteristics like place of residence [30].

Regardless of the available efforts already made to include representative data on older adults and to acknowledge specific health conditions (e.g., geriatric oncology) [52], governments, non-governmental organizations (NGOs), and international bodies are requested to reinforce efforts to ensure that older adults are included in the pursuit of the SDGs and that they are not left behind. Table 10.3 presents key connections between all the 17 SDGs and ageing while simultaneously displaying illustrative large-scale examples of such efforts.

By prioritizing age-tailored efforts, societies can promote sustainable development for all, ensuring that older adults are not only recipients of support but also

Table 10.3 Key connections between SDGs and aging and illustrative examples of efforts that specifically address each SDG in relation to the older population

SDG 1: No poverty	Older adults are at risk of poverty, especially if they lack pensions, savings, or access to employment. Ensuring financial security and affordable healthcare for ageing populations is essential to ending poverty for all. An illustrative example of efforts to address this SDG is **HelpAge International**, a global non-profit organization that works to improve the lives of older people around the world. It advocates for universal social pensions, an effort that is essential in low- and middle-income countries where formal employment and savings are less common among older people.
SDG 2: Zero hunger	Older people often face food insecurity due to economic constraints, lack of mobility, or living in food deserts. Improving food access, affordability, and nutrition for older adults can help reduce hunger and malnutrition. Examples of efforts to address this SDG include local organizations, such as **food banks and community kitchens**, that often partner with senior centers to distribute nutritious food and ensure that, older adults have access to balanced diets.
SDG 3: Good health and well-being	Health challenges increase with age, including chronic diseases, mental health issues, and disabilities. Access to age-friendly healthcare services, preventive care, and support for mental health are critical to achieving this goal. Initiatives like the **WHO's Age-Friendly Cities and Communities** program constitute a good example of an effort to address this SDG as it focuses on making urban areas more conducive to healthy ageing, and ensure that older people can access healthcare, recreation, and social support in their communities.
SDG 4: Quality education	Lifelong learning opportunities benefit older adults by promoting skills development and social inclusion. Accessible educational programs and digital literacy initiatives can enhance the quality of life for older people. Educational institutions, like the **Universities of the Third Age**, specifically address this SGD as they offer accessible courses for older adults on various subjects, enhancing their personal development, social occupation and inclusion.
SDG 5: Gender equality	Older women often face unique challenges, including higher poverty rates and limited access to resources due to gender disparities in income and employment. Policies aimed at supporting gender equity must consider their needs as they often have lower pensions and more caregiving responsibilities. Programs like the **UN Women's work on gender and ageing** advocate for policy changes that recognize and support older women who often provide unpaid caregiving, helping them access resources like respite care and financial assistance.
SDG 6: Clean water and sanitation	Older adults require safe and accessible water sources and sanitation facilities, especially those with disabilities or mobility issues. This goal ensures that all people, including those of more advanced ages, have reliable access to clean water. In urban areas, **age-friendly city initiatives** try to ensure that public sanitation facilities, including bathrooms, are accessible to older people, supporting their dignity and independence.
SDG 7: Affordable and clean energy	Access to affordable and clean energy is crucial for older adults, who may struggle with heating and cooling costs due to fixed reduced incomes. Reliable energy access is also vital for health-related equipment that older people might need. Nonprofit organizations that operate around the world like **Habitat for Humanity** offer energy-efficient home renovations programs that lowers heating and cooling costs for older people with limited incomes.

(continued)

Table 10.3 (continued)

SDG 8: Decent work and economic growth	Older adults should have access to work opportunities that are appropriate to their skills and capacities, and free from age discrimination. Flexible work arrangements and opportunities for older workers contribute to economic growth and reduce financial insecurity. Examples of efforts to address this SDG include **anti-age discrimination policies in the workplace**, ensuring that older workers have equal access to employment opportunities. Re-skilling programs that enable older adults to remain in the workforce if they choose is also an illustrative example.
SDG 9: Industry, innovation, and infrastructure	Age-friendly infrastructure and technology innovations (e.g., accessible transport and telemedicine) can improve the lives of older people. Encouraging industries/companies and research institutions to develop **age-inclusive and age-friendly products and services** like easy-to-use smartphones, fall detection devices, and smart home technology supports this SDG.
SDG 10: Reduced inequalities	Addressing age discrimination and promoting policies that support social protection for older adults are essential for reducing inequalities. Equitable healthcare, income support, and access to resources ensure that older people are included in society. The UN and WHO's **campaign to combat ageism and promote age-inclusive policies** calling for an end to stereotypes that limit opportunities for older people constitutes a renowned example of an effort to address this SDG.
SDG 11: Sustainable cities and communities	As urban populations age, cities must be designed to be age-friendly, with accessible transportation, housing, and social services. Safe, inclusive urban spaces allow older people to participate in community life. Examples of efforts to address this SDG include local intergenerational housing projects where older and younger people live together, fostering social connections and mutual support. Equally illustrative are global initiatives like the **WHO Age-Friendly Cities and Communities** program that supports cities in adapting infrastructure, public spaces, housing, and community resources to accommodate older adults, promoting active ageing and social inclusion.
SDG 12: Responsible consumption and production	Older generations play a key role in promoting sustainable consumption as they are often more conservative with resources. Supporting older people in adopting and maintaining sustainable practices benefits the environment and the economy. **NGOs that promote education on sustainable living practices** like waste reduction for older adults, encouraging them to contribute to climate efforts in everyday life exemplifies an effort to address this SDG.
SDG 13: Climate action	Older people are more vulnerable to climate impacts, like extreme weather. Climate resilience planning should consider the needs of ageing populations, especially in areas prone to natural disasters. Local governments that develop emergency response systems that prioritize vulnerable older adults during extreme weather events is a good example of an effort for addressing this SDG. Equally demonstrative is the work conducted by organizations like **AARP and the Red Cross** that offer training programs for older adults to prepare for natural disasters.
SDG 14: Life below water **SDG 15: Life on land**	While these two goals focus on environmental preservation, older adults can contribute significantly to conservation efforts and education on protecting ecosystems. Examples of efforts to address this SDG include community conservation initiatives like **tree-planting programs** and wildlife preservation, and **environmental conservation education** for older adults.

(continued)

Table 10.3 (continued)

SDG 16: Peace, justice, and strong institutions	Older adults have a right to social justice and protection from violence, abuse, and neglect. Ensuring easy access to legal support and public services safeguards their rights. **UN and other agencies** awareness campaigns against elder abuse that focuses the promotion of rights of older adults to live free from harm and the work of local organizations that provides legal assistance to older adults focusing on issues such as financial exploitation constitute examples of efforts to address this SDG.
SDG 17: Partnerships for the goals	Collaborating with organizations focused on ageing can enhance initiatives to support older adults. Partnerships between governments, NGOs, and private sectors (like the **UN Decade of Healthy Aging 2021–2030**), which coordinate efforts to improve life for older adults and integrate their needs into policy discussions is a global expressive example.

Source: Authors

active contributors to achieving these global goals. Hence, partnerships on research and data collection that focus on the older populations and help ensuring that policies and programs effectively target their specific needs and contribute to the achievement of the SDGs are to be strongly incentivized. On this matter, worthwhile mentioning is the increasing involvement of older adults as "experts by experience" / "lived expert advisors" within gerontological research [53, 54]. Increasingly seen as critical assets in community-based participatory research (CBPR), particularly in "Ageing in the Right Place Initiatives", a way of promoting inclusiveness of older adults in academia is by truly involving them throughout the research process: in identifying key issues, shaping research questions, codesigning methods that respect their preferences and capabilities, and analyzing findings and developing actionable outcomes that ensure their lived experiences and inform policies and interventions. This inclusive approach empowers older adults and enhances the relevance and impact of the research.

7 Final Remarks

The longevity revolution constitutes one of the most significant societal transformations of the twenty-first century and requires a paradigm shift in the way we view old age. It is crucial that societies focus not only on increasing life expectancy, but also on quality of life and well-being in additional years. Creating age-friendly environments, access to appropriate healthcare, ensuring financial stability and promoting social inclusion are key to ensuring that older people can thrive. The specific needs of subgroups of older adults, such as the oldest old, women and older caregivers, should be addressed through targeted policies. Combating ageism and recognizing the value of older generations are imperative to building a truly inclusive society for all ages.

References

1. UN, United Nations (2023) World social report 2023: leaving no one behind in an ageing world. UN Department of Economic and Social Affairs. ISBN 978-92-1-130458-9 https://social.desa.un.org/sites/default/files/publications/2023-02/WorldSocialReport2023.pdf. Accessed 7 Dec 2024
2. UN (2024) World population prospects 2024: SUMMARY OF REsults. UN DESA/POP/2024/TR/NO. 9. United Nations
3. EUROSTAT (2024) Demography of Europe – 2024 edition. https://ec.europa.eu/eurostat/web/interactive-publications/demography-2024#about-publication. Accessed 7 Dec 2024
4. Teixeira L, Araújo L, Paul C, Ribeiro O (2020) Centenarians in Europe. Springer, Berlin
5. UN (2022) Operationalizing leaving no one behind: good practice notes for un country teams. https://unsdg.un.org/sites/default/files/2022-04/Operationalizing%20LNOB%20-%20final%20with%20Annexes%20090422.pdf. Accessed 7 Dec 2024
6. EU, European Union (2021) Green paper on ageing. Fostering solidarity and responsibility between generations. https://commission.europa.eu/system/files/2021-06/green_paper_ageing_2021_en.pdf. Accessed 7 Dec 2024
7. Kalache A, Voelcher I, Louvison M (2021) Active aging and the longevity revolution. In: Rojo-Pérez F, Fernandez-Mayoralas G (eds) Handbook of active ageing and quality of life. Springer, Cham
8. WHO (2002) Active ageing: a policy framework. World Health Organization, Geneva
9. Ribeiro O, Paúl C (Coord.) (2018) Manual de Envelhecimento Ativo. LIDEL, Lisboa
10. Díaz J, García A (2021) "Active aging": its relevance from and historical perspective. In: Rojo-Pérez F, Fernández-Mayorales G (eds) Handbook of active ageing and quality of life. From concepts to applications. Springer, Cham
11. Rojo-Pérez F, Fernández-Mayoralas G (2021) Handbook of active ageing and quality of life: from concepts to applications. Springer, Berlin. https://doi.org/10.1007/978-3-030-58031-5
12. CIL-BR, Centro Internacional de Longevidade Brasil (2015) Envelhecimento Ativo: Um Marco Político em Resposta à Revolução da Longevidade. ILC-Brasil, Rio de Janeiro.
13. WHO (2020) UN decade of healthy ageing: plan of action. https://www.who.int/initiatives/decade-of-healthy-ageing. Accessed 7 Dec 2024
14. WHO, World Health Organization (2015) World report on ageing and health in. World Health Organization, Geneva. https://iris.who.int/bitstream/handle/10665/186468/WHO_FWC_ALC_15.01_eng.pdf?sequence=1. Accessed 7 Dec 2024
15. Keating N (2022) A research framework for the United Nations Decade of Healthy Ageing (2021-2030). Eur J Ageing 19:775–787
16. Lloyd-Sherlock P, Kalache A, Kirkwood T, McKeed M, Princee M (2019) WHO's proposal for a decade of healthy ageing. Lancet 394(10215):2152–2153
17. Gruenberg E (1977) The failure of success. Milbank Q 55:3–24
18. Fries J (1980) Aging, natural death, and the compression of morbidity. N Engl J Med 303(3):130–135
19. Fries J (2005) The compression of morbidity. Milbank Q 83(4):801–823. https://doi.org/10.1111/j.1468-0009.2005.00401.x
20. Manton K (1982) Changing concepts of morbidity and mortality in the elderly population. Milbank Q 60:183–244
21. Robine J-M, Jagger C (2005) The relationship between increasing life expectancy and healthy life expectancy. Ageing Horizons 3:14–12
22. Graham P, Blakely T, Davis P, Sporle A, Pearce N (2003) Compression, expansion, or dynamic equilibrium? The evolution of health expectancy in New Zealand. J Epidemiol Community Health 58:659–666. https://doi.org/10.1136/jech.2003.014910
23. WHO (n.d.) Healthy life expectancy (HALE) at birth. https://www.who.int/data/gho/indicator-metadata-registry/imr-details/66. Accessed 7 Dec 2024

24. Stiefel M, Perla R, Zell B (2010) A healthy bottom line: healthy life expectancy as an outcome measure for health improvement efforts. Milbank Q 88(1):30–53. https://doi.org/10.1111/j.1468-0009.2010.00588.x
25. The Lancet Respiratory Medicine (2016) Prolonging life at all costs: quantity versus quality. Lancet Resp Med 4(3):165. https://doi.org/10.1016/S2213-2600(16)00059-X
26. WHO (2020) Global 2019 life expectancy and healthy life expectancy. https://apps.who.int/gho/data/view.main.SDG2020LEXWBv?lang=en
27. Aanegola R, Nakamura S, Kumar N (2022) Longitudinal analysis of the determinants of life expectancy and healthy life expectancy: a causal approach. Healthc Anal 2:100028. https://doi.org/10.1016/j.health.2022.100028
28. National Academy (2022) National Academy of Medicine Global Roadmap for Healthy Longevity. https://nap.nationalacademies.org/login.php?record_id=26144
29. National Academies of Sciences, Engineering, and Medicine (2024) Aging, functioning, and rehabilitation: proceedings of a workshop. The National Academies Press, Washington. https://doi.org/10.17226/27763
30. WHO (2024) Making older persons visible in the Sustainable Development Goals' monitoring framework and indicators. World Health Organization, Geneva. Licence: CC BY-NC-SA 3.0 IGO
31. Serra V, Watson J, Sinclair D, Kneale D (2011) Living beyond 100: a report on centenarians. International Longevity Centre, London
32. Leung Y, Barzilai N, Batko-Szwaczka A, Beker N, Boerner K, Brayne C et al (2023) Cognition, function, and prevalent dementia in centenarians and near-centenarians: an individual participant data (IPD) meta-analysis of 18 studies. Alzheimers Dement 19(6):2265–2275. https://doi.org/10.1002/alz.12828
33. Duarte N, Teixeira L, Ribeiro O, Paul C (2014) Frailty phenotype criteria in centenarians: findings from the Oporto Centenarian Study. Eur Geriatr Med 5(6):371–376
34. Andersen-Ranberg K, Schroll M, Jeune B (2001) Healthy centenarians do not exist, but autonomous centenarians do: a population-based study of morbidity among Danish centenarians. J Am Geriatr Soc 49:900–908. https://doi.org/10.1046/j.1532-5415.2001.49180.x
35. Araújo L, Ribeiro O (2012) Centenários: que redes sociais. Rev Kairós 15(2):57–74
36. Homma S, Hirose N, Inagaki T, Suzuki M, Wakida Y (1999) Lifestyle, familial history, and social background of Japanese Centenarians. In: Tauchi H, Sato T, Watanabe T (eds) Japanese Centenarians. Institute for Medical Research, Japan
37. Martin P, MacDonald M, Margrett J, Poon L (2010) Resilience and longevity: expert survivorship of centenarians. In: Fry P, Keyes C (eds) New frontiers in resilient aging: life strengths and well-being in late life. Cambridge University Press, New York
38. Ribeiro O, Teixeira L, Araújo L, Afonso R, Pachana N (2015) Predictors of anxiety in centenarians: health, economic and social factors. Int Psychogeriatr 27(7):1167–1176. https://doi.org/10.1017/S1041610214001628
39. Jopp D, Rott C (2006) Adaptation in very old age: exploring the role of resources, beliefs, and attitudes for centenarians' happiness. Psychol Aging 21(2):266–280
40. WHO (2007) Women, ageing and health: a framework for action. ISBN 978 92 4 156352 9
41. Golaszewski N, LaCroix A, Godino J, Allison M, Manson J, King J et al (2022) Evaluation of social isolation, loneliness, and cardiovascular disease among older women in the US. JAMA Netw Open 5(2):e2146461. https://doi.org/10.1001/jamanetworkopen.2021.46461
42. Boehlen F, Maatouk I, Friederich H-C, Schoettker B, Brenner H, Wild B (2022) Loneliness as a gender-specific predictor of physical and mental health-related quality of life in older adults. Qual Life Res 31:2023–2033
43. European Parliament (2019) The gender gap in pensions in the EU. https://www.europarl.europa.eu/RegData/etudes/BRIE/2019/631033/IPOL_BRI(2019)631033_EN.pdf

44. EU (2020) Ageing Europe – looking at the lives of older people in the EU. https://ec.europa.eu/eurostat/web/products-statistical-books/-/ks-02-20-655. Accessed 7 Dec 2024
45. Herrmann F, Michel J-P, Robine J-M (2010) Worldwide decline in the oldest old support ratio. Eur Geriatr Med 1:3–8
46. AARP Public Policy Institute (2015) Caregiving in the U.S.: a focused look at caregivers age 75 and older. https://www.aarp.org/content/dam/aarp/ppi/2015/AARP1001_75orOlder_CGProfileAug26.pdf. Accessed 7 Dec 2024
47. Greenwood N, Smith R (2016) The oldest carers: a narrative review and synthesis of the experiences of carers aged 75 years. Maturitas 94:161–172
48. Milne A, Larkin M (2017) What matters to older carers: evidence from practice-related research. Innov Ageing 1(S1):1109
49. Macedo T, Sousa L, Ribeiro O (2021) Aged 70 and still a child: complexities, strains and gains of older children caring for their (near)centenarian mothers. Age Ageing 51(1):afab204. https://doi.org/10.1093/ageing/afab204
50. WHO (2021) Global report on ageism. https://www.who.int/teams/social-determinants-of-health/demographic-change-and-healthy-ageing/combatting-ageism/global-report-on-ageism. Accessed 7 Dec 2024
51. Shevelkova V, Mattocks C, Lafortune L (2023) Efforts to address the Sustainable Development Goals in older populations: a scoping review. BMC Public Health 23:456. https://doi.org/10.1186/s12889-023-15308-4
52. Mizutani T, Cheung K-L, Hakobyan Y, Lane H, Decoster L, Karnakis T et al (2024) Leave no one behind: a global survey of the current state of geriatric oncology practice by SIOG national representatives. J Geriatr Oncol 15(2):101709
53. Canham S, Weldrick R, Cartledge A, Chapple H, Danielsen C, Kestle D et al (2024) We need to be at the table: collaboration with lived experts. Prog Community Health Partnersh. https://preprint.press.jhu.edu/pchp/preprints/we-need-be-table-collaboration-lived-experts
54. Guerra S, Sousa L, Carvalho R, Melo S, Ribeiro O (2022) Understanding loneliness in older adults: reports from experts by experience to reach digital solutions. J Gerontol Soc Work 65(7):728–734. https://doi.org/10.1080/01634372.2021.2019866
55. ILC-UK (2015) The emotional well-being of older carers. University College London, London

Oscar Ribeiro is an assistant professor with habilitation in Gerontology and Geriatrics at the Department of Education and Psychology of the University of Aveiro, Portugal. He is the PI of the Ageing Cluster Research group at the Centre for Health Technology and Services Research at the Associate Laboratory RISE—Health Research Network (CINTESIS@RISE) located at the Faculty of Medicine of the University of Porto, and currently the coordinator of one of its hubs at the University of Aveiro. Main research and interest areas include successful, active, and healthy ageing, and exceptional longevity (oldest old and centenarian population). He has participated in several applied research projects in the field of ageing funded by several national and international agencies. He is a licenced clinical and health psychologist and a fellow of the Gerontological Society of America.

Lia Araújo is an assistant professor at the School of Education of the Polytechnic Institute of Viseu and a researcher at CINTESIS@RISE. She is a Gerontologist (degree and Master—U. Aveiro) with PhDs in Biomedical Sciences (U. Porto) and in Education and Behavioral Sciences (U. Vigo). She has been involved in several research projects in the areas of ageing and longevity (PT100—Oporto Centenarians), quality of life (QASP—Quality of life and Ageing in Spain, Sweden and Portugal), and intergenerationally (VIAS-Viseu InterAge Stories: developing an app to foster Social Inclusion and Healthy Lifestyles). She has interest in action research methodologies, which involve direct contact with older people, as it is happening in the COBLAGES—Using Community-Based Learning to Prepare Higher Education Students for an Ageing World (Erasmus+), in the "PERENE- Photovoice with older persons", and in the "Café Memória" (Alzheimer Portugal).

The Integration of Vulnerable Populations for Inclusive Development: Study of Disability and Gender in Spain

11

Carmen Dueñas-Zambrana and Marco A. Cruz-Morato

> *Look at me! Look at my arm. I have plowed, I have planted and I have gathered into barns. And no man could head me. And ain't I a woman? I could work as much, and eat as much as any man.*
>
> Sojourner Truth.

Abstract

Vulnerable populations, such as people with disabilities or women, normally face higher barriers to development in the labour market (being, therefore, a limitation for inclusive development). This challenges the global achievement of the SDGs, not only in developing countries, but also in developed economies, like Spain. Discrimination in the workplace has been identified as one of the main causes of this widespread social exclusion of people with disabilities, especially in the case of women, who suffer a situation of multiple discrimination (due to disability and gender). Therefore, to really overcome the situation, the reduction and elimination of this social discrimination and stigma seem crucial, as well as the promotion of positive coping responses to empower these groups of population (based on a Behavioural Economics framework, according to which inputs from Psychology are incorporated into economic decision-making analysis). In this sense, recent research is pointing to the potential of Social Marketing (the

C. Dueñas-Zambrana
Department of Social Psychology, Social Work and Social Services, and Social Anthropology. Facultad de Estudios Sociales y del Trabajo, Universidad de Málaga, Málaga, Spain
e-mail: cdz@uma.es

M. A. Cruz-Morato (✉)
Department of Economics and Management (Business Organization). Facultad de Turismo, Universidad de Málaga, Málaga, Spain
e-mail: mcruz@uma.es

B. Casais (ed.), *Integrated Science to Achieve Sustainable Development Goals*, Integrated Science 37, https://doi.org/10.1007/978-3-031-88777-2_11

use of traditional commercial marketing techniques to change behaviours for social good). The aim of this research is to study the situation, focusing on the example of Spain, where one of the main economic sectors is tourism (with more difficult labour conditions for these vulnerable populations). This study can serve as an inspiration both in the academic and professional spheres, with the objective of promoting the achievement of the SDGs.

Graphical Abstract

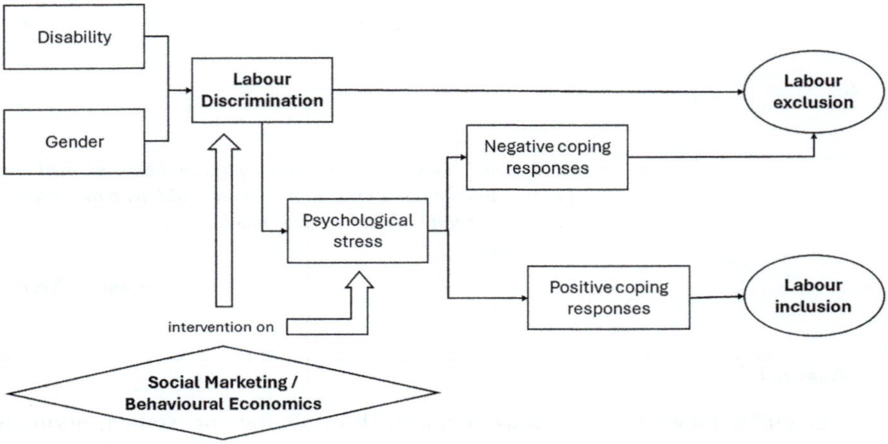

Source: Authors

Keywords

SDG · Social Inclusion · People with Disabilities · Women · Social Marketing · Behavioural Economics · Discrimination · Spain

1 Introduction

According to Gupta et al. [17], inclusive development "[…] includes marginalized people, sectors and countries in social, political and economic processes for increased human well-being, social and environmental sustainability, and empowerment". Thus, these authors exposed that inclusive development is a dynamic learning process that adapts to evolving changes and emerging risks of exclusion and marginalization. It is related to concepts such as inclusive growth and sustainable development. However, inclusive development encompasses the three dimensions of sustainable development (that is to say, economy, environment and society), focusing on social considerations.

Although there is an increasing global concern about the development of real inclusive development, as the United Nations Sustainable Development Goals

(SDGs) show, the situation is still problematic. The 2030 Agenda for Sustainable Development, endorsed by all United Nations Member States in 2015, serves as a unified framework for promoting peace and prosperity for people and the planet, both now and in the future. Central to this agenda are the 17 SDGs, representing an urgent call to action for all nations (both developed and developing) through a global partnership. The SDGs emphasize that eradicating poverty and addressing other deprivations must be coupled with strategies to enhance health and education, reduce inequality, drive economic growth, combat climate change, and protect oceans and forests [32]. However, as it has been pointed out by UN ([33], p. 2): "[...] only seventeen per cent of SDGs targets are on track to be achieved, nearly half are showing minimal or moderate progress, and progress on over a third has stalled or even regressed".

Focusing on the social inclusion dimension, labour inclusion has an important role. In this sense, vulnerable populations, such as people with disabilities and women, often encounter greater barriers in the labour market (especially combining the two elements, showing women with disabilities lower activity rates, as it will be shown). This situation implies a limitation for inclusive development, posing challenges to achieving the SDGs globally, not only in developing countries, but also in developed economies (like Spain). Therefore, even in advanced economies like Spain, people with disabilities continue to face enduring challenges related to labour exclusion [20–22], a situation exacerbated by the pandemic [18, 33].

In this sense, workplace discrimination is recognized as a primary driver of widespread social exclusion for people with disabilities (See Vornholt et al. [34]). This situation is especially problematic in the tourism industry (one of the most relevant sectors in the Spanish economy), as has been pointed out by De Sá et al. [12] and Madera et al. [25]. And it is also particularly harmful for women, who experience a situation of multiple discrimination (due to both disability and gender).

Therefore, addressing this issue effectively requires reducing and eliminating social discrimination and stigma, as well as fostering positive coping mechanisms to empower these groups. This approach aligns with a Behavioral Economics framework, integrating psychological insights into economic decision-making analysis. Related to this framework, recent studies highlight the potential of Social Marketing (using commercial marketing strategies to promote positive social change) as a tool to address these issues.

So that, this research aims to examine the general situation in Spain, where tourism is a major economic sector and where labour conditions may be especially challenging for these vulnerable populations. This example seeks to inspire academic and professional sectors, promoting SDG progress. Therefore, the next section develops a theoretical and practical examination of the context. Section 3 includes examples of Social Marketing actions in this regard. Furthermore, in the fourth section of this chapter, the issue is specifically related to concrete SDGs, citing the number and substantiating their connection. The last section includes the main conclusions of this research.

2 Theoretical and Empirical Analysis of the Situation

As it has been exposed, women usually experience a situation of multiple discrimination (due to disability and gender). This phenomenon is also called intersectionality [9], considered as the confluence of variables that lead to multiple discrimination. According to COCEMFE [6], the feminist theoretical framework provides the concept of intersectionality for understanding processes of multiple discrimination, such as those experienced by women with disabilities. This term emerged from the demands of Black feminists who advocated for an analytical lens addressing the triad of "race, class, and gender." Over time, various authors have expanded it to include specific categories of interest, such as age, disability, sedentary lifestyles, or sexuality. As defined by Brah and Phoenix [3], intersectional theory posits that individuals experience multiple forms of oppression and privilege simultaneously, resulting from the intersection of various social identities within specific historical and social contexts. In this sense, an intersectional analysis will integrate marginalized life experiences while highlighting the importance of understanding power and privilege in their multiple forms. Intersectionality theory, therefore, allows for the analysis of complex relationships of inequality [6].

According to the research previously quoted, although significant progress has been made in recent years regarding the rights of people with disabilities, the gender gap has widened. Women with disabilities face discrimination in family and educational settings, have less access to employment, encounter healthcare systems that fail to meet their needs, and receive social protection that, for most, does not alleviate poverty and social exclusion. These factors collectively hinder the development of regular and normalized life paths.

Thus, focusing on the Spanish labour situation, according to Cruz-Morato and Dueñas-Zambrana [10]: "[…] not only the labour inactivity is the main labour problem for people with disabilities, but also the situation for women is even worse than men, especially in activity rates (although the difference between the activity rates of women without disabilities and those with disabilities is smaller than for men, due to the worse situation of women without disabilities compared with men without disabilities)". Labour exclusion becomes, this way, a relevant factor in aggravating the social exclusion of women with disabilities.

In this sense, Adecco Foundation [1] exposes that the difficult labour situation of women with disabilities is caused by the intersection of barriers related to gender, disability, and the social context in which they live. In addition to the traditional obstacles faced by all women in the labour market (gender roles, motherhood stigma, etc.), they also encounter prejudices and stereotypes associated with disability (perceptions of being less capable, more costly, or less efficient, among others). This confluence of factors results in lower active participation rates in the labour market (34% compared to 36.3% for men), leading to increased exposure to poverty and social exclusion. In this sense, the type of disability (such as intellectual disability) or gender, are usually related to even higher inactivity rates [13], due to the intersectionality situation previously exposed.

Access to employment is one of the areas where inequality between men and women, particularly women with disabilities, is most evident. This directly affects their economic income and significantly limits their ability to lead an independent life. Therefore, having fewer financial resources, whether from employment or public social protection systems, as well as greater barriers to accessing education, training, employment, and healthcare services, and higher prevalence of various forms of violence, are some of the most important challenges faced by women with disabilities [6].

As it has been previously exposed, the labour participation rate of women with disabilities in Spain (34%) is lower than that of men with disabilities (36%). This disparity underscores the significant barriers faced by women with disabilities in securing employment, often stemming from lower expectations and limited access to the labour market. In fact, according to INE [22], the distribution of gender among the working-age population with disabilities is 58.1% male and 41.9% female. Furthermore, data shows that 57.7% of employed people with disabilities are men, while 42.3% are women. Women with disabilities also face greater barriers to employment in regular companies, as they only represent 41.4% of the total. According to Adecco Foundation [1], in Table 11.1 we can find more statistical information about the issue.

Data from the Observatory on the Labor Market and Statistics for People with Disabilities [28] indicates that, as in 2018, the service sector (with high relevance of tourism industry) remains the leading employer of individuals with disabilities, primarily in roles such as cleaning staff. Conversely, jobs with the lowest representation of workers with disabilities include salaried drivers of cars, taxis, and vans, as well as other elementary occupations (see Table 11.2). However, jobs in the tourism sector are typically characterized by low quality, including rigid schedules, long working hours, and highly variable working conditions [23] or [11], making these circumstances particularly challenging for people with disabilities (and much more for women with disabilities, as it has been previously exposed).

Table 11.1 Labour inequality of women with disabilities

Indicators	Men	Women
Actives	398,100	287,100
% actives	58.1%	41.9%
Employed	311,100	227,800
% employed	57.7%	42.3%
Employed in ordinary companies	191,000	135,000
% employed in ordinary companies	58.6%	41.4%
Unemployed	87,000	59,300
% unemployed	59.5%	40.5%
Activity rates	36.30%	34%
Employment rates	28.60%	26.90%
Unemployment rates	21.90%	20.70%
Receive public social benefits?	1,096,100	845,800
% receive public social benefits	56.4%	43.6%

Source: INE [22]

Table 11.2 Employed people with disabilities by type of occupation, year 2020

	Number of contracts	PWD hired (%)
Cleaning staff for offices, hotels and other similar establishments	39,092	15.7
Laborers of the manufacturing industries	23,143	9.3
Agricultural laborers (except in orchards, greenhouses, nurseries and gardens)	12,561	5.1
Salaried waiters	7739	3.1
Building custodians	7546	3.0
Other cleaning staff	5942	2.4
Freight transport laborers and unloaders	5416	2.2
Salespeople in stores and warehouses	5299	2.1
Salaried truck drivers	4363	1.8
Telemarketers	4231	1.7
Administrative employees with customer service tasks not classified under other headings	4224	1.7
Official workers and craftsmen of other trades not classified under other headings	3882	1.6
Other elementary occupations	3861	1.6
Salaried drivers of cars, taxis and vans	3841	1.5

Source: ODISMET [28]

As Adecco Foundation [1] also pointed out, the intersection of disability, gender, and unemployment creates a particularly vulnerable group of women who are at a significantly increased risk of experiencing gender-based violence, poverty, and social isolation. In this way, the invisibility problem arises. It is often challenging to accurately identify violence in these cases, as victims may misinterpret abusive behaviour as overprotective care. Abusers may convince victims that they need protection due to their disability situation. In addition, since most of the time they are confined at home, their network of contacts is very reduced, leading to a spiral of isolation and invisibility (making it more difficult to find a job). Finding a job becomes complicated, not only because of this isolation and invisibility problem, but also by the prejudices that still prevail in society, which, when transferred to companies, reduce their professional opportunities.

Thus, it leads us to a Behavioural Economics framework. This area has gained particular significance since the release of *Nudge* [31], which characterized Behavioural Economics as the concept of "nudging". According to the previous backgrounds analyzed, in order to face the labour exclusion problem of women with disabilities, it is necessary to study in depth the society's behaviours (not only of women with disabilities, but also, and especially, the behaviours of the rest of the population). There is a general social discrimination (much more in the labour contexts) of this collective, as pointed by Vornholt et al. [34]. People (especially employers and other employees in the labour market) could be developing (consciously or not) discrimination/stigmatization processes towards women with disabilities, limiting their ability to participate in the labour spheres and develop an independent life [10].

Miller and Major [27] suggest that social stigma can be a significant source of psychological stress. This stress may cause the stigmatized individual (in this case, woman with disabilities) to avoid engaging in economic activities and the labour market, thereby limiting their empowerment and worsening their social and labour exclusion problem. Social stigma causes some individuals to limit their engagement with the broader community to avoid exposure to discrimination ([8]; or [26]).

In this sense, "[...] from a psychological perspective, the person with disabilities could be suffering from stress, but whether they decide (consciously or unconsciously) to participate or not in the labour market depends on how they can or want to face the previously mentioned stress" (Cruz–Morato and Dueñas–Zambrana [10], p. 351). Compas et al. [7] provided a comprehensive classification of coping strategies, categorizing them as either positive (functional) or negative (dysfunctional). Most coping strategies are considered dysfunctional, with avoiding participation in economic activities being perceived as a less risky option. However, functional coping strategies also exist, and some individuals with disabilities choose to engage in the labour market, often associated with greater human capital and resource availability, boosting their empowerment [10].

Therefore, this context leads us to Social Marketing as an intervention tool in order to change social behaviors to increase the empowerment and labor participation of women with disabilities. In this sense, any initiative that tries to change behaviours for social good (such as Social Marketing) is implicitly assuming the need to incorporate psychological inputs (Behavioural Economics), as it was pointed out by Carvalho and Mazzon [5] or Thaler [30]. That is why Behavioural Economics and Social Marketing are so closely connected to each other (Behavioural Economics would be the basis not only for Social Marketing, but also for general Marketing discipline, due to its focus on human behaviours and the relationship with economic decisions [10]. Moreover, authors such as Lefebvre and Kotler [24] and French [15] exposed that including a Behavioural Economics framework would improve the development of the Social Marketing intervention.

3 Social Marketing Campaigns About Women with Disabilities

The two Social Marketing campaigns selected for this chapter are: "Women in on mode" (developed by Inserta and ONCE Foundation), and "Employment for all", carried out by Adecco Foundation, because they are good examples of the kind of intervention that could be developed to boost SDGs related to the social and labour inclusion of women with disabilities. A content analysis of the campaigns was conducted, analyzing the campaign message, the tone used, its purpose, graphic design, broadcasting media and the target audience (see Galan-Ladero and Galan-Ladero [16] for further information).

3.1 Women in on Mode

About this first example of Social Marketing campaign oriented to improve the labour inclusion of women with disabilities, it is necessary to remember that it has been carried out by the ONCE Foundation and Inserta Empleo.

The ONCE Foundation was established in 1988 through an agreement between the ONCE association and major organizations representing people with disabilities in Spain [29]. It was designed as a tool for cooperation and solidarity, enabling the Spanish blind community to support other disability groups in improving their situation. The Foundation also includes the Spanish Committee of Representatives of People with Disabilities (CERMI) as a member, an entity that unites over 3000 associations.

On the other hand, Inserta Empleo was established in 2009 with a strong commitment to integrating people with disabilities into the workforce [19]. This non-profit organization focuses on providing high-quality training and employment opportunities with long-term prospects, as well as fostering personal autonomy. Continuing the philosophy of the ONCE Foundation, Inserta Empleo supports a socially excluded group, helping to create a pathway toward a promising future. Its activity is mainly founded by public programs (Spanish Government and European Social Found).

Focusing on the campaign, "Women in on mode" was presented on 2018, founded by European Founds, with the objective of shedding light on the compounded disadvantages faced by women with disabilities and promoting their labour market participation. Its first video (broadcasted on YouTube: https://www.youtube.com/watch?v=KzbDkwn6JeU) focuses on the situation of double discrimination of this group, and how their talents and abilities should be oriented to reverse the situation (social barriers, prejudices, family overprotection, self-limitation or lack of knowledge of inclusive resources and tools), claiming their role in the personal as well as in the labour and social spheres.

The spot started with all the negative comments and prejudices about women with disabilities (such as "don't do it", "you are not capable", or "do not try it"). After an informative brief explanation of the intersectionality problem related to their situation, all in black colour and darkness, a woman turns on the lights, transforming every "no" into "on". Therefore, although the video started with a negative vision of the situation, it turns out, focusing on a positive perspective and resilient way to face the problem (in terms of labour inclusion, education, sport and actions of daily life). It finishes by giving the link: mujeresenmodoON.es, a job portal where women with disabilities can access to find employment.

The tone of this communication action is very emotive (focusing on the negative situation at the beginning, with black and white images, and positive and encouraging later, when the images are more colourful). It shows different women with disabilities acting on labour and social contexts, fighting every day to overcome the situation. The classical music used in the background is positive and is oriented to empower this group (one of the main target audiences of this campaign, as well as employers).

This is the first video (with a duration of 1:33 and more than 10,000 views) of a wider campaign, that encompasses other spots (such as https://www.youtube.com/watch?v=erNn_TwsM-A&t=2s), actions in social media (Facebook, Instragram, X and Linkedin) and a specific website (mujeresenmodoON.es, the job portal previously referred), which is the main resource (as well as the Social Marketing campaign itself) that they offer to overcome discrimination and improve the labour inclusion of women with disabilities.

3.2 Employment for All

The Adecco Foundation was created in 1999, as part of the Corporate Social Responsibility initiatives of the Adecco Group, a global leader in human resource management. Its primary mission is to facilitate the integration into the labour market of individuals who face significant barriers to employment, including people with disabilities, individuals over 45 who have been unemployed long-term, women with sole caregiving responsibilities or those who are survivors of gender-based violence, and other groups at risk of social exclusion.

The Adecco Foundation has been a member of the United Nations Global Compact since 2003. The 17 Sustainable Development Goals (SDGs) proposed by the Global Compact address the global challenges faced by society and serve as a framework for the Adecco Foundation's actions. Through their Employment For All Project, the Adecco Foundation directly contributes to [2]:

SDG 1 (No Poverty): Supporting the most vulnerable in our society.

SDG 5 (Gender Equality): Promoting equal opportunities for women.

SDG 10 (Reduced Inequalities): Building a more inclusive labour market.

SDG 8 (Decent Work and Economic Growth): Helping generate employment in Spain.

Thus, in this case, women with disabilities would be part of the intervention, but the aim of their actions is to act in inclusive development in a general way, including other kinds of deprived segments of the population.

About the Social Marketing campaign "Employment for all", it took place in 2015. The video (https://www.youtube.com/watch?v=Ptgx6oES0jA) shows the context of three job interviews in which three women are confronted with questions that reflect prejudice because of their status as women with disabilities, older women or single mothers. The duration of the video is 2 minutes 19 seconds, during which, up to minute 1:39, the message is mainly negative, stressing the discriminatory elements and the impact it has on these women in terms of their participation in the labour market.

However, from that moment on, the tone changes, and these women (looking at the camera and with a positive and empathetic attitude) put forward rational arguments to refute the source of the social stigma, empowering them. "When someone trusts me, my effort and commitment are doubled", says one of these three women. The spot ended with the message: "Thousands of women, great professionals, are left out of the labour market every day because of prejudice. An opportunity can change their lives. Don't put gender on it, put talent on it".

As well as the first campaign analyzed, the tone of this communication action ended with a positive message (although at the beginning is more negative and blames employers who stigmatize these women). The music is emotive and encouraging, and the graphic design is in colour since the first moment (always with subtitles). Although the target audience is the general public, it focuses on the employers' perspective (as well as women, in order to empower them to develop positive coping strategies to overcome the social stigma).

The video can be found in YouTube, with more than 215,000 views, and is part of a holistic campaign, with a specific website (https://fundacionadecco.org/empleoparatodas/8demarzo/#informe). However, as it has been previously exposed, according to the purposes of the Adecco Foundation, women with disabilities are included in the intervention, but the focus of the efforts is on promoting inclusive development more broadly, encompassing other marginalized segments of women as well.

4 Impact on Sustainable Development Goals

Focusing on how SDGs can be achieved in the topic, in this section, the most important SDGs related to this intervention will be listed, describing their connection and current situation, and also providing practical guidance for managers, public policy and other stakeholders.

Therefore, following Dueñas-Zambrana and Cruz-Morato [14], who connected this issue with SDGs number 10 (Reduce Inequalities) and number 8 (Promote sustained, inclusive, and sustainable economic growth, full and productive employment, and decent work for all), in line also with Adecco Foundation [2], we should take into consideration SDGs number 5 (Gender Equality) and even number 1 (No poverty) as well.

Regarding SDG number 5 (Gender Equality), which seeks to promote equal opportunities for women, this objective is clearly related to our topic. So that, if we focus on reducing labour exclusion of women with disabilities, this will enhance a more equal gender context for this collective. What is more, this objective also has a strong relationship with SDG 10 (Reduced Inequalities) and a strong impact on SDG number 8 (Decent Work and Economic Growth). However, as explained by the UN [33], achieving gender equality and empowering all women and girls, in a general sense, is clearly off track. The participation of women in public life, labour contexts and managerial tasks is still far from real gender equality, being the kind of approach exposed in this chapter an effective and innovative way to improve the situation.

About SDG 10 (Reduced Inequalities), building a more inclusive labour market is clearly related to our approach and this objective. Trying to increase labour participation of women with disabilities is basically a way to build a more inclusive labour market (as long as this group of population is suffering a situation of multiple discrimination or intersectionality that leads them to the exclusion of labour spheres, as it has been previously exposed). And, thus, it reduces inequality within and among countries. This objective is connected to SDG number 5, as it has been said, and also numbers 8 and 1, helping to promote more sustainable and inclusive economic growth, reducing poverty rates. Nevertheless, the global situation is still dramatic: one person in six encounters discrimination. "Racial discrimination and discrimination based on age, gender, religion or belief remain pervasive" (UN [33], p. 16). An intervention based on Social Marketing and Behavioural Economics would encompass the main variables that lead to discrimination and could offer a way out to women with disabilities (better say, a way in into the labour market).

With regard to SDG number 8 (Promote sustained, inclusive and sustainable economic growth, full and productive employment and decent work for all), this objective is also connected to our topic (it is basically the main objective of this research). Therefore, focusing on improving the labour and social inclusion of women with disabilities will develop a more decent work for this collective, motivating them to participate in economic activity, and consequently increasing inclusive and sustainable economic growth. So, it is related to SDG 5 and 10, and will also promote SDG 1 (No Poverty). However, although some economic sectors have recovered their pre-pandemic levels (such as tourism), the current situation is exacerbating income inequality and discriminating against some groups of the population (such as women), so achieving SDG 8 requires implementing policies that promote economic growth while prioritizing social justice and inclusive employment opportunities [33], as we are proposing in this research.

About SDG 1 (End poverty in all its forms everywhere), supporting the most vulnerable in our society is the essential aim of this chapter. Reducing poverty is an expected outcome of reducing inequality (SDG 10), increasing gender equality (SDG number 5), and especially, improving inclusive and sustainable economic growth (SDG 8). Nevertheless, according to UN [33], the situation is still complicated (COVID-19 pandemic, geo-political crisis and war conflicts...) so eradicating poverty by 2030 seems increasingly unattainable. Therefore, an innovative approach to face the situation, as it has been exposed, will increase real opportunities to escape the poverty trap.

5 Conclusions

When focusing on social inclusion, labour inclusion plays a crucial role. Vulnerable groups, such as people with disabilities and women, frequently face heightened barriers in the labour market [10], mainly based on discrimination. This is particularly evident when these factors intersect, as women with disabilities tend to exhibit lower participation rates.

Therefore, an intervention grounded in Social Marketing and Behavioural Economics would address the key factors contributing to discrimination, potentially providing women with disabilities a pathway into the labour market. Thus, in a similar way to the research previously quoted, that analyze this kind of intervention for all people with disabilities, from a Social Marketing/Behavioural Economics approach, it would be necessary to promote positive coping responses for women with disabilities (in order to face social stigma, by increasing their empowerment and participating in labour market). In line with Calderwood and Wellington [4], who defended specific Social Marketing strategies designed for stigmatized individuals, Social Marketing campaigns would be segmented and specifically oriented to women with disabilities (and even different groups of this collective).

However, it would also be necessary to reduce discrimination from the rest of society (as well as promote generosity) through Social Marketing/Behavioural Economics to tackle the situation of this group. As it has been analyzed in the two examples studied, it is very important to develop an informative but also positive tone for the campaign message, trying not to blame society (sometimes, discrimination is an unconscious outcome, or would be based on lack of information).

These Spanish examples aim to inspire both academic and professional sectors, fostering advancement toward the SDGs. Thus, this topic is related to SDGs number 5 (Gender Equality), 10 (Reduced Inequalities), 8 (Promote sustained, inclusive and sustainable economic growth, full and productive employment and decent work for all) and 1 (End poverty in all its forms everywhere). This is very important because, despite the growing global attention to achieving genuine inclusive development, as highlighted by the United Nations Sustainable Development Goals (SDGs), the challenges remain significant, and it is necessary to explore innovative ways to improve the situation.

References

1. Adecco Foundation (2024a) Empleo para todas. La mujer en riesgo de exclusión. Informes Fundación Adecco. Available online: https://fundacionadecco.org/wp-content/uploads/2024/03/Informe-EmpleoParaTodas-2024.pdf. Accessed on 23 Nov 2024
2. Adecco Foundation (2024b) Quiénes somos. Available online: https://fundacionadecco.org/quienes-somos/. Accessed on 23 Nov 2024
3. Brah A, Phoenix A (2004) Ain't I a Woman? Revisiting intersectionality. J Int Women's Stud 5(3):75–86. https://vc.bridgew.edu/jiws/vol5/iss3/8
4. Calderwood KA, Wellington WJ (2013) Social marketing strategies for stigmatized target populations: a case example for problem gamblers and family members of problem gamblers. Qual Rep 18(49):1–19. https://doi.org/10.46743/2160-3715/2013.1431
5. Carvalho HC, Mazzon JA (2013) Homo economicus and social marketing: questioning traditional models of behavior. J Soc Mark 3(2):162–175. https://doi.org/10.1108/JSOCM-11-2011-0080
6. COCEMFE (2019) Manual básico sobre género y discapacidad. Instituto de la Mujer. Available online: https://www.cocemfe.es/wp-content/uploads/2020/06/COCEMFE-manual-genero-discapacidad.pdf. Accessed on 23 Nov 2024
7. Compas BE, Connor-Smith JK, Saltzman H, Thomsen AH, Wadsworth ME (2001) Coping with stress during childhood and adolescence: problems, progress and potential in theory and research. Psychol Bull 127(1):87–127. https://doi.org/10.1037/0033-2909.127.1.87
8. Corrigan PW, Watson AC (2002) The paradox of self stigma and mental illness. Clin Psychol Sci Pract 9(1):35–53. https://doi.org/10.1093/clipsy.9.1.35
9. Crenshaw K (1991) Mapping the Margins: Intersectionality, Identity Politics, and Violence against Women of Color. Stanford Law Rev 43(6):1241–1299. https://doi.org/10.2307/1229039

10. Cruz-Morato MA, Dueñas-Zambrana C (2021) Disability, Labour Inclusion and Social Marketing in Spain: The ONCE foundation case. In: Galan-Ladero MM, Rivera RG (eds) Applied Social Marketing and Quality of Life, Applying Quality of Life Research. Springer, Cham. https://doi.org/10.1007/978-3-030-83286-5_21
11. Deery M, Jago L (2015) Revisiting talent management, work-life balance and retention strategies. Int J Contemp Hosp Manag 27(3):453–472. https://doi.org/10.1108/ijchm-12-2013-0538
12. De Sá MAD, Oliveira MIM, Calado Días SMR, Barbosa MLA (2017) Human resources practices and inclusion of people with disabilities in the hotel industry of Belém, Brazil: a multiple case study. REGE-Revista de Gestão 24:13–23. https://doi.org/10.1016/j.rege.2016.08.002
13. Domínguez Vila T, Alén González E (2023) Disability and the labour market: conditioning factors for the inactive population with intellectual disabilities. Int J Develop Disab. https://doi.org/10.1080/20473869.2023.2183306
14. Dueñas-Zambrana C, Cruz-Morato MA (2023) Corporate social marketing and the labor inclusion of people with disabilities. A case study of ilunion hotels. In: Galan-Ladero MM, Alves HM (eds) Social Marketing and Sustainable Development Goals (SDGs), Springer Business Cases. Springer, Cham. https://doi.org/10.1007/978-3-031-27377-3_6
15. French J (2013) Social business, social behavior and social marketing: three cornerstones of future social development. Social Business 3(4):285–296. https://doi.org/10.1362/204440813X13875569153948
16. Galan-Ladero MM, Galan-Ladero MA (2019) The importance of social Marketing in Global Health Emergencies: the case of Zika virus infection. In: Galan-Ladero M, Alves H (eds) Case studies on social marketing. Management for professionals. Springer, Cham. https://doi.org/10.1007/978-3-030-04843-3_7
17. Gupta J, Pouw NRM, Ros-Tonen MAF (2015) Towards an Elaborated Theory of Inclusive Development. Eur J Dev Res 27(4):541–559. https://doi.org/10.1057/ejdr.2015.30
18. Gupta A, Kavanagh A, Disney G (2021) The impact of and government planning and responses to pandemics for people with disability: a rapid review. Int J Environ Res Public Health 18:6505. https://doi.org/10.3390/ijerph18126505
19. Inserta Empleo (2024) Quiénes somos. Available online: https://www.insertaempleo.es/quienes/sobre-nosotros. Accessed on 23 Nov 2024
20. Instituto Nacional de Estadística, INE (2019) El Empleo de las Personas con Discapacidad. Notas de prensa 2019. Available online: https://www.ine.es/prensa/epd_2019.pdf. Accessed on 22 Sept 2021
21. Instituto Nacional de Estadística, INE (2022) El Empleo de las Personas con Discapacidad. Notas de prensa 2020. Available online: https://www.ine.es/prensa/epd_2020.pdf. Accessed on 18 June 2022
22. Instituto Nacional de Estadística, INE (2023) El Empleo de las Personas con Discapacidad. Notas de prensa 2022. Available online: https://www.ine.es/prensa/epd_2022.pdf. Accessed on 23 Aug 2024
23. Lee S, McCann D, Messenger JC (2007) Working time around the world: Trends in working hours, laws, and policies in a global comparative perspective. Routledge
24. Lefebvre RC, Kotler P (2012) Design thinking, demarketing and behavioral economics: fostering interdisciplinary growth in social marketing. In: Hastings G, Angus K, Bryant C (eds) The SAGE handbook of social marketing. SAGE Publications Ltd, London, pp 80–94. https://doi.org/10.4135/9781446201008.n6
25. Madera JM, Taylor C, Barber NA (2020) Customer service evaluations of employees with disabilities: The roles of perceived competence and service failure. Cornell Hosp Q 6(1):5–18. https://doi.org/10.1177/1938965519882315
26. Mandiberg JM, Warner R (2012) Business development and marketing within communities of social service clients. J Bus Res 65(12):1736–1742. https://doi.org/10.1016/j.jbusres.2012.02.015
27. Miller CT, Major B (2000) Coping with stigma and prejudice. In: Heatherton TF, Kleck RE, Hebl. M.R., Hull JG (eds) The social psychology of stigma. Guilford, New York, pp. 243–272. doi:https://doi.org/10.1017/S204579601700021X, 27

28. ODISMET (2020) Volumen de contrataciones a personas con discapacidad por principales ocupaciones y actividades económicas. Available online: https://www.odismet.es/indicador-basico/111volumen-de-contrataciones-personas-con-discapacidad-por-principales-ocupaciones. Accessed on 21 Mar 2022
29. ONCE Foundation (2024) Presentación. Available online: https://www.fundaciononce.es/es/quienes-somos/presentacion. Accessed on 23 Nov 2024
30. Thaler BRH (2016) Behavioral economics: past, present, and future. Am Econ Rev 106(7):1577–1600. https://doi.org/10.2139/ssrn.2790606
31. Thaler RH, Sunstein CR (2008) Nudge. Penguin Books, New York
32. United Nations, UN (2015) Do you know all 17 SDGs? Available online: https://sdgs.un.org/es/goals. Accesed on 15 Nov 2024
33. United Nations, UN (2024) Progress towards the sustainable development goals. Report of the secretary-general. Available online: https://unstats.un.org/sdgs/files/report/2024/SG-SDG-Progress-Report-2024-advanced-unedited-version.pdf. Aaccesed on 15 Nov 2024
34. Vornholt K, Villotti P, Muschalla B, Bauer J, Colella A, Zijlstra F, Corbiere M (2018) Disability and employment– overview and highlights. Eur J Work Organ Psychol 27:40–55. https://doi.org/10.1080/1359432X.2017.1387536

Carmen Dueñas-Zambrana Affiliation: Professor of Master's Degree in Health Social Work, Faculty of Health Sciences, Valencian International University. Researcher of Department of Social Psychology, Social Work and Social Services, and Social Anthropology, University of Málaga.

Education: PhD Student on Legal and Social Sciences at University of Málaga. Expert on Labour Guidance. MSc on Research and Social and Community Intervention. Degree on Social Work.

Main research topics: Disability, Labour and Social Inclusion, Social Marketing, Social Services Quality, Social Participation.

Marco A. Cruz-Morato Affiliation: Professor of the Economics and Business Administration Department (Business Management), University of Málaga since 2013.

Education: Phd on Economics and Business Administration. Post-graduate on International Cooperation and Development Policies. Post-graduate on Teaching. Degree on Administration and Business Management. Degree on Economics.

Main research topics: Business Management, Human Resources, Tourism, Welfare Economics, Corporate Social Responsibility, Social Marketing, Behavioural Economics and Disability.

Ten Gaps of Smart and Sustainable Cities 12

Maria Teresa Pinheiro Melo Borges-Tiago,
Flávio Gomes Borges Tiago,
and Sónia Margarida Moreira Avelar

> *The concept of a smart city is not just about being technologically advanced, but also about being sustainable, inclusive, and citizen-centric.*
>
> – Narendra Modi (Prime Minister of India)

Abstract

Smart and sustainable cities aim to enhance urban living by integrating technological and sustainable practices. However, several gaps have hindered their full realization. First, integrating diverse technologies and developing a robust infrastructure pose considerable challenges, requiring comprehensive strategies for seamless operation across various urban systems. Data privacy and security have emerged as critical concerns, requiring protecting citizens' information against breaches and misuse. Digital divide and inequality represent another gap, as not all populations have equal access to digital resources, exacerbating social and economic disparities. These initiatives' funding and financial models often lack the innovative mechanisms necessary to support long-term sustainability. Governance and policy frameworks must evolve to guide the development and implementation of smart city projects and ensure they meet all stakeholders' needs. Public engagement and acceptance are crucial to the success of smart initiatives, necessitating strategies that foster community involvement and buy-in. Interoperability and standards are essential for the compatibility of technologies and systems; however, the absence of universal standards complicates integration efforts. While aiming for sustainability, the environmental impact of smart cities must be carefully managed to avoid adverse effects. Skill gaps and the need for workforce development present challenges in maintaining and advancing smart city technologies. Finally, effective monitoring and evaluation

M. T. P. M. Borges-Tiago (✉) · F. G. B. Tiago · S. M. M. Avelar
University of the Azores, Ponta Delgada, Portugal
e-mail: maria.tp.tiago@uac.pt; flavio.gb.tiago@uac.pt; sonia.mm.avelar@uac.pt

B. Casais (ed.), *Integrated Science to Achieve Sustainable Development Goals*,
Integrated Science 37, https://doi.org/10.1007/978-3-031-88777-2_12

mechanisms are required to assess progress, adapt strategies, and ensure the achievement of smart and sustainable objectives. Addressing these gaps is vital for fostering the success of smart and sustainable cities.

Graphical Abstract

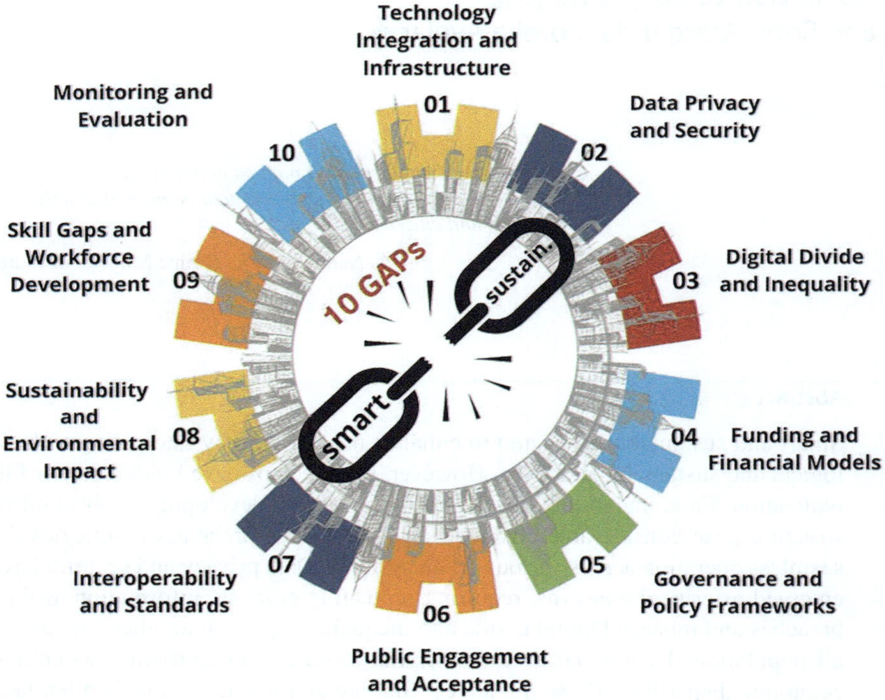

Keywords

Data privacy · Digital divides · Digital transformation · Governance · Interoperability · Skill gaps · Smart initiatives · Sustainability · Technology · Urban living

1 Introduction

Smart and sustainable cities are at the forefront of a global push toward urban environments prioritizing environmental conservation, resource efficiency, and socio-economic well-being [6, 18]. By leveraging various advanced technologies and innovative practices, these cities aim to optimize their urban infrastructure, enhance public services, and promote sustainable resource management [6]. However, despite the crucial promise of these advancements, the widespread implementation of smart and sustainable city initiatives is fraught with challenges [19]. This chapter delves into the gaps that currently limit the full realization of smart and sustainable cities, providing a structured overview of 10 gaps based on recent academic insights and empirical evidence.

2 Background

As cities worldwide embark on this ambitious path, numerous gaps and challenges impede the full realization of their potential [7]. This chapter explores ten critical gaps in smart and sustainable city development (see Fig. 12.1), which, despite widespread advancements, remain unresolved in cities worldwide.

These gaps underscore the complexities of modern urban development and the necessity for strategic frameworks that can bridge the technological, infrastructural, social, and economic divides. We delve into each of these gaps by examining the issues they present and their implications for the sustainable future of cities.

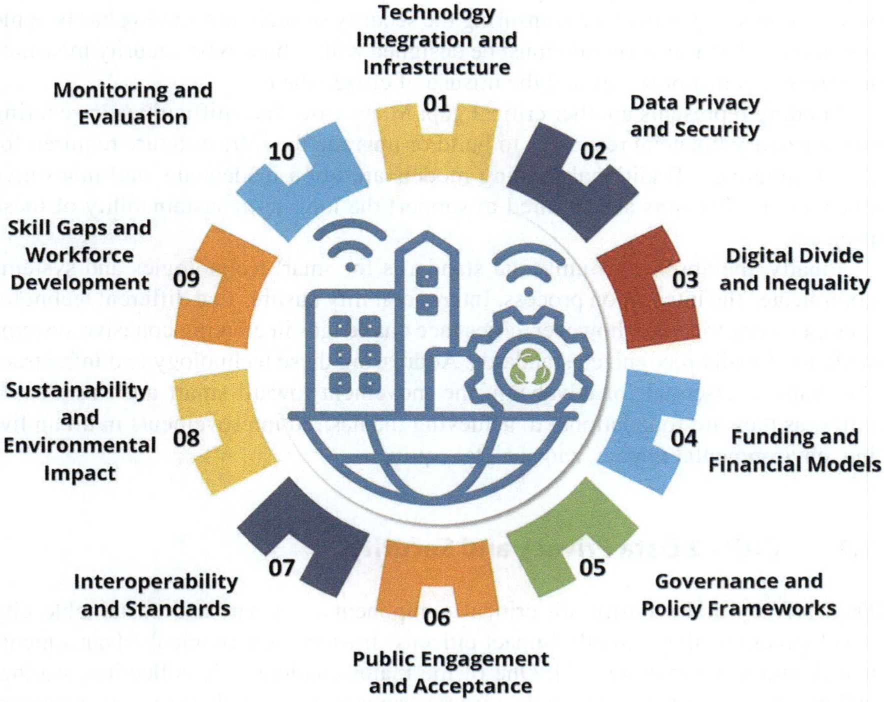

Fig. 12.1 The ten gaps. (Source: Authors)

2.1 GAP #1 Technology Integration and Infrastructure

Integrating technology and infrastructure is pivotal for developing smart and sustainable cities; however, numerous challenges remain in fully realizing this vision [16]. The integration of diverse technologies across urban systems is a critical issue. Today, cities comprise multiple infrastructure networks (e.g., transportation, energy, waste management, and water systems) that require harmonization for effective smart-city operations. This technological integration requires a comprehensive strategy to ensure seamless connectivity and interoperability, without which desired efficiency and sustainability benefits cannot be fully achieved.

Infrastructure gaps persist, particularly in developing and upgrading the physical and digital networks necessary to support smart technologies. Many cities struggle to modernize their infrastructure to handle the data-intensive requirements of smart technologies. The digital divide exacerbates this issue, as not all regions or populations have equal access to the necessary digital infrastructure, such as broadband internet or advanced data centers. This inequality can create further social and economic disparities that hamper the equitable development of smart cities. In addition to these challenges, integrating technology raises data privacy and security concerns. As cities increasingly rely on interconnected systems that collect and process vast amounts of personal data, ensuring the security of such information has become paramount. The infrastructure must be designed with robust cybersecurity measures to protect against breaches and the misuse of citizen data.

Funding represents another critical gap. Many cities face difficulties in securing the necessary financial resources to build or upgrade the infrastructure required for smart initiatives. Traditional funding models are often inadequate, and innovative financial mechanisms are required to support the long-term sustainability of these projects.

Finally, the absence of universal standards for smart technologies and systems complicates the integration process. Interoperability ensures that different technologies can work together; however, cities face challenges in creating cohesive systems without globally recognized standards. Addressing these technology and infrastructure gaps is essential for advancing the movement toward smart and sustainable cities, as they are foundational to achieving the desired improvements in urban living, environmental impact, and societal equity.

2.2 GAP #2 Data Privacy and Security

Data privacy and security are critical components in smart and sustainable city development as they directly impact citizens' trust in technological advancements and digital infrastructure [23]. One of the major challenges is collecting, storing, and processing vast amounts of data from various sources, such as sensors, cameras, smart devices, and citizens' interactions with digital services. Although these data enable smarter decision-making and improved city management, they also introduce substantial risks related to privacy and security.

A key concern is potential data breaches, which can expose sensitive personal information and undermine public trust. In a smart city environment, data are continuously collected from diverse urban systems, including healthcare, transportation, energy, and public services. The centralized nature of many of these systems and the interconnectedness of data increases their vulnerability to cyberattacks. Data protection against unauthorized access and misuse requires sophisticated cybersecurity measures, including encryption, multifactor authentication, and real-time monitoring. Without these protections, systems designed to improve urban life could become vulnerable.

Moreover, the sheer volume and complexity of data in smart cities pose considerable challenges for data governance and management. Many cities lack comprehensive policies to regulate data collection, sharing, and storage. A well-defined governance framework ensures that data are used responsibly and transparently. This includes ensuring compliance with international data protection regulations such as the General Data Protection Regulation (GDPR) in Europe, which sets strict data privacy and security standards.

Another data privacy and security gap is balancing the benefits of data-driven innovations with citizens' privacy rights. The tension between security objectives and personal privacy increases as cities deploy technologies like surveillance cameras, biometric sensors, and data analytics platforms. The challenge lies in implementing these technologies to maximize their potential without infringing on individual freedom or enabling state surveillance. Public awareness and engagement are essential to address these concerns, ensuring that citizens are informed about how their data are being collected and used and that they can opt-out or control their data where appropriate.

Finally, smart cities must develop strategies to resist data breaches and cyberattacks. This includes disaster recovery plans, regular audits, and continuous security protocol updates. Addressing data privacy and security gaps is vital for protecting citizens and fostering the sustainable growth and trust required to make smart cities successful.

2.3 GAP #3 Digital Divide and Inequality

Digital divide and inequality are critical barriers to realizing smart and sustainable cities, impacting both access to technology and the distribution of its benefits [5]. In a smart city, where technologies such as the high-speed internet, data analytics, and Internet of Things (IoT) devices are integral to managing urban systems and improving the quality of life, disparities in access to these resources can widen existing social and economic gaps.

The digital divide refers to unequal access to digital technologies and the internet across different population segments. This divide often occurs along socioeconomic, geographic, and demographic lines, with low-income communities, rural areas, and older populations typically having less access to advanced digital infrastructure. In the context of smart cities, this lack of access can mean that some citizens are left behind and unable to take advantage of the benefits of technology, such as improved healthcare services, more efficient transportation systems, and better access to education and employment opportunities.

A critical factor exacerbating this divide is the unequal availability of digital infrastructure. Many urban areas, particularly in developing countries or underfunded regions, lack high-speed internet connectivity, robust telecommunications networks, and access to smart devices, which are foundational to smart city initiatives. Without this basic infrastructure, entire populations are excluded from participating in the smart city ecosystem, reinforcing social inequities.

In addition to physical access, digital literacy critically contributes to inequality. Even in cities with a widespread digital infrastructure, a gap persists between those with the skills to use technology and those without [1, 17]. This skill gap can limit individuals' ability to benefit from smart city technologies such as e-governance platforms, digital healthcare services, and online education resources. Consequently, populations with lower digital literacy are at risk of further marginalization in a smart city environment.

Addressing the digital divide and inequality requires targeted efforts to expand digital infrastructure and improve digital literacy across all population segments. Governments and city planners must prioritize inclusive strategies that ensure all citizens can access and benefit from smart city technologies regardless of income level, age, or geographic location. This can include subsidizing internet access for low-income households, providing public Wi-Fi hotspots in underserved areas, and offering digital literacy programs to equip individuals with the skills they need to navigate the digital world. Bridging the digital divide is not only a matter of social equity but also essential for the long-term sustainability of smart cities.

2.4 GAP #4 Funding and Financial Models

Establishing a smart infrastructure with digital networks, energy-efficient systems, and other advanced technologies requires a substantial initial investment. Traditional financial models often fail to address the long-term needs for sustainable urban development, leaving cities struggling to secure sufficient funding for such projects [21]. One of the primary gaps in funding smart cities is the reliance on conventional public financing mechanisms such as government budgets and municipal bonds. Although these sources can provide initial capital, they may be insufficient to cover the scale and complexity of smart-city initiatives, particularly in cities with limited financial resources. Moreover, public budgets are often strained by competing priorities, such as healthcare, education, and basic infrastructure, making it difficult for governments to allocate the necessary funds for smart city development.

Private sector involvement offers a potential solution to this funding gap but comes with challenges. Public-private partnerships (PPPs) have emerged as a popular model for sharing financial burdens between governments and private companies. However, aligning the interests of both parties may be difficult. Private investors typically seek short-term returns on investment, whereas smart city projects require long-term commitments and may not yield immediate financial gains. This misalignment of incentives can hinder the formation of effective partnerships and slow the progress of smart city initiatives.

Innovative financial models are essential for overcoming these challenges and ensuring the sustainability of smart city projects. One promising approach is the development of outcome-based financing models such as social impact and green bonds. These models link financial returns to specific sustainability or social impact goals, thus encouraging investments in long-term outcome-driven projects. Green bonds, for instance, have been successfully used to fund renewable energy projects and sustainable infrastructure, making them viable options for smart cities seeking to fund environmentally friendly technologies.

In addition, leveraging emerging technologies such as blockchain can help improve transparency and accountability in smart city financing. Blockchain can track and verify financial transactions, ensuring that funds are used effectively and are aligned with sustainability goals. This can build trust among investors and stakeholders, making it easier to attract funding.

Cities must explore diverse and innovative funding mechanisms to support their ambitious goals [21]. Traditional financial models alone are unlikely to meet the needs of these projects; thus, creative and flexible solutions are required to bridge the funding gap.

2.5 GAP #5 Governance and Policy Frameworks

Governance and policy frameworks are essential for the development and operation of smart and sustainable cities [13]. These frameworks establish the legal, regulatory, and institutional foundations necessary to efficiently, inclusively, and sustainably implement smart city projects. However, many cities currently face substantial governance and policy gaps, hindering their ability to realize the benefits of smart technologies fully.

The rapid pace of technological advancement in areas such as artificial intelligence (AI), IoT, and big data often outstrips the ability of policymakers to develop and implement corresponding regulations. Consequently, many smart city initiatives operate in a regulatory gray area, with outdated or incomplete policies that fail to address new challenges, such as data privacy, cybersecurity, and the ethical use of technology. Moreover, governance structures in many cities are often fragmented, with responsibilities divided among multiple government agencies and departments. This siloed approach can lead to inefficiencies and a lack of coordination when implementing smart city initiatives. To illustrate, different departments may oversee transportation, energy, and public services; however, smart city technologies often require an integrated approach across these sectors. The full potential of smart cities remains unrealized without robust governance mechanisms to facilitate cross-departmental collaboration.

Additionally, smart city governance must be transparent, flexible, and adaptable. As technologies evolve, so must policies and regulations that govern their use. Rigid policy frameworks can hinder innovation and prevent cities from fully exploiting emerging technologies. To address this issue, cities must develop dynamic governance structures that allow continuous learning, adaptation, and improvement.

2.6 GAP #6 Public Engagement and Acceptance

Public engagement and acceptance are fundamental for the success of smart and sustainable city initiatives [2]. As these projects often involve substantial changes in urban infrastructure, governance, and daily life, they require broad-based support from the communities they serve [15]. However, many smart city efforts face challenges in achieving meaningful public participation and widespread acceptance, limiting their long-term success and sustainability.

A key challenge in public engagement is ensuring that citizens are adequately informed about smart city initiatives and how they impact their lives. Many smart city projects are highly technical and involve complex technologies, such as IoT, AI, and big data, which can be difficult for the average citizen to understand fully. Without clear communication from city planners and policymakers, the public may struggle to grasp the benefits of these projects or feel disconnected from the decision-making processes that shape their urban environment. This can lead to skepticism, resistance, or apathy because citizens may perceive smart city technologies as invasive or irrelevant to their needs.

Moreover, public engagement must go beyond one-way communication. Specifically, citizens should be involved in the planning, design, and implementation of smart city projects. Traditional top-down approaches to urban development, in which government officials or private companies make decisions without meaningful input from the community, often fail to capture the diverse perspectives and needs of the population. Smart city initiatives that lack citizen involvement risk overlooking important social, cultural, and local considerations, resulting in projects that may not align with the actual needs or preferences of the people they are intended to serve.

Inclusivity is another crucial aspect of public engagement. Smart city projects must ensure that all population segments, including marginalized groups, can participate in the decision-making processes. This involves addressing the digital divide, as certain populations—such as low-income individuals, older adults, or those living in underserved areas—may have limited access to the digital tools needed to engage with smart city technologies or platforms. Failure to include these voices can exacerbate existing social inequalities and lead to an uneven distribution of the benefits of smart city projects.

Public acceptance is closely linked to trust, which is built through transparency and accountability. Citizens must trust that smart city technologies are being used responsibly, particularly for data collection and surveillance. Concerns about data privacy, security, and government overreach can erode public trust if not adequately addressed through clear policies and open dialogue. Therefore, governments and city planners must prioritize transparency regarding technology deployment, data handling, and decision-making.

Fostering strong public engagement and gaining public acceptance requires creating participatory, inclusive, and transparent governance models for smart city projects. By meaningfully involving citizens, addressing their concerns, and maintaining open communication channels, cities can garner the support required to ensure that smart initiatives are sustainable, equitable, and widely embraced.

2.7 GAP #7 Interoperability and Standards

Interoperability and universal standards are critical factors in the development of smart and sustainable cities [3]. These cities rely on a wide array of technologies, from IoT devices to data analytics platforms and smart infrastructure systems, and all must work seamlessly to deliver improved urban living [14]. However, the absence of consistent and comprehensive standards and challenges related to interoperability often impede the integration and scaling of smart-city technologies.

Interoperability refers to the ability of different systems, devices, and applications to communicate, exchange data, and collaborate. In a smart city, various technologies must operate cohesively across multiple domains, such as transportation, energy, healthcare, and public safety [14]. For example, real-time data from traffic sensors must be integrated with transportation management systems to optimize traffic flows, reduce congestion, and improve public transportation services. If these systems are not interoperable, they function independently, limiting the overall efficiency and effectiveness of smart-city ecosystems.

A key challenge in achieving interoperability is the lack of standardized protocols and interfaces for smart-city technologies. Different vendors have developed numerous systems for smart cities, each using proprietary technologies, data formats, and communication protocols. This creates fragmentation and complicates the integration of different systems into a single cohesive system. Without universal standards, cities face substantial technical and financial barriers when scaling their smart infrastructures or adopting new technologies. Each new system may require custom integration efforts, which is likely time-consuming, costly, and prone to errors.

Developing and adopting universal standards for smart city technologies are essential for overcoming these barriers. Standards ensure that different systems can communicate and exchange data consistently regardless of the vendor or technology platform. This simplifies the integration of new technologies and facilitates innovation by allowing developers to build on existing systems, rather than starting from scratch. Moreover, standards promote competition by preventing vendors from locking in, allowing cities to choose the best solutions for their specific needs without being tied to a single supplier.

Organizations such as the International Organization for Standardization (ISO) and the International Telecommunication Union (ITU) are developing global standards for smart cities that cover data management, IoT communication protocols, and cybersecurity. However, the adoption of these standards has been slow because cities, technology providers, and regulatory bodies often operate under different frameworks and priorities. To address this issue, greater collaboration between governments, industry stakeholders, and standardization bodies is required to accelerate the development and implementation of universal standards.

In addition to the technical standards, regulatory frameworks must align to support interoperability. Governments and policymakers play a crucial role in creating conditions for interoperable smart city systems by adopting regulations that promote open standards and ensure that new technologies are compatible with existing infrastructure.

By ensuring that different systems and technologies work together seamlessly, cities can unlock the full potential of their smart infrastructure, enabling more efficient urban management, reducing costs, and improving the quality of life for their citizens.

2.8 GAP #8 Sustainability and Environmental Impact

Sustainability and environmental impacts are central considerations in developing smart and sustainable cities [2, 19]. These cities aim to improve urban living by incorporating advanced technologies while minimizing adverse environmental effects. However, achieving this balance is challenging because deploying new technologies and infrastructure can, depending on how they are managed, both help and hinder environmental sustainability.

One of the primary goals of smart cities is to reduce their environmental footprint by optimizing the use of resources, such as energy, water, and land. Technologies such as smart grids can enhance energy use efficiency by dynamically adjusting energy distribution based on demand, integrating renewable energy sources, and reducing waste. In addition, smart buildings equipped with sensors and automation systems can monitor and regulate energy consumption, substantially reducing greenhouse gas emissions. Similarly, smart waste management systems can optimize waste collection routes, reduce fuel consumption, and improve recycling rates, lowering the overall environmental impact.

However, although smart technologies offer substantial potential for reducing environmental impact, concerns about their sustainability remain. Many smart city systems, such as IoT devices, sensors, and communication networks, require substantial energy and resources for manufacturing, deployment, and maintenance. The widespread use of these devices can contribute to electronic waste (e-waste) as technologies rapidly become obsolete or are replaced. If not managed properly, the environmental cost of deploying smart city infrastructure may offset some of the sustainability benefits.

Renewable energy integration is another critical component of sustainable smart cities. By leveraging technologies such as solar panels, wind turbines, and energy storage systems, cities can transition to cleaner energy sources, reducing their reliance on fossil fuels. Smart grids are pivotal in this transition, enabling better integration of variable renewable energy sources and balancing supply and demand. However, cities must ensure that renewable energy systems are scalable and that energy storage and distribution infrastructure can support future growth.

Water conservation and management are crucial to the sustainability of smart cities. With growing urban populations putting pressure on water resources, smart water management systems can monitor water usage, detect leaks, and optimize water distribution to reduce waste. These systems can help cities manage their water supply more sustainably and adapt to changing environmental conditions exacerbated by climate change such as droughts or floods.

In addition, smart transportation systems contribute to sustainability by reducing emissions and improving mobility. Technologies such as electric vehicles, bike-sharing programs, and smart traffic management systems can reduce the carbon footprint of urban transportation. For example, real-time traffic monitoring and optimization can decrease congestion and vehicle emissions while promoting public transportation and reducing reliance on private cars.

However, one challenge in integrating sustainability into smart city planning is ensuring that environmental benefits are equally distributed. Green technologies and smart infrastructure are often concentrated in affluent areas, leaving lower-income neighborhoods behind. Smart city policies must prioritize inclusivity to ensure environmental justice, guaranteeing that all residents benefit from sustainability initiatives.

2.9 GAP #9 Skill Gaps and Workforce Development

Skill gaps and workforce development are critical challenges in advancing smart and sustainable cities [12]. As cities become smarter, leveraging advanced technologies such as AI, IoT, big data, and automation, the demand for a workforce with specialized skills in these areas grows [20]. However, such skilled workers are unavailable in many cities, hindering the successful implementation and operation of smart city initiatives.

Furthermore, one of the most significant challenges is the rapid pace of technological change, which often outpaces the workforce's ability to adapt [12]. Technologies critical to smart city functions, such as AI for predictive analytics, IoT for infrastructure monitoring, and data analytics for decision-making, require workers with considerable expertise. However, the supply of professionals trained in these emerging technologies has not kept up with demand, leading to skill shortages that can delay or prevent the rollout of smart city projects.

Moreover, the workforce gap is not limited to technical skills [12]. Smart cities require interdisciplinary knowledge because integrating technology into urban planning and management necessitates collaboration across engineering, urban planning, environmental science, public policy, and social sciences. Workers need to understand the technical aspects of smart technologies and how these interact with broader urban systems and citizens' needs. Bridging this gap requires a holistic education and workforce development approach, including technical and non-technical skills.

In addition to the technical expertise required to design and maintain smart city systems, cities also need workers with skills to manage the data generated by these systems. Data governance, cybersecurity, and privacy management are becoming increasingly important as cities collect vast amounts of data from sensors, devices, and citizens. Without a workforce capable of managing and securing these data, cities may face risks related to data breaches, privacy violations, and the misuse of information, which can undermine public trust and the effectiveness of smart city projects.

Workforce development strategies must focus on upgrading the existing workforce and training new generations. Ongoing professional development and retraining programs are essential for helping existing workers acquire the skills required to work with new technologies. Governments, educational institutions, and private companies should collaborate to offer targeted training programs, certifications, and courses focusing on the technologies that drive smart city innovations.

Education systems must adapt to prepare future generations of students for the demands of the smart city workforce. This includes integrating Science, Technology, Engineering, and Mathematics (STEM) education into curricula at all levels, from primary school to university, and emphasizing interdisciplinary learning. Collaboration between academia, industry, and the government can also help ensure that educational programs align with the specific needs of smart cities and provide students with the skills and experiences needed to thrive in such environments.

Finally, addressing the workforce development gap requires a focus on inclusivity. As smart city technologies transform the job market, ensuring that all population segments have access to the training and opportunities required to participate in the smart city economy is essential. Special attention must be paid to underrepresented groups, including women, minorities, and low-income populations, to ensure that workforce development efforts promote diversity and do not exacerbate existing inequalities.

2.10 GAP #10 Monitoring and Evaluation

Monitoring and evaluation (M&E) are critical for the development and success of smart and sustainable cities [4]. These processes ensure that smart city initiatives achieve their intended goals, remain adaptable to changing circumstances, and provide measurable benefits to the citizens. Effective M&E frameworks allow cities to assess the impact of their projects, adjust strategies as necessary, and ensure the efficient use of resources. However, many cities face substantial challenges in establishing and implementing robust M&E systems.

One of the main challenges is the complexity of smart city initiatives, which often involve multiple technologies, stakeholders, and objectives [14]. Monitoring the performance of diverse systems, such as smart grids, transportation networks, public services, and waste management, requires collecting and analyzing large amounts of data from various sources. Cities must have the technical capability to integrate these data, analyze them in real-time, and extract meaningful insights to inform decision-making. The lack of standardized metrics for evaluating the performance of smart technologies complicates this process, making it difficult to compare the results across different projects or cities.

Another critical aspect of smart city monitoring is the continuous tracking of environmental, social, and economic impacts. Smart cities aim to improve the quality of life, reduce environmental harm, and promote sustainability. Therefore, M&E systems must measure technical performance and broader outcomes such as reductions in energy consumption, carbon emissions, traffic congestion, and inequalities. Tracking these outcomes requires interdisciplinary approaches and tools to evaluate quantitative and qualitative data.

Moreover, the adaptability of M&E systems is crucial. Smart cities are dynamic ecosystems in which technologies, regulations, and citizen needs continuously evolve. Therefore, monitoring frameworks must be flexible and capable of adjusting to new challenges and changes in the urban environment. For example, as new data streams become available through IoT devices or AI-driven platforms, M&E systems must incorporate these innovations to maintain relevance and accuracy. Rigid or outdated monitoring systems can become ineffective quickly, limiting their ability to provide timely interventions or course corrections.

Transparency and accountability are additional key components of M&E in smart cities. Citizens must be able to observe and understand the impact of smart city initiatives, particularly when public funds or personal data are involved. Open access to the monitoring results and the inclusion of citizens in the evaluation process can help build trust in smart city projects and ensure that all stakeholders' needs are met. However, many cities struggle with transparency because the collected data are often technical and difficult for the general public to interpret. Governments must provide clear and accessible reports and actively engage communities in monitoring to foster public participation and trust.

Additionally, the effective use of M&E data in decision-making is essential for continuous improvement. It must be translated into actionable insights to inform future planning, policy adjustments, and resource allocation. Cities need to develop clear feedback loops in which M&E results are regularly reviewed and used to refine strategies and optimize performance. Without this, monitoring becomes a passive activity rather than a tool for proactive governance and management.

3 Evidence Worldwide

Various challenges shape the development of smart and sustainable cities worldwide, with ten major gaps emerging as common obstacles (see Table 12.1).

In terms of technology integration and infrastructure, cities such as New Delhi (India), face difficulties integrating new technologies because of inadequate infrastructure [10]. Despite the country's "Smart Cities Mission," the outdated and fragmented urban systems present considerable barriers. Similarly, New York City

Table 12.1 Challenges and solutions for gaps in smart and sustainable city development

Gap	Examples of challenges	Possible solutions
Technology integration and infrastructure	Integration of outdated systems (e.g., New Delhi's fragmented urban systems) and high-tech upgrades (e.g., NYC) costs.	Develop integrated digital platforms, adopt PPPs to share costs, and implement phased modernization plans.
Data Privacy and security	Surveillance concerns in Shanghai, balancing GDPR compliance with smart goals in EU cities like Barcelona.	Establish robust privacy laws, deploy decentralized data storage systems (e.g., blockchain), and enhance encryption.
Digital Divide and inequality	Limited digital infrastructure in Johannesburg, gaps between wealthy and low-income areas in San Francisco.	Expand broadband infrastructure, offer subsidized devices, and promote digital literacy programs.
Funding and financial models	Reliance on traditional financing (e.g., Rio de Janeiro) and insufficient funds for infrastructure in Detroit.	Introduce green/social impact bonds, outcome-based financing, and incentivize private sector investments through transparent PPPs.
Governance and policy frameworks	Bureaucratic inefficiencies in Ahmedabad, public concerns over governance in Toronto's quayside project.	Foster adaptive governance models, establish collaborative public-private frameworks and enhance policy transparency.
Public engagement and acceptance	Resistance to surveillance tech in London, perceived lack of inclusivity in Singapore's smart initiatives.	Conduct public consultations, improve communication about project benefits, and ensure inclusivity in decision-making processes.
Interoperability and standards	Vendor fragmentation in Berlin and lack of communication protocol standards in Tokyo.	Develop and adopt universal standards, incentivize open-source solutions, and encourage vendor-neutral platforms.
Sustainability and environmental impact	E-waste concerns in Dubai, high energy demands for smart tech in NYC despite efficiency initiatives.	Promote circular economy principles, prioritize renewable energy integration, and enforce green procurement practices.
Skill Gaps and workforce development	Shortage of IoT and AI expertise in Bangalore, reliance on foreign talent for smart tech in Sydney.	Invest in STEM education, establish training programs for reskilling, and encourage diversity in workforce development.
Monitoring and evaluation (M&E)	Lack of long-term impact frameworks in Seoul, limited ability to adjust strategies in Barcelona.	Implement real-time M&E systems, standardize metrics for performance evaluation, and establish transparent reporting.

Source: Authors

(USA) contends with the high costs associated with upgrading its infrastructure to support smart technology integration across various urban systems such as transportation and energy.

Data privacy and security are critical concerns in smart cities. For example, in Shanghai (China), the extensive use of surveillance technologies has raised substantial privacy concerns [8]. Despite technological advancements, a lack of robust data privacy frameworks can undermine public trust. Meanwhile, cities in the European Union, such as Barcelona and Amsterdam, must balance their smart city goals with strict data protection regulations, such as the GDPR, which complicates the deployment of technologies that collect vast amounts of personal data.

Another critical challenge is the digital divide and inequality. In Johannesburg (South Africa), disparities in access to digital infrastructure have exacerbated socio-economic inequality, leaving underserved communities out of the smart city ecosystem [11]. In San Francisco, a city known for its technology culture, this divide persists, with lower-income neighborhoods lacking access to essential digital services, further widening the gap between the rich and poor.

This funding and financial model gap is evident in cities such as Rio de Janeiro (Brazil), where smart city projects struggle to secure sustainable funding [22]. Reliance on PPPs introduces complications, as private sector interests may not always align with long-term public goals. Similarly, Detroit (USA) faces financial constraints that limit its ability to invest in the necessary infrastructure improvements for smart city development, considering that traditional financing methods have proven insufficient.

Governance and policy frameworks are also critical to smart city success. However, many cities lag behind. In Ahmedabad (India), bureaucratic inefficiencies slow the implementation of smart city projects, and outdated governance models cannot keep up with technological advancements. Toronto (Canada) encountered substantial governance challenges during the development of the Quayside Smart City Project, which was eventually abandoned because of concerns over data control and public involvement in decision-making processes [9].

Public acceptance plays a key role in the success of smart cities; however, public engagement and acceptance remain considerable challenges. In London (UK), the population has resisted the expansion of smart technologies, particularly those related to surveillance and data collection, and citizens express concerns about privacy and government overreach. The top-down approach to smart city planning in Singapore has led to the perception that citizens' voices are not adequately considered despite the city's technological advancements.

The absence of interoperability and standards hampers the ability of cities such as Berlin (Germany) and Tokyo (Japan) to integrate diverse technologies effectively. In Berlin, the lack of common standards among vendors has led to fragmented systems that are difficult and expensive to connect. Tokyo faces similar challenges, where the lack of standardized communication protocols across different smart city systems complicates the efforts to create a cohesive smart urban environment.

Sustainability and environmental impact are central to smart city initiatives; however, cities such as Dubai (UAE) face challenges balancing technological development with environmental concerns. The rapid deployment of smart technologies has increased concerns regarding electronic waste and energy consumption, which could undermine sustainability goals. Similarly, despite investments in energy-efficient technologies, New York City struggles with substantial energy demands for powering its smart infrastructure.

Skill gaps and workforce development necessary for smart cities present another critical challenge. Despite being a technology hub, Bangalore (India) has a shortage of workers with expertise in emerging fields such as the IoT and AI. This skills gap hampers the city's ability to fully implement its smart city initiatives. Sydney (Australia) faces similar difficulties, relying on foreign talent to fill gaps in crucial areas, such as data analysis, cybersecurity, and IoT management.

Finally, M&E is crucial for assessing the impact of smart city initiatives and ensuring that they meet their goals. Despite being a leader in smart city technology, Seoul (South Korea) lacks a comprehensive M&E framework to track long-term progress and make necessary adjustments. Similarly, Barcelona struggles to implement effective systems for evaluating the outcomes of its smart projects, limiting its ability to refine its strategies over time.

The ten gaps, which may occur independently or in combination, encompass technology integration and infrastructure, data privacy and security, the digital divide and inequality, funding and financial models, governance and policy frameworks, public engagement and acceptance, interoperability and standards, sustainability and environmental impact, skill gaps and workforce development, and monitoring and evaluation. These gaps present significant challenges to developing smart and sustainable cities, necessitating targeted actions to address and overcome them effectively (see Table 12.1).

These examples from worldwide demonstrate how the ten gaps present considerable barriers to developing smart and sustainable cities. Despite progress in some areas, these gaps illustrate the need for ongoing innovation, collaboration, and reform to ensure that smart city technologies deliver the promise of improved urban living, sustainability, and social equity.

4 Conclusion

Several key gaps must be overcome to realize the vision of smart and sustainable cities. These include technology integration and infrastructure, data privacy and security, digital divide and inequality, funding and financial models, governance and policy frameworks, public engagement and acceptance, interoperability, and standards, sustainability and environmental impacts, skill gaps and workforce development, and monitoring and evaluation. Data privacy, security, and system integration are top priorities because they are crucial in building trust, security, and efficiency across urban systems.

One of the most pressing challenges smart cities face is ensuring data privacy and security. As cities deploy interconnected systems that collect, process, and share vast amounts of data, the risk of data breaches and unauthorized access becomes a valid concern. Without proper safeguards, public trust, vital for the long-term success of smart city initiatives, can erode because of the misuse of citizen data.

To address this issue, cities must implement robust privacy frameworks and data security measures. Regulations, such as the EU's GDPR, provide an important foundation for protecting citizens' rights in a digital environment; however, cities must go beyond mere compliance. Investing in cutting-edge encryption techniques and decentralized data storage systems, such as blockchain, can ensure that data are secure and tamper-proof. Cities must simultaneously adopt real-time cybersecurity monitoring tools to detect and prevent potential breaches. Moreover, transparent data-governance policies that outline how data are collected, stored, and used can foster public trust and address privacy concerns.

System integration and interoperability are equally important. Smart cities connect various technologies across different sectors, such as transportation, energy, healthcare, and public services; however, these systems remain isolated without interoperability, limiting their effectiveness. Achieving seamless integration across these systems is essential for realizing the full potential of smart-city technologies.

The development and adoption of universal standards are crucial to overcome this challenge. Open standards allow different systems to communicate effectively, regardless of the source or vendor. Governments and international organizations must collaborate with private-sector technology providers to establish these standards and ensure that new technologies are compatible with the existing infrastructure. Open-source platforms and Application Programming Interfaces (APIs) help cities integrate diverse systems regardless of specific vendors.

Governments can encourage interoperability by promoting PPPs that adhere to open standards. These partnerships will become essential as cities expand their smart infrastructure, enabling them to integrate emerging technologies more efficiently. Governance bodies overseeing the implementation of these standards across sectors should ensure that system integration remains a priority.

The digital divide continues to be a major obstacle to realizing smart cities. Access to digital infrastructure and skills required to use smart technologies are unevenly distributed, often along socioeconomic lines. As smart cities rely on technologies such as broadband internet, IoT devices, and digital services, individuals in underserved communities risk being excluded from these technologies' benefits.

To bridge this divide, governments must prioritize investments in digital infrastructure in underserved areas. Providing affordable broadband access, creating public Wi-Fi hotspots, and subsidizing digital devices for low-income populations are crucial to ensuring that all citizens can participate in and benefit from smart city services. Digital literacy programs should also be implemented to equip citizens with the necessary skills to engage effectively with smart technology. By fostering inclusivity, smart cities can help close the gap between socioeconomic groups and promote more equitable access to digital services.

Traditional funding models are often insufficient for meeting the high capital demands of smart city projects. These projects require substantial digital and physical infrastructure investment, often beyond the public budget. To overcome this problem, cities must explore innovative financial models such as green and social impact bonds and outcome-based financing, which align financial returns with sustainability and social goals.

PPPs remain vital for securing the resources needed for smart city projects. However, these partnerships must be structured to prioritize the long-term public interest over short-term profits. Governments should ensure that PPPs are transparent with clear governance frameworks that balance the objectives of both public and private stakeholders.

Effective governance is crucial to the success of smart cities. Many cities struggle with outdated policies that fail to keep pace with the rapid technological advancements. To address this issue, cities must establish adaptive governance frameworks that are sufficiently flexible to accommodate emerging technologies and evolving citizen needs. Governments should foster collaboration among various stakeholders, including private companies, policymakers, and citizens, to ensure that policies reflect the diverse urban populations' needs.

Participatory governance models, in which citizens are actively involved in decision-making processes, are key to building trust and ensuring that smart city initiatives respond to public concerns. Digital platforms that facilitate real-time feedback from residents can enhance transparency and allow informed decision-making.

Public engagement and acceptance are crucial for the success of smart city initiatives. Without widespread support, these projects risk failing to deliver the intended benefits. For instance, adopting smart bins requires both technology adoption, integration, and behavioral engagement from citizens and tourists to ensure proper usage and waste sorting. Thus, cities must actively involve citizens in the planning, implementing, and monitoring smart technologies. Public consultations, workshops, and online forums, where residents can voice their concerns and offer suggestions, will help foster a sense of ownership and trust.

Moreover, cities need to ensure transparency regarding the use of data and technologies, such as surveillance systems, to address privacy and security concerns. Open communication channels that explain the purpose and benefits of smart-city technologies can help demystify these systems and foster public trust.

Sustainability is at the core of smart city development. To achieve environmental goals, cities must prioritize integrating renewable energy sources, smart grids, and energy-efficient technologies. By reducing energy consumption and optimizing resource management, cities can lower their carbon footprints while improving quality of life. However, the rapid deployment of smart technologies can have unintended environmental consequences such as increased electronic waste. To mitigate these impacts, cities should adopt circular economy principles to ensure that smart technologies are designed for longevity and recyclability.

Addressing the skill gap is essential for effectively deploying and managing smart city technologies. Cities must invest in education and training programs that equip their workforce with the skills to develop and maintain smart systems. This includes focusing on STEM education at all levels and providing reskilling opportunities for workers in industries transformed by smart technologies. Governments should also promote diversity and inclusivity in these programs, ensuring that underrepresented groups have access to the training required to participate in the smart city workforce.

Finally, M&E systems are essential for tracking the progress and effectiveness of smart city projects. Cities must implement comprehensive M&E frameworks that allow them to assess the impact of smart initiatives in real time and make data-driven adjustments. By openly sharing the results of these evaluations, cities can foster public trust and enhance accountability.

In conclusion, overcoming the ten gaps in smart and sustainable city development will require coordinated efforts across multiple domains, particularly in addressing data privacy concerns and improving system integration. Cities can foster governance, financing, and workforce development innovation to lay the foundation for more inclusive, secure, and efficient urban environments.

To the authors of this chapter, "Bridging the gaps in smart and sustainable city development is not merely a technological challenge but a collective endeavor requiring innovation, collaboration, and inclusivity. The cities of the future will embrace smart solutions and prioritize equity, transparency, and environmental stewardship, paving the way for a truly sustainable urban future." (authors).

Acknowledgments We gratefully acknowledge financial support from FCT- Fundação para a Ciência e Tecnologia (Portugal) through research grants UIDB/00685/2020 of the Centre of Applied Economics Studies of the Atlantic, School of Business and Economics of the University of the Azores and UIDB/04521/2020 of the Advance/CSG, ISEG—Lisbon School of Economics and Management and the support from the Regional Directorate for Science, Innovation and Development.

References

1. Arnaud J, São Mamede H, Branco F (2024) The relationship between digital transformation and digital literacy-an explanatory model: systematic literature review. F1000Research 13:253. https://doi.org/10.12688/f1000research.146991.1
2. Avelar S (2020) From a smart city to a smart destination: a case study. In: Strategic innovative marketing and tourism: 8th ICSIMAT, Northern Aegean, Greece, 2019. Springer, pp 7–14
3. Brutti A, De Sabbata P, Frascella A, Gessa N, Ianniello R, Novelli C, Pizzuti S, Ponti G (2019) Smart city platform specification: a modular approach to achieve interoperability in smart cities. In: The internet of things for smart urban ecosystems. Springer, pp 25–50
4. Caird SP, Hallett SH (2019) Towards evaluation design for smart city development. J Urban Des 24(2):188–209
5. Caragliu A, Del Bo CF (2022) Smart cities and urban inequality. Reg Stud 56(7):1097–1112
6. De Maio A, Musmanno R, Skrame A (2024) A human-centric decision-support system for smart and sustainable tourism management in urban settings. Curr Issue Tour 1-23:643–665. https://doi.org/10.1080/13683500.2024.2339957
7. Georgiadis C, Patias P, Verde N, Tsioukas V, Kaimaris D, Georgoula O, Kocman D, Athanasopoulou E, Speyer O, Raudner A (2022) State-of-play in addressing urban environmental pressures: mind the gaps. Environ Sci Pol 132:308–322
8. Guo Y, Chen J, Liu Z (2022) Government responsiveness and public acceptance of big-data technology in urban governance: evidence from China during the COVID-19 pandemic. Cities 122:103536. https://doi.org/10.1016/j.cities.2021.103536
9. Haggart B, Spicer Z (2022) Infrastructure, smart cities and the knowledge economy: lessons for policymakers from the Toronto Quayside project. Can Public Adm 65(2):295–313. https://doi.org/10.1111/capa.12460
10. Nandi S, Gamkhar S (2013) Urban challenges in India: a review of recent policy measures. Habitat Int 39:55–61. https://doi.org/10.1016/j.habitatint.2012.10.001

11. Oyedemi TD (2009) Social inequalities and the South African ICT access policy agendas. Int J Commun 3:18
12. Panagiotakopoulos T, Iatrellis O, Kameas A (2022) Emerging Smart City job roles and skills for smart urban governance. In: Fitsilis P (ed) Building on smart cities skills and competences: human factors affecting smart cities development. Springer, pp 3–19. https://doi.org/10.1007/978-3-030-97818-1_1
13. Pereira GV, Parycek P, Falco E, Kleinhans R (2018) Smart governance in the context of smart cities: a literature review. Inf Polity 23(2):143–162
14. Pliatsios A, Kotis K, Goumopoulos C (2023) A systematic review on semantic interoperability in the IoE-enabled smart cities. Internet Things 22:100754
15. Przeybilovicz E, Cunha MA, Geertman S, Leleux C, Michels A, Tomor Z, Webster CWR, Meijer A (2022) Citizen participation in the smart city: findings from an international comparative study. Local Gov Stud 48(1):23–47
16. Rani S, Mishra RK, Usman M, Kataria A, Kumar P, Bhambri P, Mishra AK (2021) Amalgamation of advanced technologies for sustainable development of smart city environment: a review. IEEE Access 9:150060–150087
17. Reddy P, Sharma B, Chaudhary K (2020) Digital literacy: a review of literature. Int J Technoethics 11(2):65–94
18. Shafiee S, Rajabzadeh Ghatari A, Hasanzadeh A, Jahanyan S (2019) Developing a model for sustainable smart tourism destinations: a systematic review. Tour Manag Perspect 31:287–300. https://doi.org/10.1016/j.tmp.2019.06.002
19. Silva BN, Khan M, Han K (2018) Towards sustainable smart cities: a review of trends, architectures, components, and open challenges in smart cities. Sustain Cities Soc 38:697–713
20. Thite M (2011) Smart cities: implications of urban planning for human resource development. Hum Resour Dev Int 14(5):623–631
21. Wolniak R, Gajdzik B, Grebski M, Danel R, Grebski WW (2024) Business models used in smart cities—theoretical approach with examples of smart cities. Smart Cities 7(4):1626–1669
22. Xia L, Semirumi DT, Rezaei R (2023) A thorough examination of smart city applications: exploring challenges and solutions throughout the life cycle with emphasis on safeguarding citizen privacy. Sustain Cities Soc 98:104771
23. Zhang K, Ni J, Yang K, Liang X, Ren J, Shen XS (2017) Security and privacy in smart city applications: challenges and solutions. IEEE Commun Mag 55(1):122–129

Maria Teresa Pinheiro Melo Borges-Tiago, PhD in Marketing, is an Associate Professor with Habilitation at the University of Azores, an invited professor at NOVA Information Management School (NOVA IMS), and a Research Fellow at the Centre of Applied Economics Studies of the Atlantic—the University of the Azores and Advance/CSG, ISEG—Lisbon University. Her main research interests include Digital Marketing, Consumer Behavior, and Tourism. She has published articles in peer-reviewed scientific international journals such as the Journal of Business Research, Business Horizons, and Tourism Management. She is an associate editor at Consumer Behavior in Tourism and Hospitality Journal. She belongs to the editorial board of the Tourism Review, the International Journal of Contemporary Hospitality Management, and the Journal of Hospitality and Tourism Insights.

Flávio Gomes Borges Tiago is an Associate Professor with Habilitation at the University of the Azores with a Ph.D. in Internet Marketing and E-business and is a Research Fellow at the Advance/CSG, ISEG—Lisbon University, and at the Centre of Applied Economics Studies of the Atlantic – Azores (Portugal). He is the regional director of science, innovation, and development for the Azores government. His main research interests include Digital Marketing, social media, consumer behavior, and Tourism. He has published articles in peer-reviewed scientific international journals such as the Journal of Business Research, Journal of Innovation & Knowledge, Technological Forecasting & Social Change, and Tourism Management.

Sónia Margarida Moreira Avelar has been an Invited Professor at the University of the Azores since 2021 and a Research Fellow at the Centre of Applied Economics Studies of the Atlantic—the University of the Azores. She has a Ph.D. in Economics and Business Sciences and a master's in international Tourism Management from the University of the Azores. She teaches tourism and human resources courses and participates in several tourism projects. Her main research interests include Tourism, Consumer Behavior, Human Resources, and Sustainability. She has published articles in peer-reviewed scientific international journals such as the Journal of Business Research and the Journal of Innovation and Knowledge.

Towards Responsible Consumption 13

Teresa Heath and Maria Lichrou

> *Our numbness, our silence, our lack of outrage could mean we end up the only species to have minutely monitored our own extinction. What a measly epitaph that would make: 'they saw it coming but hadn't the wit to stop it from happening.'*
>
> (Parkin [63], p. 7)

Abstract

This chapter discusses the concept of responsible consumption, defined to be consumption that fulfils our immediate responsibilities without harming our ability to fulfil our broader responsibilities. This can include concerns about personal, social and environmental matters and an appreciation of the moral value of ourselves, others and the planet. We consider the concept of consumer-citizen and various categories that scholars have used to categorise consumers who were judged to behave in responsible or virtuous ways, such as green, sustainable, mindful, and ethical consumption. We also note the importance of attending to contextual and structural barriers and competing personal responsibilities when discussing consumers' responsibilities. Achieving truly responsible consumption, we conclude, requires individual efforts and broader social and policy interventions to foster long-term change.

T. Heath (✉)
NIPE, School of Economics, Management and Political Science, University of Minho, Minho, Portugal
e-mail: teresa.pereiraheath@eeg.uminho.pt

M. Lichrou
University of Limerick, Limerick, Ireland
e-mail: Maria.Lichrou@ul.ie

B. Casais (ed.), *Integrated Science to Achieve Sustainable Development Goals*, Integrated Science 37, https://doi.org/10.1007/978-3-031-88777-2_13

Graphical Abstract

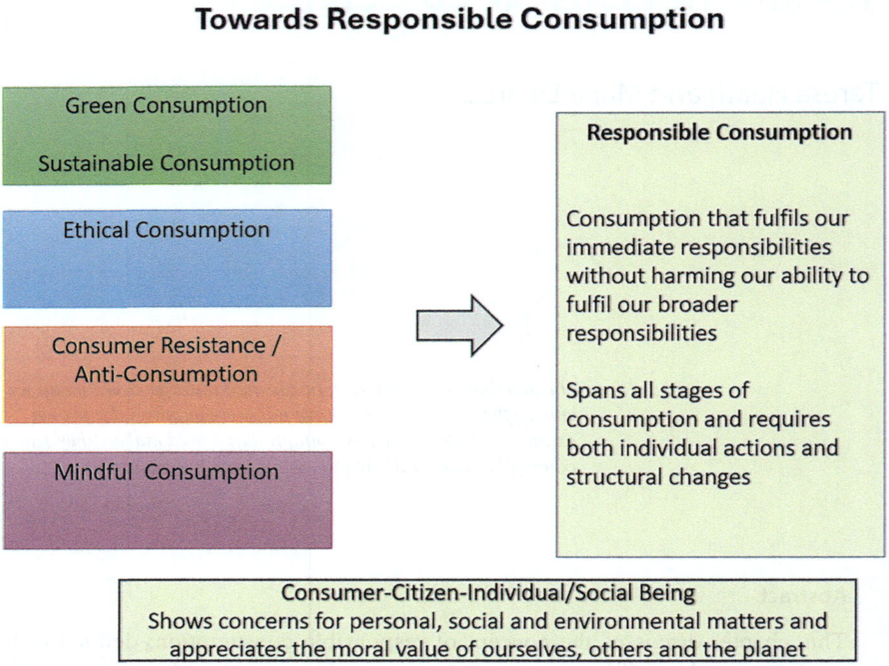

Source: Authors

Keywords

Responsible consumption · Ethical consumption · Sustainable consumption · Consumer resistance · Anti-consumption · Consumer citizen

1 Introduction

Human activity, greed and irresponsibility have harmed our planet to the verge of irreparability. Consumption practices (of some) are a central part of the problem. Repairing this calls for holistic and concerted interventions at both micro and macro levels. This necessitates efforts from individuals, businesses, governments, communities, and other institutions to encourage the acceptance and adoption of sustainable practices (see e.g [51, 68]). In particular, this requires reflexivity on behalf of any decision-maker as to how their behaviour can advance (or impair) the planet's sustainability.

With the 1987 report "Our Common Future" (also called the Brundtland Report) from the United Nations' World Commission on Environment and Development

(WCED), the concept of sustainable development emerged as key to progress towards a sustainable and equitable society globally. It defined *sustainable development* as "meet[ing] the needs of the present without compromising the ability of future generations to meet their own needs" [87]. Meeting such needs requires, amongst other things, recognition that there *are* "Limits to Growth" as long advanced by the Club of Rome [57]. Notably, "Our Common Future" represented a pressing "call for action", "an urgent notice based on the latest and best scientific evidence—that the time has come to take the decisions needed to secure the resources to sustain this and coming generations" [87]. However, we still have not got our consumption within sustainable limits. Earth Overshoot Day for 2024, the date when humanity's demand for nature's resources exceeds the planet's capacity to regenerate them for that year, fell on the first of August, meaning that humanity is currently using natural resources 1.7 times faster than the Earth's ecosystem's ability to regenerate [20]. The United Nations' Sustainable Development Goals also stress the importance of responsible consumption, with the 12th goal calling for *Sustainable Consumption and Production* Patterns.

Climate change represents the most urgent threat to sustainability and is substantially driven by burning fossil fuels for energy. Much of this energy goes to producing and transporting goods for individual consumption [22]. Increasingly, we may add to this the energy needs of the data centres that provide online services and content, and train models for Artificial Intelligence [25, 36]. Changes in energy production will be a part of any solution to this, with a rapid expansion of renewable generation and storage [22, 36] along with the electrification of transportation [92]. However, these technological developments are not, on their own, proving sufficient for the task of reining in climate change and, as the latest United Nations' Emissions Gap Report [84] indicates, we are collectively missing targets agreed upon to keep warming within safe limits. Hence, the consumption side of the equation remains vital. Importantly, the climate crisis is also a crisis of inequality [62], with a significant consumption gap prevailing between richer and poorer countries [35]. "Meeting the needs of the present" necessitates equity in access to resources [87] so that everyone's needs are met. The richer countries are responsible for using much more fossil fuels than others and rarely pay the social costs of this usage, while the poor are often located in places more vulnerable to climate change and have fewer resources to protect them against climate shocks [62].

The importance of consumer action is further underlined by patchy progress by national governments. While some countries are ahead of targets in the Paris climate agreement for decomposing their power generation [21], those targets are being missed globally. At the time of writing, news sources are claiming that US President-Elect Donald Trump is preparing to withdraw his country from the Paris Agreement entirely [72], which could make it substantially more difficult for the world as a whole to achieve the reductions needed to avoid runaway climate change. This state of affairs underscores the urgent need for profound societal transformations and a real commitment to resist attempts to continue with "business as usual" [27, p. ix].

Similarly, many other threats to sustainability, such as damage to habitats and oppressive working conditions, result from consumption choices. In addition, while consumers are often offered ethical, sustainable, or green brands, they are rarely encouraged to reflect upon the necessity of buying things in the first place. On the contrary, they are frequently made to believe that the solution to their problems (whatever these may be) resides on the market. The role of marketing in encouraging consumption (e.g [58, 81, 93]) and stimulating consumption opportunities [78] whilst discouraging reflection about the origins and end-points of the goods we consume [82] places it at the centre of severe ecological destruction [75]. Persuasive stories about consumption told via marketing channels [94] and reinforced by other elements of the culturally constituted world [96] help to link brands, goods and experiences to a range of symbolic meanings and benefits beyond the offers' instrumental value [93, 95]. Through consumption, people acquire and shape such meanings [96], driving a "profusion" of objects and waste [97], which characterises the lifestyles of many industrialised Western societies. Fast fashion, which relies on cheap production, frequent purchases and short-lived garments [98], feeds into this, providing multiple opportunities for consumers to engage in a society of consumption at an affordable price, yet at a significant social and environmental cost [4, 98].

In place of celebrations of an abundance of things and the rapidity of cycles of production-usage-disposal prevailing in today's societies, sustainability requires a renewed appreciation for moderation, durability and slowing down. The current chapter emphasises the importance of promoting responsible practices in consumption (and production). In the following sections, we will explore marketing's connection to sustainability, briefly tracing some of the key studies that reflect its evolution from early concerns about ecological issues to the development of green marketing and the broader macro considerations within the field. From there, we move to discuss the role of consumers in advancing the sustainability agenda. Additionally, the chapter addresses some tensions that arise from defining a responsible consumer before presenting key conclusions.

2 Marketing, Consumption and Sustainability Matters

In the following section, we provide a brief overview of how scholars in marketing have addressed environmental, ecological, and sustainability matters. Following Heath and McKechnie [31], this does not purport to be an exhaustive account of the literature but rather to summarise some key developments and authors in the field. Additional material on the historical development of academic marketing discussions of these matters can be found in van Dam and Apeldoorn [85], Kilbourne and Beckmann [43], Peattie [65], McDonagh and Prothero [54], Lunde [52] and Kemper and Ballantine [41].

2.1 Ecology, Marketing and Consumers: Early Steps

The relationship between marketing and sustainability is complex, yet marketing scholarship has long acknowledged the importance of addressing environmental issues on both the production and consumption sides. Lavidge [49] posited that as marketing's power increased, marketing should take greater responsibility for its broader impacts on society, identifying issues that remain of great importance today, including the effects of marketing on consumption, its intersection with issues of social justice, and the use and pollution of society's resources. A few years later, Fisk [23] identified "an unprecedented" environmental crisis and expressed concerns about rising consumption's impact on the planet. Ahead of his time, Fisk raised the need to develop a "new attitude towards the meaning of consumption" and new forms of social organisation to create such an attitude. Fisk defined *responsible consumption* as the "rational and efficient use of resources with respect to the global human population" and recognised how the environmental crisis must be tackled globally ([23], p. 24). In a similar direction, Shapiro [76] expressed the need to discuss the reduction of consumption levels and to practice ecologically responsible corporate marketing. Around this time, several marketing scholars attempted to identify and characterise *socially conscious* [1, 88], *ecologically concerned* [47], or *environmentally concerned* consumers [61]. Scales were developed for the effect, such as the environmental concern scale [89]. This signalled the managerial relevance of an "emergent" segment of consumers who seemed sensitive to social and environmental matters and would potentially employ their "purchasing power to bring about social change" ([88], p. 188; see also [1]). Some of these early studies focussed on fairly narrow issues, such as air pollution [65], and preferences for specific products [31], such as less polluting gasoline [40] or detergents [47].

Similarly to the current understanding, marketing and consumption were already recognised as part of the environmental problem and hailed as a part of a potential solution. Reflecting this, Henion and Kinnear [33] defined ecological marketing as concerned with "all marketing activities: (a) that have served to help cause environmental problems and (b) that may serve to provide a remedy for environmental problems".

2.2 Greening Marketing

In the late 1980s, the term "green marketing" was coined to refer to "activities which attempt to reduce the negative social and environmental impacts of existing products and production systems, and which promote less damaging products and services" [65 , p. 129; 67]. The concept of "green consumers" gained widespread attention with the release of Elkington and Hailes's [100] book, *The Green Consumer Guide* [65], which advised consumers on how to minimise the environmental impact of their shopping. Meanwhile, as businesses recognised the attractiveness of green offers, they strove to engage consumers who were concerned with the environment and perhaps concerned enough to pay a premium for "greener" options (see [42, 64, 99]).

However, the approach of green marketing was found inadequate or insufficient to drive the magnitude of changes required ([68], 101, [31]) for the planet. Environmental friendliness was often only a "marketing tool" ([85], p. 52). Instead of promoting responsible consumption, some companies were primarily focused on exploiting the green trend for their benefit [5]. Surface changes enabled marketers to carry on as usual [101] and consumers to feel better about their "green" purchases. This approach was mainly about replacing products rather than reducing overall consumption [68], overlooking that "green products and green consumers" still utilise resources and generate waste [44 , p. 107]. Indeed, from a purely environmental impact perspective, the "greenest" product would be no product at all [24]. Green consumers were also found to be elusive [90] in the sense that there is a significant gap between their attitudes and concerns for the planet and actual behaviour. To compound the problem further, some companies engaged in deceptive practices, seemingly adopting "green" strategies while continuing to employ unsustainable practices [26, 31, 39, 64, 67]. Overall, there was a perception that green marketing had "significantly underachieved" [67 , p. 357].

2.3 A Macro Approach to Marketing and Consumption: Towards Sustainability

From the mid-nineties on, scholars began to challenge the managerial emphasis of green marketing and adopt a broader reflection on marketing in relation to sustainability [31]. With the works of Kilbourne et al. [45], van Dam and Apeldoorn [85], and Kilbourne and Beckmann [43], amongst others, a broader and more critical stance towards marketing's relationship with society and the planet began to take shape. This body of literature recognised the limitations of the prevailing green discourse. It expanded the scope of study from individual factors, such as consumers' environmental attitudes, to encompass more significant systemic considerations at the macro and societal levels [43, 45, 64, 70, 86]. Accordingly, studies challenged the prevailing ideology of consumption ([5], 99) and considered the importance of limiting (rather than just changing) consumption [5, 41, 45]. Significantly, they promoted reflection upon the societal institutions and worldviews that underpin overconsumption (e.g., [17, 19, 44–46, 51, 75]). Thus, this critical school challenged the dominant social paradigm (DSP) and sought radical alternatives, redefining market systems and values [59]. DSP refers to the prevailing cultural beliefs, values, and practices that shape how a society is organised and interprets the world [45]. In the so-called developed capitalist economies and many parts of the world adopting similar systems, the DSP tends to be rooted in ideals and preferences for anthropocentrism, materialism and technological optimism [e.g 46] in ways incompatible with sustainability goals.

This stream of studies represented a shift from a micromarketing to a macromarketing perspective in the environmental arena [43]. Consequently, the sustainability research agenda expanded towards collective practices and discourses, networks and organisations of various forms [54, 69], and contexts in which production and consumption practices are problematised and reconfigured. For example, Chatzidakis et al. [12] show how critique and experimentation in Exarcheia, an urban neighbourhood in Athens, Greece, led to new ways of thinking and doing ecological behaviours. In a different setting, members of an Irish ecovillage use reflexive tactics that enable them to confront the DSP and enact the sustainability discourse in their everyday lives [8, 10].

Such a critical, macromarketing perspective on sustainability encompasses societal, ecological and environmental considerations and requires governments, businesses, communities and other institutions to collaborate to progress the sustainability agenda [78]. Meanwhile, growing evidence of the profound environmental crisis we are facing (e.g., extreme weather events, loss of biodiversity, plastic pollution) and an increasing consciousness of a range of concerns about social justice, inclusiveness, and equality that intersect businesses and consumption practices have further transformed marketing. With businesses growing acutely aware of the importance that their response to the challenge of sustainability represents for competitiveness [79, 108], sustainable marketing has gained central importance both for practitioners and scholars [78]. Accordingly, sustainable marketing emerges as a form of marketing in which value is intrinsically linked to environmental and social dimensions and moral considerations for consumers and a wide range of stakeholders of the present and the future. Sustainable marketing is aptly articulated by Lunde [52] as: "the strategic creation, communication, delivery, and exchange of offerings that produce value through consumption behaviors, business practices, and the marketplace, while lowering harm to the environment and ethically and equitably increasing the quality of life (QOL) and well-being of consumers and global stakeholders, presently and for future generations" (p. 94). We note previous uses of the term sustainable marketing, such as that offered by van Dam and Apeldoorn [85].

Importantly, promoting responsible consumption is a crucial part of the path to sustainability and has been identified as a key effort for companies to build a sustainable marketing strategy [78]. Indeed, consumption can be seen as the ultimate cause of all production [16]. The following section addresses the consumers' side of the equation.

3 Responsible Consumption

Consumers are increasingly encouraged to participate in sustainability efforts, with various studies discussing their shared responsibility [15, 28, 30] in promoting the betterment of the planet. Indeed, consumers significantly affect ecological and social issues directly through the emissions from their consumption and indirectly through the side effects along the value chain of the goods they buy [74].

In this direction, we have witnessed the rise of the "citizen-consumer" who displays their societal and environmental concerns through their purchasing decisions, with shopping thus becoming a means to create progressive social change [38 ,

p. 229]. Indeed, as shopping activities become increasingly intertwined with social, political and environmental causes, the concepts of "consumers" and "citizens" intersect (*ibid*). However, Davies et al. [17] note the limitations of focusing solely on consumers (or citizens) and instead advocate for developing sustainable *people* to foster sustainable development across society.

Several concepts, such as green, sustainable, mindful, and consumption, have been advanced to explain how individuals can decide and act mindfully in their capacity as responsible people. Lim [107] provides a thorough discussion of responsible consumption and related terms. Although these concepts may sometimes overlap [55, 66], they underscore important ways individuals can affect and show concern for the planet, the people and other species.

While connected to broader dimensions of sustainable development, green consumption tends to be primarily associated with environmental or ecological aspects of sustainability [66]. As articulated by Carrigan et al. [6], it is linked to "the process of avoiding certain types of products, such as those causing pollution or cruelty to animals (Schaefer and Crane 2001; [80]). It can also represent positive product choices, such as the purchase of environmentally friendly products, or recycling behaviour" (p. 401). As green marketing, the idea is to lessen (rather than solve) the harmful effects caused by the market's activities.

The concept of sustainable consumption is typically applied with a broader sense than "green consumption". It was defined by the Oslo Symposium in 1994 as "the use of goods and services that respond to basic needs and bring a better quality of life, while minimising the use of natural resources, toxic materials. and emissions of waste and pollutants over the life-cycle, so as not to jeopardise the needs of future generations" (cited in [16 , p. 370]). Like sustainable development, sustainable consumption considers the importance of the needs of future generations. It also highlights that consumers can impact each stage of a product's life. For instance, consumers may purchase clothing from slow fashion brands rather than fast fashion retailers, opt for lower washing temperatures, or recycle or upcycle garments no longer in use. Relatedly, Prothero et al. [70] articulate the potential for consumer researchers and public policymakers to advance approaches that promote sustainable consumption across the entire lifecycle. This may include encouraging practices such as product sharing, product reuse and overall consumption reduction.

Sustainable consumption can be seen as a subset of the broader area of research called ethical consumption; indeed, the terms are sometimes used interchangeably. Consumer ethics refers to "the moral principles and standards that guide the behaviour of individuals as they obtain, use, and dispose of goods and services" [60 , p. 298]. Initially focused on environmental issues, ethical consumption has expanded to encompass a broader range of "matters of conscience" [3, 6]. These considerations go beyond environmental concerns to include issues such as animal welfare, labour rights and community welfare [6], alongside more self-interested motivations about individual well-being or the welfare of one's family [102]. In particular, Strong [80] discussed how ethical consumption required concern for the people involved in the production, use and disposal of goods. In general, as aptly articulated by Crane et al. [16], ethical consumption tends to focus on decisions "beyond self-interest" (p. 365). For instance, a consumer may buy a cosmetic product from Lush because of the brand's ethical stance against animal testing, even if they can find a similar product at a lower price from a brand not focused on this issue. Moreover, ethicality can also manifest in consumers' actions independent of brands or businesses, such as how consumers respect staff or fellow consumers, as Heath et al. [32] demonstrated while studying ethics in consumption during the COVID-19 pandemic.

Although marketing scholarship and practice have long engaged with discourses of ecology, environment, and sustainability and encouraged "less harmful" forms of production, consumption, and disposal , the issue of reducing consumption remains little considered. This may be because curbing consumption is not a popular goal with established marketing theories or practices [68], nor does it align well with the ideals of unlimited economic growth, quality of life and materialism prevailing in the dominant social paradigm [17, 45, 46] of industrialised societies. Sheth et al. [79] argue strongly for the role of individual consumers' outlooks and habits in moving towards sustainability. Towards this, they propose "mindful consumption" (p. 21), in which a caring attitude towards oneself, nature and community, tempers harmful consumption habits. On the side of the firm, this is matched with "Customer-centric sustainability", which includes nurturing mindful consumption amongst one's customer base to benefit all parties. This expectation that business and consumer interests can align on sustainability may be overly optimistic today. However, Sheth et al.'s [79] argument that consumers' mindsets and habits play a significant part in sustainability remains convincing.

Relatedly, there are various ways in which consumers have shown responsibility by resisting a culture of consumption or creating alternative ways of consuming, which are more balanced and mindful of one's relationship with others and the planet. We will look at this next.

4 Consumer Resistance and Anti-consumption

Consumer resistance and anti-consumption are multifaceted and often overlapping phenomena encompassing a wide array of motivations and expressions, including opposition to the acquisition, use, and disposal of products and brands [50]. The level of action, motivations, behaviours, and means of resistance and anti-consumption are also wide-ranging. These actions can vary significantly in their scale, from individual acts to widespread collective movements, involving diverse motivations and behaviours. Examples in the literature range from practices such as voluntary simplicity [77] and culture jamming [13] to new consumer movements [48] and organised consumer collectives [2, 29].

Resistance occurs when consumers defy dominant cultural, economic or institutional forces, such as consumer culture and the marketing system. For example, voluntary simplifiers consciously resist overconsumption and strive to live a more frugal and meaningful life, less reliant on materialistic values and in greater harmony with the environment and themselves (e.g [18, 56]). Resistance can manifest in other ways: sometimes, consumers express their concerns by rejecting certain types of consumption and refusing to buy a product or brand, whereas other times, they do so by supporting certain products, brands or forms of consumption [11].

Historically, boycotts have been effective tools of social change. For example, Roux and Izberk-Bilgin [73] mention the non-importation movement (1764–1776) during the American colonial era as an early example. Consumers have more recently used both *boycotts* and *buycotts* to voice their discontent with globalisation [73]. Boycotts involve withholding patronage for brands or organisations perceived to engage in socially or environmentally objectionable practices and buycotts involve supporting companies or brands that align with people's socio-political concerns [73].

Resistance often involves open confrontation with a market actor, logic or practice. For example, activist groups like Adbusters (https://www.adbusters.org/) utilise guerrilla communication and culture-jamming to protest the ideology of consumerism and the appropriation of public and mental space by advertising [73]. Yannopoulou et al. [91] studied how, amidst a severe financial crisis in Greece, a politically motivated group called the *Indignant Citizens* crafted new forms of collective exchange less reliant on the market to express political resistance and to satisfy people's consumption needs. However, even in less confrontational situations, resisting an unsustainable market logic or practice may entail conflict with established socio-cultural norms. Guillard and Roux (2014) illuminate this issue in their case study of the phenomenon of urban *gleaning* in France. Gleaning is the practice of collecting bulky items from the pavement, such as furniture and home items, that others have disposed of, giving them a new lease of life. Consumers, both the gleaners and disposers, conflict with the hygiene norm that prevails in waste management (Guillard and Roux 2014). Casey et al. [9] found that consumers' tendency to hold on to unused electrical and electronic products, resisting calls to recycle them, relies on the perceived use potential of these objects.

Peñaloza and Price's (1993) seminal conceptualisation of consumer resistance considered the following dimensions: the level of resistance from individual to collective, the motivations for resistance from reformist to radical goals, the tactics employed by consumers from altering the marketing mix to altering the symbolic meaning of products, and the means of resistance from standing within to standing outside the institution of marketing. Drawing on Poster's treatise on consumer agency, which was in turn based on De Certeau's notion of everyday moments of tactical resistance, Penalosa and Price [104] called attention to the importance of small acts of individual resistance, such as when individuals change the meaning of goods as a tactic that resists consumer culture and the mass-produced meanings of goods. The authors note that these acts may not be as ambitious or conspicuous as more radical interventions seeking structural change, such as consumer boycotts. Yet, they argue their importance as subjective daily acts of resistance through which consumers symbolically contest the marketing system should not be ignored. These acts may be harder to trace and research because they are less conspicuous (see for example [34]).

Similarly, anti-consumption involves different motivations and expressions. Iyer and Muncy [37] offer a broad categorisation of the purpose of anti-consumption ranging from societal to personal concerns, and the focus of anti-consumption from consumption in general to specific products or brands. Chatzidakis and Lee [11] analyse the nature of motivations for anti-consumption including ethical concerns relating to the consumer's moral beliefs and values, environmental concerns, resistance concerns, and symbolic concerns. While anti-consumption and consumer resistance are not identical, it is important to note that they often share common ground. This is the case, especially in the empirical contexts in which the two phenomena have been examined [50]. For Lee et al. [50] the domain of anti-consumption revolves mainly around consumption concerns and the domain of consumer resistance revolves mainly around power concerns. These are not mutually exclusive; for example, a consumer of organic products may be motivated by an interest in healthy eating while also protesting the dominant unsustainable agriculture practices. Indeed, Pecot et al. (103: see also [105]) found that political ideology can be a strong driver of anti-consumption.

5 Final Thoughts

Taking these concepts together, we may envision responsibility in consumption to be enacted through mindful and considerate choices and practices throughout the several stages of consumption. This includes deciding whether to buy something—for example, choosing not to purchase unneeded items or renting or sharing instead. It also involves considering the origins of the goods we buy, such as whether the item is new or second-hand, the sourcing of the good or the materials used in its production, the working and living conditions of those involved in making and selling these goods, and the environmental impact of these products. Moreover, responsible consumption extends to how we buy, including our moral behaviour inside a shop; how we use the items we buy, such as minimising food waste or unplugging electronic devices when not in use; and how we dispose of goods or their components that we no longer need. This includes recycling, upcycling, or donating items to give them a second life.

However, considerations of morality in consumption should avoid judgmental categorization of consumers as responsible or irresponsible. Discussing the limitations of the attitude-behaviour gap in ethical consumption, Carrington et al. [7] warned that this may "promote erroneous notions of consumer sovereignty and responsibilization." The same principle applies here; consumers may not have the conditions to meet the standards of "responsibility" as defined by mainstream approaches. Additionally, individuals often also face more immediate responsibilities to their families or others who rely on them [32]. Responsible consumption is a broad and complex topic, as each of us has a wide range of responsibilities; we are responsible to the planet as a whole and distant and future others, but equally, to those nearest us and ourselves.

Furthermore, everything we do (even in our "productive" work lives) involves consuming resources. As a result, pinning down a clear definition of "responsible consumption" can be challenging. The sense of balance established in thedefinition of sustainable consumption proposed by the 1994 Oslo Symposium on Sustainable Consumption — "the use of goods and services that respond to basic needs and bring a better quality of life, while minimising the use of natural resources, toxic materials and emissions of waste and pollutants over the life cycle, so as not to jeopardise the needs of future generations" [106]—provides a solid starting point. We may think of consumption as responsible when it fulfils our immediate responsibilities without harming our ability to fulfil our broader responsibilities. This can include concerns about personal, social and environmental matters and an appreciation of the moral value of ourselves, others and the planet. Bringing about a state of affairs where such consumption is both possible for all and widely practised is a significant challenge and cannot be solved without considering both individual mindsets and broad social policies. However, reaching a state of responsible consumption is a precondition for securing a sustainable future.

References

1. Anderson WT Jr, Cunningham WH (1972) The socially conscious consumer. J Mark 36(3):23–31
2. Arnould EJ, Arvidsson A, Eckhardt GM (2021) Consumer collectives: a history and reflections on their future. J Assoc Consum Res 6(4):415–428
3. Auger P, Devinney TM (2007) Do what consumers say matter? The misalignment of preferences with unconstrained ethical intentions. J Bus Ethics 76:361–383
4. Brewer MK (2019) Slow fashion in a fast fashion world: promoting sustainability and responsibility. Laws 8(4):24
5. Buchholz RA (1998) The ethics of consumption activities: a future paradigm? J Bus Ethics 17(8):871–882
6. Carrigan M, Szmigin I, Wright J (2004) Shopping for a better world? An interpretive study of the potential for ethical consumption within the older market. J Consum Mark 21(6):401–417
7. Carrington MJ, Zwick D, Neville B (2016) The ideology of the ethical consumption gap. Mark Theory 16(1):21–38
8. Casey K, Lichrou M, O'Malley L (2017) Unveiling everyday reflexivity tactics in a sustainable community. J Macromark 37(3):227–239
9. Casey K, Lichrou M, O'Malley L, Fitzpatrick C (2019) Neither wasted nor wanted: theorising the failure to dispossess objects of ambiguous value. Adv Consum Res 47
10. Casey K, Lichrou M, O'Malley L (2020) Prefiguring sustainable living: an ecovillage story. J Mark Manag 36(17–18):1658–1679
11. Chatzidakis A, Lee MS (2013) Anti-consumption as the study of reasons against. J Macromark 33(3):190–203
12. Chatzidakis A, Maclaran P, Bradshaw A (2012) Heterotopian space and the utopics of ethical and green consumption. J Mark Manag 28(3–4):494–515
13. Cherrier H (2009) Anti-consumption discourses and consumer-resistant identities. J Bus Res 62(2):181–190
14. Connolly J, Prothero A (2003) Sustainable consumption: consumption, consumers and the commodity discourse. Consum Mark Cult 6(4):275–291
15. Crane A, Matten D, Glozer S, Spence L (2016) Business ethics, 5th edn. Oxford University Press, Oxford

16. Davies I, Oates CJ, Tynan C, Carrigan M, Casey K, Heath T, Henninger C, Lichorou M, McDonagh P, McDonald S, McKechnie S, McLeay F, O'Malley L, Wells V (2020) Seeking sustainable futures in marketing and consumer research. Eur J Mark 54(11):2911–2939
17. Demirel A (2022) Voluntary simplicity: an exploration through text analysis. Int J Consum Stud 46(1):75–87
18. Dolan P (2002) The sustainability of "sustainable consumption". J Macromark 22(2):170–181
19. Earth Overshoot Day/Global Footprint Network (2024) Earth overshoot day 2024 falls on August 1st – ending overshoot: humanity's critical race. https://overshoot.footprintnetwork.org/newsroom/press-release-2024-english/
20. European Environment Agency (2024) Trends and projections in Europe 2024. https://www.eea.europa.eu/en/analysis/publications/trends-and-projections-in-europe-2024
21. European Parliament (2023). https://www.europarl.europa.eu/pdfs/news/expert/2018/3/story/20180301STO98928/20180301STO98928_en.pdf
22. Fisk G (1973) Criteria for a theory of responsible consumption. J Mark 37(2):24–31
23. Fuller D (1999) Sustainable marketing: managerial-ecological issues. Sage, London
24. Gooding M (2024) Global data center electricity use to double by 2026 – IEA report. https://www.datacenterdynamics.com/en/news/global-data-center-electricity-use-to-double-by-2026-report/
25. Gordon R, Carrigan M, Hastings G (2011) A framework for sustainable marketing. Mark Theory 11(2):143–163
26. Gottlieb R (1997) The ecological community. Routledge, London
27. Hansen U, Schrader U (1997) A modern model of consumption for a sustainable society. J Consum Policy 20(4):443–468
28. Harvey J, Smith A, Goulding J, Illodo IB (2020) Food sharing, redistribution, and waste reduction via mobile applications: a social network analysis. Ind Mark Manag 88:437–448
29. Heath T, Chatzidakis A (2012) 'Blame it on marketing': consumers' views on unsustainable consumption. Int J Consum Stud 36(6):656–667
30. Heath T, McKechnie S (2019) Sustainability in marketing. In: Incorporating sustainability in management education: an interdisciplinary approach, pp 105–131
31. Heath T, Gallage S, Chatzidakis A, Hutton M (2024) Dilemmas of care (re) allocation: care and consumption in pandemic times. J Bus Ethics:1–21
32. Henion KE, Kinnear TC (1976) Measuring the effect of ecological information and social class on selected product choice criteria importance ratings. In: Ecological marketing. American Marketing Association, Chicago, pp 145–156
33. Hogg MK, Banister EN, Stephenson CA (2009) Mapping symbolic (anti-) consumption. J Bus Res 62(2):148–159
34. Huang MH, Rust RT (2011) Sustainability and consumption. J Acad Mark Sci 39:40–54
35. International Energy Agency (2024) World Energy Outlook 2024. https://iea.blob.core.windows.net/assets/60db7f34-da7f-41d7-8232-c0b718463fd0/WorldEnergyOutlook2024.pdf
36. Iyer R, Muncy JA (2009) Purpose and object of anti-consumption. J Bus Res 62(2):160–168
37. Johnston J (2008) The citizen-consumer hybrid: ideological tensions and the case of whole foods market. Theory Soc 37(3):229–270
38. Jones P, Clarke-Hill C, Comfort D, Hillier D (2008) Marketing and sustainability. Mark Intell Plan 26(2):123–130
39. Kassarjian HH (1971) Incorporating ecology into marketing strategy: the case of air pollution. J Mark 35(3):61–65
40. Kemper JA, Ballantine PW (2019) What do we mean by sustainability marketing? J Mark Manag 35(3–4):277–309
41. Kilbourne WE (1998) Green marketing: a theoretical perspective. J Mark Manag 14(6):641–655
42. Kilbourne WE, Beckmann SC (1998) Review and critical assessment of research on marketing and the environment. J Mark Manag 14(6):513–532
43. Kilbourne WE, Carlson L (2008) The dominant social paradigm, consumption, and environmental attitudes: can macromarketing education help? J Macromark 28(2):106–121

44. Kilbourne W, McDonagh P, Prothero A (1997) Sustainable consumption and the quality of life: a macromarketing challenge to the dominant social paradigm. J Macromark 17(1):4–24
45. Kilbourne WE, Dorsch MJ, Thyroff A (2018) Theorizing materialism through the institutional analysis and development framework. Mark Theory 18(1):55–74
46. Kinnear TC, Taylor JR, Ahmed SA (1974) Ecologically concerned consumers: who are they? Ecologically concerned consumers can be identified. J Mark 38(2):20–24
47. Kozinets RV, Handelman JM (2004) Adversaries of consumption: consumer movements, activism, and ideology. J Consum Res 31(3):691–704
48. Lavidge RJ (1970) The growing responsibilities of marketing. J Mark 34(1):25–28
49. Lee M, Roux D, Cherrier H, Cova B (2011) Anti-consumption and consumer resistance: concepts, concerns, conflicts and convergence. Eur J Mark 45(11/12)
50. Lim WM (2016) A blueprint for sustainability marketing: defining its conceptual boundaries for progress. Mark Theory 16(2):232–249
51. Lunde MB (2018) Sustainability in marketing: a systematic review unifying 20 years of theoretical and substantive contributions (1997–2016). AMS Rev 8(3):85–110
52. McDonagh P, Prothero A (2014) Sustainability marketing research: past, present and future. J Mark Manag 30(11–12):1186–1219
53. McDonald S, Oates CJ, Alevizou PJ, Young CW, Hwang K (2012) Individual strategies for sustainable consumption. J Mark Manag 28(3–4):445–468
54. McGouran C, Prothero A (2016) Enacted voluntary simplicity–exploring the consequences of requesting consumers to intentionally consume less. Eur J Mark 50(1/2):189–212
55. Meadows D, Meadows D, Randers J, Behrens III W (1972) The Limits to Growth: a Report for the Club of Rome's Project on the Predicament of Mankind. Universe Books, New York.
56. Merz JJ, Barnard P, Rees WE, Smith D, Maroni M, Rhodes CJ et al (2023) World scientists' warning: the behavioural crisis driving ecological overshoot. Sci Prog 106(3):00368504231201372
57. Mittelstaedt JD, Shultz CJ, Kilbourne WE, Peterson M (2014) Sustainability as megatrend: two schools of macromarketing thought. J Macromark 34(3):253–264
58. Muncy JA, Vitell SJ (1992) Consumer ethics: an investigation of the ethical beliefs of the final consumer. J Bus Res
59. Murphy PE, Kangun N, Locander WB (1978) Environmentally concerned consumers-racial variations: are middle and upper-class black females as ecologically conscious as their white counterparts? J Mark 42(4):61–66
60. Pande R (2023) The climate crisis is a crisis of inequality. Science 381(6661):eadk3500
61. Parkin S (1991) Power and green politics. Resurgence, May–June, 4–7
62. Peattie K (1999) Trappings versus substance in the greening of marketing planning. J Strateg Mark 7(2):131–148
63. Peattie K (2001) Towards sustainability: the third age of green marketing. Mark Rev 2(2):129–146
64. Peattie K (2010) Green consumption: behavior and norms. Annu Rev Environ Resour 35(1):195–228
65. Peattie K, Crane A (2005) Green marketing: legend, myth, farce or prophesy? Qual Mark Res 8(4):357–370
66. Peattie K, Peattie S (2009) Social marketing: a pathway to consumption reduction? J Bus Res 62(2):260–268
67. Prothero A, McDonagh P (2015) Introduction to the special issue: sustainability as megatrend II. J Macromark 35(1):7–10
68. Prothero A, Dobscha S, Freund J, Kilbourne WE, Luchs MG, Ozanne LK, Thøgersen J (2011) Sustainable consumption: opportunities for consumer research and public policy. J Public Policy Mark 30(1):31–38
69. Reuters (2024) Trump prepares to withdraw from Paris climate agreement, NYT reports. https://www.reuters.com/business/environment/trump-prepares-withdrawing-paris-climate-agreement-nyt-reports-2024-11-08/
70. Roux D, Izberk-Bilgin E (2018) Consumer resistance and power relationships in the marketplace. In: Arnould E, Thompson C (eds) Consumer culture theory. Sage, pp 295–317

71. Schrader U, Thøgersen J (2011) Putting sustainable consumption into practice. J Consum Policy 34:3–8
72. Scott K, Martin DM, Schouten JW (2014) Marketing and the new materialism. J Macromark 34(3):282–290
73. Shapiro SJ (1978) Marketing in a conserver society. Bus Horiz 21(2):3–13
74. Shaw D, Newholm T (2002) Voluntary simplicity and the ethics of consumption. Psychol Mark 19(2):167–185
75. Sheth JN, Parvatiyar A (2021) Sustainable marketing: market-driving, not market-driven. J Macromark 41(1):150–165
76. Sheth JN, Sethia NK, Srinivas S (2011) Mindful consumption: a customer-centric approach to sustainability. J Acad Mark Sci 39:21–39
77. Strong C (1996) Features contributing to the growth of ethical consumerism-a preliminary investigation. Mark Intell Plan 14(5):5–13
78. Tadajewski M (2019) Critical reflections on the marketing concept and consumer sovereignty. In: Tadajewski M, Higgins M, Denegri-Knott J, Varman R (eds) The Routledge companion to critical marketing studies. Routledge, London, pp 196–224
79. Tadajewski M, Hamilton K (2014) Waste, art, and social change: transformative consumer research outside of the academy? J Macromark 34(1):80–86
80. United Nations Environment Programme (2023) Broken record – emissions gap report. https://wedocs.unep.org/bitstream/handle/20.500.11822/43922/EGR2023.pdf?sequence=3&isAllowed=y
81. van Dam YK, Apeldoorn PA (1996) Sustainable marketing. J Macromark 16(2):45–56
82. Varey RJ (2010) Marketing means and ends for a sustainable society: a welfare agenda for transformative change. J Macromark 30(2):112–126
83. WCED (1987) Our common future. Oxford University Press, Oxford
84. Webster FE Jr (1975) Determining the characteristics of the socially conscious consumer. J Consum Res 2(3):188–196
85. Weigel R, Weigel J (1978) Environmental concern – the development of a measure. Environ Behav 10(1):3–15
86. White K, Hardisty DJ, Habib R (2019) The elusive green consumer. Harv Bus Rev 11(1):124–133
87. Yannopoulou N, Liu M, Xuemei B, Heath T (2019) Exploring social change through social media: the case of the Facebook group indignant citizens. Int J Consum Stud 43(4):348–357
88. Yuan M, Thellufsen JZ, Lund H, Liang Y (2021) The electrification of transportation in energy transition. Energy 236:121564
89. Alvesson M (2013) The Triumph of Emptiness. Oxford University Press, Oxford
90. Heath T and Heath M (2016) Once Upon a Time there was a Consumer…: Stories of Magic and the Magic of Stories. Journal of Marketing Management 32(9-10): 811-826
91. Gabriel Y and Lang T (2015) The Unmanageable Consumer. SAGE, London
92. McCracken G (1990) Culture and Consumption: New Approaches to the Symbolic Character of Consumer Goods and Activities. Indiana University Press, Bloomington and Indianapolis
93. Baudrillard J (1999) The Consumer Society – Myths and Structures. Sage Publications, London
94. Niinimäki K, Peters G, Dahlbo H, Perry P, Rissanen T, & Gwilt A (2020) The environmental price of fast fashion. Nature Reviews Earth & Environment 1(4), 189-200
95. Belz FM and Peattie K (2009) Sustainability Marketing: A Global Perspective. Wiley, Chichester
96. Elkington J and Hailes J (1989). The Green Consumer Guide. Gollancz, London
97. Kilbourne W (2010) Facing the challenge of sustainability in a changing world: An introduction to the special issue. Journal of Macromarketing 30(2), 109-111
98. Heath T, O'Malley L, Heath M and Story V (2016) Caring and conflicted: Mothers' ethical judgments about consumption. Journal of Business Ethics 136, 237-250
99. Pecot F, Vasilopoulou, S, and Cavallaro, M (2021) How political ideology drives anti-consumption manifestations. Journal of Business Research, 128, 61-69

100. Penaloza L and Price L (1993) Consumer resistance: A conceptual overview. Advances in consumer research, 20(1)
101. Portwood-Stacer L (2012) Anti-consumption as tactical resistance: Anarchists, subculture, and activist strategy. Journal of Consumer Culture, 12(1), 87-105
102. International Institute for Sustainable Development (2025). https://enb.iisd.org/consume/oslo004.html
103. Lim W (2017) Inside the sustainable consumption theoretical toolbox: Critical concepts for sustainability, consumption, and marketing. Journal of Business Research, 78: 69-80
104. Lubin D and Esty D (2010) The sustainability imperative. Harvard Business Review 88(5), 42-50

Teresa Heath is an associate professor with habilitation in marketing at the University of Minho. She received her PhD from the University of Nottingham. Her research focuses on consumption and its intersection with ethics, sustainability and education. She has advocated for critical and transformative approaches to marketing in her research and teaching. Her work has been published widely, including in the *Journal of Business Ethics*, the *Journal of Business Research*, *Marketing Theory*, the *European Journal of Marketing* and *Management Learning*. She is a member of the Education Committee of the Academy of Marketing and holds a position of Honorary Associate Professor at the Nottingham University Business School, University of Nottingham.

Maria Lichrou is an associate professor in Marketing at the Kemmy Business School (KBS), University of Limerick. Her research interests lie in the areas of consumption, place, and sustainability, with a particular focus on how these themes intersect with consumer identity, place-making, and sustainable living. Work on sustainability has been published in *Marketing Theory*, *European Journal of Marketing*, *Journal of Marketing Management*, *Journal of Macromarketing*, and *Resources, Conservation and Recycling*.

Climate Change, Conservation of Ecosystems and Human Rights

14

Márcia Marques and Maria Adelaide Ferreira

Never before have we had such an awareness of what we are doing to the planet, and never before have we had the power to do something about that.

– Sir David Attenborough, at the World Economic Forum Annual Meeting in Davos-Klosters, 2019

Abstract

This chapter explores the complex relationship between climate change, ocean conservation, and human rights, emphasizing the ocean's role as Earth's life support system and a critical component of global sustainability. It highlights the ecological, economic and cultural significance of the ocean while examining some of the many threats it faces from climate change, including warming, acidification, biodiversity loss, and ecosystem degradation. The chapter demonstrates how these environmental challenges directly and indirectly impact fundamental human rights, such as access to food, water, and a healthy environment.

The discussion is framed around the Sustainable Development Goals (SDGs) 13 (Climate Change) and SDG 14 (Life below water), showcasing their interdependence and their importance in addressing global challenges. International agreements are addressed as pivotal mechanisms for fostering sustainable ocean governance. Furthermore, the chapter advocates for the integration of blue economy strategies, nature-based solutions, and ecosystem restoration as pathways to mitigate climate impacts while ensuring economic growth and social equity.

M. Marques (✉)
Senior Consultant on Ocean Governance and Management (IPMA), Lisbon, Portugal

M. A. Ferreira
MARE-Faculty of Sciences of Lisbon University, Lisbon, Portugal

B. Casais (ed.), *Integrated Science to Achieve Sustainable Development Goals*, Integrated Science 37, https://doi.org/10.1007/978-3-031-88777-2_14

In conclusion, this chapter calls to the urgency of collaborative and integrated global efforts to address the climate-ocean-human rights nexus. It is possible to secure the future health of the ocean while advancing human well-being and environmental justice by promoting sustainable management practices, innovative policies, and inclusive governance.

Keywords

SDG14, SDG13, ocean health, ocean governance · Threatened life-support system · Marine sustainability · Nature's contributions to people · BBNJ · Triple planetary threat · Blue economy

1 Inroduction

As global temperatures rise, and the economies of wealthy nations continue to thrive, the economic development of poorer countries is increasingly constrained. Vulnerable nations such as the least developed countries (LDCs), landlocked developing countries (LLDCs), and small island developing states (SIDS) collectively represent more than 90 nations with a population of approximately 1.1 billion people. These countries are among the most vulnerable in the world, facing complex and multiple challenges stemming from structural issues and geographical disadvantages, including increased exposure to extreme events, such as heat waves and droughts, strong reliance on economic activities and natural resources highly sensitive to climate variability, and deficient access to risk management tools, such as air conditioning and insurance, compared to wealthier countries [1, 2]. These challenges are further exacerbated by limited institutional capacity, scarce financial resources to address emerging threats, and a high degree of susceptibility to systemic shocks. Remaining on a "business-as-usual" trajectory of rising carbon dioxide levels and rapid climate change, developing nations' average annual growth rate is expected to decline from 3.2% to 2.6% [3]. While all nations experience heightened vulnerability to climate change, some are more vulnerable than others. This effectively undermines global efforts to achieve sustainable development.

Transforming our world, for people, planet and prosperity, is the ambitious aim of the UN 2030 Agenda for Sustainable Development set forward in 2015, to be achieved by 2030, through the accomplishment of 17 Sustainable Development Goals (SDGs) and 169 targets, which, i.a., "seek to realize the human rights of all".[1] In 2021, the UN Human Rights Council, highlighted the profound interconnection between environmental health and the realization of human rights. By formalizing this recognition, individuals and communities have gained a powerful mechanism to hold governments, corporations, and other entities accountable for environmental degradation [4]. More recently, on July 26, 2022, the General Assembly of the

[1] A/RES/70/1, p. 1.

United Nations recognized that a clean, healthy and sustainable environment is a human right.[2]

It is widely recognized that all SDGs are integrated and indivisible, that progress in one directly influences outcomes in others, and that sustainable development for all can only be achieved when all SDGs are accomplished (2030 agenda).

However, not all SDGs are alike [5]. Some focus on human well-being: SDG1—No Poverty, SDG3—Good health and wellbeing, SDG4—Quality Education, SDG 5—Gender Equality, SDG 10—Reduced inequalities, and SDG 16—Peace, Justice and Strong institutions. A bigger group of SDGs focuses on sustainable production and consumption: SDG 2—Zero hunger, SDG 6—Clean water and sanitation; SDG 7—Affordable and clean energy, SDG 8—Decent work and economic growth, SDG 9—Industry, Innovation and Infrastructure, SDG 11—Sustainable cities and communities, SDG 12—Responsible consumption and production, and SDG 17—Partnerships for the goals. This goal acts as "glue" that binds the goals together, recognizing that no single entity or country can achieve sustainable development in isolation.

The three remaining SDGs focus on preserving our planet's life support system and a safe operating space for humankind: SDG 14—Life below water (also known as the ocean goal) and SDG 15—Life on land. Both SDGs focus on preserving the highly threatened web of life that sustains humanity by combating the loss of biodiversity and of essential ecosystem functions and services, such as pollination, nutrient cycling, and biological productivity. SDG 13—Climate action, focuses on urgently combating climate change and its deleterious impacts on the same biodiversity and ecosystem services, both on land and on the ocean, which make up humanity's life support ecosystems. SDG13 can be seen as an externality of human action that directly threatens the achievement of SDG14 and SDG15. Its significance is equally critical and intertwined with these two goals Fig. 14.1.

So, while sustainable development, as an anthropocentric concept, is centered on human well-being and aims to balance economic, social and environmental aspects, it is vital to recognize that action directed at securing a safe operating space for humankind, through these three foundational SDGs, must be a priority.

This chapter explores the relationship between these three SDGs, focusing on the ocean as our planet's life support system, and therefore, as the cornerstone of sustainable development. We begin by highlighting the critical ecological role and immense value of the ocean for both the planet and humanity. It then examines how the health of the ocean is increasingly threatened by anthropogenic pressures. Following this, we explore global responses to these challenges, focusing on governance frameworks and innovative economic approaches. Finally, the chapter demonstrates the intricate interconnections between SDG 14, SDG 13, and human rights.

---

[2] Decision A/76/L.75

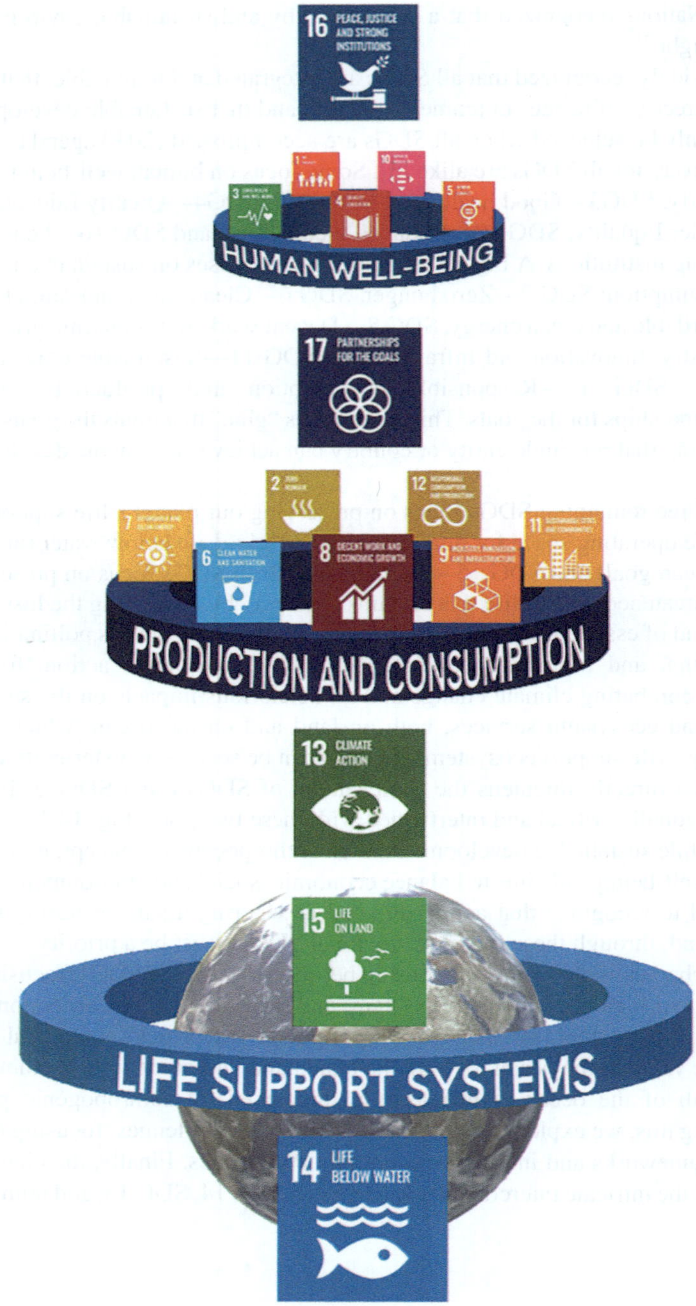

Fig. 14.1 "SDG's tree" (Source: Adapted from United Nations Environment Programme [7])—the lower tier includes the SDGs that represent Earth's life-support system—the ocean ecosystem (the focus of SDG14), and terrestrial ecosystems (SDG15—Life on Land). Climate change (SDG 13),

2 The Ocean: Earth's Life Support System

The ocean is our planet's life support system. It plays a fundamental role in maintaining the conditions necessary for life on Earth. It is the largest ecosystem on our planet, covering more than 70% of the Earth's surface, holding roughly 97% of the planet's water, and representing about 99% of the living space on Earth [8]. The "oceans" we learned about in school, the Atlantic, Indian, Pacific, Arctic and Antarctic, are in fact ocean basins, all interconnected by a global current, known as the "global conveyor belt", driven by density and temperature gradients. This global ocean circulation effectively links all these basins making up one immense and single ocean.

The ocean is teeming with life, from tiny microorganisms to the blue whale, the biggest animal ever known to have lived, and is home to an incredible variety of species living in a diverse array of habitats, from coastal shallow areas, such as coral reefs, mangroves, kelp forests, and seagrass beds, to the deepest depths, such as sponge gardens and hydrothermal vent communities, not forgetting the water column, from the surface, into the twilight zone and the abyss.

The ocean provides a plethora of essential ecosystems services which are vital for humankind:

Provisioning Services Marine and coastal ecosystems offer essential products such as fish, plants, and animals. They provide seafood, which plays a critical role in food security, supplying over 20% of the average animal protein intake *per capita* for 3 billion people and exceeding 50% in certain developing nations [9]. The ocean is home to nearly a million known species containing vast untapped potential for scientific discovery [10] Marine ecosystems yield a wide variety of biochemicals, natural medicines, pharmaceuticals, and raw materials like sand and coral. On a smaller scale, they also provide freshwater and fiber, particularly in specific coastal areas.

Regulating Services The ocean regulates the global climate system and serves as a crucial heat and carbon sink. Both the physical properties of the ocean as a body of water and its diverse marine life are vital to this process. The ocean produces an estimated 50–80% of the planet's oxygen through the photosynthetic activity of phytoplankton [11] and absorbs approximately 30% of human-produced carbon dioxide (CO_2) emissions. Atmospheric CO_2 dissolves into the ocean's surface waters, being removed through physical mechanisms like mixing and downwelling, as well as biological processes like phytoplankton photosynthesis. When phytoplankton die, sink, or are consumed by zooplankton, the carbon they contain is

Fig. 14.1 (continued) a severe externality of human activities, threatens the life-support system; the middle tier encompasses all SDGs related with sustainable production and consumption headed by partnerships, which are crucial for achieving expected results; the top tier includes the SDGs related with human well-being, the ultimate goal of sustainable development, capped by peace, justice and strong institutions [7] transferred through the marine food web. Eventually, it sinks to deeper waters, where it is decomposed by microbes, completing a critical step in the ocean's carbon cycle.

Coastal ecosystems, such as saltmarshes, mangroves, corals and seagrass beds, but also deep-sea ecosystems, are essential in carbon sequestration, and contribute to stable climate conditions, such as balanced temperatures and precipitation. These conditions support agricultural activities, preserve human health, and protect critical infrastructure. Coastal ecosystems also act as natural barriers against erosion and storms, reducing wave energy, stabilizing shorelines, and protecting coastal areas from flooding and surges. This mitigation enhances the resilience of coastal settlements to climate-related risks.

Supporting Services Marine biodiversity and ecosystems are crucial for maintaining primary productivity and driving biogeochemical cycles, such as nutrient cycling. Photosynthesis in marine and coastal ecosystems supports the conversion of solar energy into biological forms, sustaining food webs and biodiversity. Coastal ecosystems, such as saltmarshes, seagrass meadows, mangroves, kelp forests, and coral reefs, as well as oceanic and deep-sea ecosystems and habitats such as coral and sponge gardens, hydrothermal vents, and seamounts, also serve as essential reproductive habitats and nursery grounds for marine species, maintaining the biodiversity necessary for healthy marine systems.

Cultural Services Marine ecosystems offer significant non-material benefits, providing opportunities for spiritual and aesthetic experiences, recreational activities, and cognitive development. These cultural services foster human well-being and a deep connection to nature, making marine ecosystems an integral part of many cultural practices and traditions worldwide.

2.1 Valuing Ocean Ecosystem Services

The global value of ecosystem services has been estimated to exceed 150 trillion US dollars—more than twice the world's GDP [12]. Regulating services, such as climate regulation and water purification, accounted for the largest share of this value [13]. The World Bank estimates that the collapse of ecosystem services could cost the global economy up to 2.7 trillion annually by 2030 [14]. Globally, more than half of GDP is moderately or highly dependent on nature [15] but low- and middle-income countries are expected to bear the greatest burden, with some nations experiencing GDP losses as high as 10%.

The concept of ecosystem services, which emerged in the 1970s, did not immediately include marine ecosystem services. It was only in the 2000s that the ocean was also considered in this equation [16]. The ocean's economic value is undisputed: it generates jobs that support millions of livelihoods, it supplies resources that have enabled decades of industrial growth, and about 90 percent of world trade is done by sea [17]. In some least-developed nations, fish protein accounts for more than 50 percent of animal protein intake [9]. Additionally, the services that the ocean ecosystem provides are vital for the well-being of society. The ocean is deeply rooted and interwoven in many cultural practices around the world, serves as a source of inspiration for art, and offers significant recreational and aesthetic value to countless individuals [17].

The economic value of the ocean is often measured both by direct output, as well as by any indirect impacts it produces [18]. A study by the World Wildlife Fund valued the ocean at over 24 trillion dollars, with the ocean's annual "gross marine product" valued at a minimum of 2.5 trillion US dollars. If it were a national economy, this value would place the ocean as the seventh-largest economy in the world [19].

However, thinking in terms of GDP is highly limiting when considering the value of nature and of nature's contributions to people. As Robert F. Kennedy remarked in his famous address at the University of Kansas in 1968, GDP "measures everything (…), except that which makes life worthwhile" [20]. The ocean, a healthy ocean, makes all life on Earth, including human life, possible. In that sense, in the way that the ocean and marine biodiversity is existential to us, its value to humanity is incommensurable.

3 Earth's Life Support System Is Endangered

At present, our precious and irreplaceable life support system is endangered. The compounded effects of human activities are posing a pervasive and unprecedented threat on ocean health.

3.1 Ocean Warming

The ocean absorbs and retains heat at a rate over 1000 times greater than the atmosphere [21], with its upper layer holding more heat than the entire Earth's atmosphere. Since 1950, the ocean has taken in over 90% of the additional heat generated by human activities. While this capacity has mitigated some of the more severe impacts of global climate change, the ocean's ability to store excess heat is not unlimited [22]. Global ocean temperatures are rising rapidly, with recent studies showing that ocean warming is happening faster than previously estimated. Since 1993, the average rate of warming has more than doubled, according to the IPCC [23].

At the ocean's surface, rising temperatures increase heat and vapor transfer to the atmosphere. Ocean warming has profound physical consequences, including thermal expansion, which contributes to global sea-level rise. Rising sea levels exacerbate the impacts of extreme events like storm surges, leading to severe coastal consequences, including urban flooding, beach erosion, land loss, and salinization of agricultural areas. Coastal infrastructure, including sewage systems, ports, roads, railways, and cultural heritage sites, also faces significant risks from these changes [16].

Ocean warming also causes increased heat transfer to the atmosphere, which intensifies tropical and mid-latitude cyclones. These changes also disrupt marine ecosystems and food webs. Warming increases the intensity, duration, and frequency of marine heatwaves, which cause significant biodiversity loss, as observed, for example, in the Mediterranean Sea and the Gulf of Mexico over the past two decades [15]. Warming also alters species distribution, leading fish i.a, to seek cooler waters and causing certain species to migrate to higher latitudes. This shift in fish stocks composition carries known negative consequences in fisheries, when fish stocks move out of their traditional range. Not only does the fishing industry suffer from a lack of resource, it is oftentimes also faced with new species it doesn't know nor value.

3.2 Ocean Deoxygenation

Warmer waters have a lower capacity to hold oxygen, which is crucial for breathing. One of the direct consequences of ocean warming is deoxygenation, which creates an added stress for marine life, particularly on species with high metabolic rates such as sharks, and tuna, effectively shrinking the available habitat area (or volume) and eventually even creating dead zones. Dead zones are spreading around the world's ocean.

3.3 Ocean Acidification

High levels of human-induced CO_2 emissions also drive chemical changes in seawater, reducing its pH, causing ocean acidification This process depletes carbonate ions in seawater, significantly interfering in calcification processes, which are essential for calcifying organisms such as corals, shellfish, and some species of phytoplankton—the species that constitute the very basis of marine foodwebs. These organisms rely on calcium carbonate to build their shells and skeletons. Acidification threatens their survival, disrupting ecosystems and marine food webs [4]. Ocean acidification has other physical-chemical consequences, such as affecting sound transmission in seawater, and modifies the behavior of trace metals [4].

Adding to this triple threat—warming, deoxygenation, and acidification—other anthropogenic pressures are contributing to rapidly deteriorating ocean health. Other types of pollution, including excess nutrients, plastics and a plethora of contaminants reach the ocean in unprecedented amounts with unfathomable consequences. Habitat destruction and resource overexploitation lead to depleted stocks and extensive biodiversity loss.

4 Putting Ocean Conservation at the Forefront of Global Efforts

SDG 14 marked the first time the ocean was addressed in a global agenda as a separate goal, as a recognition of its importance to humankind and world prosperity. SDG 14 aims to conserve and sustainably use the oceans, seas, and marine resources for sustainable development [24]. It highlights the importance of protecting marine ecosystems, combating pollution, overfishing, ocean acidification, and habitat destruction. It stresses the interconnectedness of a healthy ocean with the broader sustainability agenda, recognizing that ocean health is crucial for food security, climate regulation, and biodiversity. Notwithstanding, and perhaps unsurprisingly, to date it has been the most underfunded and under-implemented SDGs, and one of the least studied, with major challenges remaining in all regions and income groups [25]. As of June 2024, only slightly more than ¼ of the global seafloor had been mapped [26]. Understanding the ocean at multiple spatial and temporal scales is fundamental to predicting future scenarios, mitigating the impacts of degraded ocean health, and ensuring societal adaptation [16].

In 2019, in the 25th Conference of Parties (COP) of the UN Framework Convention on Climate Change (UNFCCC) the need to strengthen the understanding and knowledge about the ocean, and action towards its improved health[3] was recognized, . Ensuing UNFCCC COP and several other high-level conferences, such as the Our Ocean and UN Ocean Conference series, or the One Ocean Summit, have helped to bring the ocean firmly into global political discussions [16].

In 2021, the UN Decade of Ocean Science for Sustainable Development (2021–2030), another UN initiative, was officially launched, aiming to catalyze a global effort to advance SDG14. This initiative focuses on conserving and sustainably using the ocean and its resources, while fostering the co-design of transformative knowledge and actions to address the challenges posed by climate change and a growing human population. In parallel, the UN declared 2021–2030 the "UN Decade on Ecosystem Restoration", underscoring the urgent need to accelerate the restoration of degraded ecosystems worldwide to combat the climate crisis, improve food security, ensure access to clean water, and protect biodiversity. Together, these efforts aim to safeguard the planet's ecological integrity and resilience in the face of growing global challenges [27].

The United Nations Convention on the Law of the Sea (UNCLOS), adopted in 1982, provides the legal foundation for maritime governance [28]. UNCLOS defines maritime zones, establishes rights and responsibilities for resource management, and promotes sustainable use of marine resources. The maritime zones closest to land (internal waters and the 12-nautical-mile territorial sea) are considered part of a coastal state's territory, where the state exercises sovereignty. Coastal states also have exclusive economic zones (EEZs), extending up to 200 nautical miles from the baseline, within which they hold sovereign rights over natural resources and jurisdiction over specific activities, including marine scientific research and

[3] FCCC/CP/2019/L.10

environmental protection. Similarly, coastal states possess sovereign rights over living and non-living natural resources on and within their continental shelf.

Beyond ocean areas within national jurisdiction lie the high seas, the water column of the wide ocean, open to all states and reserved for peaceful purposes, and the Area, the ocean floor beyond the limits of national jurisdiction. The Area, together with its resources, are the common heritage of humankind [28]. In June 2023, the United Nations adopted the Agreement on the Conservation and Sustainable use of Marine Biological Diversity of Areas Beyond National Jurisdiction—BBNJ Agreement. The agreement, represents a landmark achievement in ocean governance and underscores the need for international cooperation to address the unique challenges of marine conservation in the high seas and the Area, establishing mechanisms for marine protected areas, benefit-sharing from marine genetic resources, environmental impact assessments, capacity-building and the transfer of marine technology [29].

Efforts to conserve and sustainably use marine biodiversity align closely with initiatives under the Convention on Biological Diversity (CBD). A key focus of the CBD's work on coastal and marine biodiversity is identifying ecologically or biologically significant marine areas [30]. In 2022, the parties to the CBD adopted the Kunming-Montreal Global Biodiversity Framework, which includes the ambitious "30x30 target." This target aims to ensure that by 2030, at least 30% of the planet, including marine and coastal areas, are "effectively conserved and managed through ecologically representative, well-connected, and equitably governed systems of protected areas and other effective area-based conservation measures".[4]

In November 2024, the 29th Conference of Parties (COP29) to the UN Framework Convention on Climate Change (UNFCCC) was held in Baku, Azerbaijan. During the conference, a groundbreaking finance goal was announced, aimed at supporting nations in protecting their populations and economies from climate disasters while ensuring equitable access to the benefits of the global clean energy transition.

Focusing on climate finance, COP29 brought together nearly 200 countries and achieved a historic agreement that includes tripling financial support to developing countries, increasing the previous target to USD 300 billion annually by 2035 [5], and mobilizing efforts from both public and private sectors to scale up climate finance to USD 1.3 trillion per year by 2035. This landmark agreement, known as the New Collective Quantified Goal on Climate Finance (NCQG), was finalized after 2 weeks of intensive negotiations and years of preparatory work, requiring unanimous consensus on every detail of the text [3]. Additionally, COP29 achieved consensus on carbon markets—a critical breakthrough after several COPs had failed to reach an agreement on the matter. This progress will enable nations to implement their climate plans more efficiently and cost-effectively, accelerating efforts to halve global emissions this decade, as mandated by science.

Other global initiatives and instruments related to ocean conservation include the Convention on the Conservation of Migratory Species of Wild Animals (a.k.a., the Bonn Convention), the UN Fish Stocks Agreement (under UNCLOS), the work of

[4] CBD/COP/DEC/15/4, p. 9.

the International Seabed Authority, the Ocean Dialogue under the UNFCCC, and the ongoing negotiations for an international legally binding instrument to address plastic pollution in the marine environment [29].

4.1 Catalysts for Ocean Conservation, Climate Mitigation and Adaptation

Despite all these international initiatives, agreements, and policies, environmental degradation continues at an alarming rate. The Global Risk Report (2021) identifies extreme weather events, failure of climate action, biodiversity loss, and pollution as some of the most pressing threats to humanity over the next decade, with cascading impacts on livelihoods, health, and human rights [31]. Addressing the "triple planetary crisis" — climate change, biodiversity loss, and pollution—requires urgent action, and a rights-based approach, essential not only for protecting fundamental human rights but also for achieving the SDGs.

In this context, Table 14.1 provides a simplified summary of the relationship between human rights and SDGs 13 and 14, illustrating the close interconnection between environmental protection and human rights.

A study conducted by the World Health Organization [36] highlights several ways in which biodiversity loss directly impacts human health. These include invasive alien species outcompeting native species essential for food and medicine, deforestation increasing the risk of wildlife-to-human disease transmission, such as with the COVID-19 pandemic, and the bioaccumulation of pollutants like mercury in food chains. Access to a healthy environment, health, food, water, sanitation, cultural participation, and work are particularly vulnerable to the impacts of biodiversity loss, directly affecting human well-being.

The blue economy[5] presents numerous opportunities for mitigating and adapting to climate change, many of which are deeply rooted in nature-based solutions. Recent analyses suggest that ocean-based solutions could reduce emissions of greenhouse gases by over 11 billion tonnes annually by 2050, reducing the global emissions gap (*i.e.*, the gap between where global emissions are heading with current country commitments and where they ought to be to limit warming) up to 35% under a 1.5 °C warming pathway and by 47% under a 2.0 °C pathway [11]. Scaling up ocean-based renewable energy sources, such as offshore wind, tidal energy, and algal biofuels, presents significant opportunities for cutting greenhouse gas emissions.

Nature-based approaches leveraging marine ecosystems' capacity to sequester and store carbon offer cost-effective mitigation potential [37]. Coastal "blue carbon" ecosystems, such as mangroves, salt marshes, and seagrass beds, are particularly efficient at capturing and storing carbon, surpassing the carbon sequestration

[5] The blue economy encompasses all economic activities based on or connected to the ocean, seas, and coasts. This includes both sectoral and inter-sectoral activities, ranging from fisheries and aquaculture to renewable energy and coastal tourism [43].

Table 14.1 Implementation status of SDG 13 and SDG 14 along with their specific targets and connections to human rights [32–35]

Status	Target	Related human rights (indicative)
	Take urgent action to combat climate change and its impacts	
	13.1 Strengthen resilience and adaptive capacity to climate-related hazards	Right to life; right to security; right to adequate housing (protection from disasters)
	13.2 Integrate climate change into policies, strategies and planning	Right to development; right to sustainable development
	13.3 Improve education, awareness-raising and human and institutional capacity	Right to education; right to participation in environmental decision-making
	13.a Mobilize financial resources for mitigation	Right to equality (addressing disparities in climate impacts); right to development
	13.b Raise capacity for effective climate change-related planning and management in LDCs and SIDS	Right to equitable development; right to self-determination for vulnerable states
	Conserve and sustainably use the oceans, seas and marine resources for sustainable development	
	14.1 Prevent and significantly reduce marine pollution	Right to a clean and healthy environment; right to health (free from toxic exposure)
	14.2 Sustainably manage and protect marine and coastal ecosystems	Right to health; right to water and sanitation; right to life.
	14.3 Minimize and address the impacts of ocean acidification	Right to food (due to impact on marine food chains); right to a sustainable environment
	14.4 Effectively regulate harvesting and end overfishing, illegal, unreported and unregulated fishing	Right to work and livelihoods (for fishing communities); right to food security
	14.5 Conservation of coastal and marine areas	Right to culture (especially for indigenous coastal communities); right to biodiversity
	14.6 End harmful fisheries subsidies	Right to equitable economic opportunities; right to sustainable development
	14.7 Increase the economic benefits to SIDS and LDCs from the sustainable use of marine resources	Right to development; right to work and livelihoods (especially for SIDS and LDCs)
	14.a Increase scientific knowledge, develop research capacity and transfer marine technology, (…) to the development of developing countries, in particular SIDS and LDCs	Right to education; right to participation in environmental decision-making
	14.b Provide access for small-scale artisanal fishers to marine resources and markets	Right to work and livelihoods (for fishing communities); right to food security
	14.c Enhance the conservation and sustainable use of oceans and their resources by implementing international law as reflected in UNCLOS	Right to equitable development; right to self-determination for vulnerable states; right to participation in environmental decision-making

potential of terrestrial ecosystems [38]. These ecosystems absorb and store carbon both within the vegetation itself and in the sediments beneath. They play a crucial role in mitigating climate change by sequestering and retaining significant amounts of carbon in plant biomass and underlying sediments [39]. Globally, blue carbon ecosystems store approximately 11.5 billion tons of carbon, with mangroves holding the largest share at 6.5 billion tons [40].

Protecting and restoring these habitats provides multiple co-benefits, including supporting biodiversity, offering storm protection, and enhancing ecosystem-based adaptation (EbA) efforts. There is an immense potential for EbA, which involves conserving and restoring ecosystems that provide natural defenses against climate hazards. Examples include wetlands, mangroves, and oyster reefs, which protect shorelines, as well as strengthening ecosystems' resilience to climate impacts through biodiversity conservation and adaptive resource management, such as sustainable fisheries. Networks of Marine Protected Areas (MPAs) are essential tools for ecosystems conservation and management, while reducing stressors like land-based and marine pollution further enhances resilience [41]. Other promising mitigation strategies include expanding seaweed aquaculture to produce low-carbon food, feed, and fuel alternatives, as well as promoting shifts towards sustainably produced "blue" proteins, such as farmed bivalves. These proteins are highly nutritious and have lower environmental impacts compared to land-based protein sources.

To minimize the impacts of climate change on the ocean, the blue economy and society at large, it is essential to enhance the adaptive capacity of ecosystems, individuals, communities, sectors, nations, and regions. Effective adaptation also requires individuals and communities to have resources to rely on during crises, the flexibility to switch strategies as conditions change, the ability to organize and act collectively, the capacity to learn and respond to climate impacts, and the power to decide on appropriate responses. Adaptation strategies, including EbA, must prioritize vulnerable groups such as small-scale fishers and workers, especially women. Women are often engaged in informal and undervalued roles, such as fish processing, and are frequently excluded from policymaking processes [41].

Effectively, the blue economy represents a transformative opportunity to address climate change through integrated strategies that balance economic growth, ecological sustainability, and social equity. By leveraging both technological innovations and nature-based solutions, countries can enhance resilience, reduce emissions, and support livelihoods and human well-being. Effective governance, such as marine spatial planning (MSP), and due consideration of vulnerable groups, including women and small-scale fishers, are key to ensuring that the blue economy fulfills its potential as a cornerstone of sustainable development. In fact, MSP plays a pivotal role in optimizing the potential of the blue economy. By mapping and identifying the roles and interests of different stakeholders and sectors, MSP facilitates effective, efficient, and equitable responses to complex challenges. This approach enables countries to make informed and coordinated decisions that promote the sustainable use of marine resources while advancing efforts in climate adaptation and mitigation.

5 Concluding Remarks

The ocean lies at the core of human well-being. Despite its vital importance, policies addressing ocean health often focus narrowly on either climate or biodiversity goals, neglecting their intricate interconnections. This fragmented approach limits the effectiveness of conservation and climate action strategies. A more holistic view is needed to address the synergies between these sustainable development goals and ensure sustainable ocean management.

Climate change and its impacts are increasingly forcing many human migrations, in response to environmental and ecological changes that affect livelihoods, health, food security, and safety. While the connection between environmental crises and human migrations is not a new phenomenon, it is becoming increasingly global and urgent. In some areas entire communities are unwillingly displaced due to environmental change such as sea level rise, or by the destruction caused by abrupt disasters and extreme weather events, often worsened by climate change. In turn, human migrations caused by ecological degradation often cause social and political turmoil in the territories and societies receiving these displaced communities. In short, the ongoing planetary ecological crisis has profound deleterious implications for human rights, widening rather than narrowing the gap to achieving the SDGs.

The ocean is central to addressing the current planetary ecological crises, while striving for human rights and, ultimately, human well-being. For most of history, the ocean was considered "too big to fail". More recently, in the face of pervasive marine environmental degradation and overexploitation, the opposing narrative started to prevail considering that the ocean is simply "too big to fix" [42]. Narratives are important in that they help frame our thinking and action. Believing that the ocean is too big to fix elicits depression and disengagement, leading to inaction. Lubchenco and Gaines [42, p. 911] argue that a new narrative for the ocean is needed, one that inspires new science and effective action: "*It is time for a new ocean narrative that says, "The ocean is so central to our future. It's too important to neglect." In creating a new solution space for the ocean, we can also address broader global problems. In healing the ocean, we can heal ourselves. The ocean sustains and feeds us. It connects us. It is our past and our future. The ocean is not too big to fail, nor is it too big to fix. It is too big to ignore.*"

Acknowledgements The authors gratefully acknowledge the contribution of Maria Andrade in producing Fig. 14.1. This publication was financed by the Fundação para a Ciência e a Tecnologia (FCT) through the project UIDP/04292/2020 (https://doi.org/10.54499/UIDP/04292/2020), UIDB/04292/2020 (https://doi.org/10.54499/UIDB/04292/2020), awarded to MARE and through project LA/P/0069/2020 (https://doi.org/10.54499/LA/P/0069/2020) granted to the Associate Laboratory ARNET.

References

1. International Organization for Migration (IOM), & United Nations Office of the High Representative for the Least Developed Countries, Landlocked Developing Countries, and Small Island Developing States (UN-OHRLLS) (2019) Climate change and migration in vulnerable countries: a snapshot of least developed countries, landlocked developing countries, and small island developing states. International Organization for Migration
2. Levy BS, Patz JA (2015) Climate change, human rights, and social justice. Ann Glob Health 81(3):310–322. https://doi.org/10.1016/j.aogh.2015.08.008
3. Molony BW, Ford AT, Sequeira AMM, Borja A, Zivian AM, Robinson C, Lønborg C, Escobar-Briones EG, Di Lorenzo E, Andersen JH, Müller MN, Devlin MJ, Failler P, Villasante S, Libralato S, Fortibuoni T (2022) Editorial: sustainable development goal 14 – life below water: towards a sustainable ocean. Front Mar Sci 8:829610. https://doi.org/10.3389/fmars.2021.829610
4. Bamaniya PK, Vaghela DT, Bambhaniya I, Kirankumar J, Bhadarka M, Sureandiran B, Iqbal G (2024) Ocean acidification. In: Research and reviews in animal science, vol II. Bhumi Publishing, p 28–47. Available at: https://www.researchgate.net/publication/378868726_OCEAN_ACIDIFICATION
5. Johansen E (2020) The role of the oceans in regulating the Earth's climate: legal perspectives. In: Johansen E, Busch S, Jakobsen IU (eds) The law of the sea and climate change. Cambridge University Press
6. United Nations Framework Convention on Climate Change (UNFCCC) (2024) COP29: UN climate conference agrees to triple finance to developing countries, protecting lives and economies. Retrieved from https://unfccc.int/news/cop29-un-climate-conference-agrees-to-triple-finance-to-developing-countries-protecting-lives-and
7. United Nations Environment Programme (2021) Making peace with nature: a scientific blueprint to tackle the climate, biodiversity and pollution emergencies. Nairobi
8. NASA (2016) Understanding earth: our ocean, p 16. https://eospso.nasa.gov/sites/default/files/publications/UnderstandingEarth-OurOcean_508_0.pdf
9. Food and Agriculture Organization of the United Nations (FAO) (2018) The state of world fisheries and aquaculture 2018: meeting the sustainable development goals. FAO, Rome. Available at http://www.fao.org/3/i9540en/i9540en.pdf
10. United Nations (2020) The sustainable development goals report 2020. United Nations Department of Economic and Social Affairs. https://unstats.un.org/sdgs/report/2020/
11. Hoegh-Guldberg O et al 2019 The ocean as a solution to climate change: fve opportunities for action. Report. World Resources Institute, Washington. Available online at http://www.oceanpanel.org/climate
12. Boston Consulting Group (2021) The biodiversity crisis is a business crisis. https://web-assets.bcg.com/fb/5e/74af5531468e9c1d4dd5c9fc0bd7/bcg-the-biodiversity-crisis-is-a-business-crisis-mar-2021-rr.pdf
13. United Nations Development Programme (2024) Asia in focus: biodiversity and the business and human rights agenda. UNDP
14. Johnson J, Ruta G, Baldos UL, Cervigni R, Chonabayashi S, Corong E, Gavryliuk O, Gerber J, Hertel T, Nootenboom C, Polasky S (2021) The economic case for nature: a global Earth-economy model to assess development policy pathways. World Bank, Washington. https://doi.org/10.1596/35882
15. World Economic Forum (2020) Nature risk rising: why the crisis engulfing nature matters for business and the economy. World Economic Forum, in collaboration with PwC. https://www3.weforum.org/docs/WEF_New_Nature_Economy_Report_2020.pdf
16. European Marine Board (2024) Navigating the Future VI: placing the ocean within the wider earth system. Position Paper 28 of the European Marine Board, Ostend, Belgium. 116pp. ISSN: 0167-9309 ISBN: 9789464206265. https://doi.org/10.5281/zenodo.13329469

17. High Level Panel for a Sustainable Ocean Economy (2020) The ocean panel: benefit-cost analysis of sustainable ocean-based interventions. World Resources Institute
18. United Nations Development Programme (UNDP), United Nations Environment Programme (UNEP), & Office of the United Nations High Commissioner for Human Rights (OHCHR) (2023) What is the right to a healthy environment? Information note. United Nations
19. Guldberg O et al (2015) Reviving the ocean economy: the case for action – 2015. WWF International, Gland, Switzerland, Geneva, p 60
20. Kennedy RF (1968, March 18) Remarks at the University of Kansas. John F. Kennedy Presidential Library and Museum. Available at: https://www.jfklibrary.org/learn/about-jfk/the-kennedy-family/robert-f-kennedy/robert-f-kennedy-speeches/remarks-at-the-university-of-kansas-march-18-1968
21. Intergovernmental Panel on Climate Change (IPCC) (2013) In: Stocker TF, Qin D, Plattner G-K, Tignor M, Allen SK, Boschung J, Nauels A, Xia Y, Bex V, Midgley PM (eds) Climate change 2013: the physical science basis. Contribution of working group I to the fifth assessment report of the intergovernmental panel on climate change. Cambridge University Press
22. Intergovernmental Panel on Climate Change (IPCC) (2021) Chapter 9: ocean, cryosphere and sea level change. In Climate change 2021: the physical science basis. Available at: https://www.ipcc.ch/report/ar6/wg1/chapter/chapter-9/
23. SROCC Report, Summary for Policy Makers (n 21), at p. 8; IPCC, Climate Change 2013 (n 38), at p. 1228
24. Global Goals (n.d.) Goal 14: life below water. Retrieved January 3, 2025, from https://www.globalgoals.org/goals/14-life-below-water/
25. Haas B (2023) Achieving SDG 14 in an equitable and just way. Int Environ Agreements 23:199–205. https://doi.org/10.1007/s10784-023-09603-z
26. National Oceanic and Atmospheric Administration (NOAA) (n.d.) How much of the ocean have we explored? NOAA Ocean Exploration. Available at: https://oceanexplorer.noaa.gov/facts/explored.html
27. Waltham NJ, Elliott M, Lee SY, Lovelock C, Duarte CM, Buelow C, Simenstad C, Nagelkerken I, Claassens L, Wen CK-C, Barletta M, Connolly RM, Gillies C, Mitsch WJ, Ogburn MB, Purandare J, Possingham H, Sheaves M (2020) UN decade on ecosystem restoration 2021–2030 – what chance for success in restoring coastal ecosystems? Front Mar Sci 7. https://doi.org/10.3389/fmars.2020.00071
28. United Nations (1982) Convention on the Law of the Sea, Dec. 10, 1982, 1833 U.N.T.S. 397
29. Bansard J, Pasini O (2024) Blue leaders bulletin: summary of the blue leaders high-level event. International Institute for Sustainable Development (IISD). Available at: https://enb.iisd.org/blue-leaders-high-level-event-biodiversity-beyond-national-jurisdiction-bbnj
30. European Marine Board (2024) Navigating the future VI: placing the ocean within the wider earth system. Position Paper 28 of the European Marine Board, Ostend, Belgium, p 116. ISSN: 0167-9309 ISBN: 9789464206265. https://doi.org/10.5281/zenodo.13329469
31. World Economic Forum (2021) The global risks report 2021. 16th Edition. https://www3.weforum.org/docs/WEF_The_Global_Risks_Report_2021.pdf
32. United Nations (1966) International covenant on economic, social and cultural rights. United Nations General Assembly
33. United Nations Development Programme (2023) What is the right to a healthy environment? Information note. UNDP
34. United Nations Framework Convention on Climate Change (UNFCCC) (2015) Paris agreement. UNFCCC
35. United Nations General Assembly (2022) The human right to a clean, healthy, and sustainable environment (A/RES/76/300). United Nations
36. World Health Organization (WHO) & Secretariat of the Convention on Biological Diversity (CBD) (2015) Connecting global priorities: biodiversity and human health – A state of knowledge review. World Health Organization. ISBN: 9789241508537
37. Lecerf M, Millington-Drake M, Picourt L (2024) Blue thread: aligning national climate and biodiversity strategies. Ocean & Climate Platform, Blue Marine Foundation, p 1–13

38. McLeod E, Chmura GL, Bouillon S, Salm R, Björk M, Duarte CM, Lovelock CE, Schlesinger WH, Silliman BR (2011) A blueprint for blue carbon: toward an improved understanding of the role of vegetated coastal habitats in sequestering CO_2. Front Ecol Environ 9(10):552–560. https://doi.org/10.1890/110004
39. Rau GH (2014) Enhancing the ocean's role in CO_2 mitigation. In: Freedman B (ed) Global environmental change. Handbook of global environmental pollution, vol 1. Springer, Dordrecht. https://doi.org/10.1007/978-94-007-5784-4_54
40. Choudhary B, Dhar V, Pawase AS (2024) Blue carbon and the role of mangroves in carbon sequestration: its mechanisms, estimation, human impacts, and conservation strategies for economic incentives. J Sea Res 199:102504. https://doi.org/10.1016/j.seares.2024.102504
41. International Institute for Environment and Development (IIED) (2022) Climate change and the blue economy: a sustainable and equitable blue economy can support climate action. Policy Brief. Irish Aid
42. Lubchenco J, Gaines SD (2019) A new narrative for the ocean. Science 364:911–911. https://doi.org/10.1126/science.aay2241

Márcia Marques is a Consultant specializing in marine environment management, Ocean Governance, and Blue Economy, with over 15 years of experience in sustainable marine management, biodiversity conservation, and blue economy promotion. Márcia served the Portuguese Government as an adviser to the Minister of the Sea, Secretary of State for Ocean Affairs and Secretary of State for Fisheries between 2019 and 2024, providing technical support, particularly in marine conservation, environmental compliance, and climate change. She has significantly contributed to the development and implementation of national ocean governance policies, the advancement of international ocean management initiatives, and the coordination of numerous national and international working groups dedicated to ocean-related matters.

Currently, Márcia works as a consultant to the Portuguese Institute for Sea and Atmosphere (IPMA), specifically supporting the development and implementation of Marine Strategy Framework Directive, oceanic marine protected areas and marine ecosystem services accounting.

Maria Adelaide Ferreira, Over the last decade, Adelaide has conducted applied research on ocean governance, at the national, regional, and global levels, on marine/maritime spatial planning, and on the conservation and sustainable use of marine ecosystems and biodiversity, in close connection with UNEP and the Secretariat of the Convention on Biological Diversity. Currently, Adelaide is a researcher on public policies and ocean governance at the Portuguese Institute for Sea and Atmosphere (IPMA), focusing on the Marine Strategy Framework Directive and on oceanic marine protected areas. She is also invited assistant professor of Marine Governance and Conservation at the Faculty of Sciences of Lisbon University (FCUL) and invited professor at NOVA SBE.

Cities Environmental Assessment: Reflections for Advancing the Sustainable Development Goals Agenda

15

Maria da Luz Fernandes

Science alone does not hold the power to achieve the goal of greater sustainability, but scientific knowledge and wisdom are needed to help inform decisions that will enable society to move toward that end. A sustainable biosphere is one that is ecologically sound, economically feasible, and socially just. Scientific understanding can help frame the questions to be posed, provide assessments about current conditions, evaluate the likely consequences of different policy or management options, provide knowledge about the world, and develop new technologies.

– Lubchenko [1]

Abstract

The Sustainable Development Goals (SDGs) represent a transformative global commitment to a more inclusive and sustainable future. As rapid urbanisation and population growth continue, cities stand at the forefront of this transition. However, translating the SDGs into specific actions and policies is challenging. Strategic Environmental Assessment (SEA) offers a structured approach to integrating environmental considerations into decision-making processes. This research explores how the integration between SEA and the SDGs can be improved, explicitly addressing the urban context through the place-based conceptual framework *SEA for Sustainability*. This framework addresses the shortcomings in the literature regarding the integration between the SDGs and SEA. It emphasises governance and community empowerment as crucial to changing the

M. da L. Fernandes (✉)
Research Unit on Governance, Competitiveness and Public Policies (GOVCOPP), Department of Social Political and Territorial Sciences, University of Aveiro, Campus Universitário de Santiago, Aveiro, Portugal
e-mail: maria.luz@ua.pt

B. Casais (ed.), *Integrated Science to Achieve Sustainable Development Goals*, Integrated Science 37, https://doi.org/10.1007/978-3-031-88777-2_15

decision-making paradigm. To achieve this change, the framework promotes enhanced cross-sector collaboration, practitioner capacity building, stakeholder engagement, and knowledge exchange as key to fostering a sense of ownership among practitioners and improving knowledge and awareness throughout the SEA process. The platforms provided by the public participation processes in SEA urban planning are relevant to this effort and can be explored to create space for experimentation. This will enable new avenues for advancing the integration of sustainability, the SDGs, and SEA, provide new methodologies, and ensure the necessary alignment of policy frameworks, translating the high-level targets to local implementation needs.

Graphical Abstract

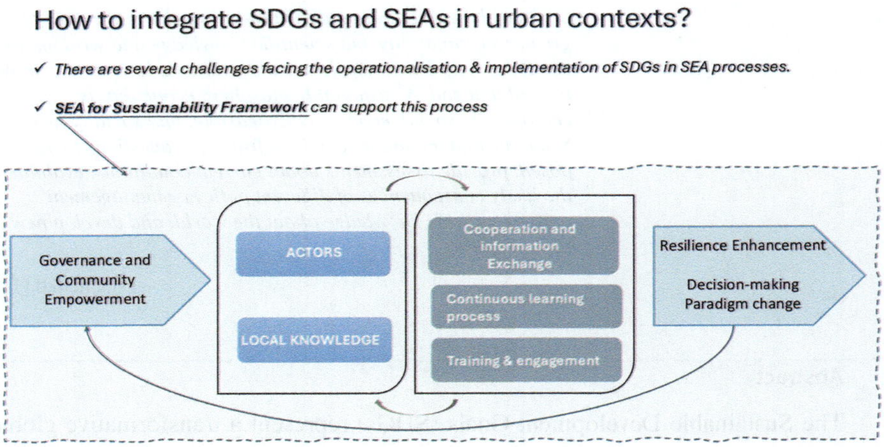

Source: Author

Keywords

Strategic environmental assessment · Urban planning · Urban transformations · Stakeholder engagement · Public participation

1 Introduction

The 2030 Agenda for Sustainable Development, with its 17 Sustainable Development Goals (SDGs), represents a transformative global commitment to fostering economic growth, social inclusion, and environmental sustainability [2]. These characteristics are joined by the need to work in a climate of peace, strong institutions and international partnership. However, translating these aspirational global targets into actionable, context-specific policies remains a significant challenge. Cities are the core front of this challenge due to the growth of the urban population and the rapid urbanisation processes, which pose increased environmental pressures and intensify the complexity of achieving Sustainable Development (SD). The UN SDGs identified a specific goal focused on cities (Goal 11), and most of the other goals and targets have urban applications and interdependencies [3].

Environmental Assessment (EA) instruments, specifically Strategic Environmental Assessment (SEA), plays a crucial role in addressing sustainability challenges [4]. SEA offers a structured approach to integrating environmental considerations into policy, plan, and program (PPPs) decision-making processes. Although scholars have identified SEA's main characteristics for providing a strategic and structured approach [5, 6], such as empowering stakeholders, and increasing transparency and accountability [7, 8], they also acknowledge the limitations of current SEA practices in driving environmental change. SEA is often perceived as a procedural requirement that lacks sufficient integration into decision-making and does not challenges predetermined policy and planning priorities [9–11]. In this scope, researchers in the SEA field have produced extensive work addressing SEA and sustainability challenges through broad, overarching conceptual frameworks. However, these frameworks are often detached from specific local contexts, even though they are usually considered as tailor-made approaches [12]. Polido [13] proposes an alternative approach, the *SEA for Sustainability* framework, which advocates for a place-based conceptual framework that demonstrates how to advance sustainability through SEA in urban settings. This framework shows that governance and community empowerment, decision-making paradigm and resilience enhancement are key to advancing sustainability through SEA.

Against this backdrop, the main aim of this research is to explore how the integration between SEA and SDGs can be improved, explicitly addressing urban contexts and relating to the place-based conceptual framework developed by Polido [13]. This chapter unfolds in four main sections. The first briefly introduces SEA, its field, and its urban planning context; the second presents the *SEA for sustainability* framework; and the third offers a literature review on the relationship between SEA and SDG integration. Finally, the fourth chapter discusses how SEA, specifically the *SEA for Sustainability* framework, can contribute to advancing the challenges of integrating SDGs into SEA. After these sections, a conclusion section summarises the main ideas covered in the chapter and brings suggestions for future research directions.

2 Cities, SEA and Sustainability

2.1 Strategic Environmental Assessment

The roots of SEA lie in the Environmental Impact Assessment (EIA) framework, first formalised in the 1969 U.S. National Environmental Policy Act (NEPA). NEPA required federal agencies to evaluate the environmental effects of major projects, marking the first instance of formal environmental assessment at a national level. EIA gained traction worldwide in the 1970s as other countries adopted similar laws to ensure that significant environmental impacts were considered before the approval of development projects. However, EIAs primarily focused on individual projects rather than broader policies, plans, or programs. After, in the 1970s and 1980s, environmental and policy experts recognised the limitations of project-based EIAs, as they needed to adequately address cumulative impacts, regional issues, or policy-level considerations. This realisation highlighted the need for a more strategic tool to evaluate the environmental consequences of policies, plans, and programs (PPPs) rather than just specific projects [14]. This broader level of assessment became known as Strategic Environmental Assessment (SEA). Early academic literature and reports advocated for SEA, highlighting its potential to integrate environmental considerations into higher-level decision-making [15, 16].

SEA is more broadly defined as a systematic process for evaluating the environmental consequences of proposed PPP initiatives to ensure they are fully included and appropriately addressed at the earliest appropriate decision-making stage with economic and social considerations [17]. However, the role of SEA varies according to the context of planning and decision-making, and therefore, it has been regarded as a family of tools or approaches. The availability of data, knowledge of impacts, and level of definition of PPP also influence the approach taken and the tools used. Therefore, SEA can be applied under different labels, such as "sustainability appraisal" or "integrated assessment", [18]. Nevertheless, one of the core attributes of SEA is the emphasis on moving toward a strategic focus instead of a snapshot, as defined by Therivel [14]. This entails considering the environmental impacts and alternatives, identifying the cumulative and synergistic effects spanning various policies and plans, and enabling decision-makers to integrate ecological and sustainability considerations at the beginning of the decision-making process [5, 8].

Since its inception, SEA has prioritised public participation and consultation with relevant authorities as fundamental aspects of its process [15]. Public involvement is considered essential, as it helps ensure that diverse perspectives are integrated into decision-making processes, ultimately enhancing both environmental and social outcomes. Essentially, SEA aims to expand the decision-makers focus to include issues beyond their primary area of concern. As such, SEA should involve various stakeholders, generally including the public, and document what has been done, why decisions have been made, and what assumptions and uncertainties exist [5, 19].

SEA is usually divided into three main steps: scoping, identification and evaluation of the effects and finally, the mitigation and monitoring of impact. The scoping phase addresses the coverage and extent of the assessment. The relevant issues are identified in this phase, and the baseline conditions and the links to the other strategic actions are analysed. Then, the identification and evaluation of the significant impacts, as well as the cumulative impacts, are followed according to the alternative options considered. In the final stage, the measures envisaged to avoid, reduce, or compensate for any significant impacts are indicated, as well as any links to EIA and monitoring measures are also put forward [14].

The use of the SEA as a policy tool is widely applied globally in at least 60 countries [20]. At the European level, the European Directive (Directive 2001/42/EC) entered into force in 2004 and has institutionalised SEA, mandating its application across Member States and reinforcing SEA's role in aligning regional policies with sustainable development objectives. The EU Directive requires that the public and environmental authorities be consulted on draft plans or programs and that the Environmental Report (ER) be prepared in the SEA process. In this scope, the public participation process is also a core focus of the Aarhus Convention, formally adopted in 2003 in Kyiv, and addresses Access to Information, Public Participation in Decision-making, and Access to Justice in Environmental Matters. However, public consultation within SEA can vary widely in scope and format, with different levels of engagement serving different purposes and utilising a range of methods and tools depending on the stage of the decision-making process [19, 21].

2.2 SEA and Urban Planning

Urbanisation processes are increasing with the rapid population growth and population shifts into cities. It is projected that 68% of the worldwide population will live in cities by 2050 [22]. Due to their relevance worldwide, they are crucial to meet the global sustainability targets, which challenge urban planning and management systems. A new perspective on governing the transformation towards sustainability is necessary, including different actors, knowledge and resources [23]. As Bai et al. [24] acknowledged, policy at the urban level will become increasingly important for solving global environmental issues, and this points to the need for processes that enhance scientific understanding of cities' socio-ecological systems and reinforce the importance of urban governance, with increased public participation and interconnections across multiple spaces and scales. Scholars have pointed out that SEA has the potential to support this paradigm shift towards sustainability [13, 25].

At the urban level, the Urban Master Plans (UMPs) are the long-term strategic documents that establish the long-term vision of city development and growth. The plans address several dimensions: land use, infrastructure, housing, transportation, environmental protection and social aspects. UMPs provide a comprehensive framework to align development with broader objectives such as sustainability, resource management, economic growth and quality of life while balancing competing interests. The SEA Directive applies to many public plans and programmes, including land use, transport, energy, waste and agriculture. According to a 2016 SEA study, spatial planning was the most common subject in SEA, with percentages ranging from 50% to 90% of SEAs concerning land use planning. SEA supports land use planning by providing structure and shaping strategic planning processes towards achieving more environmentally, socially, and economically sound and sustainable decisions [26]. It allows for identifying key issues early in the process and promotes evaluating different alternatives for development and analysing the cumulative effects [8, 13]. It improves transparency and accountability by engaging the public and relevant stakeholders in urban sustainability, enabling diverse points of view and local knowledge to inform decision-making processes [21, 27, 28]. When the planning process is long and complicated, SEA may support the non-specialists and the public in participating by outlining key environmental concerns and communicating them to the stakeholders.

Public participation is also one of the key aspects of planning [29]. It is relevant to democratic legitimacy and effectively contributes to the quality and acceptance of the planning outcomes, leading to more informed, transparent, and accountable decisions. It empowers citizens with knowledge and skills, creating a culture of active civic engagement [30–32]. Literature studying the relevance of PP in SEA of planning processes has proven that it can improve environmental quality by incorporating local knowledge and perspectives into sustainable development strategies. It allows the planning team to identify and minimise adverse environmental impacts, enhance positive impacts, and increase learning [10]. For instance, communities can provide insights into ecological challenges or risks that may not be immediately apparent to planners. This process strengthens the relationship between governments and communities, fostering collaboration and shared responsibility for urban development. However, studies have also focused on the type of public participation developed and its shortcomings. PP is generally limited to the lower forms of participation, where, according to the Arnstein [33] ladder of participation, it means only informing or consultation procedures when the plan has already been developed [10, 21].

3 SEA for Sustainability

The framework *SEA for Sustainability* (Fig. 15.1; [13, 34]) was designed to overcome the need for more research on SEA place-based and deliberative capacity for sustainability through tailored practices. It stresses the need for a place-based approach to address the context-specific issues in these processes, and it underlines the transformative capacity of SEA through the empowerment of individuals and communities. The framework was initially developed for small islands, which are bounded territorial

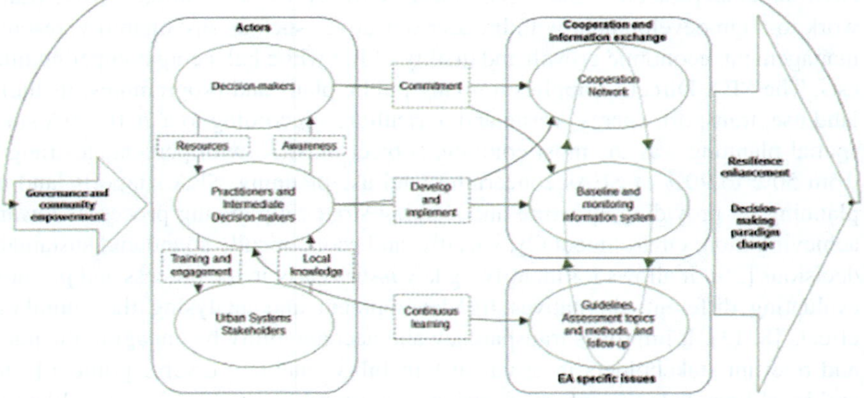

Fig. 15.1 SEA for Sustainability framework. (Source: Adapted from Polido et al. [34])

systems and enclosed units of study at the regional or sub-national level. Due to their place-based characteristics, small islands serve as effective case studies for understanding integrated sustainability approaches. The framework is adaptable to other territorial contexts and has been successfully adapted to address sustainability challenges in urban systems [13]. The main drivers of *SEA for Sustainability* are governance and community empowerment, leading to the end-point goals of resilience enhancement and change in the decision-making paradigm. As acknowledged in Polido [13], ***Governance and community empowerment*** affect the three main clusters of the framework and their components: Actors (decision-makers, practitioners, and local stakeholders), cooperation and information exchange, and SEA-specific issues. ***Actors*** are the key point in the SEA process, as they connect all the stakeholders through collaboration and co-production. In this scope, the practitioners, as the promoters of SEA, must take ownership of the process and raise awareness among decision-makers on key sustainability issues. They must engage the local stakeholders to provide their local knowledge and create an empowered, active community. ***Cooperation and information exchange*** cluster highlight the need to establish partnerships between different territories to exchange knowledge and allow an adaptative learning process from previous experiences and local knowledge inputs. According to Polido et al. [34] ***SEA specific issues*** are linked with the *Actors' cluster* due to the continuous learning process from the previous SEA experiences and local knowledge, highlighting the need for a systematised continuous learning process.

Fernandes et al. [35] supported on *SEA for Sustainability* framework explored the contributions of the experiences of SEA "Actors" cluster in 12 Urban Master Plans in Portugal (UMP). Specifically, it explored the contributions of the SEA actors' consultation process and how they influence the outcomes of SEA towards sustainability. The main results showed that the actors in the process are the SEA practitioners, UMP planners, public officers with specific environmental responsibilities and the public. While the UMP planners and SEA practitioners are responsible for drafting the plans, the public officers and the general public produce commentaries and contributions to improve the plan. The results found in the Portuguese context align with the literature [10, 12, 19] and show that public participation tends to be weak and is only sought after all decisions have been made in the planning process. The study revealed that the SEA practitioner's role is distanced from the UMP planning team, constraining their capacity to influence the plan development and to have ownership in the process.

4 How Can SDGs and SEA Integration Occur?

The relationship between SEA and sustainability has been extensively studied over the last decades, as the SDGs aim to provide a comprehensive and universal framework that aligns closely with SEA's goal of promoting sustainability in decision-making. SEA's role of integrating environmental considerations into plan-making can serve several purposes that support the strategy and decision-making towards sustainable development [6–8, 28, 34]. Despite this well-established connection, integrating SEA and SDGs is still an emerging research theme with scarce literature on the subject. Several authors have explored the relationship between SEA and SDGs, offering frameworks and reviews to clarify the existing opportunities for integration. Practitioners consider that integrating SDGs into decision-making via SEA can be a crucial factor, as it would mean that SDGs would be integrated and brought into formalised decision-making on policies, plans, and projects. Further, SEA can provide a systematic framework for understanding the effects of decisions on SDGs. The notion of using SEA as a driver for implementing the SDGs was first suggested by Nilsson and Persson (2017) and González Del Campo et al. [36] followed, due to the assumption that SEA systematic and formalised nature offers an opportunity to (1) Incorporate SDG themes within decision-making processes, (2) provide a formal and systematic approach to align SDG priorities with policy decisions, and (3) establish a framework for ongoing monitoring and evaluation of SDG achievements, which can, in a situation where resources are scarce, facilitate the efficient mainstreaming and streamlining this two key policy instruments, i.e. SDGs and SEA. These functions also suggest that SEA can play a critical role in bridging the gap between SDG objectives and practical decision-making, allowing for a coherent integration of sustainability at all policy and planning levels. However, González Del Campo et al. [36] reviewed spatial land-use development plans in Italy, Ireland, and Kenya and reflected on the low level of engagement found between SEA and SDGs. In Italy, engagement was primarily confined to the early stages of SEA, ensuring policy compatibility across different governance levels. In Kenya, limited local capacity to develop monitoring mechanisms or objective-driven approaches constrained efforts to embed SDGs into planning processes. In the same study, the mutualistic relationship between SEA and SDGs is highlighted, framing the SDGs as the "ends" and SEA as a "means" to achieve them. However, the study denotes several shortcomings in placing this relationship into practice, including the broad scope of both sustainability and SEA and a lack of awareness and technical capacity to integrate SDG targets into SEA processes effectively and translate them into operational strategies at the local or regional planning level. Findings suggest the need for a more explicit mandate for SEA to engage with SDGs, alongside capacity-building initiatives to facilitate proactive integration. These examples highlight the disconnect between high-level SDG commitments and their practical operationalisation through SEA, particularly at the local level, due to insufficient awareness and limited integration of policy instruments across decision-making tiers.

To assess the extent of SDG integration into SEA, Kørnøv et al. [37] developed a framework distinguishing three levels of integration: (1) non-integration, where SDGs are passively mentioned; (2) partial integration, where SDGs are actively considered within the existing SEA framework; and (3) radical integration, where SDGs and EA are linked in a way that goes beyond the existing EA frameworks and SDGs fundamentally reshape SEA processes and guide all assessments. The literature review identified 32 articles categorised into four distinct groups based on their approaches to connecting SDGs and EA. These categories ranged from general mentions of SDGs without exploring their linkages in depth, to approaches highlighting explicit opportunities for integrating the concepts. Other studies proposed specific mechanisms to establish connections between SDGs and EA, while some demonstrated empirical applications of SDGs within EA practices.

Building on this framework, Ravn Boess et al. [38] reviewed 45 EA reports to evaluate the practical functions of SDGs in assessments. The results revealed that 55% of reports only mentioned SDGs without substantive integration, while 44% demonstrated partial integration, with SDGs considered for scoping or performance testing. No cases of radical integration were identified. The study further elaborates on the modes SDGs that can occur in the reports, which can be done in different forms. It may appear at the beginning of the report as background information for the project or plan or while describing the relevant policies or programmes. This shows that SDGs' relevance is recognised in the EA context. The second form is within a separate chapter on sustainability considerations, meaning they are integrated into the assessment context alongside the SEA topics that will be relevant for the plans' assessment. There are also examples of reports where SDGs are found in numerous locations and with significant variation, whether considering SDGs targets or goals. Finally, the study underscored the need for a transparent methodology to guide SDG integration, including clear criteria for selecting relevant goals, defining their functions within SEA, and involving stakeholders in the process.

The lack of radical integration suggests significant room for improvement in aligning SEA with the SDG agenda. Interviews conducted in Emilia Ravn Boess and González Del Campo [39] with environmental consultants in Denmark and Ireland revealed both motivations and barriers to integrating SDGs into practice. Consultants expressed motivation to work with SDGs in EA and willingness to align SEA with strategic goals, following the societal and political discussion on the urgency of sustainability transition. However, there are several challenges, such as client unawareness of SDGs, concerns about revealing negative impacts, and the need for new methodologies hindered progress. The study emphasised that practitioner motivation alone is insufficient to drive change, highlighting the importance of fostering collaboration, improving communication, and creating spaces for experimentation to advance SDG integration in SEA.

Overall, the literature points to SEA's potential to serve as a critical tool for operationalising the SDGs by embedding sustainability objectives into planning processes. However, achieving this potential requires addressing key challenges, including gaps in awareness and knowledge, by providing training and enhancing methodological and technical expertise. Advancing the integration of SEA and SDGs will require concerted efforts to align policy frameworks at multiple governance levels—local, national and global to bridge the gap between policy and implementation, transparency and standardised approaches and promote SEA's participatory processes to increase awareness and foster cross-sectoral collaboration to bridge the gap between high-level goals and local implementation. Experimentation and knowledge sharing among practitioners inspire new approaches to integrating SDGs into SEA processes.

5 SEA for Sustainability and SDGs: The Way Forward

The literature review on advancing sustainability and further integrating the SDGs with SEA has shown several challenges to its practical implementation. These challenges are even more pressing in urban contexts facing rapid urbanisation and increased environmental threats. However, the *SEA framework for Sustainability* provides a robust structure for overcoming these challenges and supporting the integration of the SDGs in SEA urban settings. It positions governance and community empowerment as means to increase actor engagement, enhance public participation, promote transparent and accountable decision-making, and contribute to social transformation and innovative learning experiences.

One of the main challenges identified was the broad scope of sustainability in SEA and the need to "*clarify how to operationalise the different approaches, in opposition to merely describing them,*" together with the need for explicit methodologies and improved understanding by the stakeholders involved. This aligns with the focus of the *SEA for Sustainability* framework, which aims to change the decision-making paradigm through the development and enhancement of SEA knowledge by the different institutions and through the actors involved, where SEA is a continuous learning process. Crucial to this analysis is, therefore, governance and community empowerment, which are directly connected to the actors of the process. However, as the work Fernandes et al. [35] has shown in the UMP processes analysed in the Portuguese context, the actors involved are distant, and the knowledge exchange is weak throughout the process. As acknowledged by Polido [13], both stakeholder engagement and cross-sectoral collaboration facilitate capacity building and information exchange and are critical to advancing transformations towards urban sustainability. Integrating SDGs into SEA requires engaging diverse stakeholders to align the goals with local sustainability priorities. In this sense, the platforms provided by the public participation processes in SEA urban planning can be enhanced and explored to provide opportunities to create space for experimentation. This will enable new avenues for progressing the integration of sustainability, SDGs, and SEA, provide new methodologies, and ensure the necessary alignment of policy frameworks, directing the high-level targets to local implementation needs. Relevant to this process is the role of the practitioners; they are the actors that, by having ownership in the process, may influence its paradigm change by reviewing the methodologies used in the SEA process, being open to innovation and creating awareness among decision-makers and all the stakeholders in the process [34, 35].

The resilience concept is widely used in urban sustainability and is a characteristic valued in urban systems. It encourages the development of new systems and diversity by exploring potential alternative configurations and links to systems' adaptative and transformative capacities, which interact across scales and over time [23]. Within the *SEA for Sustainability* framework resilience enhancement and decision-making paradigm change are end-point goals, and to achieve it the framework highlights the importance of cooperation and adaptive learning through knowledge-sharing and feedback from past SEA cases. This provides an opportunity to produce an adaptative learning strategy that systematically aligns SEA practices with SDG objectives, therefore enabling a continuous improvement cycle.

SEA for Sustainability offers a structured framework for integrating SDGs into SEA processes and is specific for urban planning contexts. It emphasises the actors' role, the local context where it is developed, and the knowledge exchange process. Additionally, it advances community empowerment and cooperation networks, which provides a platform for addressing the shortcomings expressed by the consultants and their clients regarding the lack of awareness of SDGs and their concerns about disclosing negative impacts.

6 Conclusion

This chapter evaluated how SEA, particularly the framework *SEA for Sustainability* developed in Polido et al. [34], can be a transformative tool to advance SDGs in urban contexts. The literature regarding the SDGs and SEA integration shows several challenges in its implementation, such as the broad scope of SDGs, the lack of awareness and knowledge on the topic and the difficulties in putting it into practice. This research shows that the *SEA for Sustainability* may address its shortcomings due to its place-based conceptual approach. It bridges the gap between high-level sustainability targets and local implementation, and it supports the SEA process on transforming decision-making and align them with the 2030 Agenda goals. As the quote at the beginning reminds us, achieving sustainability requires a collective effort, innovative thinking, and a shared commitment from society. SEA is a valuable tool in this context, as it facilitates the framing of relevant questions, the assessment of options, and the evaluation of trade-offs within an open and transparent public process. It can provide guidance to move closer to realising this vision for a more resilient and sustainable future.

Acknowledgements This work was funded by the Portuguese national funds through FCT—Fundação para a Ciência e a Tecnologia, I.P., under the project ENVISION (Ref. PTDC/GES-URB/0804/2020; doi: 10.54499/PTDC/GES-URB/0804/2020). GOVCOPP is funded by Portuguese national funds through FCT (UIDB/04058/2020) + (UIDP/04058/2020). Maria da Luz Fernandes is funded by Portuguese national funds through FCT (Ref.2023.08207.CEECIND, doi: 10.54499/2023.08207.CEECIND/CP2840/CT0029).

References

1. Lubchenko J (1998) Entering the century of the environment: a new social contract for science. Science 279:5350–5497. https://doi.org/10.1126/science.279.5350.491
2. UN (2024) THE 17 GOALS | sustainable development. https://sdgs.un.org/goals
3. Bai X, Surveyer A, Elmqvist T, Gatzweiler FW, Güneralp B, Parnell S, Prieur-Richard AH, Shrivastava P, Siri JG, Stafford-Smith M, Toussaint JP, Webb R (2016) Defining and advancing a systems approach for sustainable cities. Curr Opin Environ Sustain 23:69–78. https://doi.org/10.1016/j.cosust.2016.11.010

4. Sheate WR, Dagg S, Richardson J, Aschemann R, Palerm J, Steen U (2003) Integrating the environment into strategic decision-making: conceptualizing policy SEA. Eur Environ 13(1):1–18. https://doi.org/10.1002/eet.305
5. Bina O (2007) A critical review of the dominant lines of argumentation on the need for strategic environmental assessment. Environ Impact Assess Rev 27(7):585–606. https://doi.org/10.1016/j.eiar.2007.05.003
6. Partidario MR (2015) A strategic advocacy role in sea for sustainability. JEAPM 17(1):1550015. https://doi.org/10.1142/S1464333215500155
7. Stinchcombe K, Gibson RB (2001) Strategic Environmental Assessment as a means of pursuing sustainability: ten advantages and ten challenges. JEAPM 3(3):343–372. www.worldscientific.com
8. White L, Noble BF (2013) Strategic environmental assessment for sustainability: a review of a decade of academic research. Environ Impact Assess Rev 42:60–66. https://doi.org/10.1016/j.eiar.2012.10.003
9. João E, McLauchlan A (2014) Would you do SEA if you didn't have to? Reflections on acceptance or rejection of the SEA process. Impact assessment and project appraisal.
10. González A, Therivel R, Lara A, Lennon M (2023) Empowering the public in environmental assessment: advances or enduring challenges? Environ Impact Assess Rev 101:107142. https://doi.org/10.1016/j.eiar.2023.107142
11. Therivel R, González A (2020) Is SEA worth it? Short-term costs v. long-term benefits of strategic environmental assessment. Environ Impact Assess Rev 83:106411. https://doi.org/10.1016/j.eiar.2020.106411
12. Fischer T, Gazzola P (2006) SEA effectiveness criteria-equally valid in all countries? The case of Italy. Environ Impact Assess Rev 26(4):396–409. https://doi.org/10.1016/j.eiar.2005.11.006
13. Polido A (2023) The role of strategic environmental assessment for sustainability in urban systems transformation. In: Teles EF (ed) Territorial innovation in less developed regions. Springer International Publishing, pp 181–197
14. Therivel R (2004) Strategic environmental assessment in action. Earthscan
15. Kørnøv L (1997) Strategic environmental assessment: sustainability and democratization. Eur Environ 7(6):175–180
16. Partidário MR (1996) Strategic environmental assessment: key issues emerging from recent practice. Environ Impact Assess Rev 16(1):31–55. https://doi.org/10.1016/0195-9255(95)00106-9
17. Sadler B, Verheem R (1996) Strategic environmental assessment: status, challenges and future directions. Ministry of Housing, Spatial Planning and the Environment. The Netherlands, and the International Study of Effectiveness of Environmental Assessment
18. OCDE (2006) Applying strategic environmental assessment: good practice guidance for development co-operation. Organisation for Economic Co-operation and Development
19. Rega C, Baldizzone G (2015) Public participation in Strategic Environmental Assessment: a practitioners' perspective. Environ Impact Assess Rev 50:105–115. https://doi.org/10.1016/j.eiar.2014.09.007
20. Fundingsland Tetlow M, Hanusch M (2012) Strategic environmental assessment: the state of the art. Impact Assess Proj Apprais 30(1):15–24. https://doi.org/10.1080/14615517.2012.666400
21. Gauthier M, Simard L, Waaub JP (2011) Public participation in strategic environmental assessment (SEA): critical review and the Quebec (Canada) approach. Environ Impact Assess Rev 31(1):48–60. https://doi.org/10.1016/j.eiar.2010.01.006
22. UN (2022) World cities report. 2022. Chapter 1: the diversity of cities and visions for urban futures. UN-Habitat
23. Elmqvist T, Andersson E, Frantzeskaki N, McPhearson T, Olsson P, Gaffney O, Takeuchi K, Folke C (2019) Sustainability and resilience for transformation in the urban century. Nat Sustain 2(4):267–273. https://doi.org/10.1038/s41893-019-0250-1
24. Bai X, McAllister RRJ, Beaty RM, Taylor B (2010) Urban policy and governance in a global environment: complex systems, scale mismatches and public participation. Curr Opin Environ Sustain 2(3):129–135. https://doi.org/10.1016/j.cosust.2010.05.008

25. Wolfram M, Frantzeskaki N (2016) Cities and systemic change for sustainability: prevailing epistemologies and an emerging research agenda. Sustainability (Switzerland) 8(2). https://doi.org/10.3390/su8020144
26. Gazzola P, Rinaldi A (2016) Reflecting on SEA's usefulness: a case study on Italy. JEAPM 18(04):1650021. https://doi.org/10.1142/S1464333216500216
27. Bonifazi A, Rega C, Gazzola P (2011) Strategic environmental assessment and the democratisation of spatial planning. JEAPM 13(01):9–37. https://doi.org/10.1142/S1464333211003778
28. Sinclair AJ, Diduck A, Fitzpatrick P (2008) Conceptualizing learning for sustainability through environmental assessment: critical reflections on 15 years of research. Environ Impact Assess Rev 28(7):415–428. https://doi.org/10.1016/J.EIAR.2007.11.001
29. Fung A (2015) Putting the public back into governance: the challenges of citizen participation and its future. Public Adm Rev 75(4):513–522. https://doi.org/10.1111/puar.12361
30. Dietz T, Stern PC, National Research Council (U.S.). Panel on Public Participation in Environmental Assessment and Decision Making, & National Research Council (U.S.). Committee on the Human Dimensions of Global Change (2008) Public participation in environmental assessment and decision making. National Academies Press
31. Meadowcroft J (2007) Who is in charge here? Governance for sustainable development in a complex world. J Environ Policy Plan 9(3–4):299–314. https://doi.org/10.1080/15239080701631544
32. OECD (2001) Citizens as partners: OECD handbook on information, consultation and public participation in policy-making. OECD. https://doi.org/10.1787/9789264195578-en
33. Arnstein SR (1969) A ladder of citizen participation. J Am Plan Assoc 35(4):216–224. https://doi.org/10.1080/01944366908977225
34. Polido A, João E, Ramos TB (2018) How may sustainability be advanced through strategic environmental assessment (SEA) in small Islands? Exploring a conceptual framework. Ocean Coast Manag 153(July 2017):46–58. https://doi.org/10.1016/j.ocecoaman.2017.12.002
35. Fernandes ML, Moreno Pires S, Ramos TB, Rodigues C, Teles F, Polido A (2024) Actors in the spotlight: scrutinising how actors affect strategic environmental assessment towards sustainability in municipal master plans. J Environ Policy Plan 26(6):592–607. https://doi.org/10.1080/1523908X.2024.2392680
36. González Del Campo A, Gazzola P, Onyango V (2020) The mutualism of strategic environmental assessment and sustainable development goals. Environ Impact Assess Rev 82:106383. https://doi.org/10.1016/j.eiar.2020.106383
37. Kørnøv L, Lyhne I, Davila JG (2020) Linking the UN SDGs and environmental assessment: towards a conceptual framework. Environ Impact Assess Rev 85:106463. https://doi.org/10.1016/j.eiar.2020.106463
38. Ravn Boess E, Kørnøv L, Lyhne I, Partidário MR (2021) Integrating SDGs in environmental assessment: unfolding SDG functions in emerging practices. Environ Impact Assess Rev 90:106632. https://doi.org/10.1016/j.eiar.2021.106632
39. Boess ER, González Del Campo A (2023) Motivating a change in environmental assessment practice: consultant perspectives on SDG integration. Environ Impact Assess Rev 101:107105. https://doi.org/10.1016/j.eiar.2023.107105

Maria da Luz Fernandes has a bachelor's and master's degree in environmental engineering and a PhD from the Doctoral Programme Do*Mar- Sciences, Technologies and Management of the Sea at the University of Aveiro (2021) in collaboration with the University of A Coruña. She was a researcher in the ENVISION project between 2021 and 2024, which focused on environmental assessment and urban sustainability transitions. She has participated in several national and European projects. She is the author of 12 WOS scientific articles published in international journals such as the Journal of Environmental Policy and Planning, Journal of Cleaner Production, Science of the Total Environment, and Marine Policy, among others.

(Un)Practicing Peace Through Geopolitics

16

Sandra Fernandes and David Silva Ferreira

> *The world is actively spatialized, divided up, labelled, sorted out into a hierarchy of places of greater or lesser 'importance' by political geographers, other academics and political leaders. This process provides the geographical framing within which political elites and mass publics act in the world in pursuit of their own identities and interests(Agnew and Corbridge [2], p. 3).*
>
> *Fear is at the heart of the realist theory in the sense of the fear that one State experiences in regard to the expansion of the other*
>
> (Booth and Wheeler [6])

Abstract

In the current era, addressing societal development without geopolitics is increasingly challenging. The way power relations materialize in space, in a broad sense, affects every dimension of our lives. Geopolitics is now everywhere and, as such, preparing for risks is instrumental in a very broad range of areas, permeating all United Nations sustainable development goals. This is especially evident if we consider our interdependent world, where interdependencies are increasingly weaponized, and cooperation must be combined with competition. The chapter signals two geopolitical perspectives that provide different outlooks on achieving peace and justice. Geopolitical analysis of international politics

S. Fernandes (✉)
Centro de Investigação em Ciência Política (CICP), Universidade do Minho, Braga, Portugal
e-mail: sfernandes@eeg.uminho.pt

D. S. Ferreira
Centro de Estudos Internacionais (CEI-Iscte), Iscte - Instituto Universitário de Lisboa, Lisbon, Portugal
e-mail: dsfaa11@iscte-iul.pt

B. Casais (ed.), *Integrated Science to Achieve Sustainable Development Goals*, Integrated Science 37, https://doi.org/10.1007/978-3-031-88777-2_16

tends to be fatalist in the sense that men perpetuate suffering in the logic of the "security dilemma." But there are also transcendentalists who believe that human society can build a global world that escapes the dangers of the past. Besides highlighting contrasting views, the chapter also unpacks other related academic fields of International Relations with practical societal impact. A key argument that is developed throughout the chapter is the call to place the individual (not States) at the center of international politics, where interests and identities have a key role and are transformed.

Graphical Abstract

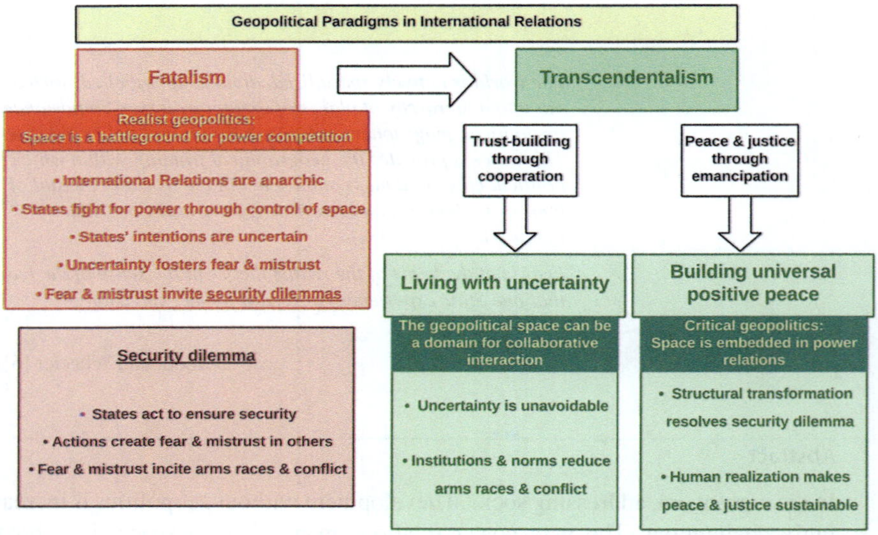

Source: Authors

Keywords

Security dilemma · Geopolitics · Positive peace · Critical theory · Fatalism · Spatialization · UN sustainable development goals

1 Introduction

Societal development is a complex problem for which security at large is a precondition. The academic field of International Relations (IR) analyses security in a spectrum including its two extreme opposite expressions of war and peace. At the inception of the IR discipline in 1919, its main purpose was to "obviate a recurrence of a war as disastrous as World War I" (Carr [9], cited in Rolf [51], p. 1). Thus, conflicts and the importance of restoring peace are the core of the discipline [51].

In practice, winning the peace has been a key political goal that has entered the global agenda since multilateral engagement became institutionalized, in particular the United Nations. The sustainable development goals set in the UN agenda 2030 showcase how peace and justice are two intertwined dimensions that shall be achieved from a human and social perspective rather than a state-centric and sovereign one.

However, addressing societal development without a geopolitical perspective is increasingly challenging. In the IR literature and the broader social environment, namely the media, geopolitics have operated a "return". The way power relations materialize in space, in a broad sense, affects every dimension of our lives. Geopolitics is now everywhere and, as such, preparing for risks is instrumental in a very broad range of areas, permeating all United Nations sustainable development goals. This is especially evident if we think about our interdependent world, where interdependencies are being increasingly weaponized, and cooperation needs to be combined with competition ("coopetition").

The "return" of geopolitics needs to be explained both as an analytical tool and a way to see the world with an impact on the possibilities to achieve peace. Both meanings entail positive and negative understandings of how international politics operate. As a result, geopolitics has served both as an instrument to practice and "unpractice" peace. The chapter delves into these two opposite dimensions to unpack how the dynamic of the "security dilemma" in IR informs the development of geopolitics in two different directions that matter a lot for prospects of peace and justice.

In the first section, we explain IR's founding "security dilemma" and how different understandings of possible solutions for this dilemma have generated fatalist and transcendent views about the behavior of international actors that promote conflictual and cooperative relations. Secondly, we delve into the implications of the fatalist perspective on the so-called ongoing "return" of geopolitics. Thirdly, we analyze how the critics of "fatalist geopolitics" have allowed for the emergence of critical studies. This strand of literature offers tools to a better account of how identities are mastered in space and, thus, to a more complex understanding of the societal underpinnings of conflicts.

Building on the differences between geopolitics as power politics (fatalists) and critical geopolitics (neutral or transcendent), our chapter demonstrates that any prospect for peace and justice is premised on the world view of decisioners and on a detailed knowledge of how specific communities form their collective identity in specific times.

2 The Security-Dilemma: An Analytical Tool for Peace and Justice

Regardless of the theoretical lenses through which one analyses IR, the security dilemma assumes a central role within the three main paradigms of the academic field (realist, liberal and constructivist). One of the assumptions underlying this notion is the existence of an anarchic international system whereby States, in the absence of a superior authority to control the use of force, have to rely upon themselves to ensure their security. What follows is a system characterized by a constant fear of being attacked due to uncertainty about the intentions of other States [23], prompting the accumulation of power to secure its own security. Consequently, a State's attempt to achieve its own security might lead to the insecurity of the other [60].

The security dilemma is fundamentally about the meaning that is attributed to a certain situation. In short, "500 British nuclear weapons are less threatening to the United States than 5 North Korean nuclear weapons" (Wendt [63], p. 73). Booth and Wheeler [6] characterize the security dilemma as a "two-level strategic predicament." Decision-makers must respond to a dilemma of interpretation of the motives and intentions of the other party, and a dilemma of response on how to react based on the previous interpretation. For Jervis [24], the security dilemma equals what he calls the "spiral model", driven by mutual misperceptions between the two parties regarding their intentions. Not all spirals are driven by security dilemmas, however. Sheer expansionist ambitions among States can be driven by their intent to threaten one another [54]. While fear is at the heart of realism, with States experiencing fear at the prospect of another's expansion, States may be simply driven by their ambitions [6].

At the core of the security dilemma lie two key aspects, "unresolvable uncertainty" [6], and fear. The former is related to the unknown intentions and motives of other States. The interpretation made by decision-makers on those intentions will define the response to be pursued [6]. Thus, the significance of the security dilemma for any geopolitical situation lies in the fact that a misperception of the other's intentions might lead to a States' own destruction [6, 24].

Despite being undertheorized in IR [11], fear is central to the security dilemma as it is rooted in a perception of threat to the national being. Booth and Wheeler [7] even go further by contending that "the international system may be conceived as a fear system" (p. 137). From this standpoint, fear emerges as a driver of States' behavior in the international system. Regardless of whether States choose power maximization strategies, as argued by Mearsheimer [35], or prioritize security concerns, as posited by Waltz [60], the underlying impetus remains, namely, reducing uncertainty, threats, and fear.

The consequences originating from the security dilemma give rise to different perspectives. Some, such as the fatalists [35], tend to consider the security dilemma as the most important source of conflict in IR and insecurity as ubiquitous. Fatalist thinking was associated with game theory's "prisoners' dilemma." States chose purely individualistic actions that generated poor outcomes because they feared operating against their short-term interests only for others not to reciprocate—the worst possible result [6]. On the contrary, transcendentalists tend to believe that human society can build a global world that escapes the dangers of the past [6, 18, 26, 30]. By trusting that others will reciprocate if they act against their short-term interests, States can mutually benefit from cooperation. While the outcome is not profit-maximizing, the suboptimal result exceeds that of purely individualistic action. If state relationships are embedded in trust, the security dilemma is transcended. In that sense, one shifts from a cyclical to a progressive account of history which does not look at the security dilemma as inevitably leading to conflict [6].

What follows from these logics is either an environment where international relations are based on permanent fear due to the uncertainty of the other's intentions that leads decision-makers to assume the worst [64], or relations founded upon trust and cooperation [6, 26, 30].

Booth and Wheeler [6] argued that the security dilemma could be a useful tool for decision-makers since awareness of it might enable them to devise strategies that mitigate dilemmas of interpretation and response. They believe that there was scope for agency within the dilemma and recommended the application of security dilemma sensibility, defined as "the ability to understand the role that fear might play in [others'] attitudes and behaviour, including, crucially, the role that one's own actions may play in provoking that fear" (Booth and Wheeler [6], p. 7). While security dilemma sensibility was not always applicable or sustainable, it could be successful if actors made an effort, took risks, and strived to cooperate [6].

3 Fatalism: The "Return" of Geopolitics

The dominance of realist IR accounts over decades has impacted the prevalence of the fatalist view of the security dilemma mentioned by focusing on the dynamics of power and war [14, 47]. A privileged focus on security studies at the expense of peace studies within the agenda of IR has emerged [14, 51], reflecting a prioritization of negative peace [21] — defined as the absence of violence [20]— over positive peace, which entails human realization [18].

The concept of positive peace is closely associated with a transcendentalist view of the security dilemma (see below), as it not only focuses on peace as the absence of violence but also underscores the promotion of cooperation and integration among different actors [14]. However, as argued by Travouillon et al. [57], "in direct comparison with conflict or violence, the concept of peace is still perceived as providing an intellectually inferior take on world politics" (p. 4).

Today, the fatalist view of international relations has been reinvigorated by a renewed focus on geopolitics. From a realist perspective, geopolitics rests upon the assumption that the geographical context sets the limits and opportunities that shape interactions in the IR [39]. However, in public discourse, geopolitics has been associated with great power competition in certain geographic spaces and material power capabilities.

Contemporary examples of geopolitical great power rivalry include Russia's full-scale invasion of Ukraine [4], a war effort assisted by Chinese exports [31, 53]. Washington, Kyiv's ally, provides it with military aid [66], having protested Beijing's "very substantial" support for Moscow's military. The U.S. has also expressed alarm over the submarine and missile technology China received from Russia in return for its assistance [31, 53] at a time when tensions between Washinton and Beijing over the South China Sea are becoming increasingly adversarial [3].

Russia and China's geopolitical priorities—Europe and the Asia-Pacific, respectively—are complementary, allowing them to reinforce one another rather than competing over the same space [52].

However, as Washington pursues a geopolitical pivot toward the Asia-Pacific amid its great power competition with China [32, 37], it might fear direct Russian involvement in a Sino-American war over U.S. ally Taiwan. Russia and China had claimed to have a "friendship without limits" and found in the U.S. a common rival, even if the region lacked great geopolitical relevance to Moscow [52] and the Sino-Russian relationship could not be described as an allyship [15].

Classical geopolitics, used as a tool for statecraft, is often associated with the realist paradigm, being concerned with rivalries over the control of geographical areas, its people, its resources, and its political problems [12, 17]. According to Waltz [59], great powers strived to influence, manage, control and direct regional or world affairs. They struggled to contend with one another, and their position of power increased their involvement in warfare, albeit not against each other, in the nuclear age. Per Waltzian realism, the security dilemma, while unsolvable, could be managed by nuclear weapons [59]. Under certain circumstances, their spread would foster peace because the priority of rational nuclear-armed actors—survival—would be jeopardized by warfare. If self-help States sought security, rather than conquest, nuclear weapons could foster peace under anarchy [22, 59, 61]. Their unfitness to deliver the second goal allowed "neighbors [to] have more peace of mind" (Waltz [61], p. 6). The critical literature of geopolitics associated the term with imperialist discourses of the nineteenth century. In the late twentieth century, in turn, geopolitics were linked to great power rivalry between the US and the Soviet Union over their spheres of influence [41].

Contrary to Western expectations, the collapse of the Soviet Union did not lead to the end of geopolitics [34]. In their views, the end of the Cold War would replace the pursuit for power in certain geographic areas by international economic cooperation, especially, liberal economic interdependence. However, the growing power rivalry between the U.S., China and Russia, above-mentioned, enhanced by the war in Ukraine and the rise of Beijing, led to the perception of the return of geopolitics [39]. The term thus evolved into a banal, "vague catch-all term" [39] to refer to power competition.

While Bull [8] viewed order, which included the absence of direct violence, and justice as separate concepts, his work included reflections on structural violence—including the absence of justice. He concluded that a study of the former was incomplete without the latter, which endowed his work with transcendentalist tones. His relative detachment from the concept of power was acknowledged in transcendentalist literature [12], some of which we review below. This body of research, which thrived after the Cold War, more closely integrated the concepts of peace and justice, criticizing the dominant trend of studying (great) power(s), states, and war, in peace science and IR [12].

4 Optimism: Understanding the Spatialization of Identities

War and peace have been central in IR thinking long before it became an academic discipline in the early twentieth century [21]. The same is true about non-fatalist outlooks on how to achieve peace and justice. In the eighteenth century, Immanuel Kant proposed a series of steps through which responsible governments could not only end aggression but also build lasting peace. His program, featured in the book *Perpetual Peace*, would become the most influential transcendentalist work in IR [6, 46].

In his essay, Kant's perspective rejects the realist assumption that structure (i.e., an asymmetrical and anarchical International System) prevailed over human agency. He believed that individuals could make choices. They could produce ideas and act according to them, shaping the system's structure. Humans could operate rationally in pursuit of the highest good, and eventually build a peaceful world society. One in which competition remained present but within a legalized context and where people had freedom of movement but also the duty of being hospitable toward foreign visitors. Justice should be universal, playing a role in maintaining order, and thus the conditions for peace [5, 46].

Despite the influence of Kant's work on peace in European and American political thinking [25], it was not until the 1950s that an academic discipline was created to systemic research the conditions of peace [21]. During that decade, Scandinavian peace studies related to the Peace Research Institute Oslo tried to overcome criticisms by turning its back to IR and welcoming researchers from areas that were more committed to positivist methods [51].

Its American counterpart, in contrast, more focused on conflict resolution and connected to the Center for Research on Conflict Resolution, tried to balance peace studies and security studies [51]. Despite integrating the research agenda of peace studies, researchers tried to focus on the conflict resolution dimension because of the ubiquity of peace in several political, social, and academic realms [21]. In their early days, both traditions of peace research directed their attention to the Cold War and the threat of a nuclear apocalypse. Researchers focused on the prevention of global war and the reduction of interstate conflict, neglecting one-sided (including structural) and non-state violence [21].

Galtung [18] was responsible for widening the scope of the discipline by expanding the concept of peace, which he defined as the negation of all forms of violence. Not just direct violence, which emanates from individuals or groups, but also structural violence, which derives from the structure of a social system [18, 21]. In his seminal work [19], he presented imperialism as a system of dominance able to perpetuate both direct and structural violence. In the first case, the means of human realization were destroyed; in the second, they were withheld. Inequality was a core type of structural violence. Since structural violence could be referred to as a condition of social injustice, peace could be understood as the absence of violence and the presence of social justice [18, 19].

This implicit need for emancipation, particularly in the post-Cold War period, led peace researchers to focus increasingly more on how to create peace conditions rather than on the causes of war [5]. They directed their attention to the study of violence in society, including the presence of injustice, oppression and exploitation, issues that had previously received little attention [5, 10, 21]. War became understood as a comprehensive socio-economic process that required a holistic approach. For the most part, eliminating war would not be achieved by strengthening international institutions, but instead by building up a "comprehensive structure of social justice." The spotlight on Human Rights and liberation—from all violence and barriers to human realization—shifted the key unit of analysis from the State to the individual (Booth [5], p. 68).

As Booth and Wheeler [6] argued, there is a very wide spectrum of relations between fatalism and transcendence. Mitigation, a middle ground between the two, can occur through policies aimed at fostering cooperation between States. By focusing on negative peace, peace research mostly strived, during the Cold War, to reduce the impact of the security dilemma, rather than to transcend it. In fact, the end of the détente in 1979 shifted the focus back to the threat of nuclear conflict and how to prevent it [5, 21]. At the same time, the changes brought about by telecommunications, fast travel, technological progress, and flourishing economic and social transactions during the 1970s and 1980s led IR theorists to consider the implications of greater interdependence on State behavior, including regarding the use of force [27].

The end of the Cold War widened not just the scope of the field of peace studies, but also of various disciplines contributing to its multidisciplinary body of research—IR included. The era was marked by the emergence of various branches of critical social science, such as critical geopolitics, which commonly drew on IR theories [17]. This "critical turn" in the social sciences brought newfound visibility to issues such as non-state actors, gender, colonialism, the environment, and many others whose interconnectedness to a broader concept of peace had become increasingly acknowledged [5, 50]. The focus on the prevention of war was replaced, in the eyes of some, by optimism regarding the possibility of transcending the security dilemma or even escaping it altogether. On the other hand, constructivists sought to reconcile classical geopolitics' narrow conceptualization of peace with the broader understanding of the space of critical geopolitics. While the former subordinated justice to order in the service of the interests of the powerful, the latter was associated with the spatialization and social construction of identities and interests, whereby trust could replace fear and eradicate prospects for war. Their contributions paint the most optimistic picture of the world Humanity can create.

5 Transcending the Security Dilemma: Living with Uncertainty or Building Universal Positive Peace?

Influenced by the concept of "positive peace"—advanced by Galtung and advocated by Martin Luther King Jr. as "the presence of justice"—geographers began exploring peace as a socio-cultural phenomenon [28, 36]. Critical geopolitics provided a strong critique of the classic perspectives of geopolitics and how space was conceptualized by them. The field produced a wide variety of scholarly rebuttals to the "ways in which political space was written, read and practiced" (Ó Tuathail and Dalby [42] cited in Dalby [13]).

Peace was understood as "contextual and embedded in power relations" (Donaldson [16], p. 102). One needed to ask who peace was for and how space was uttered and manipulated for peace [36]. Borders—be they cartographic or conceptual, real or imaginary, social or aesthetic [42] were invariably part of broader social action and often grounded in "othering" processes, which entailed creating cultural or symbolic divisions between "us" and "the other" [44], which were forms of spatial inclusion and exclusion [17]. Other dichotomies, such as democratic and non-democratic, civilized and uncivilized, were also used, as well as descriptions such as "zones of turmoil" or "rogue states" [13, 17, 33].

Indeed, discourse was central in space construction within societies, being utilized by politicians, scholars, and practitioners to express their geopolitical worldviews and advance their geopolitical interests. In organizing, dividing, and categorizing the geographical space, they established hierarchies of places. It was within their spatial framing, rooted in power relations, that the elites and the public acted and defined their own identities and interests. That active "spatialization" of the world impacted the social dynamics both inside and outside specific boundaries [2, 17]. The process oversimplified and concealed the nuances and local contexts of war, political struggle, globalization, and others [13]. Boundary-drawing practices led to the spatialization of identities, a process whereby actors and collectivities became socialized as members of the demarcated space, learning and reproducing the associated images and narratives [44].

As such, geographers questioned who received "what kind of peace, where is peace (re)produced, and how is peace realized" (Megoran et al. [36], pp. 129–130). They urged spatial sensitivity to peace, since it "[meant] different things at different scales, as well as to different groups, and at different times and places" (Koopman [29], p. 194). The meanings ascribed to space were not fixed or universal but shaped by historical events, and thus endlessly undergoing changes and transformations [43–45, 62]. Space was not an "objectively given spatial structure," but a subjective and negotiable variable influencing policy. It was created and recreated in people's daily interactions and conversations (Fard [17], p. 29). Thus, peace-building efforts needed to link the concept of peace to local ideas, including understandings of justice, that people could relate to [65].

Across the field of area studies, several experts agreed that local needs, priorities, and understandings of peace needed to be incorporated into peace-building efforts, which should not focus solely on promoting elements of liberal peace within communities (e.g., good governance, democracy, transparency). Peacebuilding practices should respect local differences, foster connections, and establish institutions able to effectively mediate political power [48, 56]. A balance needed to be negotiated between local justice, law, sources of political legitimacy and economic systems, on the one hand, and international law, the liberal peace system, and neoliberal economic development, on the other. Otherwise, the practice of peacebuilding would remain a contentious issue tied to colonial legacies [49].

Believing that geography had failed to transcend its role as a tool for statecraft, Ó Tuathail called for a critical approach that questioned the understandings and practices upheld by traditional geography concerning peace, war, violence, and the state system. A new research agenda was necessary to confront structural violence problems and question the dogmatic properties of the realist views of international politics, whereby struggles for power precluded the creation of alternative worlds [12, 40]. In contrast with the narrow understanding of peace of classic, realist geopolitics, Ó Tuathail's understanding aligned with Galtung's [18] broader conceptualization of peace. Narrow perspectives were concerned with the immediate cessation of conflict or with the medium-term imposition of order to prevent or postpone conflict. Ó Tuathail called for longer-term peace, which involved transforming and establishing social structures concerned with non-violence and justice (Taylor [55], cited in Dalby [12]).

A further point of criticism vis-a-vis short- and medium-term "peaces" concerned how they could hinder prospects of lasting peace. The former were often imposed by the victor and served its political and economic interests, being unfair to the loser and thus prone to causing a new conflict. However, change was perceived as disruptive, challenging, and dangerous, and thus often neglected in favor of stasis, even when situations were extremely unjust and inherently violent (Taylor [55], cited in Dalby [12]). A similar point on the hierarchy of order and justice had been made by Bull [8].

IR scholars attempted to reconcile the classical and critical approaches to geopolitics using constructivist lens. They argued that State action, grounded on its identities and interests, was both shaped by the geographical and the ideational elements of spaces. The social production and reproduction of ideas about spaces occurred, after all, within unique geographical contexts [17]. Interests and identities, formed within material-ideational spaces, explained why states established cooperative-reciprocal relationships with one another, constructing peace and moderating anarchy [17, 48].

Adler and Barnett argued that States could establish communities with one another, which shaped individual security policies. As a result, States could develop a peaceful demeanor. They argued that transnational security communities emerged "whenever states become integrated to the point that they have a sense of community, which, in turn, creates the assurance that they will settle their differences short of war," creating a stable peace (Adler and Barnett [1], p. 3). The authors understood peace as the absence of war [1, 58]. Western Europe was a classic example of a security community [58].

States within security communities shared fundamental values rooted in common institutions, mutual responsiveness, identity, and "we-feelings." Change through peaceful means could be reliably expected [1]. In Western Europe's case, there were also robust economic ties, healthy institutional development, and miscellaneous political, cultural and social transactions, with a European identity having been created. Despite the challenges of the European integration process and the persistence of mutual suspicions between States, the creation of trust between them had eliminated the fear of armed attack [6]. Adler and Barnett also argued that international organizations such as the UN and the Organization for Security and Cooperation in Europe contributed to the development of security communities, promoting the development of transnational linkages and spreading norms with the aim of establishing regionalized identities and mutual trust to advance the pursuit of peace [1].

Booth and Wheeler [6, 7] considered that security communities met the criteria of transcendentalist logic because they were characterized by embedded trust between states, which differentiated them from mitigator efforts. The security dilemma was mitigated when contingent cooperation was established between political leaders. Cooperation depended on their relationship, which might not be replicable once leaders were replaced. Security competition could be reduced but not eliminated.

Transcending the security dilemma, on the other hand, required the replication of positive relations between leaders at the intersocietal level. Because identities were not fixed, but socially constructed, they could evolve from relationships of enmity into relationships of trust. The development of mutual positive feelings between societies turned war and violence into unthinkable means for resolving disputes. The authors considered that policymakers could use common security and trust-building strategies to identify common values and interests, which could form the basis for constructing new identities. If governments with defensive intentions and motives took such steps while working with a progressive civil society, they might succeed in transcending the security dilemma.

The authors presented an optimistic view of human agency: cooperation and trust could replace fear and weapons. Humans had created a global political reality marked by division and suspicion, but that was not an inevitable outcome. The ideas guiding humanity toward the conflictual logic of anarchy could be universally replaced [6, 7]. Still, understanding the security dilemma as "the existential condition of unresolvable uncertainty in human affairs" (Booth and Wheeler [6], p. 1) they deemed it impossible to escape truly. Skeptical about the transformation of the deep structures of world politics, Booth and Wheeler posited that the path towards "peaceful uncertainty" included norms, laws, institutions, interdependence, multi-level interactions between societies and institutions (above and below the state), cosmopolitan sensibilities and trust-affirming commitments [6, 7]. While cooperation was possible if actors were willing to pursue it, the authors stressed that that did not mean forgiving or accepting, living with, or compromising with someone else's version of reality [6].

Other IR scholars adopted a critical approach to the study of peace, seeking the fundamental transformation of international politics. Critical voices were not a monolith, and they seldom focused on the security dilemma, perceiving it as a byproduct of the structures of international politics. Some critical studies contemplated the end of the state system, capitalism, the patriarchy, or governments, which could bring about a new international society, wherein the political conditions of trust would be present, allowing Humanity to escape uncertainty altogether [6].

Critical IR scholars often denounced the "liberal peace" promoted by Western and developed countries [48]. Liberal peacebuilding entailed "the promotion of democracy, market-based economic reforms and a range of other institutions associated with "modern" states as a driving force for building 'peace'" (Newman et al. [38], p. 3). They argued that liberal accounts of peace endorsed the discursive and hegemonic framework of the states of the neo-liberal empire, serving the interests of the powerful while dominating and dehumanizing the non-Western locals. The knowledge system through which daily life was interpreted was disconnected from local realities, reflecting Western localities and historical privileges [48].

Some contributions explored a post-Westphalian peace that was compassionate, emancipatory, and that engaged with everyday life, arguing that it likely needed to be developed through a bottom-up approach. Laws and institutions aiming to build peace should not replace local sources of legitimacy with dominant structures that lack flexibility and conceal local realities. Institutions and laws should provide sufficient economic, political, and social resources to meet not only the demands of the local but also of an international community that acts as a stakeholder. A social ontology, possibly indigenous, which recognizes peace as a process, should shape peace-building institutions and laws so that they can respond to the needs on the ground. Global norms and institutions should be mediated locally by peace actors, exploring several different blends of peace practices and local understandings. There was no single way to achieve peace, and an ontology of peace could combine multiple ideas and identities, although power relations were inevitable [48].

6 Conclusion

This chapter mapped the contrasting contributions made by scholars of IR to the question of how to manage the security dilemma in a way that constructs peace. The answer to that question is multifaceted, as different understandings of peace and the degree to which it can be pursued were uncovered. Some fatalists believe that the structure of the international system creates fear among States since the intentions of others cannot be known and thus cannot be trusted. Military power could be the key to peace, assuming rational nuclear-weapon states strived for security rather than conquest, seeing as the primary goal of states—survival—was always in jeopardy.

Other scholars were more optimistic about the prospects of managing the security dilemma via long-term cooperation rather than by the threat of mutual destruction. Peace research saw positive signs that the U.S.-Soviet nuclear arms regime could prevent war, identifying mechanisms that fostered confidence between the two states. IR scholarship on regimes, grounded on the liberal paradigm, argued that as self-interested states became more interdependent, especially economically, the use of force became too costly. Norms changed identities and interests, enabling peaceful relations and mitigating the security dilemma. Still, fear persisted due to mistrust. Power and anarchy remained preponderant variables in explaining state behavior.

Constructivist approaches moved further away from uncertainty-driven fear, understanding world politics as a social creation. States could build communities with one another based on common values and institutions. As a result of social interactions, state interests, and ideas could change to the point where it would be unthinkable to resolve differences using force. Peace would ensue, rooted in embedded trust which allowed the security dilemma to be transcended. Political leaders could play a crucial role in that regard by taking the initiative to improve state relationships, but they would not be able to succeed in building trust alone: multilevel societal efforts were required to build trust among people, rather than simply leaders.

The approaches above had in common a generally narrow understanding of peace. Other scholars, on the other hand, drew on a broader concept derived from peach research: the understanding of peace as the absence of direct violence as well as structural violence. Critical studies in IR and geography questioned who practiced peace, what kind of peace, where, how, and for whom. They denounced how space, and the peace promoted therein, reflected the interests and identities of the powerful and their societies, rather than those of the locals. In such cases, efforts to construct peace could fail. Peace and justice went hand in hand. The former was often dictated by the victor and its terms could be used to inflict injustice upon the loser. Social injustice should not be tolerated for the sake of maintaining order. Some scholars called for structural transformation, understanding the security dilemma as a mere byproduct of the deep structures of the system—such as capitalism, patriarchy, or the state system. Fear would disappear, replaced by trust, possibly among individuals, rather than states, and there would be no more security dilemmas to speak of.

The various approaches retrieved can be mapped out on a spectrum. We started from inevitable fatalism, moved towards mitigation, reached transcendence, and finally escaped the security dilemma altogether. As we progressed from one end of the spectrum to the other, the concept of peace became less narrow and more universal, albeit unfortunately also more difficult to achieve.

UN Sustainable Development Goal 16 understands peace and justice as two sides of the same coin while emphasizing the importance of strong institutions. This holistic approach to peace mirrors the recommendation of several authors in our analysis. They also stressed the importance of accounting for local understandings when attempting to build peace, for which various approaches existed. A balance should be found between local structures, interests, and identities, on the one hand, and international law and global institutions, on the other. Peace should be understood as a process focusing on the needs of the individual, not limited to his protection, but amplified to enable his personal realization. Order should not override social injustice; justice and peace are mutually reinforcing, and one cannot be built without the other.

Critical scholarship has produced crucial insights on how power dynamics shape the practice of peace, and the importance of ensuring that adjustments are made so that efforts serve local needs. To that end, greater participation, involvement, and integration of the recipients of "peace," living within specific spaces, in institutions of global governance, would ensure that their unique interests and identities are represented throughout the international decision-making processes that affect them at the local level.

Strengthening local institutions has security dilemma implications that are both internal and external. Weak institutions that fail to fulfill the needs of the people and to protect their rights can foster social unrest and violence. The result may be fear and uncertainty between citizens and domestic groups, as well as between neighboring states. Strong institutions, on the other hand, foster trust between domestic and international actors, mitigating the security dilemma.

According to our review, the security dilemma can be mitigated when actors share something with others: interests, identities, values, norms—or at least the willingness to find them or build them. Lasting cooperation that is rooted in rational egoism is likely unsustainable, but identities and interests are not fixed and can abandon the logic of anarchy-driven conflict. While interdependence could be used to prevent conflict, embedded trust between states requires further engagement between societies, which political leaders should incentivize. Security communities between states allowed for a level of integration between them that removed conflict from consideration as a means to resolve conflicts. In spreading norms and promoting transnational linkages, the UN and other international organizations can contribute toward the construction of peace.

However, relations of interdependence and security communities might pursue goals incompatible with universal peace and justice despite precluding conflict between member states. In pursuing certain regime or community agendas, States might perpetuate direct or structural violence at the intrastate level or elsewhere in the world. While transcending the security dilemma is a desirable goal in a vacuum, one must keep in mind that its achievement may not always be compatible with, and could even negatively impact, the promotion of human realization at a global level. This will remain the case until the deep structures of international politics addressed by critical theory are transformed.

The limitations of norms in restraining State behavior remains one of the quintessential questions in IR and in geopolitics, for which there are no easy solutions. States can be driven by ambition, having no intention of stopping their spiral of violence. This chapter does not attempt to address such cases, since they do not constitute security dilemmas. Security dilemmas are created by security concerns over the actions of others; they do not explain all forms of violence in international politics, direct or structural.

Our analysis has uncovered two key points: (1) Cooperation is possible when there is the willingness to pursue it, and it can be built upon by actors trapped within a logic of fear. (2) Humanity could have done much better in the past and may yet do so in the future. Contextual changes cannot be predicted, but what geopolitical analysis does allow us to do is highlight the logic of continuity in international politics. The security dilemma is a useful tool to understand state behavior, and its recognition by political leaders may open the door for attempts at mitigation or transcendence. The chapter identified the fatalists who believe that men perpetuate suffering in the logic of the security dilemma and the transcendentalists who believe that human society can build a global world that escapes the dangers of the past.

The future of world politics has not yet been written, but "kill or be killed" seems to be a lasting political option in the hands of the powerful, to the detriment of visions capable of generating trust and cooperation to replace fear. In democracies, at least, it is possible to choose governing elites who want to do things better and, above all, differently.

References

1. Adler E, Barnett M (2000) Security communities in theoretical perspective. In: Adler E, Barnett M (eds) Security communities. Cambridge University Press, Cambridge, pp 3–28
2. Agnew J, Corbridge S (2003) Mastering space: hegemony, territory and international political economy. Routledge, New York
3. Bicker L (2024) South China Sea tensions force US and Beijing to talk more. Available at: https://www.bbc.com/news/articles/cqvvxzv24pqo. Accessed 24 Oct 2024
4. Blann S (2024) Western leaders rally around Kyiv to mark 2 years since Russia's full-scale invasion. Available at: https://apnews.com/article/russia-ukraine-war-second-anniversary-65088ba9eb9bd729cf8c677e2115cb35. Accessed 24 Oct 2024
5. Booth K (2007) Theory of world security. Cambridge University Press, Cambridge
6. Booth K, Wheeler NJ (2008a) The security dilemma: fear, cooperation and trust in world politics. Palgrave Macmillan, New York
7. Booth K, Wheeler NJ (2008b) Uncertainty. In: Williams PD (ed) Security studies: an introduction. Routledge, New York, pp 133–150
8. Bull H (2002) The anarchical society. A study of order in world politics, 3rd edn. Palgrave, New York
9. Carr EH (1939) The twenty years' crisis. Papermac, London
10. Carroll BA (1972) Peace research – cult of power. J Confl Resolut 16(4):585–616. https://doi.org/10.1177/002200277201600409
11. Crawford NC (2000) The passion of world politics: propositions on emotion and emotional relationships. Int Secur 24(4):116–156. https://doi.org/10.1162/016228800560327
12. Dalby S (1991) Critical geopolitics: discourse, difference, and dissent. Environ Plann D Soc Space 9(3):261–283. https://doi.org/10.1068/d090261
13. Dalby S (2000) A critical geopolitics of global governance. International Studies Association: 41th Annual Convention. Los Angeles. 14–18 March, 2000. Available at: https://ciaotest.cc.columbia.edu/isa/das01/. Accessed 25 Oct 2024
14. Diehl PF (2016) Exploring peace: looking beyond war and negative peace. Int Stud Q 60:1–10. https://doi.org/10.1093/isq/sqw005
15. Dizikes P (2023) Foreign policy scholars examine the China-Russia relationship. Available at: https://news.mit.edu/2023/foreign-policy-scholars-examine-china-russia-relationship-1117. Accessed 24 Oct 2024
16. Donaldson J (2014) Re-thinking international boundary practices: moving away from the 'edge. In: McConnell F, Megoran N, Williams P (eds) Geographies of peace. I.B. Tauris, New York, pp 87–108
17. Fard R (2021) Towards a new concept of constructivist geopolitics: bridging classical and critical geopolitics. Centr Eur J Int Sci Stud 15(1):26–57. https://doi.org/10.51870/CEJISS.A150102
18. Galtung J (1969) Violence, peace, and peace research. J Peace Res 6(3):167–191. https://doi.org/10.1177/002234336900600301
19. Galtung J (1971) A structural theory of imperialism. J Peace Res 8(2):81–117. https://doi.org/10.1177/002234337100800201
20. Galtung J (1964) An editorial. J Peace Res 1:1–4. https://doi.org/10.1177/002234336400100101
21. Gleditsch NP, Nordkvelle J, Strand H (2014) Peace research – just the study of war? J Peace Res 51(2):145–158. https://doi.org/10.1177/0022343313514074

22. Halliday F, Rosenberg J (1998) Interview with Ken Waltz. Rev Int Stud 24(3):371–386. https://doi.org/10.1017/s0260210598003714
23. Herz JH (1950) Idealist internationalism and the security dilemma. World Polit 2(2):157–180. https://doi.org/10.2307/2009187
24. Jervis R (2017) Perception and misperception in International Politics, new edn. Princeton University Press, Princeton
25. Kane J (2012) Democracy and world peace: the Kantian dilemma of United States foreign policy. Aust J Int Aff 66(3):292–312. https://doi.org/10.1080/10357718.2012.672950
26. Keohane RO, Nye JSJ (1973) Power and interdependence. Survival 15(4):158–165. https://doi.org/10.1080/00396337308441409
27. Keohane RO, Nye JSJ (1989) Power and interdependence. HarperCollins Publisher, New York
28. King ML (1963) Letter from Birmingham Jail. Available at: https://teachingamericanhistory.org/document/letter-from-birmingham-city-jail-excerpts/. Accessed 24 Oct 2024
29. Koopman S (2011) Let's take peace to pieces. Polit Geogr 30:193–194. https://doi.org/10.1016/j.polgeo.2011.04.013
30. Krasner SD (1982) Structural causes and regime consequences: regimes as intervening variables. Int Organ 36(2):185–205. https://doi.org/10.1017/s0020818300018920
31. Lau S (2024) US accuses China of giving 'very substantial' help to Russia's war machine. Available at: https://www.politico.eu/article/united-states-accuse-china-help-russia-war-kurt-campbell/. Accessed 24 Oct 2024
32. Lieberthal KG (2011) The American Pivot to Asia. Available at: https://www.brookings.edu/articles/the-american-pivot-to-asia/. Accessed 24 Oct 2024
33. Martini A (2022) Deconstructing geopolitics in the classroom. Grasping geopolitical codes through active learning. Revista Española de Ciencia Política 60:145–173. https://doi.org/10.21308/recp.60.05
34. Mead WR (2014) The return of geopolitics. Foreign Aff 93(3) April:69–74. Available at: https://www.foreignaffairs.com/articles/china/2014-04-17/return-geopolitics. Accessed 24 Oct 2024
35. Mearsheimer JJ (2001) The tragedy of great power politics. W. W. Norton & Company, New York
36. Megoran N, McConnell F, Williams P (2016) Geography and peace. In: Richmond OP, Pogodda S, Ramović J (eds) The Palgrave handbook of disciplinary and regional approaches to peace. Palgrave Macmillan, New York, pp 123–138
37. Mitchell AW, Grygiel J (2024) US strategy should be Europe first, then Asia. Available at: https://foreignpolicy.com/2024/09/06/us-strategy-geopolitics-china-russia-europe-asia-threat/. Accessed 24 Oct 2024
38. Newman E, Paris R, Richmond OP (2009) New perspectives on liberal peacebuilding. United Nations University Press, Tokyo, pp 3–25
39. Nickel C (2024) What do we talk about when we talk about the 'return' of geopolitics? Int Aff 100(1):221–239. https://doi.org/10.1093/ia/iiad295
40. Ó Tuathail G (1987) Beyond empiricist political geography: a comment on Van Der Wusten And O'Loughlin. Prof Geogr 39(2):196–197. https://doi.org/10.1111/j.0033-0124.1987.00196.x
41. Ó Tuathail G (1997) Thinking critically about geopolitics. In: Dalby S, Routledge P, Ó Tuathail G (eds) The geopolitics reader. Routledge, New York, pp 1–12
42. Ó Tuathail G, Dalby S (eds) (1998) Rethinking geopolitics. Routledge, London
43. Paasi A (2003) Territory. In: Agnew J, Mitchell K, Ó Tuathail G (eds) A companion to political geography. Blackwell, Oxford, pp 109–122
44. Paasi A (2005) The changing discourses on political boundaries: Mapping the backgrounds, contexts and contents. In: van Houtum H, Kramsch O, Zierhofer W (eds) B/Ordering Space. Ashgate Publishing, Aldershot, pp 17–32
45. Paasi A (2009) Bounded spaces in a "borderless world": border studies, power and the anatomy of territory. J Power 2(2):213–234. https://doi.org/10.1080/17540290903064275

46. Reiss HS (2003) Kant: political writings. Cambridge University Press, Cambridge
47. Richmond OP (2008) Reclaiming peace in International Relations. Millenniu 36(3):439–470. https://doi.org/10.1177/03058298080360030401
48. Richmond O (2016) Introduction. In: Richmond OP, Pogodda S, Ramović J (eds) The Palgrave handbook of disciplinary and regional approaches to peace. Palgrave Macmillan, New York, pp 1–19
49. Richmond O, Pogodda S, Ramović J (2016) Peace in international relations theory. In: Richmond OP, Pogodda S, Ramović J (eds) The Palgrave handbook of disciplinary and regional approaches to peace. Palgrave Macmillan, New York, pp 57–68
50. Roach SC (2019) Critical theory of international relations. In: International Relations. https://doi.org/10.1093/obo/9780199743292-0095
51. Rolf JN (2023) The first 100 years: IR, critical security studies and the quest for peace. Int Politics 60(3):554–571. https://doi.org/10.1057/s41311-022-00393-w
52. Rumer E (2024) Taiwan and the limits of the Russia-China friendship. Available at: https://carnegieendowment.org/research/2024/08/taiwan-and-the-limits-of-the-russia-china-friendship?lang=en. Accessed 24 Oct 2024
53. Sher N (2024) Behind the scenes: China's increasing role in Russia's defense industry. Available at: https://carnegieendowment.org/russia-eurasia/politika/2024/05/behind-the-scenes-chinas-increasing-role-in-russias-defense-industry?lang=en. Accessed 24 Oct 2024
54. Tang S (2009) The security dilemma: a conceptual analysis. Secur Stud 18(3):587–623. https://doi.org/10.1080/09636410903133050
55. Taylor P (1991) If Cold War is the problem, is hot peace the solution? In: Kliot N, Waterman S (eds) The political geography of conflict and peace. Belhaven Press, London
56. Tom P (2016) Peace in West Africa. In: Richmond OP, Pogodda S, Ramović J (eds) The Palgrave handbook of disciplinary and regional approaches to peace. Palgrave Macmillan, New York, pp 299–311
57. Travouillon K, Lemay-Hébert N, Wallis J (2023) An emotions agenda for peace: connection beyond feelings, power beyond violence. In: Cooperation and conflict, pp 1–14. https://doi.org/10.1177/00108367231184725
58. Wæver O (1998) Insecurity, security, and asecurity in the West European non-war community. In: Adler E, Barnett M (eds) Security communities. Cambridge University Press, Cambridge, pp 69–118
59. Waltz K (1979) Theory of international politics. Addison-Wesley Publishing Company, Reading
60. Waltz K (1988) The origins of war in neorealist theory. J Interdiscip Hist 18(4):615–628. https://doi.org/10.1017/CBO9780511601033.003
61. Waltz KN (2003) More may be better. In: Sagan SD, Waltz KN (eds) The spread of nuclear weapons: a debate renewed, 2nd edn. W.W. Norton, pp 3–45
62. Weaver D (2020) Spatiality and world politics. In: Oxford research encyclopedia of international studies. https://doi.org/10.1093/acrefore/9780190846626.013.562
63. Wendt A (1995) Constructing international politics. Int Secur 20(1):71–81. https://doi.org/10.2307/2539217
64. Mearsheimer JJ (2014) Anarchy and the Struggle for Power. In: Elman C, Jensen MA (eds) Realism Reader. Routledge, New York, pp 179-187
65. Williams P, Megoran N, McConnell F (2014) Introduction: geographical approaches to peace. In: McConnell F, Megoran N, Williams P (eds) Geographies of Peace. I.B. Tauris, New York, pp 1–25
66. Baldor LC, Lee M (2024) US to send $375 million in military aid to Ukraine, including medium-range cluster bombs. Available at: https://www.independent.co.uk/news/ukraine-ap-pentagon-washington-joe-biden-b2618268.html . Accessed 24 Oct 2024

Sandra Fernandes is an Associate Professor with Tenure at the University of Minho (Portugal). She holds a PhD in Political Science from Sciences Po (Paris). Her research interests include European studies, the post-Soviet space, the relationship between the European Union and Russia, foreign policy analysis, international security, and multilateralism. She has published books, book chapters and papers, including Institutional Inertia and Change: Explaining the Czech and Portuguese Engagement in European Defence Market Integration. Journal of Common Market Studies (2023), with T. Weiss e M. Pisklová).

David Silva Ferreira is a Ph.D. candidate in Political Science at ISCTE—University Institute of Lisbon. He holds a master's degree in international studies from the same institution and a bachelor's degree in public administration from the University of Minho. He is a researcher at the Centre for International Studies (CEI-Iscte) and was awarded a scholarship from the Portuguese Foundation for Science and Technology. His research interests include nuclear weapons, U.S. foreign and domestic politics, U.S.-Russian relations, European politics, and security studies. His most recent publication is Portugal in the nuclear realm: a case of broad 'multilateralization' (2023, with S. Fernandes).

Collaborative Networks: A Strategy for Advancing Social Development

17

Senay Sadic, Emre Demir, and José Crispim

> *Collaborative networks enable organizations to pool their unique resources and capabilities, fostering innovation and resilience necessary to address complex and interconnected challenges posed by sustainable development goals*
>
> — Luís M. Camarinha-Matos

Abstract

Collaborative Networks (CNs) consist of independent entities that collaborate by sharing resources and responsibilities in pursuit of a common goal. The United Nations, through its 2030 Agenda, introduced the 17 Sustainable Development Goals (SDGs) in 2016, with SDG 17 focusing on "Partnerships for the Goals." This goal promotes global and organizational collaboration to drive sustainable action. Despite frequent references to CNs in the context of sustainable development, there is limited research addressing how these networks facilitate the equitable and sustainable distribution of value to reduce poverty and inequality. CNs are shaped by their organizational structures, business models, and supporting technologies. A Systematic Literature Review (SLR) was conducted, following the PRISMA guidelines. The findings from the SLR form the foundation of a proposed conceptual framework—Context-Interventions-Mechanisms-Outcomes (CIMO)—for CNs. The developed CIMO framework acts as a means

S. Sadic
Department of Industrial Engineering, Antalya Bilim University, Antalya, Turkiye

E. Demir
Department of Civil Engineering, Antalya Bilim University, Antalya, Turkiye

J. Crispim (✉)
NIPE, Escola de Economia, Gestão e Ciência Política, Universidade do Minho, Braga, Portugal
e-mail: crispim@eeg.uminho.pt

B. Casais (ed.), *Integrated Science to Achieve Sustainable Development Goals*, Integrated Science 37, https://doi.org/10.1007/978-3-031-88777-2_17

to understand different partnership types for accomplishing the UN social goals. The review of the 28 selected articles provides an understanding of how the economic sector, type of research, and research focus are related; the design of predictive rules that reflect the research conducted; and identification of the business models, the decision support models, and the digital architectures present in CNs when the purpose is the social sustainable development. Future research should focus on studying new forms of collaboration and socially sustainable business models.

Graphical Abstract

Collaborative Networks: A Strategy for Advancing Social Development

Keywords

Circular economy · Collaborative business model · CIMO · Partnerships · SDGs · Social sustainability · Sustainable business models

1 Collaborative Networks: Interlinkages, Challenges, and Opportunities for Social Sustainability

Collaborative networks (CNs) commonly take forms such as partnerships, alliances or coalitions are groups of independent partners who come together to achieve a common goal, sharing resources and roles. CNs are formed by various members [1], and act as a team under predetermined rules to gain mutual benefits [2]. These networks are formed when companies face complex challenges that exceed their capacities [3] or need to adapt to market changes [4].

In 2015, 193 UN members settled on the 2030 agenda, approving the Sustainable Development Goals (SDGs) as a vision for their actions and strategies. The UN vision includes 17 SDGs with 169 specific targets to promote global prosperity while protecting the planet [5]. To build a sustainable future, businesses should synchronize their strategic aims and operational activities with the SDGs [6]. Specifically, SDG 17, "Partnerships for the Goals," highlights the critical role of collaboration between nations and organizations in driving progress. However, how CNs contribute to SDGs remains underexplored and researchers have begun to address this gap. For example, Stott and Murphy [7] underscore the crucial role of partnerships in achieving the SDGs and suggest adopting a strategy that is more inclusive and centred around relationship building. Also, Leal Filho et al. [8] explore the prominence of collaboration in SDG implementations and highlight the obstacles that block executing them successfully. Additionally, Di Vaio et al. [9] examine the role of Artificial Intelligence (AI) in advancing Sustainable Business Models (SBM) and their connection to the SDGs. Moreover, Dantas et al. [10] focus on the association of Industry 4.0 and Circular Economy (CE) in supporting the SDGs achievement. Furthermore, Giannetti et al. [11] investigate cleaner production approaches as a means to achieve the SDGs. Likewise, Chauhan et al. [12] find collaboration in a network, involving diverse stakeholders including businesses, governments, consumers, and society, plays a significant role, with stakeholder pressure identified as a key driver of SDG initiatives. These studies underscore the critical role of partnerships and collaborations in advancing the SDGs, reflecting the interconnected nature of sustainable development efforts.

Organizations are facing growing global and regional social challenges due to increasing stakeholder engagement issues and rapid social changes and only recently started including social aspects in their sustainability discussions, having previously focused mainly on economic and environmental issues (often only if it helped reduce costs by protecting the environment) [13]. For some authors, the social pillar of sustainability is defined as fundamental to sustainable development [14], but there is limited literature available on social sustainability [13, 15] due to ignorance of what social sustainability is, focus on financial growth and focus on the environment by society pressure, and the incapacity in quantifying and communicating social sustainability actions [16]. From the perspective of supply networks, the SDGs relevant to social sustainability focus on creating responsible, fair, and inclusive practices throughout the entire supply network. In our perspective the relevant SDGs include: the SDG1: No Poverty by contributing to poverty eradication by paying fair wages, providing employment opportunities, and investing in local communities along the supply network; the SDG3: Good Health and Well-being by ensuring that supply network workers have access to appropriate occupational health and safety conditions, as well as wellness programs that support their physical and mental health; the SDG5: Gender Equality by ensuring gender equality is respected throughout the supply chain by promoting the equitable participation of women and ensuring that suppliers adopt non-discrimination policies; the SDG8: Decent Work and Economic Growth by promoting safe and dignified working conditions throughout the supply network, including the elimination of child labour and forced labour, and ensuring fair pay and working conditions; the SDG10: Reduced Inequalities through working with suppliers from diverse backgrounds and sizes, especially from vulnerable communities, to promote economic inclusion and reduce social inequalities; the SDG12: Responsible Consumption and Production by encouraging sustainable practices throughout the supply chain, such as reducing waste, using resources responsibly, and minimizing negative environmental and social impacts; the SDG16: Peace, Justice, and Strong Institutions by promoting transparency, ethics, and responsible governance in all supply chain operations, combating corruption, and ensuring fair business practices, and, obviously the SDG17: Partnerships for the Goals by establishing partnerships with suppliers, NGOs, governments, and other stakeholders to promote sustainable and responsible practices throughout the supply chain.

In the literature, there is a consensus that the SDGs are strongly interconnected [17], and any SDG can generate positive (synergistic) or negative (trade-off) interlinkages [18]. Examples are: for positive linkage, between SDG13 (Climate Action) and SDG14 (Life below water) [19], and for negative, SDG2 (Zero Hunger) or SDG8 (Decent work and economic growth) related to economic development can jeopardize other SDGs related to the environment [20]. According to the review of Issa et al. [17], SDG1 (No poverty), SDG3 (Good health and well-being), and SDG10 (Reduced inequalities) were reported to be highly dependent on other goals. In high-income countries, the emphasis was placed on addressing inequality (SDG10), while low-income economies were encouraged to prioritize poverty reduction (SDG1), to positively affect effects on other SDGs [5].

However, more studies are needed to identify and interpret these interlinkages between the goals, targets, and indicators of the SDGs [21].

CNs, in their creation and operation, need to define: (1) the SBM that describes how an organization generates, delivers, and captures value, and how collaboration is fostered between organizations, i.e., how activities are aligned towards social sustainability (e.g., CE) [22]; (2) the level of technology that supports collaboration (e.g., digital platforms that gather real-time information, support group decision-making, and offer a new perspective on resource management and operational effectiveness [23]; (3) the involvement of diverse stakeholders that put pressure in the alignment of the CNs and the SDGs. CNs offer a crucial interdisciplinary structure for achieving the SDGs, however, several challenges remain unclear at the formation level (business models and technology), the CNs and social sustainability relationship, and the stakeholder roles.

This article proposes a Systematic Literature Review (SLR) that aims to consolidate existing knowledge and construct a solid foundation for future research or practical applications, facilitating the understanding and implementation of the interlinkages between CNs and social sustainability goals. A conceptual Context-Interventions-Mechanisms-Outcomes (CIMO) methodology is adopted from social sciences to create a framework [24]. The CIMO framework for CNs for social sustainability is introduced based on the SLR results, as a means for understanding the collaboration forms applicable to contribute to the UN's social SDGs.

2 Methodology

The study aims to propose a structure for understanding the part of CNs in achieving SDGs. The CIMO methodology was employed to organize and structure the literature on how CNs contribute to the implementation of SDGs. It involves Context- the features of CNs; Interventions - factors and models influencing the research; Mechanisms - the business models and ICT tools used; and Outcomes—SDGs and the results of SLR. The CIMO methodology clarifies how to achieve specific goals by detailing what actions to take in a given context, using certain interventions and mechanisms.

This SLR follows the Preferred Reporting Items for Systematic Reviews and Meta-Analyses (PRISMA) guidelines and addresses the research question defined as: "How do CNs advance social SDGs?". Data was gathered from Web of Science (WoS) and Scopus using the following keywords in the search string [in the title, abstract, or keywords] "collaborative network*" "social sustainable development"OR "collaborative network*" "SDG*" OR "collaborative business model*" "social sustainable development"OR "collaborative business model*" "SDG*". In respect to study eligibility, the inclusion criteria followed were: research with applications or CN models for social sustainability, publications that contribute to SDG-related literature, and studies featuring advanced infrastructures or ICT platforms assisting CN operations. Figure 17.1 shows the PRISMA flow diagram with the identification of the studies via databases.

The data extraction process was performed independently by all reviewers. When uncertainties arose, consensus was reached through discussion. The data extraction includes the authors, publication year, journal name, research topic or referenced SDG, sustainability dimension, identified nexus, research type, research focus, methods used, IT platform, decision support system development, IT technology, SBM types, CN design, and sector. The proposed framework in its 4 phases was used to guide literature research: in context, we identified the characteristics of the studies (e.g., industry, location, disciplines underlined); in intervention, the research nature and the models proposed (e.g., research type, dimensions of sustainability involved, focus), in mechanisms, the mechanisms established to assist the CN (e.g., new business models, ICT platforms), and in outcome the outcomes in terms of SDGs (e.g., initiatives, number of contributions to each SDG, SDGs interactions).

3 Results

The CIMO typology context findings comprise the CNs studies features as CN designation and industry. The variety in the given designations is wide (23 designations out of 28 studies). The *"agri-food supply chain"* is discussed in [25]. Research on *"business models for sustainability"* can be found in [26, 27]. *"Circular business models"* are explored by [28], while the *"circular economy"* is extensively analysed in studies by [29–33]. The *"circular economy business model"* is specifically examined by [34]. The concept of the *"collaborative economy"*, including

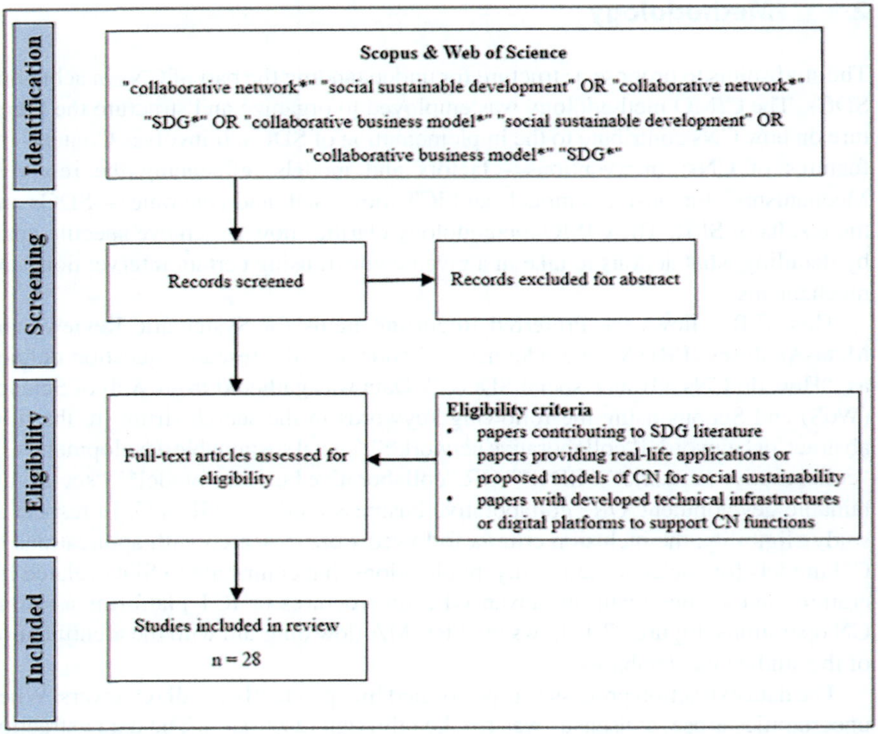

Source: Authors

Fig. 17.1 Prisma Flow Diagram

car-sharing, peer-to-peer business models, and crowdsourcing, is explored by [35]. *"Cooperative business models"* are discussed by [36]. *"Cross-sectoral partnerships"* and *"sustainable supply chains"* are analysed by [37], while [38] examines the *"cluster"* and *"innovation ecosystems"*. The *"Earth Market"* and *"collaborative enterprises"* are investigated by [39]. The *"entrepreneurial ecosystem"* is explored by [40], while *"farmer market organizations"* are studied by [41]. The *"food supply chain"* is covered by [42, 43] and Sánchez-Teba et al. [43]. The study of [44] focuses on *"industrial symbiosis"* and *"eco-industrial clusters"*. *"Multi-stakeholder refugee response partnerships"* are discussed by [45], and *"open innovation"* through university start-up collaboration is examined by [46]. The study of [47] addresses the concept of a *"product club"*, while *"regional collaboration"* is explored by [48]. *"Resilient Regional Food Supply Chain"* is discussed by [49]. The study of [50] focuses on *"sustainable business models"*, and the *"tourism product club"* is covered by [51]. *"Virtual factories"* are studied by [52], and *"collaborative entrepreneurship"* is analysed by [53]. Given the significant mix-up in naming these collaborations, we sought to create a categorization that groups the terms used into categories and highlights the need for greater consensus in the adopted designations to consolidate this research field. Table 17.1 organizes the terms into categories based on their proximity and relatedness to each other.

Regarding industry, we observed that the primary sector includes the agriculture industry [25, 36, 38, 41, 49]. The food industry is explored by [30, 34, 37, 39, 43, 54]. The construction industry is discussed by [33, 44, 55]. The chemical sector is covered by [44]. Pharmaceuticals are analysed by [50]. Forest bioenergy is studied by [48], while Fast-Moving Consumer Goods (FMCG) are examined by [32]. Manufacturing is explored by [52], and the textile industry by [29]. In the tertiary sector, the HoReCa industry is discussed by [56], and tourism by [47, 51]. Financial services are covered by [44]. In the quaternary sector, education is studied by [46]. The platform economy is explored by [26] and the collaborative economy by [35]. In the Quinary sector, smart city is explored by [57] and non-profit organizations by [45]. Other sectors involve multiple industries, as studied by [28], and entrepreneurship across all sectors, as discussed by [40, 53]. Such diversity of sectors allows us to conclude that social issues in development are not a concern specific to certain economic sectors but are instead transversal to all of them.

The CIMO Interventions comprise the sustainability dimension and the research focus and type. The focuses of the research reveal that CE and Waste Management

Table 17.1 CN designation categorization

Category	Terms
Business Models and Sustainability	Business models for sustainability Circular business models Circular economy business model Cooperative business models Collaborative business models Sustainable business models Product club Tourism product club
Supply Chains and Food	Agri-food supply chain Food supply chain Resilient Regional Food Supply Chain
Circular Economy and Symbioses	Circular economy Industrial symbiosis Eco-industrial clusters
Innovation and Ecosystems	Innovation ecosystems Entrepreneurial ecosystem Open innovation Virtual factories Farmer market organizations Earth Market Cluster
Partnerships and collaboration	Collaborative economy Cross-sectoral partnerships Regional collaboration Multi-stakeholder refugee response partnerships Collaborative enterprises Collaborative entrepreneurship

Source: Authors

is discussed by [28, 31–33, 44]. Food Loss and Waste Management is covered by [25, 34, 41, 43, 54, 56]. Business Models for Sustainability are analysed by [26, 39]. Frameworks and Industrial Transitions to Sustainability are examined by [29, 30, 50, 55]. Technology and Innovation is studied by [52]. Sustainable Supply Chain is considered by [49]. Collaboration and Partnerships are explored by [35–38, 40, 46–48, 51, 58, 59]. Table 17.2 shows the relation between the economic sector and the type and focus of the research.

The type of research includes: case study (17 studies out of 28) [25, 26, 28, 29, 34, 36–41, 44, 45, 47–49, 51]; Technical paper (2 studies): [30, 52]; Literature Review (7 studies) [32, 33, 35, 43, 54, 56, 59]; Conceptual Paper (2 studies) [46, 53]; and Perspective Paper (2 studies): [31, 50]. Concerning the sustainability dimension involved except for two studies: [52] focused on economic and [28] focused on Economic and Environmental dimensions, all the other studies were focused on the 3 dimensions (Economic, Environmental, Social). Table 17.3 shows the relation between the type of the research and its focus.

The set of research focus was categorized (Table 17.4) and separated into the terms that represent business models (approaches to sustainability and management) and that act as tools (methods or systems used to achieve these models). Studies in business models are lacking.

The CIMO mechanisms comprise business models, decision support system (DSS) frameworks and ICT platforms. We observe the development of 4 business models with focus on: 1) create value from waste through industrial symbiosis [38, 44], Circular Economy (CE) [28, 29, 31, 33, 34], and Sharing assets (shared ownership and collaborative consumption) [26, 35]; 2) encourage sufficiency through slow food models [39]; 3) repurpose for society or environment through social enterprise [26], cooperative ownership [36, 41], not for profit models [37, 45]; and 4) develop scale-up solutions through collaborative approaches [49, 51, 52] and incubators and entrepreneur support models [40, 46]. Only two papers develop DSS for collaborative planning: for solid waste management transition [30] and network formation in sustainable collaborative partner selection [60]. Only two papers create an ICT platform: a virtual factory platform incorporating a service-oriented framework, a multi-tier architecture, an interactive dashboard, and cloud-based data storage [52] and a virtual marketplace (Farmers market Riceville) for online direct-to-consumer retail model [49].

In CIMO outcomes was observed that 10 studies out of 28 specify the SDG in text and for the others the SDGs nexus was determined. Only four studies point to a unique SDG: the SDG12 [39, 54]; and the SDG17 [46, 59]. The other studies refer to various SDGs: SDGs 2 and 12 [43]; SDGs 7 and 17 [45]; SDGs 1, 2, 3, 12 and 17 [41]; SDGs 2, 3, 8, 11 and 12 [49]; SDGs 1, 2, 3, 5, 6, 12, 15 and 17 [37]; all excepting SDGs 6, 10, and 16 [31]. From the CIMO structure, prescribed rules can be designed (Table 17.5). These rules allow for a more consistent synthesis of the purpose of the study and the context in which it took place, the type of research conducted, as well as the mechanisms developed in light of the desired outcome. In this case, we specify the relevant SDG and the respective target. Regarding the mechanisms, the presented synthesis follows the SBM archetypes developed by Bocken et al. [61].

Table 17.2 Studies type and research focus according the economic sector

Economic sector	Industry	Research type					Research focus						
		Perspective Paper	Conceptual paper	Literature Review	Technical paper	case study	Food Loss and Waste Management	Partnerships and collaboration	SSC	Frameworks and transitions to sustainability	Business Models for Sustainability	Circular Economy and Waste Management	Technology and Innovation
1	Agriculture					[25, 36, 38, 41, 49]	[25, 41]	[36]	[38, 49]				
2	Food industry			[43, 54]	[30]	[34, 37, 39]	[34, 43, 54]	[37]		[30]	[39]		
	Construction			[33]		[44]	[33]	[48]		[29]		[44]	
	Chemical					[44]						[44]	
	Pharmaceutical	[50]								[50]			
	Forest bioenergy					[48]		[48]					
	Fast moving consumer goods			[32]								[32]	
	Manufacturing				[52]								[52]
	Textile					[29]				[29]			
	Multiple industries					[28]						[28]	
3	HORECA			[56]			[56]						
	Tourism					[47, 51]		[47, 51]					
	Financial services					[44]						[44]	
4	Education		[46]					[46]					
	The platform economy					[26]					[26]		
	Collaborative economy			[35]				[35]					
	Entrepreneurship		[53]			[40]		[40, 53]					
5	Smart city											[57]	
	NPO					[45]		[45]					
Total (28 studies)		1	2	6	2	17	7	10	1	3	2	4	1

Source: Authors

Table 17.3 Type and focus of the research

	Food loss and waste management	Partnerships and collaboration	SSC	Frameworks and industrial transitions to sustainability	Business models for sustainability	Circular economy and waste management	Technology and innovation
Perspective paper				[50]			
Conceptual paper		[46, 53]					
Literature review	[33, 43, 54, 56]	[35]				[32]	
Technical paper				[30]			[52]
Case study	[25, 34, 41]	[36, 37, 40, 45, 47, 48, 51]	[38, 49]	[29]	[26, 39]	[28, 44]	
Total (28 studies)	7	10	2	3	2	3	1

Source: Authors

Table 17.4 Research focus categorization

Category	Terms
Business models	Business Models for Sustainability Circular Economy and Waste Management SSC (Sustainable Supply Chains) Industrial Transitions to Sustainability
Tools	Food Loss Partnerships and collaboration Framework Design Technology and Innovation

Source: Authors

Most of the studies propose the development of new business models, followed by sustainable supply chains (only two studies suggest the creation of agricultural clusters [38, 41] as a way to achieve the SDGs. In most cases, scale-up solutions are sought through the implementation of new SBMs (three studies suggest the use of ICT platforms, specifically the use of a virtual factory [52], product club [51], or an entrepreneurial ecosystem [53] as a way to achieve scale-up), followed by value from waste, either through new SBMs or collaborations and partnerships. To achieve repurpose for society, they suggest adopting new collaborations and partnerships. Finally, the two studies that examine the encouragement of sufficiency suggest the use of new SBMs [39, 43].

4 Conclusion

Collaborative networks (CNs) are ways for companies to overcome the limitations imposed by their limited resources, and in this sense, it is important to understand whether this new form of organization implies and allows for better social sustainability. This systematic review makes use of some of the UN's SDGs as evidence of social sustainability. Although all contribute to better social sustainability, the selection was based on the fact that the chosen ones have a more direct contribution. What we know from this review of 28 studies: a) most of the included studies are case studies (17), and in these, the main focus of the research is on studying partnerships and collaborations (7) in the five economic sectors. Literature reviews (6) are the second most used research type, with a greater focus on food loss. The design of predictive rules through CIMO allows us to see what has already been studied and how it was studied, thus providing a future research agenda for what has not yet been explored. For a better understanding and to more effectively identify areas lacking studies, two categorizations were added (CN designations and Research focus categorizations).

This study establishes a basis for comparison for future research in two ways: a) in the development of new collaborative networks (type, business model, and technological support base), and b) in terms of social sustainable development (to achieve the targets advocated by the SDGs).

Table 17.5 Prescribed rules identified

If Outcome	Context	Interventation	Mechanism	Article
If you want to achieve SDG 8 & 9	In the context of manufacturing & BM development	Then use intervention type technical paper, eco.	Through the development of ICT platforms for scale-up solutions in virtual factory for new SMEs collaboration and Partnerships solutions	[52], Virtual factory business model for SME collaboration—Target 8.3; target 9.4
If you want to achieve SDG 3 & 9	In the context of pharmaceutical & BM development	Then use intervention type perspective paper, eco.	Through designing scale-up solutions as new SBM	[50], Partnerships for sustainable vaccine development - target 3.b; target 9.4
If you want to achieve SDG 8 (4)	In the context of tourism & BM development	Then use intervention type case study, TBL	Through the designing scale-up solutions in new product club collaboration and partnerships solutions	[47], Cycle tourism as a form of sustainable tourism—Target 8.9
				[51], New BM for sustainable tourism product Club—Target 8.9
	In the context of entrepreneurship & BM development	Then use conceptual type perspective paper, TBL	Through designing scale-up solutions as new SBM	[53], Collaborative entrepreneurship for SD—Target 8.3
		Then use intervention type case study, TBL	Through designing scale-up solutions in new entrepreneurial ecosystem	[40], Inclusive entrepreneurial ecosystem framework design—Target 8.1
If you want to achieve SDG 2 & 8	In the context of agriculture & BM development	Then use intervention type case study, TBL	Through designing environmental solutions or repurpose for society in new Partnerships and collaboration	[36], Business models for family farming cooperatives - target 2.4; target 8.3

If you want to achieve SDG 12 (15)	In the context of agriculture & Agri-food SC development	Then use intervention type case study, TBL	Through the creation of value from waste in new collaboration and Partnerships solutions	[25], Circular economy for food waste prevention—Target 12.3
	In the context of agriculture & agriculture clusters			[38], 2022, min waste innovation ecosystem—Target 12.4
				[41], Collaborative framework for solid waste management—Target 12.4
	In the context of the food industry & SSC development	Then use intervention type LR, Env.	Through the encouragement of sufficiency in new SBM	[43], Food waste reduction—Target 12.3 [54], decision support systems food waste reduction—Target 12.3
		Then use intervention type case study, TBL		[39], Slow food BM for sustainable consumption—Target 12.3
			Through creating value from waste with new partnership and collaboration solutions	[34], A circular economy business model from agriculture sector—Target 12.3
		Then use intervention type technical paper, TBL	Through ICT platforms in collaborative planning for transitioning industries for sustainability with new CE BMs	[30], Collaborative framework for solid waste management—Target 12.4
	In the context of textile & BM development	Then use intervention type case study, TBL	Through creating value from waste for transitioning industries for sustainability with new CE BMs	[29], Challenges in the textile industry circular economy transition—Target 12.2,12.5
	In the context of fast moving consumer goods & CE development	Then use intervention type LR, Env.		[32], Circular economy in FMCG sector—Target 12.2,12.5
	In the context of HoReCa industry & food loss and waste management	Then use intervention type LR, Env.		[56], Food waste reduction in HoReCa industry—Target 12.3
	In the context of collaborative economy & BM development	Then use intervention type LR, TBL	Through capturing value from waste with new partnership & collaboration solutions	[35], Sustainability in the collaborative economy collaborative consumption - target 12.1
		Then use intervention type case study, TBL	Through the emergence of creating value from waste with new SBM and environment solutions or repurpose for society	[26], Business model innovation for sustainability collaborative consumption - target 12.1
	In the context of multiple industries & BM development	Then use intervention type case study, eco & Env.	Through the creation of value from waste in new CE BM	[28], Business models for circular economy transitions—Target 12.2,12.5
	In the context of manufacturing & BM development	Then use intervention type case study, Env.	Through the development of repurpose for society through creation of CE in new collaboration & partnership solutions	[44], The new integrated process to design new industrial Symbiosis clusters - target 12.1
	In the context of the construction industry & BM development	Then use intervention type LR, TBL		[33], Collaborative framework for solid waste management—Target 12.4

(continued)

Table 17.5 (continued)

If Outcome	Context	Interventation	Mechanism	Article
If you want to achieve SDG 17 (4)	In the context of the food industry & SSC development	Then use intervention type case study, TBL	Through the design of environmental solutions in new CE BM or repurpose for society	[37], Sustainable coffee trade through cross-sectoral partnerships—Target 17.11
	In the context of forest bioenergy & BM development	Then use intervention type case study, TBL	Through the emerging scale-up solutions in new collaboration & partnerships	[48], Strategic collab between Indochina countries towards sustainable forest development—Target 17.6
	In the context of NPO & BM development	Then use intervention type case study, TBL	Through the design of environmental solutions or repurpose for society in new refugee response partnerships solutions	[45], Refugee response via a multi-stakeholder partnership—Target 17.6
	In the context of education & BM development	Then use intervention type conceptual paper, TBL	Through the proposal of scale-up solutions with new collaboration and Partnerships solutions	[46], University start-up collaboration for SDGs—Target 17.6

Source: Authors

We suggest for 'Where can we go from there?' three fundamental areas for social CNs to investigate: new business models for social sustainability, the contribution of technology and innovation in this path, how the SGDs can conflict and poses difficulties in achieving the targets, and how different forms of organization of companies in CNs, particularly SSCs, impact the goals of social sustainability.

References

1. Camarinha-Matos LM, Rocha AD, Graça P (2024) Collaborative approaches in sustainable and resilient manufacturing. J Intell Manuf 35(2):499–519
2. Nof SY (2007) Collaborative control theory for e-work, e-production, and e-service. Annu Rev Control 31(2):281–292
3. Yoon SW, Nof SY (2011) Affiliation/dissociation decision models in demand and capacity sharing collaborative network. Int J Prod Econ 130(2):135–143
4. Yilmaz I, Yoon SW, Seok H (2017) A framework and algorithm for fair demand and capacity sharing in collaborative networks. Int J Prod Econ 193:137–147
5. Lusseau D, Mancini F (2019) Income-based variation in sustainable development goal interaction networks. Nat Sustainability 2(3):242–247
6. Pohlmann CR et al (2020) The role of the focal company in sustainable development goals: a Brazilian food poultry supply chain case study. J Clean Prod 245:118798
7. Stott L, Murphy DF (2020) An inclusive approach to partnerships for the SDGs: using a relationship lens to explore the potential for transformational collaboration. Sustain For 12:1. https://doi.org/10.3390/su12197905
8. Leal Filho W et al (2022) Relevance of international partnerships in the implementation of the UN sustainable development goals. Nat Commun 13(1):613
9. Di Vaio A et al (2020) Artificial intelligence and business models in the sustainable development goals perspective: a systematic literature review. J Bus Res 121:283–314
10. Dantas TET et al (2021) How the combination of circular economy and industry 4.0 can contribute towards achieving the sustainable development goals. Sustainable Prod Consumption 26:213–227
11. Giannetti BF et al (2020) Cleaner production for achieving the sustainable development goals. J Clean Prod 271:122127
12. Chauhan C et al (2022) Supply chain collaboration and sustainable development goals (SDGs). Teamwork makes achieving SDGs dream work. J Bus Res 147:290–307
13. Kumari A, Singh MP (2023) A journey of social sustainability in organization during MDG & SDG period: a bibliometric analysis. Socio Econ Plan Sci 88:101668
14. Granillo-Macías R (2021) Logistics optimization through a social approach for food distribution. Socio Econ Plan Sci 76:100972
15. Dempsey N et al (2011) The social dimension of sustainable development: defining urban social sustainability. Sustain Dev 19(5):289–300
16. Sajjad A, Shahbaz W (2020) Mindfulness and social sustainability: an integrative review. Soc Indic Res 150(1):73–94
17. Issa L, Mezher T, El Fadel M (2024) Can network analysis ascertain SDGs interlinkages towards evidence-based policy planning? A systematic critical assessment. Environ Impact Assess Rev 104:107295
18. Mainali B et al (2018) Evaluating synergies and trade-offs among sustainable development goals (SDGs): explorative analyses of development paths in South Asia and sub-Saharan Africa. Sustain For 10. https://doi.org/10.3390/su10030815
19. Wu X et al (2022) Decoupling of SDGs followed by re-coupling as sustainable development progresses. Nat Sustainability 5(5):452–459

20. Bennich T, Weitz N, Carlsen H (2020) Deciphering the scientific literature on SDG interactions: a review and reading guide. Sci Total Environ 728:138405
21. Bie Q et al (2023) Progress toward sustainable development goals and interlinkages between them in Arctic countries. Heliyon 9(2):e13306
22. Boons F, Lüdeke-Freund F (2013) Business models for sustainable innovation: state-of-the-art and steps towards a research agenda. J Clean Prod 45:9–19
23. Scholz J et al (2018) Digital Technologies for Forest Supply Chain Optimization: existing solutions and future trends. Environ Manag 62(6):1108–1133
24. Denyer D, Tranfield D (2009) Producing a systematic review. In: The Sage handbook of organizational research methods. Sage, Thousand Oaks, CA, pp 671–689
25. Ciccullo F et al (2021) Implementing the circular economy paradigm in the agri-food supply chain: the role of food waste prevention technologies. Resour Conserv Recycl 164:105114
26. Sinthupundaja J et al (2020) Investigating business model innovation for sustainability: cases from Thailand. Int J Innovation Sustainable Dev 14(3):313–329
27. Stål HI, Bengtsson M, Manzhynski S (2022) Cross-sectoral collaboration in business model innovation for sustainable development: tensions and compromises. Bus Strateg Environ 31(1):445–463
28. Veleva V, Bodkin G (2018) Corporate-entrepreneur collaborations to advance a circular economy. J Clean Prod 188:20–37
29. Franco MA (2017) Circular economy at the micro level: a dynamic view of incumbents' struggles and challenges in the textile industry. J Clean Prod 168:833–845
30. Oliveira Silva WD, Morais DC (2021) Transitioning to a circular economy in developing countries: a collaborative approach for sharing responsibilities in solid waste management of a Brazilian craft brewery. J Clean Prod 319:128703
31. Sharma HB et al (2021) Circular economy approach in solid waste management system to achieve UN-SDGs: solutions for post-COVID recovery. Sci Total Environ 800:149605
32. Stewart R, Niero M (2018) Circular economy in corporate sustainability strategies: a review of corporate sustainability reports in the fast-moving consumer goods sector. Bus Strateg Environ 27(7):1005–1022
33. Wijewickrama MKCS, Rameezdeen R, Chileshe N (2021) Information brokerage for circular economy in the construction industry: a systematic literature review. J Clean Prod 313:127938
34. Zucchella A, Previtali P (2019) Circular business models for sustainable development: a "waste is food" restorative ecosystem. Bus Strateg Environ 28(2):274–285
35. Ertz M, Leblanc-Proulx S (2018) Sustainability in the collaborative economy: a bibliometric analysis reveals emerging interest. J Clean Prod 196:1073–1085
36. Giagnocavo C, Galdeano-Gómez E, Pérez-Mesa JC (2018) Cooperative longevity and sustainable development in a family farming system. Sustain For 10. https://doi.org/10.3390/su10072198
37. van Hille I et al (2020) Cross-sector partnerships for sustainability: how mission-driven conveners drive change in National Coffee Platforms. Sustain For 12. https://doi.org/10.3390/su12072846
38. Spicka J (2023) Cooperation in a minimum-waste innovation ecosystem: a case study of the Czech Hemp Cluster. Int J Emerg Mark 18(10):4320–4342
39. Hatipoglu B, Inelmen K (2021) Effective management and governance of Slow Food's earth markets as a driver of sustainable consumption and production. J Sustain Tour 29(11–12):1970–1988
40. Zhao W et al (2021) Investigating inclusive entrepreneurial ecosystem through the lens of bottom of the pyramid (BOP) theory: case study of Taobao village in China. Chin Manag Stud 15(3):613–640
41. Moggi S, Bonomi S, Ricciardi F (2018) Against food waste: CSR for the social and environmental impact through a network-based organizational model. Sustain For 10. https://doi.org/10.3390/su10103515

42. Adams D, Donovan J, Topple C (2021) Achieving sustainability in food manufacturing operations and their supply chains: key insights from a systematic literature review. Sustainable Prod Consumption 28:1491–1499
43. Sánchez-Teba EM, Gemar G, Soler IP (2021) From quantifying to managing food loss in the agri-food industry supply chain. Food Secur 10. https://doi.org/10.3390/foods10092163
44. Baldassarre B et al (2019) Industrial Symbiosis: towards a design process for eco-industrial clusters by integrating circular economy and industrial ecology perspectives. J Clean Prod 216:446–460
45. Moreno-Serna J et al (2021) Feedback loops and facilitation: catalyzing transformational multi-stakeholder refugee response partnerships. Sustain For 13. https://doi.org/10.3390/su132111705
46. Jirapong K, Cagarman K, von Arnim L (2021) Road to sustainability: University–start-up collaboration. Sustain For 13. https://doi.org/10.3390/su13116131
47. Gazzola P et al (2018) Cycle tourism as a driver for the sustainable development of little-known or remote territories: the experience of the Apennine regions of Northern Italy. Sustain For 10. https://doi.org/10.3390/su10061863
48. Bruckman VJ et al (2018) Sustainable forest bioenergy development strategies in Indochina: collaborative effort to establish regional policies. Forests 9. https://doi.org/10.3390/f9040223
49. Marusak A et al (2021) Resilient regional food supply chains and rethinking the way forward: key takeaways from the COVID-19 pandemic. Agric Syst 190:103101
50. Rappuoli R, Hanon E (2018) Sustainable vaccine development: a vaccine manufacturer's perspective. Curr Opin Immunol 53:111–118
51. Ribarić R, Stipanović C (2019) Stakeholder collaboration based on an innovated tourism product club model - an empirical investigation of the Parenzana product club. World J Entrep Manag Sustain Dev 15(5):539–559
52. Hao Y, Helo P, Shamsuzzoha A (2018) Virtual factory system design and implementation: integrated sustainable manufacturing. Int J Syst Sci: Oper Logist 5(2):116–132
53. Schaltegger S, Beckmann M, Hockerts K (2018) Collaborative entrepreneurship for sustainability. Creating solutions in light of the UN sustainable development goals. Int J Entrep Ventur 10(2):131–152
54. Somlai R (2022) Integrating decision support tools into businesses for sustainable development: a paradoxical approach to address the food waste challenge. Bus Strateg Environ 31(4):1607–1622
55. Balasubramanian S et al (2024) Construction industry 4.0 and sustainability: an enabling framework. IEEE Trans Eng Manag 71:1–19
56. Buczacki A, Gładysz B, Palmer E (2021) HoReCa food waste and sustainable development goals—a systemic view. Sustain For 13. https://doi.org/10.3390/su13105510
57. Bhati A, Upadhayaya A, Sharma A (2016) National disaster management in the ASEAN-5: an analysis of tourism resilience. Tour Rev 71(2):148–164
58. Emanuelsson L et al (2013) Ambulance personnel adherence to hygiene routines: still protecting ourselves but not the patient. Eur J Emerg Med 20(4):281–285
59. Vazquez-Brust D et al (2020) The governance of collaboration for sustainable development: exploring the "black box". J Clean Prod 256:120260
60. Govindan K et al (2019) Environmental management partner selection for reverse supply chain collaboration: a sustainable approach. J Environ Manag 236:784–797
61. Bocken NMP et al (2014) A literature and practice review to develop sustainable business model archetypes. J Clean Prod 65:42–56

Senay Sadic received her BSc degree in Management Engineering and her MSc degree in Industrial Engineering from Istanbul Technical University. While doing her MSc studies, she worked as a research and teaching assistant at Istanbul Technical University, Industrial Engineering department. Later, she further obtained her PhD degree in Engineering Design and Advanced Manufacturing from the MIT Portugal program, which is a collaborative program between the

Portuguese government and the Massachusetts Institute of Technology, Boston. During her PhD, she also worked as a research scientist at Inesc Porto, Enterprise Systems Modeling/Engineering center and contributed to several projects on manufacturing networks and SME collaboration. Her research interests include supply chain optimization and modeling, innovative business models, data science and smart manufacturing.

Emre Demir received the B.S. degree in civil engineering from Boğaziçi University, Istanbul, Turkey, in 2007, the M.S. degree in transport engineering and operations from Newcastle University, Newcastle upon Tyne, UK, in 2008, and the Ph.D. degree in civil engineering from the University of Missouri, Columbia, MO, USA, in 2013. He is currently an Associate Professor at the Faculty of Engineering and Natural Sciences, Antalya Bilim University, Antalya, Turkey. His current research interests include transportation analysis, fuzzy systems in transportation, optimization, modeling, and transportation geography.

José Crispim is an Associate Professor of Management and a member of NIPE - Center for Research in Economics and Management at the University of Minho. He is the Director of the Master in Management at the School of Economics and Management (EEG). His research concentrates on the application of operations and supply chain management in environments where complexity may emerge from factors such as human behavior, network structures, or risk. Namely, in risk analysis, value-based healthcare, digitalization of healthcare services, collaborative networks, sustainable and resilient supply chains, and performance measurement and management. He has a PhD in Industrial Engineering and Management from the Faculty of Engineering, University of Porto.

Index

B. Casais (ed.), *Integrated Science to Achieve Sustainable Development Goals*, Integrated Science 37, https://doi.org/10.1007/978-3-031-88777-2

9783031887765